A

BIBLIOGRAPHY OF

William Carlos Williams

BY

EMILY MITCHELL WALLACE

Texts mount and complicate themselves, lead to further texts and those
to synopses, digests and emendations. So be it.
Paterson, Three, II, 156

Wesleyan University Press

MIDDLETOWN, CONNECTICUT

Library of Congress Catalog Card Number: 68-27541

Manufactured in the United States of America

FIRST EDITION

FOR FLOSS
"Are facts not flowers
and flowers facts"

Contents

Illustrations

Introductory Note

WILLIAM CARLOS WILLIAMS'
"COMPLETE COLLECTED EXERCISES TOWARD A POSSIBLE POEM"

He says in *Paterson*, "It is dangerous to leave that which is badly written. A chance word, upon paper, may destroy the world. . . . Only one answer: write carelessly so that nothing that is not green will survive."[1] "But," of course, "you cannot be/an artist/by mere ineptitude."[2] He obviously intends "write carelessly" in a special sense opposed to "badly written." It is, in fact, his quality of "careless truth,"[3] plus his refusal to use the traditional *ex machina* props of poetry, that has puzzled some readers and critics: there seems so little to say, in the usual ways, about many of the poems. We shall be learning, for some time to come, new ways to talk about his immaculate craft. But we can recognize in his analysis of a Polish woman's comment to her daughter, "You bust your coat with your fifty sweaters," some characteristics he associated with "careless truth" and achieved in his writing:

> What's that: You bust your coat with your fifty sweaters?
> Its immediacy, its sensual quality, a pure observation, its lack of irritation, its lack of pretense, its playful exaggeration, its repose, its sense of design, its openness, its gayety, its unconstraint. It frees, it creates relief. In the great it is the same, or would be if ever it existed, a delicious sincerity (in greater things of course) not a scheme, nor a system of procedure—but careless truth.[3]

"Delicious sincerity," "careless truth" have to be qualities of the total man. "It isn't just 'honesty.' . . . First it's human character that decides."[4] And in *Paterson:*

---

1. *Paterson, Three*, III, 155. (1949) [Abbreviations used in these footnotes are explained on page 3. The date given for each quoted phrase, statement, or poem is the year it was written or spoken, when that can be determined; otherwise the date of first publication is given.]

2. *Paterson, Five*, II, 258. *JL*, 18. *PB*, 135. (1955)

3. *AG*, 206. (1923–1924)

4. *SE*, 181. (1937?)

ix

What more clear than that of all things
nothing is so unclear, between man and
his writing, as to which is the man and
which the thing and of them both which
is the more to be valued [5]

Everything he wrote is not of course of equal value, but every thing he wrote helps us to understand the design and character of his work because he tried always simply ("carelessly") to tell the truth, his truth of the present moment. Perhaps this is partially what he means in the first sentence of his autobiography, "I was an innocent sort of child and have remained so to this day." Although a Williams poem may be complex or, as he says of Homeric verse admiringly, "multiplex, efflorescent, varied as the day in its forms," [6] the poem reveals no *effort* at complexity or at profundity. He insists that "for the poet words come first and the ideas are caught, perhaps, among them. . . . It does not go the other way." [7] Any thing that is felt on the pulses is a subject for poetry, if the poet has a "bitter seriousness" [8] about his technique—"which means saying what he means and not saying what he does not mean" [8]—if the "words will/bite/their way/home" [9]:

The world of the senses lies unintelligible on all sides. It is only interpretable by the emotions. . . .

I must write, I must strive to express myself. I must study my technique, as a Puritan did his Bible, because I cannot get at my emotions in any other way. There is nothing save the emotions: I must write, I must talk when I can. It is my defiance; my love song: *all of it.*[8]

Not only the size of the bibliography but other sources indicate that Williams believed in writing all the time he could steal from being "a good first line doctor." [10] Wallace Stevens, for example, wrote to a publisher: "I think that Williams, who is really a prodigious theorist, would do what you want very well. . . . Williams, I believe, writes every day or night or both,

---

5. *Paterson, Three*, II, 140. (1949)

6. *A Dream of Love* (Norfolk, Conn., 1948) 103.

7. "In Praise of Marriage," *The Quarterly Review of Literature*, II. 2 ([1945]) 147.

8. "Notes from a Talk on Poetry," *Poetry*, XIV. 4 (July 1919) 212–213. Italics added. "No ideas but in things," Williams insists.

9. "The Wind Increases," *CEP*, 68. (1930)

10. The beneficial tension created by the pressure of the two careers is memorably described in the autobiographical *A Voyage to Pagany* (New York, 1928) 12–13.

and his house must be full of manuscripts, but it is quite different with me." [11] From many other comments about his constant activity, here is one that the doctor and poet scribbled in one of his notebooks:

> Periodicity of psychologic and imaginative energy—Work *all* the time—manic depression but learn to use yourself: when up drive in—when down assume the clerk—there's plenty of room for both.[12]

What "assume the clerk" meant to him may be inferred from his description of prose and poetry in *Spring and All*:

> prose: statement of facts concerning emotions, intellectual states, data of all sorts—technical expositions, jargon, of all sorts—fictional and other—
> poetry: new form dealt with as a reality in itself
> The form of prose is the accuracy of its subject matter—how best to expose the multiform phases of its material
>   the form of poetry is related to the movement of the imagination revealed in words—or whatever it may be—
>   the cleavage is complete
> . . .
>   The cleavage goes through all the phases of experience. It is the jump from prose to the process of imagination that is the next great leap of the intelligence. . . .[13]

Prose to Williams was what he wrote when he was unable to make the "great leap" from accuracy of subject matter to "the dynamisation of emotion into a separate form." [13] He thought "there is no use denying that prose and poetry are not . . . the same IN INTENTION," [14] but that prose could lead to (inspire) or follow (to enlighten) the poetry.

All the prose kept him verbalizing his experiences and ideas, thus releasing his imagination. "Why do you write?" is the question at the end of "Conversation as Design"; the answer:

> For relaxation, relief. To have nothing in my head—to freshen my eye by that till I see, smell, know and can reason and be.[15]

---

11. Letter to Ronald Lane Latimer, Nov. 28, 1934. Harriet Monroe Collection, University of Chicago. Published, except for the first sentence, in *Letters of Wallace Stevens,* edited by Holly Stevens (New York, 1966).
12. Undated ["10/22/30" several pages before], *YALC.*
13. *Spring and All* (Paris, 1923) 67–68.
14. *Ibid.,* 77–78.
15. *SE,* 101. (1929)

The experimental writing (like *Kora in Hell, The Great American Novel, A Novelette and Other Prose*) kept him alert to the possibilities of a more fluid and flexible form for poetry. He defended the Improvisations: "Their excellence is, in major part, the shifting of category. It is the disjointing process." [16] "Get into the fluid state," he says in *Short Story* [*Notes*], "for unless you do, all you will say will be valueless." [17] Ezra Pound praised *The Great American Novel*: ". . . a new sort of unity has been achieved . . . the parts are more definitely 'of' the entirety than they had been in earlier sorts of poem [*sic*] which could be taken piecemeal or in quotation." [18] Williams' prose kept his mind ready (*set*, as the psychologists term it) for the quest of the poems.

Williams used the prose also to explore all the phases of "the form of poetry [which] is that of language": "all art first," "then . . . certain essential characteristics of language," then "words," and "finally . . . everything among all the categories of knowledge among which the social attributes of a time occur." [19]

All art first. Among the listings of the bibliography are many statements about painters, sculptors, musicians, dancers, photographers; translations from French and Spanish, Greek (he did not know Greek but, entranced by the rise and fall of the beat of the original poems as read to him by Greek scholars, he translated some Theocritus and Sappho) and Chinese (made in collaboration with Chinese scholars); editorials for little magazines, numerous prefaces and postscripts to the volumes of other poets, and many other essays about writers living and dead, American and European. It is noteworthy too that he illustrated his medical school yearbook (in 1906) and painted a self-portrait in oil (early in 1914).[20] The medical school yearbook, with its line drawings signed "W. C. Williams" and its photograph of "Billy" Williams as an actor in a long white beard, reminds one that the young man gave considerable thought to the choice of an art on which to concentrate. That writing won, but that he remained involved with the other arts, is thoroughly documented by his bibliography.

---

16. "Juan Gris," *A Novelette and Other Prose* (*1921–1931*) (Toulon, France, 1932) 25.

17. *SE*, 307. (1949)

18. *Profile, an Anthology Collected in MCMXXXI*, edited by Ezra Pound (Milan, 1932) 127.

19. Letter to Kay Boyle [1932], *SL*, 131.

20. The self-portrait is reproduced facing page 36 of this book.

His lifelong comparison of the arts was closely linked to the imagistic, dramatic, and musical aspects of his poems. "A poet should take his inspiration from the other arts too." [21] Consider, as an example, one of the last poems he wrote:

Still Lifes

All poems can be represented by
still lifes not to say
water-colors, the violence of
the Iliad lends itself to an arrangement
of narcissi in a jar.
The slaughter of Hector by Achilles
can well be shown by them
casually assembled yellow upon white
radiantly making a circle
sword strokes violently given
in more or less haphazard disarray[22]

The multiple image of the flowers and the dramatic fight between Hector and Achilles cross, stasis and violent activity united, through the measured tautness of the short lines and the strength of the natural language. The poem is a whole, the sharp converging and crossing of lines establishing a point about the relation of one art to another and of art to life.[23] There is no final period: the image of swords and narcissi remains a moment, the sound lingers.

Certain essential characteristics of language. Words. "I have been working with prose," he wrote Kay Boyle in 1932, "since I didn't know what to do with poetry. Perhaps I have been in error. Maybe I should be slaving at verse. But I don't think so. Prose can be a laboratory for metrics. It is lower in the literary scale. But it throws up jewels which may be cleaned and grouped." [24] In 1949: "The short story is a wonderful medium for prose experimentation. You may, economically, try devices—varied devices —for making the word count toward a particular effect." [25] In an essay on measure in 1959, he says that if the poetic measure is "to take its part

---

21. *SL,* 133. ([1932])
22. *The Hudson Review,* XVI. 4 (Winter 1963–1964) 516.
23. See his comment about poetry and mathematics in *SE,* 122. (1925)
24. *SL,* 130.
25. *SE,* 305.

among other measures in the assemblies of the age," it must be "broken away from its ankylosed conditions," and one way to achieve this is: "To use cadences dictated by the American idiom. All that I have learned in prose composition [is] to get as much as I can in the fewest possible words, trimming wherever it is possible to make the sense come through without tautology, balancing the words against that. . . . That's where the test comes. What is and what is not permitted. Mere eccentricity is not permitted." [26] His prose, then, offered an opportunity for study, exciting in itself, of the words and cadences of the American idiom, the nervous, vital rhythm of speech that he used to measure the new line of his poems.

All the categories of knowledge among which the social attributes of a time occur. To understand these, he, as all writers must, began with himself, going from the local to the universal.[27] On the dust jacket of the 1948 edition of *In the American Grain,* he says the book is "a clutch of rough sketches of . . . men and women put down in an attempt to orient myself in the conditions." In an essay in that book: "I seek the support of history but I wish to understand it aright, to make it SHOW itself." [28] In *A Voyage to Pagany* he wrote about his travels and the life of an American doctor and writer to which he would return. In the Stecher trilogy (*White Mule, In the Money, The Build-Up*) he wrote about his wife from her infancy to girlhood. In the short stories he explored his relation to his patients and the other people of his community. The tension between his American environment and his French and Spanish heritage produced the translations (of Soupault's *Last Nights of Paris,* Quevedo's *The Dog and the Fever,* short stories and poems), which also helped him to become better acquainted with his parents when he enlisted their aid in the translating. In *Yes, Mrs. Williams* he wrote about his mother. He sought to understand, he declares in "Fierce Singleness," the "single significance of every minutest gesture of my life of which I am a part only." [29]

The prose cannot be dismissed, however, as merely self-discovery, self-therapy, experimentation, theorizing about art, though Williams did use the prose for those purposes. *In the American Grain,* for one example, is

---

26. "Measure," *Spectrum,* III. 3 (Fall 1959) 155.
27. In his *Autobiography,* 391, Williams gives credit to John Dewey and Keyserling for the idea, "The local is the only universal, upon that all art builds."
28. *AG,* 116. (1924)
29. *A Novelette,* 34. (1929?)

a "new form dealt with as a reality in itself." [30] Nor is it fair to consider Williams' interest in the prose deficient because he felt the poems were more important. He would have liked to write The Great American Novel. He taught a workshop and wrote about the art of the short story. He loved the theater, built a stage in his back yard, acted in a play in Greenwich Village, was thrilled to have his plays produced formally or informally. He set demanding standards for criticism: to focus on the object for criticism, to avoid the merely personal, "to hold up (or to condemn) in particular that it may (or may not) go on to develop." [31] He considered the possible forms of the essay from a fluid association of ideas and sensations to "the perfect essay" with "every word numbered, say as the bones in a body and the thoughts in the mind are fixed. . . . Then there could be no confusion." [32] Much of the prose is distinguished in its own particular forms, which have been and will be discussed by other critics.

Whatever its other virtues, the prose is singularly interesting and valuable, all of it, as a revelation of the rigorous process of a poet's art. Prose and poetry together offer a compelling portrait of a man unsparingly channelling his energy toward the poem, learning to release the force of our language in the poem effortlessly ("carelessly," like Mr. T.'s perfectly achieved *entrechat* in the poem "The Artist" [33]). In helping us to understand the design and scope of Williams' creativity, it also shows us its source:

> . . . a moral source . . . peculiarly sensitive and daring in its close embrace of native things. His sensitive mind. For everything his fine sense, blossoming, thriving, opening, reviving—not shutting out—was tuned. He speaks of his struggles with . . . language, its peculiar beauties, *"je ne sais quoi d'énergique,"* he cited its tempo, the form of its genius with gusto, with admiration, with generosity.[34]

The poet "is not a moralist" [35] in choice of subject, Williams maintains,

---

30. *Spring and All* (1923) 67. The essay on Raleigh, *AG*, 59–62, is published as a poem in *100 Modern Poems,* selected by Selden Rodman (New York, 1949) 92–98.
31. "George Antheil and the Cantilène Critics," *SE*, 59. (1927)
32. "An Essay on Virginia," *A Novelette*, 73. (1925)
33. *DM*, 43. *PB*, 101. (1953)
34. "Père Sebastian Rasles," *AG*, 121. (1924)
35. *I Wanted*, 79. (1957)

because "the province of the poem is the world," [36] and "as poets all we can do is to say what we see and let the rest speak for itself." [37] To be moral ("to be positive, to be peculiar, to be sure, generous, brave" [38]) rather than to be a moralist is different, and he was moral in his devotion to poetry as "the crystallization of the imagination—the perfection of new forms as additions to nature." [39] "Everything we know and do is tied up with words, with the phrases words make, with the grammar which stultifies, the prose or poetical rhythms which bind us to our pet indolences and medievalisms. . . . This is a moral question at base, surely but a technical one also and first." [40] He argues that it is "sheer bastardy" [41] to borrow the much used forms of the past. "Unless he [the artist] discovers and builds anew he is betraying his contemporaries in all other fields of intellectual realization and achievement and must bring their contempt upon himself and his fellow artists." [41] "There is no use pretending that we live in a closed 'poetic' world in which we do not need to know what is going on about us and then think we can invent poetry. . . . In the form, the form of the line (of which diction is a part) it must have room for the best of Joyce—the best of all living, terminal, bud-end reflection of thought and—Einstein—the Soviets." [42] "The moral issue must finally be faced. What is a poet? A magpie? An owl? Possibly, in one phase, but he had better be a man if he wants to be hung. . . . Either it is a basic demand of life and the age that a man write well or we are the worst fools in the world to be disturbed by him." [43]

---

36. *Paterson, Three,* I, 122. (1949) For this reason Williams objected to Wallace Stevens' statement (in the Preface of Williams' *Collected Poems 1921–1931*) that Williams was interested in the "anti-poetic."

37. Letter to Marianne Moore, June 23, 1951. *SL.*

38. See *AG*, 121. (1924) This dazzling paragraph about Rasles, beginning "He was a great MAN," presents a concept of *to be moral* similar to Aristotle's group of moral virtues. I do not mean to say that Williams was deliberate about this—and in any case his language is extraordinarily different—but he had read Dante's *Convivo* and "a little of Spenser," and both refer to the eleven or twelve moral virtues named by Aristotle. Dante says they are some fruits by which we can recognize Nobleness. Spenser attributes to Magnificence, represented by Prince Arthur in *The Faerie Queen,* a virtue that essentially embodies the others.

39. *Spring and All* (1923) 77.

40. *SE,* 163. (1934)

41. *SE,* 217. (1939)

42. *SL,* 135. ([1932])

43. "The Later Pound," typescript dated Jan. 13, 1950, *YALC.*

Curiously, even his first book, *Poems, 1909*, indicates a vague awareness of the need for new forms. The quotations from Keats and Shakespeare on the title page both contain the word "new." Consider also the unorthodox way Edgar Williams, the designer of the title page, divided the lines, with his brother's approval:

> —HAPPY MELODIST—FOR-
> EVER PIPING SONGS FOR-
> EVER NEW.—Keats.—
> —SO ALL MY BEST IS DRESS-
> ING OLD WORDS NEW—
> —SPENDING AGAIN WHAT-
> IS ALREADY SPENT.—.—
> —Shakespeare—

It looks like a fitful tracing of the new line to come, measured by the "variable foot." [44] The title page promised more than the old-fashioned, imitative poems inside offered (Williams never allowed them to be reprinted), but the forecast, even if offered unconsciously, was eventually fulfilled. "Dressing old words new" is not an inclusive description, however, of Williams' later aims. New words must be recognized, as he does in a delightful passage in *The Great American Novel:* "This is no place to talk that way. What a word to use. I'm new said the sudden word." [45] And new forms must be *invented* "to build our vitally important celebrations of the present." [46] Williams thought of himself, accurately, as a revolutionist:

> CRRRRRASH.—Down comes the world. There you are gentlemen. I am an artist.
>
> . . .—To me beauty is purity. To me it is discovery, a race on the ground. And for this you are willing to smash—

---

44. Williams did not begin using the phrase *variable foot* until 1954 or 1955. Several years earlier in rereading his poem "The Descent," he had "discovered" the form that inspired him to find a term to describe a measure which is flexible, musical, natural in language, and avoids both the formlessness of free verse and the restrictiveness of fixed feet. He said in conversation (1959) that the earlier poems "were all instinctive." One of his essays about the variable foot is "Poetry and the Making of the Language: How Verse Forms Create Something New," *The New Republic,* CXXXIII. 18 (Oct. 31, 1955) 16–17.

45. (Paris, 1923) Chapter II, 13.

46. Typescript, undated, of talk Williams gave at Bread Loaf [1951?], *YALC.*

Yes, everything.—To go down into hell.—Well, let's look. . . .

Here's a man wants me to revise, to put in order. My God what I am doing means just the opposite from that. There is no revision, there can be no revision.

Down came the rain with a crash. . . .

Living we fail to live but insist on impaling ourselves on fossil horns.[47]

An artistic revolution is never easy because living in the present moment is never easy. The reaction he noted toward George Antheil's strange, new music was symptomatic of the general reaction toward the new poetry: "'It's all wrong, it's all wrong,' kept repeating the woman back of me. Of course it is. We are not used to it, therefore, it must be so. But we are not quite yet dead. Everything new must be wrong at first since there is always a moment when the living new supplants that which has been and still is right and is thus sure to be wrong in transit, or until it is seen that that which was right is dead." [48] "It is not to be boastful that I strike out against the old, but because I must," he wrote in 1919. "It is one effort—to remain aware. In the presence of some rhymed master-piece of antiquity I am humble; in its beauty I take refuge. But one is never safe; no sooner is one a little at ease than life comes back to the slugging match." [49] In 1950 he asked again: "What is the problem? It is the universal one today . . . : To win for the language, the language as it stands, not as it stood three centuries ago, but today, a subtlety and time-liness (in a special sense) a speed and a flexibility (as only the poem can show in full use) comparable to the greatness of the past." [50]

Although Williams admired the new forms of the poems of Ezra Pound, E. E. Cummings, and other poetic revolutionists, he was never complacent about his own victories. His attempt to measure the significance of his own poems was not motivated by vanity[51]—he wanted to measure an Ideal Poem for our time, a measure that might be used by other poets.

---

47. *The Great American Novel* (1923) Chapter III, 21; Chapter V, 26; Chapter XVI, 66.

48. *SE,* 60. (1927)

49. "Notes from a Talk on Poetry," *Poetry,* XIV. 4 (July 1919) 216.

50. "The Later Pound," *YALC.*

51. At the very beginning he wrote to his brother Edgar that his interest in poetry was "bigger than [personal] success" (unpublished letter, postmarked Feb. 7, 1906, *YALC*). And see "The Pink Locust," *JL,* 24–26. *PB,* 140–142. (1954–1955)

Introductory Note

After his first stroke he wrote an essay headed, "What has sustained me and made me feel in the face of the troubles of our time that it was worth-while going on," in which he says:

> When I am convinced that I have contributed something to the art of the poem, the total poem, the poem as it did not exist before I was born, I am happy in my innermost heart and continue happy for days or months at a time or as long as I can continue in this belief.
>
> That stimulates me, drives me with the inexorable fire to go on. Without that feeling of happiness or the possibility of it I would not write another word. But granted with that drive constantly uppermost in my mind I cannot quit.[52]

Among his unpublished manuscripts is a typed sheet in the form of a title page for a group of his writings: "THE COMPLETE COLLECTED | EXERCISES | TOWARD A POSSIBLE | POEM | (in 2 vols) | by | W. C. W." Following the title and author's initials are *"Six Books"*:

1. The River
2. Kora in Hell: Improvisations
3. Spring and All
4. The Wedge
5. The Poem as a Machine
6. A New Way of Measuring

At the foot of the page is the description: "(Preceded in each case by a statement, a brief statement, by the author describing his mode of attack together with his appraisals of success and defeat as indifferent alternatives.)" and "Note: Each 'book' will be a heading for a complete sweep through the available material of the poems, from beginning to end, for a cohesive arrangement." [53]

Of the "six books" listed, *Kora in Hell* is marked out in pencil; it is included on another similar typed sheet and also crossed out in pencil. The reason for his uncertainty can only be guessed. He liked the book but was not sure he could explain its significance; he told Edith Heal, "Although I did not call the book Prose Poems I believe that is what it is. It has no stated form. I have always been puzzled by it. I realized it had poetic quality but without any form. I was willing to let it stand by itself

---

52. Typescript, *YALC*. Published in "Faiths for a Complex World," *The American Scholar*, XXVI. 4 (Autumn 1957) 453–457.

53. Undated, but certainly written some time after 1944, *YALC*.

and later I felt I could not include any of it in any anthology of my poetry." [54] In the first "book" he may have intended to contrast the different forms of his poems and prose about the river, including the poem "The Wanderer" (1914), the short poem "Paterson" (which won the Dial Away in 1926), possibly a short story from *Life Along the Passaic River* (1938), and culminating in selections from the epic *Paterson*, a poem (with prose sections) about the river and language. The third and fourth "books" can be identified as collections of poems, but prose passages are interspersed in *Spring and All* (1923), and *The Wedge* (1944) begins with one of his favorite essays about poetry. The "mode of attack" in the last two "books" is indicated by their titles, and apparently they would have contained poems with prose to elucidate the method of the poems.

The evidence of this typed sheet suggests that Williams might not have objected to calling the entire body of his writing *The Complete Collected Exercises Toward a Possible Poem*. Certainly he would have agreed that the "exercises" were, in their bounty and variety, sustained from beginning to end by his concern for "the art of the poem, the total poem, the poem as it did not exist before [he] was born."

His last poems complete the design. Many of them are among the best poems of our time. Many of them are intensely personal and express "tragic winter/thoughts." [55] Yet the emotion is measured inexorably, impersonally, as though something beyond the emotion compelled his concentration and protected him—perhaps the new place he had created where "love and the imagination . . . avoid destruction." [56] Each poem stands alone, and can bear with ease the scrutiny of even the sternest New Critics. Yet there is something that no approach to the individual poems can reach, as though they are the "isolate flecks" [57] of beauty given off from the larger design.

His "Possible Poem" is "a miracle of varied work,/a thing for you to marvel at," [58] and "there is no detail extraneous/to the composition." [59]

---

54. From Edith Heal's unpublished notes for *I Wanted*, YALC. (1957)
55. "The Woodthrush," *PB*, 16. (1961)
56. "Asphodel, That Greeny Flower," *JL*, 83–84. *PB*, 179. (1954)
57. "To Elsie," *CEP*, 272. (1924)
58. "Theocritus: Idyl 1," *DM*, 67–68. *PB*, 106. (1954)
59. "The Parable of the Blind," *PB*, 11. (1960)

Acknowledgments

Samuel Johnson said of the lexicographer's task "that one enquiry only gave occasion to another, that book referred to book, that to search was not always to find, and to find was not always to be informed; and that thus to persue perfection, was, like the first inhabitants of Arcadia, to chace the sun." So it has been with this bibliography. But many persons have helped, and the faults of this book are fewer because of the quality and quantity of that assistance.

Dr. Williams, with an amused shrug, disclaimed any interest in his bibliography, but invited me to explore, "for what there may be in it," the attic where once he had had his study and where boxes and trunks of little magazines and first editions (now in library collections) had accumulated to provide days of discovery and delight. Mrs. Williams agreed with her husband that finding everything he had published would be impossible, but in her alert and gentle way proceeded to turn up dozens of rare items, and she has continued over the past six years to tell me of new publications, to give prompt, precise answers to questions, and to offer warm hospitality. We shared not only facts but the enchantment of Greece where together we saw the wild flowers, the goatherds, the rugged rocks, the dancing that Dr. Williams had seen in his imagination, and listened to the language of which he had heard an inner measure. In words from "Asphodel," one of the many poems written for her, this bibliography, "for what there may be in it," is dedicated to Mrs. Williams.

James Laughlin, as the publisher of Williams' books, was burdened with time-consuming requests for a considerable amount of publishing data from New Directions files. He gallantly and painstakingly responded with the available information and with copies of books from the beginning to the point where we stopped; we did not reach the end because the demand for Williams' books increases, and several new printings or editions are in process even as this bibliography goes to press, including a fourth impression, bound in hard covers, of the complete *Paterson,* and an enlarged edition of the *Selected Poems.* (Also, forthcoming English editions of Williams' books have been announced by MacGibbon & Kee, London; and an English edition of *I Wanted to Write a Poem,* first published by Beacon Press, Boston, has recently been issued by Jonathan Cape Ltd, London.)

Donald C. Gallup, Assistant Professor of Bibliography and Curator of the American Literature Collection at Yale, has been an invaluable source of bibliographic information and wise counsel. His bibliographies of T. S. Eliot and Ezra Pound were my models, and his answers to my questions saved me many hours and mistakes.

Norman Holmes Pearson, Professor of American Studies at Yale, encouraged me at the beginning to go ahead, and generously allowed me to examine his collection of Williams' books (now in the Yale American Literature Collection) and some unpublished letters, which he has given me permission to quote. As he was also the first reader of an early typescript of the bibliography, and he recommended it to the publisher, I am deeply indebted to him for constructive and friendly advice.

Mary K. Woodworth, Professor of English at Bryn Mawr College, has been a stimulating teacher and advisor. From my last year as an undergraduate to the present, she has heartened and criticized me, always with kindness and tact.

Warner Berthoff, through his persuasive insistence on the historical existence and continuance of literature—"Time's rendings, time's blendings," in Hart Crane's metaphor—helped to shape my attitude toward scholarly inquiry, and, more directly, first suggested to me that a bibliography of Williams' published work was needed.

My earliest debt is to Robert Wallace, who twelve years ago gave me a book of Williams' poems inscribed "in place of flowers," followed later by a bouquet of other books and pamphlets that became the center of my Williams collection.

I am grateful also to Barry Casselman, who voluntarily searched the University of Pennsylvania Archives for Williams' student publications; to Joel O. Conarroe for his record of typographical changes in *Paterson* and for other suggestions; to Ruth Koehler, who supplied much of the information about the recordings in the Free Public Library of Rutherford; to Morse Peckham, who advised on some problems of style; to John C. Thirlwall, the editor of Williams' *Selected Letters,* who kindly lent me his card index of periodicals and other publications containing material by Williams; to Humphrey Tonkin, who wrote in Esperanto to acquaintances in

Acknowledgments

East European countries for information about translations; to Gerald Weales, who remembered theater programs with statements by Williams; to Michael Weaver, who shared the discoveries of his careful and original research with me; and to the following persons who also helped in various ways: Michael Anania, Charles Angoff, Alan W. Armstrong, Edward Bassett, John Bernstein, Mr. and Mrs. Graham Berwind, E. Sculley Bradley, James E. Breslin, James Broderick, Tram Combs, James A. Decker, Isota Tucker Epes, Vincent Di Fiore, Mr. and Mrs. James P. Foley, Robert Francis, Mr. and Mrs. Roland M. Frye, Jack Gerber, the late David Green, Mr. and Mrs. William Gratwick, Edith Heal, Caroline Robbins Herben, Daniel Hoffman, Herbert Howarth, Samuel Hynes, Maurice Johnson, Hugh Kenner, Mr. and Mrs. Ralph Kramer, Richmond Lattimore, Mr. and Mrs. John H. Lewis, A. Walton Litz, Richard Ludwig, David Lyle, Katharine E. McBride, Jerre Mangione, the late William Marshall, Louis L. Martz, Mary H. Merrick, J. Hillis Miller, N. Richard Miller, Prewitt Evans Mitchell, Leslie G. Nicholson, Henry Niese, Mr. and Mrs. Barry Peril, Katherine E. Read, Emanuel Romano, M. L. Rosenthal, Clyde Ryals, Arthur Scouten, Seymour Shapiro, Mr. and Mrs. Ferdinand Schoettle, Mr. and Mrs. Christoph Schweitzer, Joseph Evans Slate, Mary Ellen Solt, Arthur Colby Sprague, Elizabeth Spitzer, Frank Stamato, K. Laurence Stapleton, Edmond Strainchamps, Gael Turnbull, Linda W. Wagner, Monroe Wheeler, Edgar I. Williams, Vera Zlotnikova, Marguerite Zorach, Louis Zukofsky. For kind hospitality and help abroad I am grateful to the late Sylvia Beach, Mrs. Eugene Jolas, and Stuart Gilbert, Paris; Cristina Campo and John L. Brown, Rome; Boris and Mary de Rachewiltz and Mrs. Ezra Pound, Brunnenburg, Tirolo (Merano), Italy.

I am indebted to many libraries, and I wish particularly to express thanks to Oscar Silverman and Anna Russell of the Lockwood Library at Buffalo for their kindness in making available in the most useful way the resources of the Poetry Collection, including its fine collection of little magazines; to Robert H. Land, Chief, General Reference and Bibliography Division, The Library of Congress; to Neda M. Westlake, Curator of Rare Books, Van Pelt Library, University of Pennsylvania; to Mrs. Paul Eckardt, Director of the Free Public Library, Rutherford, New Jersey; and to Donald Gallup and Anne Whelpley of the Beinecke Rare Book and Manuscript Library at Yale for their exceptional courtesy and resourcefulness in locating the material I needed. I also appreciate the courtesies extended by other staff

xxiii

members, both those listed and those whose names I did not learn, of these libraries: The American Library, Paris (Ian Forbes Frazer); Bibliothèque Nationale, Paris; Biblioteca Universitaria Alessandrina, Rome; British Museum, London; Bryn Mawr College (Janet Agnew, Pamela Reilly, Yildiz van Hulsteyn); State University of New York at Buffalo (David Posner, Kathleen Hagan, Paul Carpenter); Cambridge University, England; University of Chicago (Robert Rosenthal, Pearl Freiberg); College of Physicians of Philadelphia; Columbia University; The Library of Congress (Reed Whittemore, Consultant in Poetry); Fairleigh Dickinson University, Rutherford (Robert J. Stanbury); Harvard University (Houghton: Rodney G. Dennis, Helen D. Willard; Harvard College: Foster M. Palmer); University of Michigan; the New York Public Library (Paul Myers); The Public Library, Newark (William Urban); University of Pennsylvania (Rudolf Hirsch, Lyman Riley, Cicely Baker, Barbara Mumma; Archives: Don Kayash); Free Library of Philadelphia (Jerry Post); Princeton University; Free Public Library, Rutherford (Bernice W. Reid); St. John's University (Anna M. Donnelly); Swarthmore College (Catherine J. Smith); Sweet Briar College; University of Virginia; Yale University (Peter Bunnell, Margaret N. Coons).

In addition, I am indebted to the following art galleries, book stores, museums, and publishers for their cooperation in answering inquiries, supplying copies of books, and other assistance: Alicat Book Shop (Oscar Baron); George Allen & Unwin, Ltd. (M. Jay Hill); Appleton-Century-Crofts (Burton Frye); The Art Galleries, University of California at Los Angeles (Doris Coke); Asphodel Book Shop (James R. Lowell); Ballantine Books, Inc. (Ian Ballantine); Bantam Books, Inc. (E. R. Little); Beacon Press (Arnold Tovell, Roberta Fitzsimmons, Jennifer Dawes); Bryn Mawr College Bookshop (Jessica Valentine); Caedmon Records, Inc. (Mrs. Mantell); City Lights Booksellers & Publishers (Lawrence Ferlinghetti, Richard McBride); Columbia Records (C. R. Jenkins); Columbia University Press (Jean-Louis Brindamour); Louis Carré [Gallery] (Yolanda Le Witter); Corinth Books, Totem Press (Elias Wilentz); Thomas Y. Crowell Company (Richard Arber); The Devin-Adair Company (Martin Cooley); The Dial Press, Inc. (Donna Schrader); Definition Press (Martha Baird); Dennis Dobson, Publishers (Alan England); Doubleday & Company, Inc. (Robert Smith); Editorial La Nueva Salamanca (Charles Toth); André Emmerich Gallery (André Emmerich); Farrar, Straus, and Giroux (Richard Holland); Gotham Book Mart (Frances Steloff, Andreas Brown); Grune &

Acknowledgments

Stratton, Inc. (Duncan Mackintosh); Harcourt, Brace & World, Inc. (Gerald Vaughan, Rita Vaughan); Bruce Humphries, Publishers (Edmund R. Brown, Evelyn Beck); Alfred A. Knopf, Inc. (William Finn, Herbert Weinstock); Kootz Gallery (Samuel M. Kootz); Kraft Publishing Company (Gertrude Sobel); The Macaulay Company (Eva B. Lieberman); MacGibbon & Kee, Ltd. (Timothy O'Keeffe, Patricia Connolly, Cornelia Lichtner); David McKay Company, Inc. (Virginia Noe); The Macmillan Company (Emily Tucker); The Metropolitan Museum of Art (Joan Foley); The Museum of Modern Art (Inga Forslund); University of Nebraska Press (Bruce Nicoll, Sue Kripps); New Directions Publishing Corporation (James Laughlin, Robert M. MacGregor, Else B. Lorch); The New York Public Library (William Crahley); *The New York Review of Books* (Alexandra T. Emmet); The Newark Museum (Mildred Baker); W. W. Norton & Company (Eugene Healy); Origin Press (Cid Corman); Peter Owen, Ltd. (Peter Owen); Oxford University Press (Fon W. Boardman); Pennsylvania Book Center (Richard Beard, Peter Nickles); Phoenix Book Shop (Robert Wilson); Bern Porter; Princeton University Press (Julie Anderson); Random House, Inc. (Albert Erskine, Ruth Fenichel, A. L. Friedman); Schenkman Publishing Company, Inc. (Judith Skeist); Seven Gables Book Shop (John S. Van E. Kohn); The Shoe String Press, Inc. (Frances T. Ottemiller); *Sparrow* (Felix Stefanile); Stanford University Press (James W. Torrence, Jr.); Steuben Glass (Isobel C. Lee); Arthur H. Stockwell, Ltd.; the late Alan Swallow; Terrain Gallery (Dorothy Koppelman); Twayne Publishers (Joel Saltzman); United States Information Agency (Ruth Walter); Vanguard Press (James Henle); Villiers Publications, Ltd. (James Boyer May); Henry Wenning; H. W. Wilson Company (A. L. Remley); World Publishing Company (Robert Taylor); Yale University Art Gallery; Yoseloff, Inc., Publishers (Thomas Yoseloff).

For help with typing, checking, and proofreading, I greatly appreciate the assistance of Bobbi Berger, Susan Browder, Joel Conarroe, Grant Cooper, Helene Hollander, Mary Ann Lewis, Patricia Mallory, Laurel Mollett, Julian R. Pace, Enid Bok Schoettle, Catherine Schweitzer, Natalie Terrell, and especially the organizational skill and cheerful dependability of Betsy Samuelson, who helped every day of one long summer. This enterprise has also had the advantage of the incisive wit and logic of Gregory M. Harvey, which helped prevent many errors and inconsistencies. The Computer Center of Haverford and Bryn Mawr Colleges speeded the making of the index; I am indebted to the institutions involved, to John Pruett for his advice about the process, and to Hazel Pugh and Jacqueline Segal for showing me how to use the various machines.

To Bryn Mawr College I am also grateful for the Workman Travel Fellowship awarded to me at the start of this project, and to the University of Pennsylvania and Swarthmore College for faculty research grants that aided in its completion.

I wish to thank Florence Williams, James Laughlin of New Directions Publishing Corporation, Astor-Honor, Inc., and Beacon Press for permission to quote from the writings of William Carlos Williams, as specified on the copyright page of this book. James Laughlin has also given me permission to quote from his letters to me about the books, and to reprint material from dust jackets and editorial sections of books by Williams. Grateful acknowledgment is also made to Mrs. Williams and to Yale University Library for permission to quote from unpublished material in the Yale American Literature Collection, and to reproduce the title page of *Poems,* 1909. A photograph of William Carlos Williams, 1926, by Charles Sheeler is reproduced by permission of Mrs. Williams. Williams' self-portrait in oil, 1914, is reproduced by permission of the University of Pennsylvania Library from the original, a gift from Mrs. Williams.

For the courtesy of permission to quote excerpts from *The Letters of Ezra Pound 1907–1941,* edited by D. D. Paige (New York: 1950), acknowledgment is made to Harcourt, Brace & World, Inc.; for quotations from *Robert McAlmon, Expatriate Publisher and Writer* by Robert E. Knoll (Lincoln: 1959), acknowledgment to University of Nebraska Press; for descriptions from *Glossary of the Book* by Geoffrey Ashall Glaister (London: 1960), acknowledgment to George Allen & Unwin Ltd. Two other books, which have been helpful and from which brief statements are quoted, are *The Little Magazine, A History and Bibliography* by Frederick J. Hoffman, Charles Allen, and Carolyn F. Ulrich (Princeton: Princeton University Press, 1946) and *Being Geniuses Together 1920–1930* by Robert McAlmon (London: Secker & Warburg, 1938), recently published in a revised edition with supplementary chapters by Kay Boyle (Garden City, N.Y.: Doubleday & Company, Inc., 1968).

Some parts of the Introductory Note appeared in my article "William Carlos Williams' Bibliography," *The Literary Review,* IX. 4 (Summer 1966) 501–512, and are reprinted here with the permission of *The Literary Review.* The excerpt from the Wallace Stevens letter is quoted with the

Acknowledgments

permission of Holly Stevens, Alfred A. Knopf, Inc., and the University of Chicago Library. The poem "Still Lifes," first published in *The Hudson Review*, XVI. 4 (Winter 1963–1964) 516, is reprinted here with the permission of Mrs. Williams.

EMILY M. WALLACE

Philadelphia
1968

A BIBLIOGRAPHY OF
William Carlos Williams

* Throughout the bibliography an asterisk before a title indicates that the item is not in one of the collections by Williams listed below.

Kora: KORA IN HELL: IMPROVISATIONS (1920)

AG: IN THE AMERICAN GRAIN (1925)

CEP: THE COLLECTED EARLIER POEMS (1951)

CLP: THE COLLECTED LATER POEMS (1950)

CLP²: THE COLLECTED LATER POEMS, Revised (1963)

SE: SELECTED ESSAYS (1954)

DM: THE DESERT MUSIC (1954)

JL: JOURNEY TO LOVE (1955)

SL: THE SELECTED LETTERS (1957)

I Wanted: I WANTED TO WRITE A POEM (1958)

FD: THE FARMERS' DAUGHTERS (Collected Stories, 1961)

PB: PICTURES FROM BRUEGHEL (Collected Poems, 1954–1962; includes *DM* and *JL*, 1962)

Reader: THE WILLIAM CARLOS WILLIAMS READER (1966)

Page-number references to PATERSON are to the complete collected PATERSON (1963–A49g), designated thus: *Paterson, Five,* II, 262–265. Editions of the books of PATERSON published individually are designated thus: *Paterson (One).*

YALC: Yale American Literature Collection

A

BOOKS AND PAMPHLETS WRITTEN OR
TRANSLATED BY WILLIAM CARLOS WILLIAMS

Section A describes in detail all American and English editions of books and pamphlets by Williams. In addition to the bibliographical descriptions, notes (quotations whenever possible) from published and unpublished material are offered as a representative selection of Williams' attitudes toward the problems and pleasures of preparing each book for publication.

The labeling of the various printings of the books is based on the following definitions:†

edition: the whole number of copies of a work printed from the same set of type (or from stereos and electros of that type) and issued at any time. An edition may consist of a number of impressions if the matter is not altered to any appreciable extent.

impression: all copies printed at one time from the same type or plates. An edition may be published in several impressions, with only slight alterations at the beginning and end of the book or with no alterations.

issue: part of an edition; being copies made up from sheets run off for the first printing but with new matter or arranged matter. Before "issue" can be applied, copies of the work without any changes now involved must already have been published.

state: part of an edition; being certain copies of a book differing from other copies of the same printing by alterations in the make-up or typesetting, either made during the running off of the sheets or at any subsequent stage before first publication.

"Stamped . . . on cover and spine" means that a publisher's device or some ornamentation is added to the title and author's and publisher's

---

† These definitions are taken, with some slight changes in wording, from Geoffrey Ashall Glaister, *Glossary of the Book* (London: George Allen and Unwin, 1960).

names. "Lettered . . ." means that the words appear without ornamentation.

The method of describing collation is a modification of the system used by the American Library Association and the Library of Congress. Following are some examples. For a book of twenty-five printed leaves with page numbers that correspond exactly to the number of leaves, the notation would be simply 50 pp. If, however, the printed preliminary leaves do not count up as pages to the first numbered page of the book, the description might be "2 blank leaves, 2 leaves, 7–50 pp.," indicating that the printed preliminary material counts up to only four pages. When the first numbered page is the verso of a leaf, the number of the recto is given within square brackets: "2 blank leaves, 2 leaves, [7]–50 pp.," thus indicating that 8 is the first page numbered. The collation of "49, [1] pp.," indicates that the text ends on the unnumbered page [50] or that other printed matter appears on that page. The collation of "49 pp., 1 leaf" indicates that the text ends on page 49 and that additional material not a continuation of the text appears on a final, unnumbered leaf, either recto or verso or both being printed.

Significant cross references are given within each section, and the index supplies all references. An asterisk before a title means that that poem or prose piece is not included in any of the major published collections of Williams' work. Abbreviations used are listed on page 3.

a. First edition, first state:

[*The title page, designed by Edgar Williams, the author's brother, has a double line border, a decorative design of flowers around the title and author, and is hand lettered:*] POEMS | BY | W. C. WILLIAMS. | —HAPPY MELODIST—FOR- | EVER PIPING SONGS FOR- | EVER NEW. —KEATS.— | —SO ALL MY BEST IS DRESS- | ING OLD WORDS NEW— | —SPENDING AGAIN WHAT— | IS ALREADY SPENT.—.— | —SHAKESPEARE— | [*decorative flowers*] | 1909 [*Printed for the author by Reid Howell, Rutherford, N.J.*]

1 blank leaf, 2 leaves, [7]–22 pp., 1 blank leaf. 7 × 4 3/8 inches. Brown paper covers printed in black on front; stapled.

Never published, but originally intended for publication March, 1909, at 35¢; 100 copies printed. Two are known to have survived. One, with the inked corrections of the author and his father, is at the University of Pennsylvania; the other, with penciled corrections, is at Yale.

Contents: *Innocence—*To Simplicity—*June—*Ballad of Time and the Peasant—*To His Lady with a Queer Name—*The Uses of Poetry —*The Quest of Happiness—*July—*Imitations, I–II—*Love—*To a Friend (Sweet Lady, sure it seems)—*To My Better Self—*A Street Market, N. Y., 1908—*September—*The Loneliness of Life—*Wistful-ness in Idleness—*On Thinking of a Distant Friend—*To a Lady—*To the Unknown Lady—*November—*On a Proposed Trip South—*The Folly of Preoccupation—*The Bewilderment of Youth—*The Bewilder-ment of Age—*Hymn to the Spirit of Fraternal Love—*Hymn to Per-fection.

Notes: [Unpublished letter, YALC, to Edgar Williams, March 18, 1909:] "The book is on the press now I think or will be in a day or two. I think I shall keep about fifteen copies only for myself and put the rest on sale at thirty-five cents at Garraway's old place. It scares me when I think of it. Only one hundred copies. Could you make a sign to glue on cardboard: Size 1 foot by 1 1/2

Poems by William C. Williams
Limited Edition
On sale now

No price. Let 'em go in and ask."

[*I Wanted,* p. 10:] ". . . what a devil of a time the printer had setting it. Mr. Howell, a Rutherford printer, looked over the script and agreed to do it for around $50. The local journeymen, never having set up anything like it in their lives, must have been completely baffled. When I saw the first copy I nearly fainted. It was full of errors."

[*Autobiography,* p. 107:] ". . . about half errors—like the Passaic River in its relationship to the sewage of that time. I notice, by looking over that disastrous first issue (which never appeared), that it bears the marks of Pop's corrections and suggestions all over it—changes most of which I adopted."

b. First edition, second state:

Misprints are corrected, punctuation altered, and some words changed. The first typographical alterations are in line 5 of the first poem, "Innocence," where "of youth himself, all rose-y-clad," is changed to "of youth himself all rose-yclad."

Published May, 1909, at 25¢; 100 copies printed. Nine copies of this second state have been located: 1. Brown University, 2. University of Buffalo, 3–4. Library of Congress (both deposit copies), 5. University of Pennsylvania, 6. Yale University, 7–9. private collections.

Notes: [Review in *Rutherford American,* Rutherford, N.J., XXXIV. 977 (Thurs., May 6, 1909) Supplement, 4:] "Verses by Dr. W. C. Williams. | POEMS COMPOSED IN ODD MOMENTS BY ONE OF RUTHERFORD'S BRIGHT YOUNG MEN | A neat little booklet, from the press of Reid Howell, lies before us, and the handsome title page bears the inscription 'Poems by W. C. Williams.' At odd moments Dr. Williams, one of the bright young men of whom Rutherford is justly proud, has wooed the muse to good effect, and the result is highly creditable. We are much reminded of that Dr. Williams of an older generation in Rutherford, whose graceful verse won Queen Victoria's praise, and, although no tie of relationship exists, can imagine how proud that gentle soul, long passed away, would have been of a Rutherford boy who is also a poet. . . . [¶]It may well be hoped that, in his busy professional life, Dr. Williams will find more odd moments in which to record his open-eyed interest in the things of beauty, the mind and the spirit. We are reminded that the father wields a graceful poetic pen, and are pleased to notice how gracefully the mantle of good literary expression falls upon the son." Three poems are quoted in the review: "The Quest of Happiness — Love — A Street Market, N.Y., 1908." Williams did not allow any of the 1909 poems to be reprinted, except "The Uses of Poetry" (C528).

[*Autobiography,* pp. 107–108:] "I . . . took a dozen or so of the books to Garrison's Stationery Store in town to offer them for sale. . . . [¶]There . . . they lay for a month or so; there had been four purchasers: one dollar. The rest I brought home, giving them about the family. The stock, a hundred or so copies, Mr. Howell wrapped in a neat bundle (I may have been in Germany by that time) and put away for safekeeping. They were inadvertently burned after they had reposed ten years or more on a rafter under the eaves of his old chicken coop."

[Inscription by the author in one copy:] "William C. Williams | to | Mr. Howell May 20 –09" [Inscription by Reid Howell in the same copy:] "Presented to Yale University Library | Reid Howell | printer | Rutherford, N.J. | Nov. 18, 1940" [Unpublished letter, from WCW to Norman Holmes Pearson, November 18, 1940:] "This is the only one signed by the printer and the author and a presentation copy by the author to the printer at that. I hope you're sufficiently impressed, something had to be done to make up for the quality of the poems (?)."

A2 THE TEMPERS 1913

First edition:

THE TEMPERS | BY | WILLIAM CARLOS WILLIAMS | LONDON | ELKIN MATHEWS, CORK STREET | M CM XIII
31, [1] pp. 5 3/16 × 3 7/8 inches. Pale yellow paper boards lettered in gold on cover and upward on spine; end papers; fore and bottom edges untrimmed; glassine dust jacket.

Published September 13, 1913, at 1*s*. (price raised to 1*s*. 6*d*. soon after publication; dust jacket of *Sour Grapes,* 1921, advertises *The Tempers:* "A few copies only are now available for sale in the United States. Net $1.00"); probably 1000 copies printed. *Imprint at foot of p.* [*32*]: "Printed by William Clowes and Sons, Limited."

Contents: Peace on Earth—Postlude—First Praise—Homage—The Fool's Song—From "The Birth of Venus," Song—Immortal—Mezzo

Forte—An After Song—Crude Lament—The Ordeal—The Death of Franco of Cologne: His Prophecy of Beethoven—Portent—Con Brio— Ad Infinitum—*Translations from the Spanish, "El Romancero": I. Although you do your best to regard me II. Ah, little green eyes III. Poplars of the meadow IV. The day draweth nearer—Hic Jacet— Contemporania—To Wish Myself Courage.

Notes: Dedication: "To Carlos Hoheb." Hoheb, a brother of Williams' mother, was a surgeon in Puerto Rico, Haiti, and Panama.

The inscription by the author in Florence Williams' copy is dated "Nov. 4, 1913."

All the poems may be found in *CEP* except "Translations from the Spanish, 'El Romancero' "; the third and fourth translations are of the same poems as the third and fifth translations in *Adam & Eve & the City,* 1936. The difference in idiom is noticeable; for example, the first line of one poem is translated "The day draweth nearer" in 1913 and "The dawn is upon us" in 1936. (See A17, Notes.)

[*I Wanted,* p. 17:] "It was Ezra Pound who arranged for the publication of *The Tempers.* I paid $50 to Elkin Mathews, the English publisher . . . ."

[Review by Ezra Pound, *The New Freewoman,* London, I. 12 (Dec. 1, 1913) 227:] "Mr. Williams' poems are distinguished by the vigour of their emotional colouring. He makes a bold effort to express himself directly and convinces one that the emotions expressed are veritably his own, wherever [*sic*] he shows traces of reading, it would seem to be a snare against which he struggles, rather than a support to lean upon. It is this that gives one hopes for his future work . . . . His metres also are bold, heavily accented, and built up as part of himself. . . . [¶]One is disappointed that Mr. Williams has not given a larger volume, and one hopes for more to come."

A3   AL QUE QUIERE!   1917

First edition:

A BOOK OF POEMS | AL QUE QUIERE! | BY | WILLIAM CARLOS WILLIAMS | [*device*] | BOSTON | THE FOUR SEAS COMPANY | 1917
87 pp. 6 5/16 × 4 9/16 inches. Yellow-orange paper boards printed in black on cover and downward on spine; end papers. White dust

jacket printed in blue with a long comment on the front, headed "To Whom It May Concern!" Glassine dust jacket. Some copies are slightly larger (6 7/16 × 4 11/16 inches) with tan paper boards and the author's name misspelled *Willams* on the spine. [Letter from the publisher, Edmund R. Brown, August 8, 1963:] "I do not remember more than one issue of *Al Que Quiere,* and I do not think that there was one. It is quite possible that the edition was bound in a couple of different lots and one binding might be slightly smaller in size."

Published December 21, 1917, at $1.00 (dust jacket of *Sour Grapes,* 1921, lists the price of *Al Que Quiere!*: "Net $1.25"); 1000 copies printed.

Contents: Sub Terra—Pastoral (When I was younger)—Chickory and Daisies—Metric Figure (There is a bird in the poplars)—*Woman Walking—Gulls—Appeal—In Harbor—Winter Sunset—Apology—Pastoral (The little sparrows)—Love Song (Daisies are broken)—M. B. —Tract—Promenade—El Hombre—Hero—Libertad! Igualdad! Fraternidad!—Canthara—Mujer—Summer Song—Love Song (Sweep the house clean)—*Foreign—A Prelude—History—Winter Quiet—Dawn—Good Night—Danse Russe—Portrait of a Woman in Bed—Virtue—Conquest —*Portrait of a Young Man with a Bad Heart—Keller Gegen Dom— Smell!—Ballet—Sympathetic Portrait of a Child—The Ogre—Riposte —The Old Men—Pastoral (If I say)—Spring Strains—Trees—A Portrait in Greys—*Invitation (You who had the sense)—*Divertimiento— January Morning—To a Solitary Disciple—Dedication for a Plot of Ground—K. McB.—Love Song (I lie here thinking of you)—The Wanderer.

Notes: All the poems are in *CEP* except "Woman Walking," "Foreign," "Portrait of a Young Man with a Bad Heart," "Invitation," and "Divertimiento."

On front of dust jacket: "To Whom It May Concern! | This book is a collection of poems by William Carlos Williams. You, gentle reader, will probably not like it, because it is brutally powerful and scornfully crude. Fortunately, neither the author nor the publisher care much whether you like it or not. The author has done his work, and if you *do* read the book you will agree that he doesn't give a damn for your opinion. . . . And we, the publishers, don't much care whether you buy the book or not. It only costs a dollar, so that we can't make much profit out of it. But we have the satisfaction of offering that which will outweigh, in spite of its eighty small pages, a dozen volumes of pretty lyrics. We have the profound satisfaction of publishing a book in which, we venture to predict, the poets of the future will dig for material as the poets of today dig in Whitman's *Leaves of Grass*."

[*Autobiography*, pp. 157–159:] ". . . *Al que Quiere* . . . means, unless I am much mistaken, *To Him Who Wants It*. Alfred Kreymborg noticed that the cacophony was a re-echoing of his name and felt complimented. We were very close friends then and I think his surmise was a proper one. . . . [¶]For each of these three books [*Al Que Quiere!, Kora in Hell*, and *Sour Grapes*] I paid the Four Seas Company of Boston something in the neighborhood of two hundred and fifty dollars. They paid the remainder of the publication costs. I never received a penny, so far as I remember, on sales."

[*I Wanted*, p. 18:] "This, the third book, also took $50 out of my pocket. . . . No, it was more than $50, but some of the money could be considered toward my fourth book, *Sour Grapes,* which the Four Seas Company published with no further donation from me. [¶]The figure on the cover was taken from a design on a pebble. To me the design looked like a dancer, and the effect of the dancer was very important—a natural, completely individual pattern. The artist made the outline around the design too geometrical; it should have been irregular, as the pebble was."

A4   KORA IN HELL: IMPROVISATIONS   1920

a. First edition:

KORA IN HELL: IMPROVISATIONS | BY | WILLIAM CARLOS WILLIAMS | [*device*] | BOSTON | THE FOUR SEAS COMPANY | 1920

1 leaf, frontispiece leaf of coated paper tipped in, 3 leaves, 9–86 pp., 3 blank leaves. 9 5/8 × 6 5/16 inches. Gray paper boards printed in black on front and downward on spine; end papers. Orange dust jacket printed in black; glassine wrapper on some copies. Drawing on front cover and front of dust jacket suggested by author. Frontispiece drawing by Stuart Davis.

Published September 1, 1920, at $1.50 (price raised to $2.00 soon after publication and is so listed on the jacket of *Sour Grapes,* 1921); 1000 copies printed by The Four Seas Press, Boston.

Contents: Prologue—Improvisations, I–XXVII.

Notes: Dedication: "To Flossie"

Some improvisations are in *Reader* (A50).

[Letter to Marianne Moore, March 23, 1921, *SL:*] "It should be *tough cords* not *touch cords* [in Prologue]. It is one of the few errata in the book . . . ."

[*Autobiography,* p. 158:] "I decided that I would write something every day, without missing one day, for a year. I'd write nothing planned but take up a pencil, put the paper before me, and write anything that came into my head. Be it nine in the evening or three in the morning, returning from some delivery on Guinea Hill, I'd write it down. . . . [¶]Not a word was to be changed. I didn't change any, but I did tear up some of the stuff."

[*I Wanted,* p. 27:] "Some were unintelligible to a stranger and I knew that I would have to interpret them. I was groping around to find a way to include the interpretations when I came upon a book Pound had left in the house, *Varie Poesie* dell' Abate Pietro Metastasio, Venice, 1795. I took the method used by the Abbot of drawing a line to separate my material. First came the Improvisations, those more or less incomprehensible statements, then the dividing line and, in italics, my interpretations of the Improvisations. The book was broken into chapters, headed by Roman numerals; each Improvisation numbered in Arabic."

[*I Wanted,* pp. 28–29:] "The cover design? It represents the ovum in the act of being impregnated, surrounded by spermatozoa, all trying to get in but only one successful. I myself improvised the idea, seeing, symbolically, a design using sperms of various breeds, various races let's say, and directed the artist to vary the shadings of the drawing from white to gray to black. The cell accepts one sperm—that is the beginning of life. I was feeling fresh and I thought it was a beautiful thing and I wanted the world to see it. [¶]The frontispiece? I had seen a drawing by Stuart Davis, a young artist I had never met, which I wanted reproduced in my book because it was as close as possible to my idea of the Improvisations. . . . Floss and I went to Gloucester and got permission from Stuart Davis to use his art—an impressionistic view of the simultaneous." [A photograph of the Stuart Davis drawing is in *Briarcliff Quarterly*, III. II (Oct. 1946) opposite p. 193.]

b. Second edition, first impression ([*1957*]):

KORA | IN HELL | Improvisations | William Carlos Williams | THE POCKET POETS SERIES | Number Seven | CITY LIGHTS BOOKS | San Francisco
83 pp. 6 5/16 × 4 7/8 inches. Red and white paper covers.
  Published August 1, 1957, at $1.25; 1500 copies printed. *Imprint at foot of recto of back cover:* "Printed in England at the Press of Villiers Publications, Holloway, London."
  A two-page Prologue signed "William Carlos Williams, Rutherford, N.J., March 1957" replaces the twenty-two-page Prologue of 1920.
c. Second impression ([*1958*]):
Published December, 1958; 1500 copies printed.
d. Third impression ([*1960*]):
Published March, 1960; 1500 copies printed.
e. Fourth impression ([*1962*]):
Published October, 1962; 1500 copies printed.
f. Fifth impression ([*1964*]):
Published April, 1964; 2000 copies printed.
g. Sixth impression ([*1967*]):
Published January, 1967; 3000 copies printed.
  In these impressions of the second edition, minor changes only are made on the verso of the title page, on the back cover, and in the imprint, which is moved to the foot of p. [84]. There may have been other printings; although the 1967 impression is labeled "Sixth Printing" on the verso of the title page, records at City Lights indicate that there was a printing January, 1966, of 3000 copies, and perhaps there were three or four other printings not listed above.

A5   SOUR GRAPES   1921
First edition:

SOUR GRAPES | A Book of Poems | [*device*] | BOSTON | THE FOUR SEAS COMPANY | 1921
78 pp., 1 blank leaf. 7 3/4 × 5 1/4 inches. Olive green paper boards

with white paper label printed in olive green on spine; end papers. White dust jacket printed in green with comments about the poems of Williams on the front, about books of Williams on the back.

Published December 9, 1921, at $2.00; 1000 copies printed by The Four Seas Press, Boston.

Contents: The Late Singer—March—Berket and the Stars—A Celebration—April (If you had come away with me)—A Goodnight—Overture to a Dance of Locomotives—Romance Moderne—The Desolate Field —Willow Poem—Approach of Winter—January—Blizzard—To Waken an Old Lady—Winter Trees—Complaint—The Cold Night—Spring Storm—[*prose*] *The Delicacies—Thursday—The Dark Day—Time the Hangman—To a Friend (Well, Lizzie Anderson!)—The Gentle Man —The Soughing Wind—Spring—Play—Lines—The Poor (By constantly tormenting them)—Complete Destruction—Memory of April—Epitaph —Daisy—Primrose—Queen-Ann's-Lace [*sic*]—Great Mullen—Waiting —The Hunter—Arrival—To a Friend Concerning Several Ladies— Youth and Beauty—The Thinker—The Disputants—The Tulip Bed— The Birds—The Nightingales—Spouts—Blueflags—The Widow's Lament in Springtime—Light Hearted William—Portrait of the Author —The Lonely Street—The Great Figure.

Notes: Dedication: "To Alfred Kreymborg"

All the poems are in *CEP*, though not all are in the section *Sour Grapes;* "Complete Destruction," "The Nightingales," and "The Great Figure" have changes. [*I Wanted,* p. 35:] "For some reason I included a short prose piece called 'The Delicacies'—an impression of beautiful food at a party, image after image piled up, an impression in rhythmic prose." "The Delicacies" is not reprinted. "A Goodnight," written for Marion Strobel, is not the same poem as "Good Night" in *Al Que Quiere!.*

[*Autobiography,* pp. 157–158:] "I got it from all quarters: '*Sour Grapes,* yes, that's regret. *Sour Grapes*—that's what you are, and that's what you amount to.' But all I meant was that sour grapes are just the same shape as sweet ones: Ha, ha, ha, ha!"

[*I Wanted,* pp. 34–35:] "This is definitely a mood book, all of it impromptu. When the mood possessed me, I wrote. Whether it was a tree or a woman or a bird, the mood had to be translated into form. To get the line on paper. To make it euphonious. To fit the words so that they went smoothly and still said exactly what I wanted to say.

That was what I struggled for. To me, at that time, a poem was an image, the picture was the important thing. As far as I could, with the material I had, I was lyrical, but I was determined to use the material I knew and much of it did not lend itself to lyricism."

The poem "The Great Figure" inspired Charles Demuth's painting (oil on composition board), "I Saw the Figure 5 in Gold," 1928, which in turn influenced Jasper Johns's painting (encaustic on canvas), "The Black Figure 5," 1960. The poem is reprinted in *The Metropolitan Museum of Art Bulletin,* New York (April 1965) 296, together with black and white photographs of both paintings, in Henry Geldzahler's article, "Numbers in Time: Two American Paintings," pp. 295–299; also in Geldzahler's *American Painting in the 20th Century,* The Metropolitan Museum of Art, New York, 1965 (236 pp., incl. 163 plates; $7.50, cloth covers; $2.95, paper covers); the poem is on p. 137.

A6   THE GREAT AMERICAN NOVEL   1923

a. First (limited) edition:

The Great | American Novel | by | William Carlos Williams | [*device*] | PARIS | Three Mountains Press | 1923
[*Some copies have a rectangular slip covering the name of the press, printed:*] Contact Editions | 29, Quai d'Anjou, Paris
79, [1] pp. 10 5/8 × 6 3/4 inches. Green cloth on spine and one-sixth of gray paper boards; gray paper label printed upward in black on spine; end papers; fore and bottom edges untrimmed.

Published summer, 1923, at $2.50. *On p.* [*8*]: "Three hundred copies of this book were printed on Rives handmade paper and the type distributed. This copy is Number . . ." *On p.* [*80*]: "Finished printing in May, 1923, by Herbert Clarke and William Bird, at Paris and in St. Louis' Island."

Contents: Nineteen chapters, untitled, except for Chapter I, "The Fog." Although Williams describes the book in his *Autobiography* (p. 237) as "a satire on the novel form in which a little (female) Ford car falls more or less in love with a Mack truck," the book contains many sketches of other subjects, improvisations, bits of autobiography, and comments about art; it could be described as an attempt to explore, in a phrase from the book (p. 47), "the background of American life."

A: Books and Pamphlets

Notes: Chapters I ("The Fog"), II, VI, X, and XI are reprinted in *Reader.*

[Letter to WCW from Ezra Pound, Paris, August 1, 1922, *The Letters of Ezra Pound,* edited by D. D. Paige (London: Faber and Faber, 1951)]: "Cher Bull: There's a printer here wants me to supervise a series of booklets, prose (in your case perhaps verse, or whatever form your new stuff is in). Gen. size about 50 pages (??? too short for you). Limited private edtn. of 350 copies. 50 dollars down to author, and another 50 later. . . . [¶]Also the printing will be good, as the chap is doing it himself. (His name is Willyum Bird.) [¶]The series is OPEN: Though I don't at the moment see much more than half a dozen names: Hueffer [later Ford Madox Ford], you, Eliot, Lewis, Windeler, Hemingway, et moi même. (That's seven.) [¶]I take it Marianne [Moore] never has anything but verse??? [¶]This is a prose series. General success or point of the thing wd. lie in its being really interesting."

The series edited by Pound finally included six books printed in the following order on a hand press, with the exception of Ford's book, which Bird had printed elsewhere: *Indiscretions; or, Une revue de deux mondes,* Ezra Pound, 1923; *Women & Men,* Ford Madox Ford, 1923; *Elimus: a story,* B. C. Windeler, 1923; *The Great American Novel,* William Carlos Williams, 1923; *England,* B. M. G. Adams, 1923; *in our time,* Ernest Hemingway, 1923.

[Pound's "Postscript" to *Indiscretions,* p. 62:] "They [the five other authors] have set out from five very different points to tell the truth about *mœurs contemporaines,* without fake, melodrama, conventional ending. The other MSS. are considerably more interesting than is this one of mine, which couldn't have come anywhere else in the series, and which, yet, may have some sort of relation to the series, and even a function, if only as a foil to Bill Williams' *The Great American Novel.*"

[Robert E. Knoll, *Robert McAlmon, Expatriate Publisher and Writer* (B81), p. 34:] "Hemingway introduced Bird to McAlmon in 1922. When he and Bird joined forces, Bird printed a list of books headed 'Contact Editions, including books printed at the Three Mountains Press.' Bird planned that the Three Mountains was to be a printing office, Contact Editions was to be a publishing house. Books produced on his press were to bear the Three Mountains Press label, and the others were to be marked Contact Editions. The distinction was never maintained, however, primarily because of McAlmon's impatience with detail. McAlmon put both labels on almost everything he published. By 1924 Bird's printing office at 29, Quai D'Anjou, Ile Saint-Louis, became the headquarters of Contact Editions—Three Mountains Press."

[Letter to WCW from Ezra Pound, Rapallo, 9 February 1923, *Letters of Pound:*] "Deer Bull: The 3 Mts. printing is beautiful as the feet of young damsels on the hills (or rather better). . . . [¶]I do NOT advise you to pay for having vol. of poems printed. You *can't* sell a vol. You can get it published on royalty basis—that's all anyone can do except possibly Kipling. [¶]L'Oiseau [William Bird] is putting so much energy and cash into making 3 Mts. printing the A-1 double X, that I don't know how the press will survive the prose series. IF it does go on and if your *Gt. Am. Nov.* sells 200 copies, I think he might do the poems (yours)." [Contact Publishing Company did publish the poems (A7) the same year.]

[Letter to Kate Buss from Ezra Pound, Paris, 12 May 1923, *Letters of Pound:*] "Re Three Mts. Press: Your friend can get, or shd. be able to get copies in a hurry from the trade agents in N. Y. . . . Hueffer's book is just out, and the next two [Windeler and Williams] at the binders."

b. New edition, AMERICAN SHORT NOVELS [1960]:

American Short Novels | [*ornament*] Edited by R. P. Blackmur | PRINCETON UNIVERSITY | Thomas Y. Crowell Company · New York · Established 1834

4 leaves, 398 pp. 9 1/4 × 6 1/8 inches. Green paper covers printed in black and white on front and back and downward on spine. Book design by Laurel Wagner.

Published March 3, 1960, at $2.75; 7500 copies printed by Vail-Ballou Press, Inc., Binghamton, N.Y.

The Great American Novel is on pp. 307–343. The other novels are Herman Melville's *Billy Budd,* Mark Twain's *The Man That Corrupted Hadleyburg,* Stephen Crane's *Maggie: A Girl of the Streets,* Henry James's *Washington Square,* Gertrude Stein's *Melanctha,* and Elinor Wylie's *The Venetian Glass Nephew. American Short Novels* is one of five books in a series called "American Literary Forms," William Van O'Conner, General Editor.

American Short Novels was also issued separately, out of the series, in hard covers: "Princeton University" is deleted from title page. 9 7/16 × 6 3/16 inches. Light green cloth boards stamped in blind on front and in black, gold, and bright green on spine; end papers. Green, black, and white dust jacket.

Published 1960 at $5.95; number of copies printed not available.

A7   SPRING AND ALL   [1923]

a. First (limited) edition:

Spring and All | by | William Carlos Williams
[*On verso of title page:*] Published by | Contact Publishing Co. [*Paris*]
3 blank leaves, 3 leaves, 93 pp., 1 leaf, two blank leaves. 7 3/8 × 4 3/4 inches. Blue paper wrappers lettered in black on front, flapped at top, bottom, and fore over first and last blank leaves. Glassine dust wrapper.

Published fall, 1923, at $2.00; about 300 copies printed, but many of these may not have been distributed (see Notes). *Imprint on recto of last printed leaf:* "Printed at Dijon by Maurice Darantière M.CM.XXIII"

Contents: Prose passages interspersed with poems. The poems are numbered, without titles; the title later chosen is given in brackets. POEMS: I [Spring and All]—II [The Pot of Flowers]—III [The Farmer]—IV [Flight to the City]—V [The Black Winds]—VI [To Have Done Nothing]—VII [The Rose (The rose is obsolete)]—VIII [At the Faucet of June]—IX [Young Love]—X [The Eyeglasses]—XI [The Right of Way]—XII [Composition]—XIII [The Agonized Spires] —XIV [Death the Barber]—XV [Light Becomes Darkness]—XVI [To an Old Jaundiced Woman]—XVII [Shoot it Jimmy!]—XVIII [To Elsie]—XIX [Horned Purple]—XX [The Sea]—XXI [Quietness]— XXII [The Red Wheelbarrow]—XXIII [Rigamarole]—XXIV [The Avenue of Poplars]—XXV [Rapid Transit]—XXVI [At the Ball Game] —XXVII [The Wildflower].

Notes: Dedication: "To Charles Demuth"

All the poems are in *CEP;* prose passages that have been reprinted are two paragraphs (pp. 1–2), which are in *I Wanted* (p. 38), a prose paragraph (p. 8), which was printed as an untitled poem in *Broom* (Nov. 1923—C88), a selection for the *Reader,* and see *b* below.

[Robert McAlmon, *Being Geniuses Together* (London: Secker & War-

19

burg, 1938), pp. 270–271:] "Paris bookshops did not show much interest in limited editions, and such books as we published and tried to send to England or America were held up at the docks and in most cases we were not notified. In America the books were seldom commented on and if mentioned, they were mentioned as Paris and expatriate productions, even if their authors were living and had been living steadily in America. . . . Possibly Contact Editions might more than have paid expenses had we concentrated upon the commercial aspect. As it was, with great portions of each edition being lost at the docks the venture only lost money, and so long as the mere printing of books abroad caused them to be censored we let the matter drop. However, I wish now I had a few copies of each of the books published, because booksellers in America want some ten to twenty times what we charged for copies of most of these editions. And the works of Ezra Pound, Mary Butts, Robert Coates, Gertrude Stein, Hemingway (his first two books to appear anywhere), John Herrmann [*sic*], Gertrude Beasley, H. D., Ford Madox Ford, Mina Loy, William Carlos Williams etc., were all on the list of Contact Editions."

[*I Wanted,* pp. 36–37:] "Nobody ever saw it—it had no circulation at all—but I had a lot of fun with it. It consists of poems interspersed with prose, the same idea as Improvisations. It was written when all the world was going crazy about typographical form and is really a travesty on the idea. Chapter headings are printed upside down on purpose, the chapters are numbered all out of order, sometimes with a Roman numeral, sometimes with an Arabic, anything that came in handy. . . . But the Poems were kept pure—no typographical tricks when they appear—set off from the prose."

b. Reprint of prose ([*1963*]):

The prose passages of *Spring and All,* pp. 1–4, 26–30, 34–38, 41–45, 48–51, 67, 68, 86, 90–93, with omission of some passages on these pages, and with the correction of a few obvious misprints, are included in *William Carlos Williams: A Collection of Critical Essays,* edited by J. Hillis Miller (Englewood Cliffs, N.J.: Prentice-Hall, Inc., 1966), pp. 15–26. This collection of essays is part of Twentieth Century Views, a series edited by Maynard Mack (paper covers, $1.95; cloth covers, $3.95).

A8   GO GO   [1923]

First edition:

[*First printed leaf:*] MANIKIN | NUMBER TWO | [device] | MONROE | WHEELER | NEW YORK CITY | 206 EAST 18 STREET
[*Second printed leaf:*] GO | · | GO | WILLIAM CARLOS | WILLIAMS

    1 blank leaf, 11 unnumbered leaves. 6 7/16 × 5 1/16 inches. Gray cardboard covers printed in blue on front; tied with blue string in stabbed holes at fold.

    Published late in 1923; 150 copies printed. *On verso of last leaf:* "The price of Manikin is a quarter—or a shilling." However, Monroe Wheeler reports that the book sold for 75¢.

    On verso of last leaf: "MANIKIN—A model of the human body, showing the tissues, organs, and skeleton, commonly in detachable pieces. . . . Manikin Number Three will contain new verse by Marianne Moore."

    Contents: Flight to the City—The Rose (The rose is obsolete)—At the Faucet of June—The Eyeglasses—Light Becomes Darkness—The Sea—The Hermaphroditic Telephones—The Red Wheelbarrow—Rigmarole—The Wildflower.

    Notes: All the poems are in *CEP*. Everything except "The Hermaphroditic Telephones" had appeared in *Spring and All* (A7).

A9   IN THE AMERICAN GRAIN   1925

a. First edition, first impression:

IN THE | AMERICAN GRAIN | BY | WILLIAM CARLOS WILLIAMS | [*device (Pan)*] | NEW YORK | ALBERT & CHARLES BONI | 1925

    1 blank leaf, 4 leaves, 235 pp., 1 blank leaf. 9 1/4 × 6 1/8 inches. Black cloth boards stamped in gold on spine; end papers; top edges stained charcoal. Green dust jacket printed in dark blue; statement by Williams about the purpose of the essays on front.

    Published November 9, 1925, at $3.00 (price raised to $3.50 soon after publication); number of copies printed unknown. *On verso of title page:* "Printed in the United States of America by J. J. Little and Ives Company, New York."

Contents: Red Eric—The Discovery of the Indies: Christopher Columbus—The Destruction of Tenochtitlan: Cortez and Montezuma—The Fountain of Eternal Youth: Juan Ponce de Leon—De Soto and the New World—Sir Walter Raleigh—Voyage of the "Mayflower"—The Founding of Quebec: Samuel de Champlain—The May-pole at Merrymount: Thomas Morton—Cotton Mather's Wonders of the Invisible World: I. Enchantments Encountered II. The Trial of Bridget Bishop at Salem; The Trial of Susanna Martin III. Curiosities—Père Sebastian Rasles—The Discovery of Kentucky: Daniel Boone—George Washington—Poor Richard: Benjamin Franklin—Battle between the Bon Homme Richard and the Serapis: John Paul Jones—Jacataqua—The Virtue of History: Aaron Burr—Advent of the Slaves—Edgar Allan Poe —Abraham Lincoln.

Notes: Nine of the chapters appeared in periodicals and "Sir Walter Raleigh" was also printed as a poem (B55). Six chapters are in *Reader.*

[Statement on jacket front:] "In these studies I have sought to rename the things seen, now lost in chaos of borrowed titles, many of them inappropriate, under which the true character lies hid. In letters, in journals, reports of happenings I have recognized new contours suggested by old words so that new names were constituted. Thus, where I have found noteworthy stuff, bits of writing have been copied into the book for the taste of it. Everywhere I have tried to separate out from the original records some flavor of an actual peculiarity the character denoting shape which the unique force has given. Now it will be the configuration of a man like Washington, and now a report of the witchcraft trials verbatim, a story of a battle at sea—for the odd note there is in it, a letter by Franklin to prospective emigrants; it has been my wish to draw from every source one thing, the strange phosphorus of the life, nameless under an old misappellation."

[Letter to Horace Gregory, July 22, 1939, *SL:*] ". . . how I came to write the book. Of mixed ancestry, I felt from earliest childhood that America was the only home I could ever possibly call my own. I felt that it was expressly founded for me, personally, and that it must be my first business in life to possess it; that only by making it my own from the beginning to my own day, in detail, should I ever have a basis for knowing where I stood. I must have a basis for orienting myself formally in the beliefs which activated me from day to day. [¶]Nothing in the school histories interested me, so I decided as far as possible to go to whatever source material I could get at and start my own valuations there: to establish myself from my own reading, in my own way, in the locality which by birthright had become my own. . . . [¶]The book is as much a study in styles of writing as anything else. I tried to write each chapter in the style most germane to its sources or at least the style which seemed to me appropriate to the material. To this end, where possible, I copied and used the original writings, as in the Cotton Mather chapter, the Benjamin Franklin chapter and in the Paul Jones chapter, of which no word is my own. I did this with malice aforethought to prove the truth of the book, since the originals fitted into it without effort on my part, perfectly, leaving not a seam."

[*Autobiography*, pp. 236–237:] "It was my first book by a commercial publisher and I was dancing on air—because to that point nothing I was writing had any market: I had either paid for it myself or had it accepted, for the most part, without pay. The Bonis made a beautiful book of it, for which I shall be forever grateful, but, as far as marketing it, they did next to nothing. [¶]. . . In no time at all the thing was remaindered and I began to pick up copies wherever I could. [¶]However, I made some friends. Stieglitz found the book somewhere and wrote enthusiastically to me about it. He even said it had given him the name, An American Place, when he moved to the new site for his gallery on Madison Avenue. . . . [¶]Another good friend I made through my book was Martha Graham, who wrote me saying she could not have gone on with her choreographic projects without it. This was extremely moving."

[*I Wanted*, pp. 42–43:] "The first chapter in the book, 'Eric the Red,' was based on a translation of a Norse saga, *The Long Island Book*. Obviously I couldn't imitate the Norse but I chose a style that was barbaric and primitive, as I knew Eric the Red to be. 'The Voyage of Columbus' came next. I used the Columbus Journal, and I had a devil of a job making the chapter end with the discovery. . . . It meant turning everything around, ending with the beginning. [¶]The Tenochtitlan chapter was written in big square paragraphs like Inca masonry. I admired the massive walls of fitted masonry—no plaster—just fitted boulders. I took that to be a wonderful example of what I wanted to do with my prose; no patchwork. . . . [¶]'Ponce de Leon, Fountain of Eternal Youth' is lyrical, extravagant, romantic on purpose. The chapter on De Soto was used by Hart Crane in 'The Bridge'—he took what he wanted, why shouldn't he—that's what writing is for. . . . [¶]The whole book was written in an excited frame of mind. Floss helped with the research; I was working against time. She is solely responsible for Aaron Burr; she told me what she had read, told it so graphically and vividly I sat down and wrote the whole thing in one sitting."

[Letter to Selden Rodman, November 14, 1949, *SL:*] "It was a startling and original thought of yours to include my 'Raleigh' as a poem [in *One Hundred Modern Poems*]. Yes, I've known from the first that it was exceptionally regular in its meter, but I never looked at it as anything but what it set out to be: an 'imitation' of Raleigh, Raleigh caught in the mesh of his own period's forms. . . ."

b. Second impression ([1939]):

WILLIAM CARLOS WILLIAMS | IN THE | AMERICAN GRAIN | With an introduction by | Horace Gregory | THE NEW CLASSICS | NEW DIRECTIONS | NORFOLK, CONN. [*James Laughlin*]

1 blank leaf, 10 leaves, 235 pp., 3 blank leaves. 7 1/4 × 4 13/16 inches. Yellow cloth boards lettered in red on spine; end papers. Yellow dust jacket printed in green and red; design by Albert Erskine, Jr.

Published December, 1939, at $1.00; 1120 copies printed by offset by The Reehl Litho Co., New York, from the 1925 Boni edition, but reduced in size.

c. Third impression ([*1948*]):

Collation as in *b.* 7 1/4 × 4 11/16 inches. Tan cloth boards lettered in sienna downward on spine (or orange Mactex boards lettered in black downward on spine); end papers. White dust jacket printed in brown and black; design by Alvin Lustig; on back flap is "a recent statement by the author [not published elsewhere] about this book, which is one of his favorite productions."

Published October, 1948, at $1.50; 2200 copies printed by offset by The Reehl Litho Co., New York (1914 bound October 29, 1948, and

986 bound October 13, 1949, by Chas. H. Bohn & Co., Inc., New York). On back flap of dust jacket of second binding is an announcement of *Selected Poems,* published in 1949.

d. Fourth impression—first paperbook printing ([*1956*]):

IN THE | AMERICAN | GRAIN | BY | WILLIAM CARLOS WILLIAMS | A New Directions Paperbook [New York, James Laughlin]

> 1 blank leaf, 6 leaves, 235 pp., 2 leaves, 1 blank leaf. 7 1/8 × 4 1/8 inches. Heavy white paper covers printed in black and white; photograph by R. Johnson on front cover and spine of the palm of a hand against a background of flowers; printed in white downward on spine; comment about book on back cover.

> Published August 22, 1956, at $1.25; 10,000 copies printed by offset by Murray Printing Co., Forge Village, Mass. *On verso of title page:* "First published in 1956 as New Directions Paperbook No. 53"

> Williams' statement about the purpose of the book, first printed on the dust jacket of the 1925 edition, is reprinted on the fourth unnumbered leaf at the beginning, and Horace Gregory's Introduction is omitted.

e. Fifth impression—second paperbook printing ([*1964*]):

IN THE | AMERICAN | GRAIN | BY | WILLIAM CARLOS WILLIAMS | With an introduction by | Horace Gregory | A New Directions Paperbook [*New York, James Laughlin*]

> 10 leaves, 235 pp. 8 × 5 3/8 inches. Front cover same as previous edition; changes in text on back cover include the addition of "Second Printing."

> Published March 20, 1964, at $1.65; 5169 copies printed by offset, but enlarged in size from previous edition. *On verso of title page:* "First published in 1956 as New Directions Paperbook No. 53 | Second Printing"

> The unnumbered leaves are differently arranged than in previous edition: a biographical note is omitted; Horace Gregory's Introduction from the 1925 and 1939 editions is restored; two leaves of advertising at the end are omitted.

f. Revised edition—third paperbook printing ([*1966*]):

IN THE AMERICAN GRAIN | ESSAYS BY | WILLIAM
CARLOS WILLIAMS | Introduction by Horace Gregory | A NEW
DIRECTIONS BOOK [*New York, James Laughlin*]

8 × 5 3/8 inches. xx, 234 pp., 1 blank leaf. Front cover as in previous
edition; changes on back cover include replacing "Second Printing" with
"Third Printing."

Published November, 1966, at $1.95; 5043 copies printed in type face
matching the recent New Directions editions of WCW's collected poems,
stories, novels, and plays (also 1000 sets of sheets printed for clothbound copies—see *g* below, and 2000 sets of sheets for MacGibbon &
Kee, London—see *h* below). *On verso of title page:* "First published
in 1956 as New Directions Paperbook No. 53 | Third Printing"

g. Revised edition—clothbound issue ([*1967*]):

Title page and collation as in *f*. 8 1/4 × 5 1/2 inches. Tan paper boards
stamped in blind with publisher's device on front and lettered in gold
on spine; end papers. White and sienna (or white and blue-green) dust
jacket. Design matches other recent clothbound editions of books by
WCW published by New Directions.

Published January 20, 1967, at $5.00; 1000 copies printed (see *f* above).

h. English issue ([*1967*]):

IN THE AMERICAN GRAIN | ESSAYS BY | WILLIAM CARLOS
WILLIAMS | Introduction by Horace Gregory | [*device*] | [*rule*]
| MacGibbon & Kee [*London*]

Collation as in *f* and *g*. 8 1/4 × 5 7/16 inches. Brown paper boards
stamped in gold downward on spine; end papers. Russet-yellow dust
jacket printed in black and sienna. Design matches other books by WCW
published by MacGibbon & Kee.

Published March 23, 1967, at 30*s*.; 2000 copies printed by New Directions for MacGibbon & Kee; bound and jacketed in England. *On verso
of title page:* "First published in Great Britain by MacGibbon & Kee
Ltd 1966 | Manufactured in the United States of America" *On back
flap of dust jacket:* "Printed in Great Britain"

i. Revised edition, second impression—fourth paperbook printing ([1967?]):

Scheduled for publication, November, 1967; 5000 copies to be printed (also 1000 sets of sheets for clothbound copies).

j. Revised edition, second impression—clothbound issue ([1967–1968]):

Scheduled for publication in late 1967 or early 1968; 1000 copies—see *i* above.

A10   A VOYAGE TO PAGANY   1928

First edition:

[*Within ornamental sienna border:*] A VOYAGE | TO PAGANY | WILLIAM CARLOS WILLIAMS | [*ornament*] | NEW YORK | THE MACAULAY COMPANY | 1928

3 leaves, v–vi pp., 1 leaf, 11–338 pp., 1 leaf. 8 3/8 × 5 5/8 inches. Tan cloth boards stamped in dark brown and black on cover and spine; end papers; top edges stained brown. White dust jacket printed in black, green, and orange with a design by Edgar Williams of a serpent encircling the globe.

Published September 7, 1928, at $2.50; number of copies printed unknown. *On p. [339]:* "This book was designed by Robert S. Josephy and printed under his supervision by the J. J. Little & Ives Company, New York."

Contents: PART ONE, OUTWARD BOUND: I. Outward Bound—II. Paris Again—III. Looking About—IV. Sis—V. The Supper—VI. Carcassone—VII. Marseilles—VIII. The Riviera—IX. The Villa of St. Dennis—X. First Days—XI. Certain Days—XII. Last Night at Ville Franche. PART TWO, AT THE ANCIENT SPRINGS OF PURITY AND PLENTY: XIII. Through to Italy—XIV. Night—XV. The Arno —XVI. Florence—XVII. To Rome—XVIII. In Rome—XIX. South to Naples and Return—XX. Venice and Northward. PART THREE, THE RETURN: XXI. Vienna—XXII. The Doctors—XXIII. The Routine—XXIV. First Week—XXV. Old Vienna—XXVI. Bach—XXVII. A New Place to Meet—XXVIII. Schönbrun—XXIX. The New Room—XXX. Reitschüle—XXXI. Walküre—XXXII. Prater—XXXIII. Goodby Vienna

—XXXIV. The Mountains—XXXV. Lucerne and Interlaken—XXXVI. Geneva and Dijon—XXXVII. Paris Once More—XXXVIII. Seine Sister —XXXIX. Cherbourg.

Notes: Some of the chapters were first published in periodicals— C65, 112, 119, 121. Chapter III and part of V are in *Reader.*

Dedication: "To | the first of us all | my old friend | EZRA POUND | this book is affectionately | dedicated"

[Letter to Florence Williams, June 19, 1928, *SL:*] "I've just finished correcting the last of the galley proofs of the novel this minute. . . . I'm glad it will not be out till you are home. . . . [¶]Less than four weeks now. . . .''

[Letter to Sylvia Beach, June 24, 1928, *Sylvia Beach* (B92), pp. 114– 116:] "The novel is now being page proofed. It will appear after Labor Day, the first week in September. But you shall have copies at least a month before that. Won't you, in fact, send me a few addresses, of those to whom you think I should have advance copies sent. Joyce, of course. Also yourself and Adrienne, naturally. But there must be some others. I have always had a good feeling for Soupault. . . . Then there is Hem. Shall I send a copy to Ford? . . . [¶] . . . The people who are publishing my novel have ordered another for the Fall of 1929."

[*Autobiography*, p. 237:] "It was published by a man from Passaic, N.J., operating under the title of the Macauley [*sic*] Publishing Company. My brother did the jacket—'The Worm' encircling the world. It didn't sell either."

[*I Wanted,* p. 45:] ". . . my first serious novel. The protagonist, Evans, is supposed to have gone on a first trip to Europe alone, an American convinced Europe was turning pagan. He was going there loaded up with Americana—his love of America—to see what was going on in Europe. The protagonist was, of course, myself; his experiences, in a measure, mine. In the actual trip, Floss accompanied me, and the women figures in the story are frequently my conception of my wife. . . . [¶]Macaulay saw the manuscript and felt it was too long. I thought 'The Venus' was the best chapter in the book so I decided to cut that out and use it separately as a short story. It appeared in the early prose collection *A Novelette and Other Prose,* published in 1932 by TO Publishers. It was reprinted in 1950 in . . . *Make Light of It,* published by Random House." (See A19, 32, 46, 50, and C121.)

A11   LAST NIGHTS OF PARIS   1929

First edition:

[*Ornamental green border at top and bottom of page:*] LAST NIGHTS OF PARIS | PHILIPPE SOUPAULT | TRANSLATED FROM THE FRENCH BY | WILLIAM CARLOS WILLIAMS | [*ornament in green*] | THE MACAULAY COMPANY | NEW YORK MCMXXIX

11 pp., 1 leaf, 17–230 pp. 7 9/16 × 5 1/16 inches. Green cloth boards stamped in gold and blind on front and spine; the device of Transatlantic Library stamped on spine (or gray cloth boards stamped in blue and blind on front and spine, without the device of Transatlantic Library on spine; green border and ornament omitted on title page); end papers. Blue and yellow dust jacket printed in blue.

Published September 6, 1929, at $2.50; number of copies printed unknown.

Contents: [*I Wanted*, pp. 47–48:] "It was about a very wonderful little French whore, very intellectual, exotic, strange—one couldn't capture her mood in any way at all—contradictory, amusing."

Notes: "A Note on Philippe Soupault" by Matthew Josephson precedes the translation (pp. [5]–11).

[Unpublished letter, YALC, to Louis Zukofsky, March 4, 1929:] ". . . the translation of Soupault's novel must be in by April 15 which means that I must do at least two pages every day from now to then."

[*I Wanted*, pp. 47–48:] "I had met Soupault in Paris. He was a very amusing person, really amusing, all wound up in Dadaism. I didn't understand what Dadaism was but I liked Soupault. The French edition of his book came out in 1928. I got a copy of it and admired it. . . . I worked with my mother on the translation. She knew French well and it pleased her to work with me. We worked and worked, intently."

A12   A NOVELETTE AND OTHER PROSE   [1932]
                 (1921–1931)

First edition:

A NOVELETTE | AND | OTHER PROSE | (1921–1931) | BY | William Carlos Williams | TO | PUBLISHERS [*Toulon, France*]

1 blank leaf, 2 leaves, [7]–126 pp., 1 leaf. About 8 3/4 × 5 1/2 inches (size varies according to the trimming of the leaves; some copies have untrimmed leaves). Pale green paper covers printed in black on front and upward on spine.

Published January 1, 1932, at $1.25 (advertised price was first 50¢, then 75¢, but custom duties compelled raising the price to $1.25); about 500 copies printed. *Imprint on verso of last leaf:* "Toulon | Imprimerie F. Cabasson | Rue de l'Ordonnance | 1932" *Stamped in red or black below or above imprint in most copies:* "Made in France"

Contents: JANUARY, A NOVELETTE: I. *A Paradox—II. The Simplicity of Disorder—III. A Beautiful Idea—IV. *Juan Gris—V. Conversation as Design—VI. *The Waltz—VII. *Fierce Singleness—VIII. *Anti-Allegory—IX. In Sum (1921–1931): The Accident—Marianne Moore—A Matisse—*An Essay on Virginia—*A Memory of Tropical Fruit—The Venus—A Note on the Recent Work of James Joyce—*The Somnambulists—The Work of Gertrude Stein—George Antheil and the Cantilene Critics: A Note on the First Performance of Antheil's Music in New York City: April 10th, 1927—Kenneth Burke—*Water, Salts, Fat, etc.—*Statement.

Notes: Many of the essays and stories appeared in periodicals. The unstarred items are in *SE* or *FD*, and "The Venus," "Marianne Moore," and "A Matisse" are also in *Reader.* *"Water, Salts, Fat, etc." is a review of *The Human Body* by Logan Clendening [misspelled Clandening in text].

Notes: [Unpublished letter, YALC, to Louis Zukofsky, January 25, 1929:] "While tearing around tending the sick I've composed a Novelette in praise of my wife whom I have gotten to know again because of being thrown violently into her arms and she in mine by the recent epidemic—though not by the illness of either of us, quite the contrary."

[Letter to Ezra Pound, March 13, 1930, *SL:*] "I've been up since 5.30 certifying the death of a man's wife (he cried) and now finishing the correction of the *Novelette.* [¶]The latter will go forward to you by the next mail. It is the prime provocation for this letter. [¶]Naturally Nancy [Cunard] will not want to print two books by me this year. And the poem should come first if she prints either. But the *Novelette* is very close to my heart—and no one will handle it here. You see what I mean. [¶]The *Novelette* contains something I have been trying for half my life, yet—well, that's about enough of that. I hope you like the thing and that you will be able to find something in it suitable for *Variétés*. . . . [¶]Oh, [Eugene] Jolas will be using the first four chapters of the Novelette in *transition*. . . ."

[Inscription in a copy in YALC:] "Gertrude Stein | with appreciations | —and apologies | W. C. Williams | 4/12/32 | —unfortunately full | of typographical | errors."

[*I Wanted,* pp. 48–49:] "TO Publishers, made up of a group of objectivist poets—Louis Zukofsky, Charles Reznikoff, and others—got together and decided to publish some books. *A Novelette and Other Prose* was one of the first to appear. . . . The same method as in the *Improvisations* [*Kora in Hell*] but the material has advanced; it is more sophisticated."

On recto of back cover of *A Novelette* is a list of authors to be published by TO: Ezra Pound, [Carl] Rakosi, [Charles] Reznikoff, [Kenneth] Rexroth, [Louis] Zukofsky, and Basil Bunting.

[Article by Louis Zukofsky, " 'The Best Human Value,' " *The Nation,* CLXXXVI, 22 (May 31, 1958) 501:] "The names of our presses were my ideas: *To*—as we might say, a health to—*To.* I have this that you [WCW] said about it: 'I never knew *To* was a noun gosh all hemlock. I'll have to look that up. Anyway, it's not a bad name for publicity— nobody can understand it or keep from thinking about it once they see it.' " [The letter by WCW (now in the University of Texas library), from which the above statement is taken by Louis Zukofsky, is punctuated differently.]

A13   THE KNIFE OF THE TIMES AND   [1932] OTHER STORIES

First (limited) edition:

The Knife of the Times | And Other Stories | by WILLIAM CARLOS WILLIAMS | [*device (dragon)*] | THE DRAGON PRESS | ITHACA, N. Y. [*Some copies have a rectangular slip tipped in near the foot of the page, printed:*] THE DRAGON PRESS, publishers, | DUFFIELD & GREEN, distributors [*New York*]

[*Half title on recto of first leaf:*] THE DRAGON SERIES | Edited by Angel Flores | THE KNIFE OF THE TIMES | AND OTHER STORIES

5 leaves, 3-164 pp. 7 11/16 × 5 3/16 inches. Blue-green cloth boards with white paper labels printed in dark green on front cover and spine; end papers. Glassine dust jacket covered by gray paper dust jacket printed in blue.

Published March, 1932, at $1.50. *On verso of title page:* "The edition consists of five hundred copies for the subscribers to The Dragon Series and for sale."

Contents: The Knife of the Times—A Visit to the Fair—Hands Across the Sea—The Sailor's Son—An Old Time Raid—The Buffalos—Mind and Body—The Colored Girls of Passenack, Old and New—A Descendant of Kings—Pink and Blue—Old Doc Rivers.

Notes: All the stories are in *FD,* A46. See also A32. The only story printed first in a periodical is "The Colored Girls of Passenack, Old and New," C168.

[Letter to Marianne Moore, June 2, 1932, *SL:*] "A certain Angel Flores who is in Ithaca has published a book of short stories of mine. He's a good friend."

[*Autobiography,* pp. 298-299:] ". . . It made an attractive little collection with which I felt rather pleased; but that was the end of it. Few books were sold and I never heard of Angel Flores again. . . ." A doctor friend of Williams found "a hundred or more" copies of the book for sale for fifteen cents each on the boardwalk at Atlantic City, and Williams asked him to buy "all of them." "So I got a crate of them a few weeks later, but unfortunately let them slip through my fingers as usual."

[*I Wanted,* pp. 49-50:] "This is the first book of short stories. The stories are all about people I knew in the town, portraits of people who were my friends. I was impressed by the picture of the times, depression years, the plight of the poor. . . . I wrote it down as I saw it. The times —that was the knife that was killing them. I was deeply sympathetic and filled with admiration. How amusing they were in spite of their suffering, how gaily they could react to their surroundings. I would have done anything for them, anything but treat them for nothing, and I guess I did that too."

"A Visit to the Fair" is reprinted in AMERICANS ABROAD | An Anthology | edited by | PETER NEAGOE | WITH AUTOGRAPHED PHOTOGRAPHS AND | BIOGRAPHIC SKETCHES OF THE AUTHORS | 1932 | THE SERVIRE PRESS [*ornament*] THE HAGUE

(HOLLAND). According to Neagoe's Foreword, p. xi, ". . . this anthology is devoted to those American artists who have been living and working, during the after-war decade, in Europe—all of that time or part of it." Published December 1, 1932, at $2.50, 5.90 florins, 12s. 6d., 60 francs. The story is at the end of the book, pp. 469–475, and is preceded on p. 468 by a brief statement by Williams about himself, not published elsewhere, together with photograph and bibliography.

A14   THE COD HEAD   1932

First (signed) edition:

The Cod Head | William Carlos Williams | [*printed circularly over device of sickle and wheat:*] HARVEST | [*device*] | PRESS | San Francisco :: 1932

4 pale green leaves, first and last blank. 10 1/16 × 6 3/8 inches. Gray-green rough paper covers with untrimmed fore edge on front; white paper label printed in black on front; stapled.

Published probably summer, 1932. *On verso of title page:* "125 copies only printed at The Harvest Press for the friends of *Contempo:* Chapel Hill, N. C."

Contents: The Cod Head. [Small drawing of a fish between title of poem and text; signature "William Carlos Williams" at end of poem.]

Notes: Inscription in Florence Williams' copy: "Souvenir of Labrador | Summer 1931 — | what a time! | Floss with love —from Bill"

[Letter to Marianne Moore, June 2, 1932, *SL:*] "I met the two children [Milton Abernethy and A. J. Buttitta] who edit *Contempto* [*sic*] from Chapel Hill, N. C."

The poem was first published in *Contempo,* a semimonthly "literary newspaper," April 1, 1932. It appeared in a slightly different version in *Contact,* a magazine edited by WCW, May, 1932. The pamphlet version described above has other changes and the book publications of the poem still other revisions.

Wallace Stevens cites "The Cod Head" in his Introduction to Williams' *Collected Poems 1921–1931* as an example of Williams' "conjunction" of the "sentimental and the anti-poetic," a description with which Williams did not agree: [*I Wanted,* p. 52:] "I was pleased when Wallace Stevens agreed to write the Preface but nettled when I read the part where he said I was interested in the anti-poetic. I had never thought consciously of such a thing. As a poet I was using a means of getting an effect. It's all one to me—the anti-poetic is not something to enhance the poetic—it's all one piece. I didn't agree with Stevens that it was a conscious means I was using. I have never been satisfied that the anti-poetic had any validity or even existed."

[Unpublished letter, YALC, to Kenneth Burke, Sunday [1945]:] "I am sorry but I know the cod head was a cod head and not just a fish head—for I knew that cod was the only thing being caught at that place and had seen many of the assistant fishermen cutting up the fish preparatory to laying the flesh out on prepared boards to be sun-dried.† You might, in the same poem have wondered about the 'red cross.' But there is actually a plainly marked red cross, just like the ordinary 'plus' mark in arithmetic figured on the back of the large jelly-fish or stingeree, seen so commonly in the waters of Labrador. [*Footnote by WCW:*] †I saw hundreds of the heads thrown back into the sea."

A15   COLLECTED POEMS 1921–1931   1934

First edition:

WILLIAM CARLOS WILLIAMS | Collected Poems | 1921–1931 | WITH A PREFACE BY WALLACE STEVENS | THE OBJECTIVIST PRESS | 10 WEST 36 STREET, NEW YORK | 1934

viii, 134 pp., 1 blank leaf. 7 11/16 × 5 1/4 inches. Crimson cloth boards with white paper label printed in black on spine; end papers; fore edges untrimmed. Gray dust jacket printed in crimson. Front of jacket has comments by Marianne Moore, Ezra Pound, and René Taupin about Williams; front flap has "Biographic Note."

Published January 20, 1934, at $2.00; 500 copies printed. *On verso of title page:* "Printed in the United States of America by J. J. Little and Ives Company, New York"

Contents: POEMS: All the Fancy Things—Hemmed-in Males—Brilliant Sad Sun—Young Sycamore—It Is a Living Coral—To—This Florida: 1924—The Sun Bathers—The Cod Head—Struggle of Wings—Down-town—Winter—The Waitress—The Bull—In the 'Sconset Bus—Poem (As the cat)—The Jungle—The Lily—On Gay Wallpaper—The Source, I–III—Nantucket—The Winds—Lines on Receiving the Dial's Award—The Red Lily—The Attic Which Is Desire—Interests of 1926—This Is Just to Say—Birds and Flowers—Full Moon. PRIMAVERA:

Della Primavera Transportata al Morale: April (The beginning)—The Trees—The Birds' Companion—The Sea-Elephant—Rain—The House —Death—The Botticellian Trees. SPRING AND ALL: Flight to the City—At the Faucet of June—The Pot of Primroses—The Eyeglasses— Composition—Light Becomes Darkness—The Red Wheelbarrow—Rapid Transit—The Avenue of Poplars—At the Ball Game—Rigamarole—To Elsie. THE DESCENT OF WINTER: 9/29 (My bed is narrow)— 10/10 (Monday)—10/21 (the orange flames)—10/22 (and hunters still return)—10/28 (On hot days)—10/29 (The justice of poverty)—11/1 (The moon, the dried weeds)—11/2 A Morning Imagination of Russia —11/28 (I make very little money). THE FLOWER: The Flower (A petal, colorless). (PRIOR TO 1921): At Night—To Mark Anthony in Heaven—Transitional—Man in a Room—A Coronal—Sicilian Emigrant's Song—The Revelation—Portrait of a Lady.

Notes: All the poems are in *CEP:* "Down-town" is retitled "New England"; "Full Moon" has ten additional lines; "April" is printed under the title "Della Primavera Trasportata al Morale"; "The Pot of Primroses" is retitled "The Pot of Flowers"; 10/22 in "The Descent of Winter" section is dated 11/22, and 10/21 is changed, beginning "In the dead weeds a rubbish heap."

[*On back of dust jacket:*] "The Objectivist Press is an organization of writers who are publishing their own work and that of other writers whose work they think ought to be read. . . . Advisory Board: Ezra Pound, William Carlos Williams, Louis Zukofsky, Sec'y" The writers listed "to be published": "Basil Bunting, George Oppen, Carl Rakosi, Charles Reznikoff, René Taupin, Louis Zukofsky, Tibor Serly and others"

[*I Wanted,* pp. 51–52:] "The Objectivist Press was the same group who originally called themselves TO. George Oppen, a wealthy young man, was the angel. . . . The suggestion to collect my poems was a lovely gesture from my own gang and I was deeply moved by it. Louis Zukofsky did most of the work of making the collection. Needless to say, it didn't sell at all."

[*Autobiography,* pp. 264–265:] "The Objectivist theory was this: We had had 'Imagism' (*Amygism,* as Pound had called it [after Amy Lowell]), which ran quickly out. That, though it had been useful in ridding the field of verbiage, had no formal necessity implicit in it. It had already dribbled off into so called 'free verse' which, as we saw, was a misnomer. There is no such thing as free verse! Verse is measure of some sort. 'Free verse' was without measure and needed none for its projected objectifications. Thus the poem had run down and became formally non extant. [¶]But, we argued, the poem, like every other form of art, is an object, an object that in itself formally presents its case and its meaning by the very form it assumes. Therefore, being an object, it should be so treated and controlled—but not as in the past. For past objects have about them past necessities—like the sonnet— which have conditioned them and from which, as a form itself, they cannot be freed. [¶]The poem being an object (like a symphony or cubist painting) it must be the purpose of the poet to make of his words a new form: to invent, that is, an object consonant with his day. This was what we wished to imply by Objectivism, an antidote, in a sense, to the bare image haphazardly presented in loose verse. [¶] . . . I for one believe that it was Gertrude Stein, for her formal insistence on words in their literal, structural quality of being words, who had strongly influenced us."

See A14, Notes, for comment about the Preface by Wallace Stevens.

A16   AN EARLY MARTYR AND OTHER POEMS   1935

First (signed) edition:

AN EARLY MARTYR | and | Other Poems | BY | WILLIAM CARLOS WILLIAMS | aetate suae | 52 (in September) | NEW YORK | THE ALCESTIS PRESS | 551 Fifth Avenue | 1935
2 blank leaves, 68 pp., 1 blank leaf, 1 leaf with colophon, 2 blank leaves. 9 7/16 × 6 5/16 inches. Pale yellow stiff paper wrappers printed in black on front and downward on spine, flapped at top, bottom, and side over the first and last leaves; fore and bottom edges untrimmed. Glassine dust jacket. Green slipcase for 135 copies, yellow slipcase for 20 copies.

Published September, 1935, at $7.50; 165 copies printed. *Colophon, p.* [*71*]: "This first edition of An Early Martyr is strictly limited to 165 copies, signed by the author. Twenty copies, numbered I–XX are printed on Duca di Modena, an Italian Handmade Paper, for Presentation Purposes; 135 copies, numbered 1–135 on Strathmore permanent all-rag paper, are for sale, and 10 copies, marked out of series, are for review. Published by J. Ronald Lane Latimer at his Alcestis Press in September,

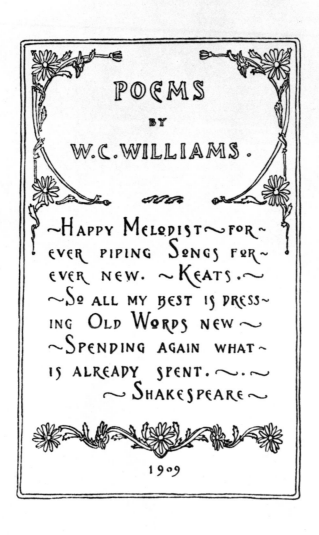

TITLE PAGE OF *POEMS*, 1909
Designed by Edgar Williams.
Photograph by courtesy of the Yale American Literature Collection.

1935. This copy is Number . . . [*signed*] William Carlos Williams."

Contents: An Early Martyr—Flowers by the Sea—Item—The Locust Tree in Flower (Among/of/green)—View of a Lake—To a Mexican Pig-bank—To a Poor Old Woman—*The Sadness of the Sea—Late for Summer Weather—Proletarian Portrait—Tree and Sky—The Raper from Passenack—Invocation and Conclusion—*Genesis—*Solstice—The Yachts—Young Romance—Hymn to Love Ended—An Elegy for D. H. Lawrence—Sunday—The Catholic Bells—The Auto Ride—Simplex Sigilum Veri—The Dead Baby—The Immemorial Wind—The Farmer—The Wind Increases—To Be Hungry Is to Be Great—A Poem for Norman Macleod—You Have Pissed Your Life.

Notes: Dedication: "To John Coffee" (An article by Williams about John Coffey [sic], "A Man Versus the Law," was published in *The Freeman,* June 23, 1920 [C50]).

All the poems in this book are in *CEP* or *CLP* except "The Sadness of the Sea," "Genesis," and "Solstice." "Young Romance" is retitled "Young Love"; "The Auto Ride" is "The Right of Way"; and "The Immemorial Wind" is "The Black Winds," first published in *Spring and All,* 1923.

[*Autobiography,* p. 299:] ". . . Ronald Lane Latimer, of Columbia University . . . started to issue a few books under the insigne, The Alcestis Press. And John Coffee was being thrown out of basement bars when he began to prate his social sermons there. He had been a fur thief working the big department stores, selling the furs afterward to give to charity and his impoverished friends. [¶]It was the depression, I'll say! [¶]Latimer published for me *An Early Martyr,* superbly, lavishly printed on rag paper, dedicated to John Coffee, who had been arrested and sent to Matteawan Hospital for the criminally insane—without trial—to prevent him from getting up in court and saying his say as he had intended to do, that he was not insane, but that he was robbing to feed the poor since the city was doing nothing for them. I visited him there. Later he was let go in charge of his brother. The place was overcrowded." [*I Wanted,* p. 56:] "The poem 'An early martyr' tells about it, the factual details. The title poem is, in effect, a dedication."

A17   ADAM & EVE & THE CITY   1936

First (signed) edition:

ADAM | & EVE | & THE | CITY || WILLIAM | CARLOS | WILLIAMS || ALCESTIS | PRESS | PERU, VT. || MCMXXXVI [*Title within a square of double rules; author's name, on left of page, and place of publication, on right of page, are separated by ornamental rules; the date is centered on a separate line below.*]

2 blank leaves, 5 leaves, 15–69 pp., 1 blank leaf. 9 7/16 × 6 3/8 inches. Olive green paper wrappers printed in black on front and downward on spine, flapped at top, bottom, and side over the first and last leaves. Green slipcase.

Published 1936 at $5.00; 167 copies printed. *Colophon, p. 69:* "This first edition of ADAM AND EVE AND THE CITY by WILLIAM CARLOS WILLIAMS is strictly limited to 167 copies signed by the author. Twenty copies, numbered I to XX are printed on DIDOT paper for presentation purposes; 135 copies, numbered 1 to 135 on WORTHY CHARTA paper are for sale; and 12 copies, marked 'out of series' are for review and copyright. Designed and printed by VREST ORTON, and published by J. RONALD LANE LATIMER at his ALCESTIS PRESS. This is number . . . [*signed*] William Carlos Williams." (The out-of-series copies are unbound. The cover is a single sheet folded vertically, composed of the title leaf, which is omitted inside, and a blank leaf. 4 leaves, 15–69 pp., 2 blank leaves. 10 × 6 5/8 inches.)

Contents: To a Wood Thrush—Fine Work with Pitch and Copper—Young Woman at a Window—The Rose (First the warmth)—La Belle Dame de Tous les Jours—A Chinese Toy—Adam—Eve—St. Francis Einstein of the Daffodils—The Death of See—To an Elder Poet—From the Poem "Patterson" [*sic*] (1. Your lovely hands 2. When I saw 3. I bought a new 4. Better than flowers)—The Crimson Cyclamen—Translations from the Spanish (1. Cancion 2. Stir your fields to increase 3. The dawn is upon us 4. Tears that still lacked power 5. Poplars of the meadow)—Perpetuum Mobile: The City.

Notes: Dedication: "To my wife"

All the poems are in *CEP* except "From the Poem 'Patterson'" and numbers 2, 3, 4, 5 of "Translations from the Spanish" (See A2, Notes).

"Translations from the Spanish" were made from *Poesías Selectas*

38

Castellanas, recogidas y ordenadas por D. Manuel Josef Quintana, Nueva Edición, Tomo Segunda (Madrid: Gomez Fuentenebro y Compañía, 1817). Ezra Pound inscribed a copy of the book: "on loan to doc Williams. | return plez ultimately | to | via Marsala – 12/5 | Rapallo."

[*Autobiography,* p. 299:] ". . . in '36 Latimer brought out my *Adam and Eve & The City.* But still nothing sold. I think Latimer did a Stevens book before he went broke and quit."

[*I Wanted,* p. 57:] "The book is a companion piece to *An Early Martyr.* 'Adam' and 'Eve' are tributes to my father and mother."

A18   WHITE MULE   1937

a. First edition, first impression:

[*Within a border of three rules:*] WILLIAM CARLOS WILLIAMS | [*long rule*] | WHITE | MULE | NEW | [*short rule*] | DIRECTIONS | [*device*] | NORFOLK | [*short rule*] CONN. | 1937 [*NEW DIRECTIONS is at left of device, place at right, and date beneath*]

4 leaves, [1]–293 pp., 1 leaf. 7 5/8 × 5 3/16 inches. White cloth boards lettered in black on front cover and spine (or gray cloth lettered in crimson on spine); end papers; top edges stained charcoal. White dust jacket printed in sienna; comment about book on front and back flaps. Book and jacket design by Sherry Mangan. Postscript to book, pp. 292–293, by James Laughlin.

Published June, 1937, at $2.50; 1100 copies printed (500 copies bound in June, 300 in July, and the remaining 300 bound probably in late summer or early fall, 1937). James Laughlin, the publisher, reports that the date "June 10" at the bottom of the front flap of the dust jacket is the same as the date of the Plimpton Press (Norwood, Mass.) bill, and the publication date would therefore have been later than June 10. Copyright date: June 1, 1937.

Contents: I. To Be—II. A Flower from the Park—III. To Go on Being—IV. To Start Again Once More—V. The Boundaries of Thought —VI. Summer Days—VII. Conflict—VIII. Men—IX. Strike!—X. The Giveaway—XI. Ständchen—XII. A Visit—XIII. The Flirtation—XIV. Gurlie and the Jewess—XV. One Year Old—XVI. Flight—XVII. The Country—XVIII. The Payson Place—XIX. Country Rain—XX. The

Soundout—XXI. Fourth of July Doubleheader—XXII. The Ferry Children.

Notes: Dedication: "To the Kids"

On verso of title page: "Chapters of White Mule were first published in the magazines of *Pagany* and *The Magazine.*" Chapters I and III are in *Reader.*

[Letter to Marsden Hartley [Fall, 1932†] *SL:*] "The 'health' of your views about art is still sticking by me, it helped me greatly to—or it, the 'health' I mean, helped me greatly in the writing of still another chapter of a book I have in hand, the story of an infant who is getting herself up to the age of ten months in the thirteenth chapter now. I'll be sending you the book some day if we both live long enough. . . . [¶]A book of poems should be coming out this spring, the work of the last ten years. The rest of this year I want to spend on my novel, of which I spoke earlier, *White Mule.* Here's hoping."

New Democracy, a periodical established in 1933 with Gorham B. Munson as editor, had a poetry section called "New Directions," which James Laughlin, then a student at Harvard, edited. Later Laughlin used the name for his publishing house, which from 1937 to the present has published more of Williams' books than any other publisher. Also, many of Williams' contributions were published in Laughlin's annual anthology, *New Directions in Prose and Poetry.* [Frederick J. Hoffman, Charles Allen, and Carolyn F. Ulrich in *The Little Magazine, A History and a Bibliography* (Princeton: 1946), p. 215:] ". . . we must think of the entire New Directions front as a noncommercial, altruistic publishing venture. . . . New Directions is a logical result of the widening stream of experimental literature. A channel devoted exclusively to its needs was to be expected; but though there was the pressure of a widening stream, that pressure was not so great that it might not have subsided had not a man of intelligence and sympathy responded to it."

[Letter to James Laughlin, October 27, 1936, *SL:*] "Dear God: You mention, casually, that you are willing to publish my *White Mule,* that you will pay for it and that we shall then share, if any, the profits! My

---

† The date of the letter may be later than fall, 1932. The book of poems is *Collected Poems 1921–1931,* published January, 1934. The thirteenth chapter of *White Mule* was published in May, 1934 (C201), and Williams says in *I Wanted,* p. 61, "The book was written serially and like Dickens I was always just up to the publication deadline."

God! it must be that you are so tall that separate clouds circle around that head, giving thoughts of other metal than those the under sides of which we are in the habit of seeing. [¶]Anyhow, nothing could give me greater pleasure than for you to undertake that task. I accept the offer quickly but without any thought of a time limit of any kind. Think the thing over, going at your own pace, and when you are ready for the script let me know. [¶]There is one point I have to make. The present script, or the script as it stands, amounts to about 22 chapters, about 300 typed pages. It is the first part only of a much longer book which may or may not someday be written. This book is a unit. It has a beginning and a fairly satisfactory end. It will be called Book I. It needs touching up toward the end, something I have clearly in mind to do at once. In a month (or less) it will be ready subject to your call."

[Unpublished letter, YALC, to Louis Zukofsky, July 18, 1937:] "White Mule is selling slowly, so I've heard. They're printing up—no, binding another 300, but that only makes 800 in all so far. That ain't many! But if it pays for itself I'll get another book and so it has always gone with me. It wouldn't be healthy at my age to burst suddenly into blatant bloom."

[*Autobiography*, p. 301:] "That it was a hit of a day with the critics was at least a compliment to us both—my first real success."

[*I Wanted*, pp. 60–61:] "After all I was a physician and not only that I was a pediatrician and I'd always wanted to write a book about a baby. . . . Why not write about Floss's babyhood, combining all the material I had learned about her with all that I had learned about babies. I had spent several days a week over a period of three years doing clinical work with babies: a year and a half at the Postgraduate Hospital in New York and a year and a half at the Babies' Hospital. I was filled up with babies and I wanted to write about them. The devil was in me. What should I call the book? Then it came to me: *White Mule*. Floss, I knew, was a mule. And she was white. There was another meaning. At that time, during the Depression, we were drinking White Mule. Floss was like a shot of whiskey to me—her disposition cantankerous, like all wives, riding her man for his own good whether he liked it or not. [¶]The book was written serially . . . . The installments appeared in a magazine called *Pagany*. . . . Richard Johns in Boston . . . was crazy about my novel *A Voyage to Pagany*. . . . He came to me and asked if I had anything to go in the first issue. I told him I had just started a piece of prose and he said, 'Let me publish it.' I was all excited, a busy physician never free of any case that might come up but with the incentive of monthly dates of publication."

b. First edition, second impression (1937):

The first and second impressions of *White Mule* seem identical. [Letter from James Laughlin, October 8, 1963:] ". . . perhaps . . . the 'June 10th' that appears at the bottom of the inside jacket flap was not repeated on the reprint later that year. If you have a copy that does not have this 'June 10th' date on the jacket flap, then I would say that you can be sure that you have a second printing. But, I'm afraid, the fact that the date is there would not necessarily mean that you had a first, because it might well have been kept on the jackets of the second printing, or jackets from the first printing may have been kept right over to the second, or something of that kind." A copy without the "June 10th" on the jacket has not been found.

Published December 29, 1937, at $2.50; 1000 copies printed. [Letter from James Laughlin, July 15, 1963:] "It appears that only 300 copies were bound up at once, and that the balance of 700 was held until . . . they were combined with sheets from *In the Money* to make *First Act*. A memo of 2/15/45 from American Book–Stratford Press records the destruction, on my authorization, of 200 folded sheets of *White Mule*. This seems to tie in with the 500 sheets of *In the Money* listed in their report of 9/25/42 and would mean that about 500 *First Acts* were bound.

c. Reissue with IN THE MONEY ([1945]): See First Act, A21b.

d. English edition ([1965]):

WILLIAM CARLOS WILLIAMS | [*long rule*] | White Mule | [*device*] | MACGIBBON & KEE [*London*]
266 pp., 1 blank leaf. 7 11/16 × 5 5/16 inches. Brown paper boards stamped in gold on spine; end papers. Blue-green dust jacket printed in black and sienna. Design matches other books by WCW published by MacGibbon & Kee.

Published July 26, 1965, at 30s., 2000 copies printed. *On verso of title page:* "First published 1965 by MacGibbon & Kee Ltd | . . . Printed in

42

Great Britain by | Bristol Typesetting Co. Ltd | Barton Manor – St Philips | Bristol 2"

e. First edition, third impression—clothbound copies ([1967]):

WHITE MULE | A NOVEL BY | WILLIAM CARLOS WIL-LIAMS | A NEW DIRECTIONS BOOK [*New York, James Laughlin*]

> 5 leaves, [1]-291 pp., 1 leaf. 8 1/4 × 5 1/2 inches. Dark brown cloth boards stamped in blind with publisher's device on front and lettered in gold on spine; end papers. White, black, and gray dust jacket. Design matches other recent clothbound editions of books by WCW published by New Directions. Comments on *White Mule* from the reviews of the first edition on back of dust jacket. Table of Contents reset.
> Published March 28, 1967, at $4.95; 1490 copies bound.

f. First edition, third impression—paperbook copies ([1967]):

> Title page and collation the same as *e.* 8 × 5 7/16 inches. White and black paper covers; design by David Ford. Comments on *White Mule* from the reviews of the first edition on recto of first leaf.
> Published simultaneously with the clothbound copies at $1.95; 4929 copies bound. *On verso of title page:* "First published as New Directions Paperbook 226 in 1967."

A19   LIFE ALONG THE PASSAIC RIVER   1938

First edition:

[*Within a border of three rules:*] WILLIAM CARLOS WILLIAMS | [*long rule*] | LIFE ALONG THE PASSAIC RIVER | NEW | [*short rule*] | DIRECTIONS | [device] | NORFOLK | [*short rule*] | CONN. | 1938 [*NEW DIRECTIONS is at left of device, place at right, and date beneath*] [*James Laughlin*]

> 4 leaves, [3]-201 pp. 7 3/4 × 5 1/8 inches. White cloth boards lettered in black on front cover and spine; end papers; top edges stained charcoal. White dust jacket printed in blue; comments about this book on front flap; reviewers' statements about *White Mule* on back. Design of book similar to *White Mule.*
> Published February 21, 1938, at $1.75; 1006 copies printed (505 bound

January 31, 1938, and 501 bound October 27, 1938). Printing and binding by Vail-Ballou Press, Inc., Binghamton, N.Y.

Contents: Life Along the Passaic River—The Girl with the Pimply Face—The Use of Force—A Night in June—The Dawn of Another Day—Jean Beicke—A Face of Stone—To Fall Asleep—The Cold World —Four Bottles of Beer—At the Front—The Right Thing—Second Marriage—A Difficult Man—Danse Pseudomacabre—The Venus—The Accident—Under the Greenwood Tree—World's End.

Notes: All the stories are in *FD,* A46. See also A32. Most of the stories appeared first in periodicals: C48, 62, 121, 147, 164, 170, 180, 189, 192, 194, 195, 202, 212, 236.

[*Autobiography,* p. 299:] "The depression had struck us. Fred Miller was out of employment: a tool designer living precariously over a garage in Brooklyn, he had started a magazine *Blast* (not after Pound's London adventure in Vorticism) to which I was contributing the short stories that later went in *Life Along the Passaic River."*

[Letter to Babette Deutsch, July 28, 1947, *SL:*] "In reply to your letters I must say that I have found little I wanted to say about the labor violence which has had Paterson as its scene during the last thirty or, perhaps, hundred years. You found 'The Strike' [a section of 'The Wanderer,' *CEP,* pp. 6–7]. Good. You will find more in the prose of *Life Along the Passaic River,* especially the first account contained therein."

[*I Wanted,* p. 63:] "This is a continuation of the stories in *The Knife of the Times.* I was still obsessed by the plight of the poor. The subject matter is the same as that of the earlier stories but I had matured as a writer. I was much freer. I could say what I had to say. The best stories were written at white heat. I would come home from my practice and sit down and write until the story was finished, ten to twelve pages. I seldom revised at all."

A20 THE COMPLETE COLLECTED POEMS [1938]
1906–1938

a. First edition, ordinary copies:

[*Star in red*] | THE | COMPLETE | COLLECTED POEMS OF | WILLIAM CARLOS | WILLIAMS | 1906-1938 | [*star in red*] | New Directions: Norfolk, Connecticut [*James Laughlin*]

1 blank leaf, 4 leaves, 3–317 pp., 1 blank leaf. 9 7/16 × 6 1/16 inches. Dark green cloth (later dark blue cloth) stamped in gold on spine; end papers. Black, yellow, and red dust jacket. Book and jacket design by Peter Beilenson.

Published November, 1938, at $3.00; about 1500 copies printed (506 copies bound October 20, 1938, in "legal Buckram," the dark green cloth; and 310 bound February 8, 1939, also in the dark green; 400 bound January 20, 1940, in "Bancroft Buckram," the dark blue cloth, and the remaining 250 may have been bound April, 1945). Printing by Walpole Printing Office, Mt. Vernon, N.Y.; binding by George Mc-Kibbin and Sons.

b. Signed copies:

Collation the same as *a*, except that a colophon is added to last leaf. 9 11/16 × 6 3/8 inches. Dark blue cloth boards stamped in gold on spine; end papers; top edges gilt; fore and bottom edges untrimmed; Hazelbourn paper. Pale blue slipcase.

Published simultaneously with the ordinary copies, November, 1938, at $7.50; 52 copies bound. *Colophon, on recto of last leaf:* "Of THE COMPLETE COLLECTED POEMS of William Carlos Williams fifty copies have been printed . . . and signed by the poet. This is number . . . [*signed*] William Carlos Williams"

Contents: SECTIONS: The Tempers—Transitional—Al Que Quiere —Sour Grapes—Spring and All—The Descent of Winter—Collected Poems—An Early Martyr—Adam & Eve and the City—Recent Verse— Longer Poems—Index of the Poems. POEMS IN SECTIONS: THE TEMPERS, 1913: Peace on Earth—Postlude—First Praise—Homage— The Fool's Song—From "The Birth of Venus," Song—Immortal— Mezzo Forte—Crude Lament—An After Song—The Ordeal—Appeal— Fire Spirit—The Death of Franco of Cologne: His Prophecy of Beethoven —Portent—Ad Infinitum—Contemporania—Hic Jacet—Con Brio—To Wish Myself Courage. TRANSITIONAL, 1915: To Mark Anthony in Heaven—Transitional—Sicilian Emigrant's Song—Le Médecin Malgré Lui—Man in a Room—A Coronal—The Revelation—Portrait of a Lady. AL QUE QUIERE (To Him Who Wants It), 1917: Sub Terra —Spring Song—The Shadow—Pastoral (When I was younger)—Chickory and Daisies—Metric Figure (There is a bird in the poplars!)—Pas-

WILLIAM CARLOS WILLIAMS

toral (The little sparrows)—Love Song (Daisies are broken)—Gulls—
Winter Sunset—In Harbor—Tract—Apology—Promenade—Libertad!
Igualidad! [sic] Fraternidad!—Summer Song—The Young Housewife
—Love Song (Sweep the house clean)—Dawn—Hero—Drink—El
Hombre—Winter Quiet—A Prelude—Trees—Canthara—M. B.—Good
Night—Keller Gegen Dom—Danse Russe—Mujer—Portrait of a Woman
in Bed—Virtue—Smell!—The Ogre—Sympathetic Portrait of a Child—
Riposte—K. McB.—The Old Men—Spring Strains—A Portrait in Greys
—Pastoral (If I say I have heard voices)—January Morning—To a
Solitary Disciple—Ballet—Dedication for a Plot of Ground—Conquest—
Love Song (I lie here thinking of you). SOUR GRAPES, 1921: The
Late Singer—A Celebration—April (If you had come away with me)—
At Night—Berket and the Stars—A Goodnight—Overture to a Dance of
Locomotives—The Desolate Field—Willow Poem—Approach of Winter
—January—Blizzard—Complaint—To Waken an Old Lady—Winter
Trees—The Dark Day—Spring Storm—Thursday—The Cold Night—
Time the Hangman—To a Friend (Well, Lizzie Anderson!)—The
Gentle Man—The Soughing Wind—Spring—Play—Lines—The Poor
(By constantly tormenting them)—Complete Destruction—Memory of
April—Daisy—Primrose—Queen-Ann's-Lace [sic] —Great Mullen—
—Epitaph—Waiting—The Hunter—Arrival—To a Friend Concerning
Several Ladies—The Disputants—The Birds—Youth and Beauty—The
Thinker—The Tulip Bed—Spouts—The Widow's Lament in Springtime
—The Nightingales—Blueflags—Light Hearted William—The Lonely
Street—Portrait of the Author—The Great Figure. SPRING AND ALL
I–XXVIII, 1923: [The poems are in the same order as in the 1923
volume (A7), except that XXI is Quietness and XXII is The Red
Wheelbarrow, the reverse of their original position, and a new poem,
XXVII, The Hermaphroditic Telephones, has been added before the
last poem, The Wildflower, which is now XXVIII.] THE DESCENT
OF WINTER: 9/29 (My bed is narrow)—9/30 (There are no perfect
waves)—10/9 (and there's a little blackboy)—10/10 (Monday)—10/21
(In the dead weeds a rubbish heap)—10/22 (that brilliant field)—
10/28 (On hot days)—10/28 (in this strong light)—10/29 (The justice
of poverty)—10/30 (To freight cars in the air)—11/1 (The moon, the
dried weeds)—11/2 (Dahlias)—11/2 A Morning Imagination of Russia—11/7 (We must listen)—11/8 (O river of my heart polluted)—
11/10 (The shell flowers)—11/20 (Even idiots grow old)—11/22 (and

46

hunters still return)—11/28 (I make really very little money)—12/15 (What an image in the face of Almighty God is she). COLLECTED POEMS, 1934: All the Fancy Things—Hemmed-in Males—Brilliant Sad Sun—It Is a Living Coral—To—This Florida: 1924—Young Sycamore—The Cod Head—New England—Winter—The Bull—In the 'Sconset Bus—Sluggishly—The Jungle—Between Walls—The Lily —On Gay Wallpaper—The Source, I–II—Nantucket—The Winds— Lines on Receiving the Dial's Award—The Red Lily—Interests of 1926—The Attic Which Is Desire—This Is Just to Say—Birds and Flowers—Della Primavera Transportata [*sic*] al Morale: 1. April (the beginning)—2. Full Moon—3. The Trees—4. The Wind Increases—5. The Birds' Companion—6. The House—7. The Sea-Elephant —8. Rain—9. Death—10. The Botticellian Trees. AN EARLY MARTYR, 1935: An Early Martyr—Flowers by the Sea—The Locust Tree in Flower (Among/of/green)—Item—View of a Lake—To a Mexican Pig-Bank—To a Poor Old Woman—Late for Summer Weather—Proletarian Portrait—Tree and Sky—The Raper from Passenack—Invocation and Conclusion—The Yachts—Hymn to Love Ended—Sunday—The Catholic Bells—The Dead Baby—A Poem for Norman Macleod. ADAM & EVE AND THE CITY, 1936: To a Wood Thrush—Fine Work with Pitch and Copper—Young Woman at a Window—The Rose (First the warmth)—A Chinese Toy—La Belle Dame de Tous les Jours—Adam —Eve—St. Francis Einstein of the Daffodils—The Death of See—To an Elder Poet—Perpetuum Mobile: The City—Cancion. RECENT VERSE, 1938: Classic Scene—Autumn—The Term—Weasel Snout—Advent of Today—The Sun—A Bastard Peace—The Poor (It's the anarchy of poverty)—To a Dead Journalist—Africa—Lovely Ad—The Defective Record—Middle—Unnamed: From "Paterson" (1. Your lovely hands 2. When I saw 3. I bought a new 4. Better than flowers)—At the Bar— Graph for Action—Breakfast—To Greet a Letter-Carrier—These. LONGER POEMS, 1910–1938: Morning—An Elegy for D. H. Lawrence—Paterson: Episode 17—The Crimson Cyclamen—The Waitress —The Flower (A petal, colorless)—Romance Moderne—Paterson— March—The Wanderer.

Notes: All the poems are in *CEP,* though not always in the same order or even in the same section; and some changes have been made in some of the poems.

[Unpublished letter, YALC, to James Laughlin, February 11, 1938:]

"The poems won't be hard to get together. I want them to come out in subdivisions of the original books as they appeared, chronologically. A very few alterations will have to be made and a few of the poems will need to be omitted for lack of value but the rest had better just follow along as they first appeared. You fix the date of their appearance to suit yourself. I don't give one whoop in hell—so long as you are interested."

[Unpublished letter, YALC, to James Laughlin, August 1, 1938:] ". . . I think it might be a useful thing to place a date after each of the subheadings through the book, such as The Tempers, 1913, etc. etc. What do you say? That shouldn't be much trouble."

[*Autobiography*, p. 374:] "One young man [at Reed College, 1950] brought a volume of my *Collected Poems 1938* for me to autograph. [¶] 'Where did you get this?' I asked. [¶] 'At the University of Oregon Co-op,' he said to me. [¶] 'Are there any more there?' because I was bound there over the week-end. [¶] 'No,' he said, 'this was the last one.' [¶] 'How much did you pay for it?' [¶] 'Seventy-five cents.' [¶] I offered him ten dollars for it. In New York it was unobtainable at any price, but he refused. It was a perfect copy."

[*I Wanted,* pp. 65–66:] "The *Collected Poems* gave me the whole picture, all I had gone through technically to learn about the making of a poem. . . . All art is orderly. Yet the early poems disturbed me. They were too conventional, too academic. Still, there was orderliness. My models, Shakespeare, Milton, dated back to a time when men thought in orderly fashion. I felt that modern life had gone beyond that; our poems could not be contained in the strict orderliness of the classics. The greatest problem was that I didn't know how to divide a poem into what perhaps my lyrical sense wanted. Free verse was not the answer. From the beginning I knew that the American language must shape the pattern; later I rejected the word language and spoke of the American idiom—this was a better word than language, less academic, more identified with speech. As I went through the poems I noticed many brief poems, always arranged in couplet or quatrain form. I noticed also that I was peculiarly fascinated by another pattern: the dividing of the little paragraphs in lines of three. I remembered writing several poems as quatrains at first, then in the normal process of concentrating the poem, getting rid of redundancies in the line—and in the attempt to make it go

48

faster—the quatrain changed into a three line stanza, or a five line stanza became a quatrain. . . ."

A21   IN THE MONEY   [1940]

a. First edition, first issue:

[*Within a border of three rules:*] WILLIAM CARLOS WILLIAMS |
[*long rule*] | IN THE MONEY | WHITE MULE—PART II |
[*device*] | [*long rule*] | A NEW DIRECTIONS BOOK | NORFOLK
– CONNECTICUT [*James Laughlin*]
    382 pp., 1 blank leaf. 7 3/4 × 5 5/16 inches. Dark blue cloth boards
stamped in silver on spine; end papers. White, blue-gray, and dark blue
dust jacket. Design of book after Sherry Mangan. Jacket design by James
Laughlin.
    Published October 29, 1940, at $2.50; about 1500 copies printed (1008
bound October 15, 1940) by American Book–Stratford Press, N.Y.
    Contents: I. To Wave Goodbye—II. Back to the City—III. Boss's
Party—IV. Home Again—V. On the Block—VI. The Newspapers—
VII. A House in the Suburbs—VIII. Threatening Clouds—IX. The
Four Leafed Clover—X. Vaccination—XI. Introducing the Boys—XII.
The Low Down—XIII. Hotel Room Symphony—XIV. The Faces—
XV. A Final Offer—XVI. The Two Generations—XVII. Night—
XVIII. Inks, Presses and Personnel—XIX. Uncle Oswald—XX. Christ-
mas Again—XXI. Lunch at the Club—XXII. New Year's Jabber—
XXIII. Two Years Old—XXIV. Country Cousins—XXV. Adventure—
XXVI. Happy Days—XXVII. The Miracle.
    Notes: On verso of title page: "In the Money *is a sequel to* White
Mule. *The political pitch of the novel is several years later than the first;
the theme continues as before.*"
    Dedication: "To Richard Johns"
    Chapter II, Back to the City, was first published in *Partisan Review*
(Spring 1939). Chapters XIII, XVII and part of IX are in *Reader.*
    The publication date is printed on a card of invitation from The
Gotham Book Mart and New Directions to meet William Carlos Williams at The Gotham Book Mart on Tuesday, October 29th, 1940.
    [Letter to Robert McAlmon, May 25, 1939, *SL:*] "Driving myself to
it, I've plugged on through the first six chapters of *White Mule* [*In the*

Money] and the seventh is half written. But it's a hell of a job. I wonder whether I'll ever get twenty-four such new chapters written this
year. Not that I don't like what I've done or the prospects of more, but
what in hell am I going to do for time? I'm sunk before I start. As soon
as the typist has finished with what I've just given her I'll bundle it off
to you. Better return it, as there will only be two copies besides the
original script."

[Letter to James Laughlin, June 7, 1939, *SL*:] "Tooraloo, must get
at the new *White Mule*. By the way, I've decided on the title for volume
two: 'A Taste of Fortune.' It has a somewhat musty flavor at that but
it goes, I think, with the story. I did think of using, 'In the Money.'
Like that better? The second is snappier and more up to date."

[*I Wanted*, p. 67:] "Floss is still a baby, as mysterious as ever in her
own way. It is the story of Flossie's family, specifically the success story
of her father and the establishing of his own business in New York as a
printer. The facts are true, the situations fictionalized. I hoped it would
be a good book but it doesn't come up to *White Mule*. I do not appear
in the story; the time sequence takes place long before Floss and I met."

b. IN THE MONEY reissued with WHITE MULE ([FIRST ACT,
1945]):

The title pages for *White Mule* and *In the Money* are the same as the original ones, and no additional title page has been added.
[*On the front of the dust jacket:*] FIRST | ACT | BY WILLIAM
CARLOS WILLIAMS | Williams' two novels—WHITE | MULE
and IN THE MONEY—now | issued together, are landmarks | in
modern American prose.

4 leaves, [1]–293 pp., 1 leaf || 382 pp., 1 leaf. 7 5/8 × 5 1/8 inches.
Gray cloth boards stamped in crimson on spine; end papers. Rough,
gray paper dust jacket printed in dark blue.

Published January, 1945, at $3.50; 445 sets of sheets of *White Mule*
(A18b) and of *In the Money* (A21a) bound together.

Notes: On the back of the dust jacket: "A Note by the Author | The
purpose of this reissue, of *White Mule* and *In the Money*, is to pose a
problem for the gentle-reader—for, as a matter of fact, the present day
reader has again become gentle—a problem as to whether or not a man
should use quotation-marks in fiction. What is the purpose of such
parentheses? It is to indicate that certain words in the text are being

spoken by a specific character. Well now, that's something, something like perspective in painting, outmoded. . . . I can't for the life of me see why one should particularly designate what is being said by whom—at least that is how the writing of *White Mule* presents it. Is *In the Money* a better book by virtue of quotation-marks, or otherwise? Any individual is twenty persons of all ages and sexes, any one of which might say anything."

[*I Wanted,* p. 67:] "I asked Dr. Williams about the 1946 title. He said that it was his and that his inflection of the phrase was: *first* act."

c. English edition ([*1965*]):

WILLIAM CARLOS WILLIAMS | [*long rule*] | In the Money | [*device*] | MACGIBBON & KEE [*London*]

352 pp. 7 11/16 × 5 1/4 inches. Brown paper boards stamped in gold on spine; end papers. Pale blue dust jacket printed in black and crimson. Design matches other books by WCW published by MacGibbon & Kee.

Published February 7, 1966, at 30s.; 2000 copies printed. *On verso of title page:* "First published 1966 by | MacGibbon & Kee Ltd | . . . Printed in Great Britain by | Bristol Typesetting Co. Ltd | Barton Manor, St Philips | Bristol 2"

d. First edition, second impression—clothbound copies ([*1967*]):

IN THE MONEY | A NOVEL BY | WILLIAM CARLOS WIL-LIAMS | A NEW DIRECTIONS BOOK [*New York, James Laughlin*]

382 pp., 1 blank leaf. 8 1/4 × 5 1/2 inches. Black cloth boards stamped in blind with publisher's device on front and lettered in gold on spine; end papers. White, black, and gray dust jacket. Design matches other recent clothbound editions of books by WCW published by New Directions; colors of jacket same as jacket of *White Mule,* to which *In the Money* is a sequel. Table of Contents reset.

Published October 16, 1967, at $4.95; 953 copies bound. *On verso of title page:* "First published by New Directions in 1940."

e. Second impression—paperbook copies ([*1967*]):

382 pp., 1 leaf. 8 × 5 3/8 inches. White and black paper covers; design by David Ford same as for *White Mule.*

Published simultaneously with the clothbound copies at $2.75; 5094 copies bound. *On verso of title page:* "First published as New Directions Paperbook 240 in 1967."

A22 THE BROKEN SPAN [1941]

First edition:

William Carlos Williams | [*title in sienna within ornamental border in sienna and black:*] the Broken Span | The Poet of the Month | [*star in sienna*] | NEW DIRECTIONS | Norfolk, Connecticut [*James Laughlin*]

Three bindings: i. 20 leaves, 2 and 19 blank, first and last pasted down as lining for cover. 9 3/8 × 6 1/4 inches. Gray paper boards printed in black and fuchsia; fore edges untrimmed. Dust jacket same color and design; front flap has comments about book; back flap lists twelve Poet of the Month pamphlets, *The Broken Span* being the first. Book design by Norman W. Forgue. Title page decoration by Paul Hazelrigg.   *ii.* 16 leaves. 9 1/16 × 6 inches. Blank stiff white paper covers. Gray dust jacket as in *i.*   *iii.* 20 leaves, first two and last two of different paper. 8 13/16 × 6 inches. Yellow paper wrappers flapped at sides, not attached at spine; printed in black.

Published January 2, 1941, at $1.00 for *i*, 35¢ for *ii*, and probably 50¢ for *iii*; 2000 copies printed (300 hardbound, *i*, by American Book–Stratford Press; 1500 paperbound, *ii*, by John M. Gettler, Inc., New York; 189 originally intended for binding like *i* were sent to Gettler April 26, 1943, for binding like *ii*, but there were no jackets for 100 of these, which were probably those bound as described in *iii*). *Colophon, on verso of eighteenth leaf:* ". . . Completed at Chicago during December 1940." Printing by The Norman Press (Norman W. Forgue), Chicago.

Contents: A Love Song, First Version: 1915—The Last Words of My English Grandmother (1920)—Impromptu: The Suckers (1927)—A Marriage Ritual (1928)—The Men (1930)—For the Poem Patterson [*sic*]: [*See below*]—Illegitimate Things—The Predicter of Famine—A Portrait of the Times—Against the Sky—The Last Turn.

For the Poem Patterson *contains fifteen poems prefaced:*
A man like a city and a woman like a flower—who are in love. Two women. Three women. Innumerable women, each like a flower. But only one man—like a city.

1. Detail (Her milk don't seem to)—2. Sparrows Among Dry Leaves—
3. St. Valentine—4. Love, the Tragedian—5. In Sisterly Fashion—6.
Detail (I had a misfortune in September)—7. Raleigh Was Right—8.
The Unknown—9. Fertile—10. Detail (Hey!)—11. The Thoughtful
Lover—12. The End of the Parade—13. Detail (Doc, I bin looking for
you)—14. A Fond Farewell—15. The A B and C of It.

Notes: All the poems are in *CEP, CLP,* or *Paterson (One).* "Sparrows
Among Dry Leaves" has eighteen lines in *The Broken Span* and in *CEP;*
the poem is arranged in eight lines in *The Wedge* (A23) and *CLP;*
it is titled "Sparrow . . ." in *CEP.* "Love the Tragedian" is retitled
"Sometimes It Turns Dry and the Leaves Fall before They Are Beautiful" in *CLP.*

[*Autobiography,* pp. 304-305:] "The Second World War had begun
in Europe, but we had not yet entered it. After printing the *Collected
Poems,* Laughlin stopped for a while, but he continued to publish my
plays, articles and poems in the anthology *New Directions,* and did a
paperbound collection of poems, *The Broken Span.*"

A23   THE WEDGE   1944

First (limited) edition:

William Carlos Williams | THE WEDGE | [*on solid blue green
wedge is a design in black of a wedge, a sundial, a sphere colored
orange, and various other curved and straight lines*] | MCMXLIV |
The Cummington Press [*Cummington, Mass.*]

1 blank leaf, 21 leaves, 5-109, [1] pp. 5 9/16 × 4 3/8 inches. Orange
paper (either striped or swirled as in finger painting) boards with the
wedge design in black on front and lettering in black upward on spine;
end papers; fore edges untrimmed. Glassine dust jacket.

Published September 27, 1944, at $3.50; 380 copies printed. *Colophon,
on verso of last leaf:* "The Wedge has been set up by hand in Centaur
& Arrighi types and first printed on Dacian paper. The edition is
limited to 380 copies. The device on the title and cover is from a drawing by Wightman Williams, who decorated the cover-papers. Cummington, Massachusetts, completed August, 1944."

Contents: Author's Introduction—A Sort of a Song—Catastrophic
Birth—Paterson: The Falls—The Dance (In Breughel's great picture)—
Writer's Prologue to a Play in Verse—Burning the Christmas Greens—

In Chains—In Sisterly Fashion—The World Narrowed to a Point—The
Observer—A Flowing River—The Hounded Lovers—The Cure—To
All Gentleness—Three Sonets [sic]—The Poem (It's all in the sound)
—The Rose (The stillness of the rose)—Rumba! Rumba!—A Plea for
Mercy—Figueras Castle—Eternity—The Hard Listener—The Contro-
versy—Perfection—These Purists—A Vision of Labor: 1931—The Last
Turn—The End of the Parade—The A, B & C of It—The Thoughtful
Lover—The Aftermath—The Semblables—The Storm—The Forgotten
City—The Yellow Chimney—The Bare Tree—Raleigh Was Right—
The Monstrous Marriage—Sometimes It Turns Dry and the Leaves
Fall before They Are Beautiful—Sparrows Among Dry Leaves—Pre-
lude to Winter—Silence—Another Year—The Clouds, I.—A Cold
Front—Against the Sky—An Address—*The Gentle Negress (Wander-
ing among the chimneys)—To Ford Madox Ford in Heaven.

Notes: All the poems are in *CLP* except "The Gentle Negress," which
was originally titled "Lillian" (see C333); "Author's Introduction" is
in *SE*. "Sparrows Among Dry Leaves" has eight lines in *The Wedge*
and *CLP*; an earlier version in *The Broken Span* (A22) and *CEP* has
eighteen lines, and in *CEP* is titled "Sparrow . . . ."

Dedication: "L. Z." [Louis Zukofsky]

[Unpublished letter, YALC, to Louis Zukofsky, May 11, 1943:]
"After considerable thought and the discovery of several poems which
I had forgotten about, a decision to include several which I had rejected
and a final determination to cut out the prose bits entirely, the collection
has been finally made up—after considerable effort. This was the sort
of thing I wanted to avoid but I couldn't escape. If it doesn't involve
heart searching and hard work nothing evolves satisfactorily. After I
have made sure that I have a copy of everything I'll ship the book to
Simon & Schuster. They'll probably reject it and then the game will
be on."

[Letter to Robert McAlmon, September 4, 1943, *SL*:] "I've been trying everywhere to find a publisher for my next book of verse, probably
the best yet. They all say they're so sorry but that they have no paper.
I've tried about all. Jim Laughlin, who promised me that he would
print anything I wrote, merely said he'd like to do the book but that
he also could not get the paper for it. I've merely put the script aside."

[*Autobiography,* p. 306:] "When Laughlin ran out of paper for a
new book, I was fortunate in finding two young men, Harry Duncan

and Paul Williams, associates of the Cummington Press, to rescue me once more. I had a script of twenty or thirty poems."

[*I Wanted,* pp. 70–71:] "There were two young men living in Cummington, Massachusetts, running the Cummington Press. They were interested in publishing small volumes of poetry. They were very poor, living in a big house that was part of some sort of summer colony. They lived there all year in order to get along. They manned their own press, had a good simple set-up. We met and they decided to do the book for me."

[Unpublished letter, YALC, to Louis Zukofsky, September 11, 1944:] "Most important along this direction is that the small book The Wedge will be out tomorrow. It has been plain hell to get it printed and bound. It was promised for last March. Finally a binder was dug up (by me) so that the infant will be born—or may be born—it has to go back to Cummington and from there be shipped back to me—then to you."

[*I Wanted,* p. 70:] "I have always been proud of this book. The Introduction, written in the most forthright prose, is an explanation of my poetic creed at that time—for all time as far as that goes. It was written, as always, in a period of great conviction and excitement. I was convinced I had something to say about poetry."

The Author's Introduction to *The Wedge* begins: "The War is the first and only thing in the world today. . . . Then why poetry? . . ."

A24   PATERSON (BOOK ONE)   [1946]

a. First (limited) edition:

PATERSON | (BOOK ONE) | [*the following 4 lines within a border of 5 rules:*] A NEW | DIREC– | TIONS | BOOK | WILLIAM CAR-LOS | WILLIAMS [*Norfolk, Conn., James Laughlin*]

28 leaves, first two and last two blank, first and last pasted down as end papers. 9 7/16 × 6 1/4 inches. Tan cloth boards with PATERSON lettered in gold on front; lower two-thirds of title superimposed on narrow black rectangle stamped across front, spine, and back; fore and bottom edges untrimmed. Yellow-green dust jacket printed in sienna. Book and jacket design by George W. Van Vechten, Jr.

Published June 1, 1946, at $2.50; 1063 copies printed (952 bound for publication date; 111 bound April, 1948). *Colophon, on verso of twenty-sixth leaf:* "Of this first edition of PATERSON: BOOK I, one thousand copies have been printed for New Directions by the Van Vechten Press in Metuchen, New Jersey. . . . The printing was completed in January, 1946." Binding by J. F. Tapley Co., Moonachie, N.J.

Notes: [*Autobiography,* pp. 60–61:] " 'The Wanderer,' featuring my grandmother, the river, the Passaic River . . . —my first 'long' poem, which in turn led to *Paterson.* It was the 'line' that was the key—a study in the line itself, which challenged me."

[*Autobiography,* p. 243:] "The *Dial's* award, though it was given for general excellence in writing during the year (1926) was specifically pointed up by their publication of a four- to six-page poem of mine, *Paterson,* on which I based the later and more extended poem."

[Comments to John C. Thirlwall, January 5, 1959, *New Directions 17* (1961), pp. 269–270:] "There were two or three abortive beginnings, associated with 'The Folded Skyscraper' [1927 (B9)], various half-remembered names—I may have been contemplating a play of some sort, realistic jottings from the conversation of some striking female encountered in my practice, positively not an intellectual. . . . [¶]One of my short stories, 'Four Bottles of Beer' [1930 (C147)], gives the milieu. It's always the same thing. I suppose it all comes from my first poem, 'The Wanderer,' concerned with my English grandmother."

[Letter to Ezra Pound, November 6, 1936, *SL:*] "And then there's that magnum opus I've always wanted to do: the poem PATERSON. Jeez how I'd like to get at that. I've been sounding myself out in these years working toward a form of some sort...."

["Patterson [*sic*]: Episode 17" was published in 1937 (C245).]

[Unpublished letter to Robert McAlmon, July 18, 1939:] "I'm always eager to write. Never get enough of it and never catch up with myself. I could keep it up pretty steadily, do two books a year or so—and do real research (Pound's slogan: Nobody wants to do exercises so that they can keep up their technique!). I am crazy to finish the long poem I started years ago: Paterson. I'd really like to *do* that one, really go to work on the ground and dig up a Paterson that would be a true Inferno. But I'm a doctor and don't seem to be able to free myself as Pound has freed himself from the importunities of daily existence."

[Letter to Horace Gregory, January 1, 1945, *SL:*] "All this fall I have wanted to get to the 'Paterson' poem again and as before I always find a dozen reasons for doing nothing about it. I see the mass of material I have collected and that is enough. I shy away and write something else. The thing is the problems involved require too much work for the time I have at my disposal."

[Letter to Horace Gregory, February 8, 1945, *SL*:] "Had my dear friend Kitty Hoagland . . . type out the first finished draft of the 1st quarter of the 'Paterson' thing two days ago—she and Flossie were both curiously impressed and agreed that I should have my pants kicked —a good sign."

[Letter to Norman Macleod, July 25, 1945, *SL*:] ". . . already I have been informed that *Paterson* will not be accepted because of its formlessness, because I have not organized it into some neo-classic *recognizable* context. Christ! Are there no intelligent men left in the world?"

[Inscription in Florence Williams' copy:] "Floss: A long wait for this but we've got all the time there is my dear—with my love. Bill"

[*I Wanted*, p. 74:] "Writing continuously for eight years, I brought out each Part as it was completed. There was a great deal of publicity; gratifying things were said. I had thought about it all a long time. I knew I had what I wanted to say. I knew I wanted to say it in *my* form. I was aware that it wasn't a finished form, yet I knew it was not formless. I had to invent my form . . . . I respected the rules but I decided I must define the traditional in terms of my own world."

[Unpublished letter to Norman Holmes Pearson, January 21, 1959:] "Book I of Paterson . . . gives the very bones of the argument without which the whole will fall apart."

For other editions, see descriptions below under *Paterson* [Collected] —A49.

A25   PATERSON (BOOK TWO)   [1948]

a. First (limited) edition:

PATERSON | (BOOK TWO) | [*the following 4 lines within a border of 5 rules:*] A NEW | DIREC- | TIONS | BOOK | WILLIAM CARLOS | WILLIAMS [*Norfolk, Conn., James Laughlin*]

32 leaves, first two and last one blank, first and last pasted down as end papers. 9 7/16 × 6 1/4 inches. Tan cloth boards with PATERSON lettered in gold on front; lower two-thirds of title superimposed on narrow green rectangle stamped across front, spine, and back; fore and bottom edges untrimmed. Yellow-green dust jacket printed in green. Book and jacket design by George W. Van Vechten, Jr.

Published April, 1948, at $3.00; 1009 copies printed (1002 bound April 1, 1948; 7 bound April 13, 1948). *Colophon, on recto of thirty-first leaf:* "Of this first edition of PATERSON: Book II, one thousand copies have been printed for New Directions by the Van Vechten Press in Metuchen, New Jersey. . . . The printing was completed in January, 1948."

Notes: [Letter to Robert McAlmon, March 9, 1947, *SL:*] "Of late I've been plugging hard, every available moment, on *Paterson*. Book II. The whole of the four books has been roughly sketched out for several years. I've finished Book I. So now Book II is up. During January and February I worked on assembling the notes I had on this book and connecting them up in some sort of order. I'm no stenographer so that as I must do all the work myself, at odd moments, on what amounts to composition; I've been extremely busy. Yesterday I finally got the 90 odd pages of the 'full' version—as I call it—down on paper. It's pretty loose stuff, but the thread, I think, is there. It's there, in other words—such as it is. [¶]Now comes the job of cutting and clarifying. I dread the job of retyping the stuff and no one can help me. If I feel a bit optimistic things go well. You know the feeling. But if I hit a low spot and the whole business seems a redundant heap of garbage, the work stops short."

[Unpublished letter, YALC, to Kenneth Burke, June 20, 1947:] "Meanwhile Paterson II has been completed—more or less—and sent to Laughlin for the printer. It contains the 'prayer' you wanted me to write."

[Letter to Babette Deutsch, July 28, 1947, *SL:*] "In Part or Book II, soon to appear (this fall, I think), there will be . . . much more relating to the economic distress occasioned by human greed and blindness —aided, as always, by the church, all churches in the broadest sense of that designation—but still, there will be little treating directly of the rise of labor as a named force. I am not a Marxian."

For other editions, see descriptions below under *Paterson* [Collected] —A49.

A26 THE CLOUDS 1948

First (limited) edition:

William Carlos Williams | THE CLOUDS, | Aigeltinger, Russia, &. | Published jointly by The Wells College Press | and The Cummington

A: Books and Pamphlets

Press. Mcmxlviij. | 3 [*all of the above printed on the top quarter of the page, except for the number 3*]

4 blank leaves, 64 pp., 4 blank leaves, first and last leaves pasted down as end papers. 9 3/8 × 5 13/16 inches (size of unsigned copies varies slightly). Slate cloth boards with gray paper label printed upward in black on spine; fore edges untrimmed. Signed copies have slipcase covered with matching cloth and blue-gray paper.

Published summer, 1948; 310 copies printed, I through LX on English handmade paper, signed and in cases at $12.50; 61 to 310 on all-rag paper, without cases, at $5.00. *Colophon, on recto of p. 1:* "[*signed*] William Carlos Williams | This is number . . . of 310 copies printed, I through LX being signed by the author." *On verso of p. 64:* "Excusum Aurorae in Novo Eboraco mensibus Aprili & Maio Mcmxlviij. H.D. & W.W. finxerunt & fecerunt propter liberalitatem Victoris Hammer. Cornelia & Petrus Franck conglutinerunt. | Habere & dispertire." (The out-of-series copies are unbound. Blue wrapper. Same collation and size of leaves as bound copies.)

Contents: i. Aigeltinger—ii. Franklin Square—iii. Labrador—iv. The Apparition—v. The Light Shall Not Enter—vi. A Woman in Front of a Bank—vii. The Night Rider—viii. Chanson—ix. The Birdsong—x. The Visit—xi. The Quality of Heaven—xii. To a Lovely Old Bitch—xiii. The Bitter World of Spring—xiv. Lament—xv. A History of Love—xvi. Mists over the River—xvii. When Structure Fails Rhyme Attempts to Come to the Rescue—xviii. Education a Failure—xix. The Banner Bearer—xx. The Goat—xxi. Two Deliberate Exercises: 1. Lesson from a Pupil Recital 2. Voyages—xxii. The Mirrors—xxiii. His Daughter—xxiv. Design for November—xxv. The Manoeuvre—xxvi. The Horse—xxvii. Hard Times—xxviii. The Dish of Fruit—xxix. The Motor-Barge—xxx. Russia—xxxi. The Act—xxxii. The Savage Beast—xxxiii. The Well Disciplined Bargeman—xxxiv. Raindrops on a Briar—xxxv. Ol' Bunk's Band—xxxvi. Suzanne—xxxvii. Navajo—xxxviii. Graph—xxxix. The Testament of Perpetual Change—xl. The Flower (This too I love)—xli. For a Low Voice—xlii. The Words Lying Idle—xliii. Lear—xliv. Picture of a Nude in a Machine Shop—xlv. The Brilliance—xlvi. A Unison—xlvii. The Semblables—xlviii. The Hurricane—xlix. The Province—l. The Mind's Games—li. The Stylist—lii. Note to Music: Brahms 1st Piano Concerto—liii. The Injury—liv. The Red-Wing Blackbird—lv. A Place (Any Place) to Transcend All Places—lvi. The Old

House—lvii. The Thing—lviii. The Mind Hesitant—lix. Tragic Detail —lx. Philomena Andronico—lxi. The Clouds.

Notes: All the poems are in *CLP*, though not all are in the section *The Clouds.* Two poems, "The Brilliance" and "The Province," are also in *CEP*. A brief commentary by WCW about the title poem, "The Clouds," is in *Modern Poetry, American and British*—B61.

[*I Wanted*, p. 75:] "The two young men [Harry Duncan and Paul Wightman Williams] who had brought out *The Wedge* on their hand press were given the opportunity to use the Wells College Press in the making of *The Clouds.*"

[Unsigned review in *The New Yorker*, XXIV. 49 (Jan. 29, 1949) 72:] "Two fine hand presses have combined forces to produce this beautifully bound and printed limited edition of Dr. Williams' latest lyrics. The poems are as musical, unexpected, and wittily varied as ever."

A27   A DREAM OF LOVE   [1948]

First edition:

A DREAM OF LOVE | A Play In Three Acts And Eight Scenes | WILLIAM CARLOS WILLIAMS | Direction | SIX [*New Directions, Norfolk, Conn., James Laughlin*]

107, [1] pp., 2 leaves. 9 1/2 × 6 5/16 inches. Brown heavy paper covers printed in black on front; designed by Alvin Lustig.

Published September 16, 1948, at $1.50; 1700 copies printed. *On verso of title page:* "Printed by Dudley Kimball | at the Blue Ridge Mountain Press | Parsippany, New Jersey" Binding by Joseph Brown.

On p. [2]: "Direction | The magazine is published quarterly by New Directions, each number being devoted to a single long work by one author, or to a group of his shorter pieces." The works published included: *Joseph Conrad* by Albert Guerard, Jr., *Nine Stories* by Vladimir Nabokov, *Toward Balzac* by Harry Levin, *Who Has Been Tampering with These Pianos?* by Montagu O'Reilly, and *The Skin of Dreams* by Raymond Queneau.

Notes: A Dream of Love is in *Many Loves and Other Plays* (A47). Act I, scene 1, is in *Reader.*

["Notes on William Carlos Williams as Playwright," by John C. Thirlwall, *Many Loves* (A47), pp. 433–434:] "*A Dream of Love* 'floated' about for two years, in and out of the hands of agents. To one agent who had delicately refused the play as not fully dramatic, Williams wrote: 'There are plays less dramatic in movement that are well capable of holding audience interest for two hours of an evening—an intelligent interest which is quite legitimate. The drama in *A Dream of Love* lies in this sector, not so much in conflict (there is very little conflict in *The Cherry Orchard*) as in revelation, development of the Doctor's situation. How far will he go and what will be the effect on some of the other characters?' [¶]In July of 1949, in the middle of one of New York's worst heat waves, *A Dream of Love* was put on at the Hudson Guild Playhouse by an off-Broadway little theatre group called 'We Present.' . . . William Saroyan gave the play a rave review in the *New York Herald Tribune,* but there was no air-conditioning in the theatre and it survived for only two weeks. . . . [¶]*A Dream of Love* has since been staged by Clinton Atkinson at Wesleyan University [D20], and there were public readings in February, 1961, at the National Arts Club by the Mannahatta Theatre Club, directed by Fred Stewart . . . ."

A28   SELECTED POEMS   [1949]

a. First edition, first impression:

WILLIAM CARLOS | WILLIAMS | SELECTED POEMS | with an introduction by Randall Jarrell | The New Classics Series [*New Directions, Norfolk, Conn., James Laughlin*]
xix, 140 pp. 7 3/16 × 4 7/8 inches. Tan cloth boards lettered in sienna downward on spine. Black and orange-brown dust jacket printed in white; tan end papers. Jacket design by Alvin Lustig.
    Published March, 1949, at $1.50; 3591 copies printed (1997 bound March 31, 1949; 1594 bound January 31, 1950) by Vail-Ballou Press, Inc., Binghamton, N.Y.
    Contents: To Mark Anthony in Heaven—A Coronal—Portrait of a Lady—El Hombre—Tract—Pastoral (The little sparrows)—The Young Housewife—Danse Russe—Smell!—Spring Strains—January Morning, I–XV—Dedication for a Plot of Ground—Love Song (I lie here thinking of you)—Overture to a Dance of Locomotives—Complaint—To Waken an Old Lady—Queen-Ann's-Lace [sic]—Great Mullen—Waiting —The Hunter—Arrival—The Widow's Lament in Springtime—The

Lonely Street—The Term—The Attic which Is Desire—The Last Words of My English Grandmother—From the Wanderer: A Rococo Study (Paterson The Strike)—Spring and All: I [Spring and All], II [The Pot of Flowers], VII [The Rose (The rose is obsolete)], XVIII [To Elsie], XXI [The Red Wheelbarrow], XXVI [At the Ball Game]—This Is Just to Say—Proletarian Portrait—The Locust Tree in Flower (Among/of/green)—The Descent of Winter: 9/30 (There are no perfect waves), 10/22 (That brilliant field), 10/28 (in this strong light)—Impromptu: The Suckers—All the Fancy Things—It is a Living Coral—Young Sycamore—The Cod Head—The Bull—Poem (As the cat)—Between Walls—On Gay Wallpaper—The Lily—Nantucket—The Red Lily—The Trees—The Wind Increases—The Birds' Companion—The Sea-Elephant—Rain—Death—The Botticellian Trees—Flowers by the Sea—To a Poor Old Woman—The Yachts—The Catholic Bells—Fine Work with Pitch and Copper—Adam—St. Francis Einstein of the Daffodils—Perpetuum Mobile: The City—These—An Elegy for D. H. Lawrence—Paterson: The Falls—Paterson: Episode from Book III—A Marriage Ritual—A Sort of a Song—Franklin Square—The Dance (In Breughel's great picture)—Raleigh Was Right—The Poor (It's the anarchy of poverty)—The Semblables—Burning the Christmas Greens—To Ford Madox Ford in Heaven—Choral: The Pink Church—April 6 The Quality of Heaven—The Visit—A Unison—The Injury—Ol' Bunk's Band—The Clouds, I–IV—The Lion, I–II—Lear—The Horse Show.

Notes: Inscription in Florence Williams' copy: "Floss from Bill on March 14, 1949."

All the poems are in *CEP* or *CLP*. "Paterson: Episode from Book III" is retitled "Paterson: Episode 17" in *CEP;* "April 6" is retitled "Aigeltinger" in *CLP*. The poems from *Spring and All* are numbered but untitled in *Selected Poems;* the bracketed titles are those in *CEP*.

b. First edition, second impression ([1950]):

Minor changes only: the end papers are white instead of tan; added to the dust jacket is the announcement: "The National Book Award for Poetry was won in 1950 by William Carlos Williams for Paterson & Selected Poems"

Published spring, 1950, at $1.75; 4000 copies printed (2000 bound April, 1950; 1000 bound February 12, 1959; 1000 bound December 22, 1960).

c. Third impression—first paperbook printing ([1963]):

WILLIAM CARLOS | WILLIAMS | SELECTED POEMS | with an introduction by Randall Jarrell | A New Directions Paperbook
> Same collation as *a* and *b*. 7 1/8 × 4 5/16 inches. Heavy paper covers printed in black and white; photograph of WCW on front by Tram [Combs]; design by David Ford.
>
> Published January, 1963, at $1.50; 6751 copies printed by Vail-Ballou Press, Binghamton, N.Y. *On verso of title page:* "First published in New Directions *New Classics* Series, 1949. First published paperbound as New Directions Paperbook Number 131, 1963."

d. Fourth impression—second paperbook printing ([1964]):

> Published March 11, 1964; 8121 copies printed.

e. Fifth impression—third paperbook printing ([1965]):

> Published August 21, 1965; 7803 copies printed.

f. Sixth impression—fourth paperbook printing ([1966]):

> Published July 21, 1966; 10,028 copies bound.

g. Seventh impression—fifth paperbook printing ([1967]):

> Published June 28, 1967; 11,894 copies bound.

A29   THE PINK CHURCH   1949

First (limited) edition:

[*Title and ornament in brown and author's name in sienna on a blue square; all else in sienna below the square:*] THE | PINK CHURCH | [*ornament*] | WILLIAM | CARLOS | WILLIAMS | GOLDEN GOOSE CHAP BOOK I | Published by | Golden Goose Press | Columbus Ohio: 1949
> 14 unnumbered leaves. About 9 1/8 × 6 1/8 inches (height of the book varies). Blank white paper covers with wrapper in two shades of blue, flapped at sides, printed in brown and sienna; fore edges untrimmed; stapled.
>
> Published April 1, 1949, at $2.00 for signed copies, $1.00 for unsigned

copies; 400 copies printed. *Colophon, on verso of last leaf:* "Of this first edition 400 copies were printed . . . and the first 25 copies signed by the author. This is copy number . . . [*signed*] William Carlos Williams." *At foot of front flap of jacket:* "Golden Goose chap books are published by Richard Wirtz Emerson and Frederick Eckman at the Golden Goose Press . . . Columbus 12, Ohio."

At top of front flap: "The publishers are proud to begin their series of chap books with this group of poems by one of the three finest poets writing in the English language in this century. The title poem stands out as one of the best poems in Dr. Williams' full writing career, and the others in the collection demonstrate the diversity that marks a major poet."

Contents: Choral: The Pink Church—The Lion, I–II—Mama—New Mexico—A Rosebush in an Unlikely Garden—Song (If I/could count the silence)—The Words, The Words, The Words—Venus over the Desert—"I Would Not Change for Thine"—Mists over the River—The Love Charm.

Notes: Dedication: "To James Laughlin"

All the poems are in *CLP.*

Celia Thaew (Mrs. Louis Zukofsky) set the title poem to music— C374.

[*I Wanted,* pp. 76–78:] "I have always been enthusiastic about *The Pink Church* because it expressed my resentment against not necessarily a political situation but a state of affairs. It is a Christian poem, very definitely. The Pink Church stands for the Christian Church. To use the word *pink* as a derogatory term as some people chose to think was absurd and the farthest thing from my mind. I used the word imagistically; the first line of the poem suggests the first pink image: 'Pink as dawn in Galilee.' The poem goes on to other images. But the contemporary associations with the word *pink* are prejudiced. No doubt it got me into trouble. I was never one to duck trouble if it came to me in a fair way, not a lying way. My conception of Christ as a socialistic figure, related to a generous feeling toward the poor, also confused many. Like Dean Inge of the Church of England I am not at all convinced that communism in its original meaning is any more communistic than Christ's own doctrine. I am obviously not talking about today's meaning of communism and its associations. In the previous book of poems, *The Clouds,* I had included a poem called 'Russia' which was also misunderstood. . . . [¶]A poet is used to being misread, but this kind of misreading hurt me deeply. It was just at this time that I received the appointment for the Chair of Poetry at the Library of Congress. I had had a stroke at the time, not a bad one, but crippling for a brief period. Floss wrote them, and they said to take my time. When I was well enough to take care of the duties in Washington—I was anxious to live up to the obligations of this honor—they didn't want me. A release from *The New York Post* Home News of August 4, 1949, more or less tells the story:

> A congressional move to reorganize or abolish the fellows of the Library of Congress was revealed today in the continuing controversy over the award of a poetry prize to Ezra Pound...Javits (Rep.) pointed out that the Ezra Pound clique among the library fellows has been strengthened by the appointment of William Carlos Williams as a member.

. . . [¶]It's all in the past now but I should like to say for the record that I have always hated today's version of communism...I was approached years ago, before communism was known to have its current frightening connotations, and even then I said this is not for me."

A30 PATERSON (BOOK THREE) [1949]

a. First (limited) edition:

PATERSON | (BOOK THREE) | [*the following 4 lines within a border of 5 rules:*] A NEW | DIREC– | TIONS | BOOK | WILLIAM CARLOS | WILLIAMS [*Norfolk, Conn., James Laughlin*]

32 leaves, first two and last two blank, first and last pasted down as end papers. 9 7/16 × 6 1/4 inches. Tan cloth boards with PATERSON lettered in gold on front; lower two-thirds of title superimposed on narrow dark blue rectangle stamped across front, spine, and back; fore and bottom edges untrimmed. Yellow-green dust jacket printed in sienna. Book and jacket design by George W. Van Vechten, Jr. "A Note on Paterson: Book III" by WCW, dated "September 28, 1949," is on the back flap.

Published December 22, 1949, at $3.00; 999 copies bound. *Colophon, on verso of thirtieth leaf:* "Of this first edition of *PATERSON:* Book III, one thousand copies have been printed for New Directions by the Van Vechten Press in Metuchen, New Jersey. . . . The printing was completed in September, 1949." Binding by Russell-Rutter Company, Inc., N.Y.

Notes: [Letter to Robert McAlmon, January 12, 1949, *SL:*] ". . . I am now 65, which means that I have been retired from active work at the hospital, not even allowed to be on any committee. So that's that. So here I am whipping myself into action on *Paterson III*—but for the moment doing nothing."

[Unpublished letter to Norman Holmes Pearson, February 3, 1949:] "Book III is now up for composition. But composition is sickness and I wonder when I shall fall sick again. But surely the sickness will come when, like ambergris in the whale's belly, the lump will be formed and finally spewed forth. Then will come Book IV if the old whale has not expired by then."

[Publisher's Note on front flap of dust jacket:] "Dr. Williams is now at work on Book IV, the final section, and we hope to publish it by 1951."

A fragment of fourteen lines (*Paterson, Three,* III, 162), beginning "(the water two feet now on the turnpike)" and ending "Speed against the inundation," is reprinted in *Object and Image in Modern Art and Poetry,* an essay by George Heard Hamilton (16 leaves, including plates) published for an exhibition at the Yale University Art Gallery, 30 April 1954 through 14 June 1954 (New Haven), p. [10].

For other editions, see descriptions below under *Paterson* [Collected] —A49.

A31   THE COLLECTED LATER POEMS   [1950]

a. First edition, ordinary copies:

The Collected Later Poems of | WILLIAM | CARLOS | WIL-LIAMS | A NEW DIRECTIONS BOOK [*Norfolk, Conn., James Laughlin*]

7 leaves, 3–240 pp., 2 blank leaves; a section of 8 leaves, stapled at fold, numbered 233–245, is inserted loose in the first binding and bound in at the appropriate place in later bindings ("Publisher's Note," on verso of first leaf: "The poems of the section 'The Rose' were omitted from the first printing of 'The Collected Later Poems' through an oversight on the part of a typist."). 8 3/16 × 5 7/16 inches. Crimson cloth boards lettered in gold on spine; end papers. Yellow, black, and red dust jacket

with Charles Sheeler photograph of WCW on back. Book design by Maurice Serle Kaplan. Jacket design after Peter Beilenson who designed jacket of *The Complete Collected Poems 1906–1938.*

Published November 30, 1950, at $3.00; 4700 copies printed (1993 bound November, 1950; 1497 bound July 5, 1951; 944 bound June, 1956) by The Haddon Craftsmen, Scranton, Pa. Some copies, evidently bound in June, 1956, have the same binding as the Horace Mann School edition (*c*), but omit the Horace Mann School seal and lettering, and in all other ways, including collation and dust jacket, are the same as *a*.

b. Signed copies:

Collation the same as *a*, except that another leaf, for the colophon, is tipped in before the last 2 blank leaves; "The Rose" section is not bound in. 8 1/4 × 5 1/2 inches. Crimson cloth boards lettered in gold on spine; pale yellow end papers; buff-colored leaves; top edges stained blue. Blue slipcase with tan paper label printed in black.

Published simultaneously with the unsigned copies, November 30, 1950, at $7.50. *Colophon, on recto of first leaf after p. 240:* "One hundred copies of this first edition of 'The Collected Later Poems' have been specially bound, and signed by the author . . . [*signature*]William Carlos Williams | This is number . . ."

Contents: SECTIONS: The Wedge—The Clouds—Ballad of Faith—All That Is Perfect in Woman—The Rat—Choral: The Pink Church—Incognito—The Birth of Venus—14 New Poems (1950)—Two Pendants: for the Ears—The Rose. POEMS IN SECTIONS: THE WEDGE: [*essay*] Author's Introduction (1944). A Sort of a Song—Catastrophic Birth—Paterson: the Falls—The Dance (In Breughel's great picture)—Writer's Prologue to a Play in Verse—Burning the Christmas Greens—In Chains—In Sisterly Fashion—The World Narrowed to a Point—The Observer—A Flowing River—The Hounded Lovers—The Cure—To All Gentleness—Three Sonnets—St. Valentine—The Young Cat and the Chrysanthemums—The Poem (It's all in/the sound)—Rumba! Rumba!—A Plea for Mercy—Figueras Castle—Eternity—The Hard Listener—The Controversy—Perfection—These Purists—Fertile—A Vision of Labor: 1931—The Last Turn—The End of the Parade—The A, B & C of It—The Thoughtful Lover—The Aftermath—The Storm—The Forgotten City—The Yellow Chimney—The Bare Tree—Raleigh Was Right—The Monstrous Marriage—Sometimes It Turns Dry and the Leaves Fall before They Are Beautiful—Sparrows Among Dry Leaves—Prelude to Winter—Silence—Another Year—A Cold Front—Against the Sky—An Address—The Gentle Rejoinder—To Ford Madox Ford in Heaven. THE CLOUDS: Aigeltinger—Franklin Square—Labrador—The Apparition—The Light Shall Not Enter—A Woman in Front of a Bank—The Night Rider—Chanson—The Birdsong—To a Lovely Old Bitch—The Bitter World of Spring—Lament—A History of Love—When Structure Fails Rhyme Attempts to Come to the Rescue—Education a Failure—The Banner Bearer—The Goat—Two Deliberate Exercises: 1. Lesson from a Pupil Recital 2. Voyages—The Mirrors—His Daughter—Design for November—The Manoeuvre—The Horse—Hard Times—The Dish of Fruit—The Motor-Barge—Russia—The Act —The Savage Beast—The Well Disciplined Bargeman—Raindrops on a Briar—Suzanne—Navajo—Graph—The Testament of Perpetual Change —The Flower (This too I love)—For a Low Voice—The Words Lying Idle—Picture of a Nude in a Machine Shop—The Hurricane—The Mind's Games—The Stylist—Note to Music: Brahms 1st Piano Concerto—The Red-Wing Blackbird—A Place (Any Place) to Transcend All Places—The Old House—The Thing—The Mind Hesitant—Tragic Detail—Philomena Andronico—The Woodpecker—The Girl (with big breasts)—The Clouds. BALLAD OF FAITH: Ballad of Faith—And Who Do You Think "They" Are?—The Non-Entity—Childe Harold to the Round Tower Came—Io Baccho!—The Centenarian. ALL THAT IS PERFECT IN WOMAN: All That Is Perfect in Woman. THE RAT: The Rat—Jingle—Every Day—The Unfrocked Priest—For G.B.S., Old—The Words, the Words, the Words—Lustspiel—April Is the Saddest Month—To Be Hungry Is to Be Great—The Complexity—A Note —Drugstore Library—The R R Bums. CHORAL: THE PINK CHURCH: Choral: the Pink Church. INCOGNITO: Incognito—3 A.M. | The Girl with the Honey Colored Hair—A Crystal Maze, I–II —New Mexico—Seafarer—The Sound of Waves—Venus over the Desert —Mists over the River—"I Would Not Change for Thine"—The Pause —Mama—The Love Charm—Approach to a City—Song (If I/could count the silence)—A Rosebush in an Unlikely Garden—The Lion (1) —The Lion (2)—An Eternity—The Three Graces—The Horse Show. THE BIRTH OF VENUS: The Birth of Venus. 14 NEW POEMS (1950): May 1st Tomorrow—Après le Bain—Spring Is Here Again, Sir.—The Hard Core of Beauty—Tolstoy—Cuchulain—Twelve Line

Poem—Nun's Song—Turkey in the Straw—Another Old Woman—Wide Awake, Full of Love—Song (Pluck the florets)—Song (Russia!)—Convivo. TWO PENDANTS: FOR THE EARS: The Lesson—Two Pendants: for the Ears I. The particulars of morning are more to be desired than night's vague images. II. Elena—To Close. THE ROSE: The Rose —The Visit—Ol' Bunk's Band—Lear—A Unison—The Quality of Heaven—The Province—The Injury—The Brilliance—The Semblables.

Notes: Dedication: "To James Laughlin"

On front flap of dust jacket: "The Collected Earlier Poems of William Carlos Williams (his work in verse from 1906 to 1939) will be re-issued in a revised and enlarged edition in 1951 as companion volume to the present Collected Later Poems."

[Unpublished letter, YALC, to Babette Deutsch, January 4, 1951:] "The edition [*CLP*] was of 5000 copies. Only 2500 of these have been bound. When the others follow them to the binder the above mentioned signature ["The Rose"] will be incorporated."

c. Horace Mann School edition, ordinary copies ([*1956*]):

9 leaves, 3–240 pp., 2 blank leaves; "The Rose" section is not bound in. 8 3/16 × 5 7/16 inches. Maroon cloth on spine and one-eighth of gray cloth boards; stamped in maroon on front with the seal of the Horace Mann School and lettered in gold on spine; end papers. Plain brown dust jacket with circular cutout to reveal school seal.

Published May, 1956; 505 copies printed (488 bound May 25, 1956; 17 bound June 3, 1956) from the plates of the first edition.

The seventh and eighth leaves contain "A Note on William Carlos Williams | For the Horace Mann School Edition | by Louis Untermeyer," dated 1956 at the end. A footnote says: "The above note was revised by Mr. Untermeyer, especially for the Horace Mann School Edition, from his paragraphs preceding William Carlos Williams' poems in *Modern American Poetry,* edited by Louis Untermeyer and published by Harcourt, Brace and Company."

d. Horace Mann School edition, signed copies ([*1956*]):

[*In red on page facing title page:*] HORACE MANN SCHOOL EDITION

11 leaves, 3–245 pp.; "The Rose" section is bound in. 7 3/4 × 4 15/16

inches. Burgundy cloth boards lettered in gold on front and with black cloth label lettered in gold on spine; end papers. Gray slipcase with seal of Horace Mann School printed in charcoal on front.

Published simultaneously with the unsigned copies May, 1956; 52 copies printed. *Colophon, on recto of third leaf:* "This edition of 'The Collected Later Poems of William Carlos Williams,' which was printed especially for the Horace Mann School, is limited to fifty copies, each of which is signed by the author . . . [*signed*] William Carlos Williams | This is number . . ."

Note, on verso of third leaf: "This limited edition of 'The Collected Later Poems of William Carlos Williams' contains a hitherto unpublished poem, titled 'Sonnet in Search of an Author,' and the Cycle of Poems entitled 'The Rose.' " The poem "Sonnet in Search of an Author," on the recto of the fourth leaf, was first printed in *Kavita,* December, 1950, and is in *PB,* but not in other editions of *CLP.*

e. Revised edition, first impression ([1963]):

The Collected Later Poems of | William | Carlos |Williams | Revised Edition | A New Directions Book [*Norfolk, Conn., James Laughlin*] 7 leaves, 3–276 pp. 8 3/16 × 5 1/2 inches. White cloth boards lettered in blue on spine; end papers. Blue-green, white, and olive green dust jacket. Design by Maurice Serle Kaplan matches other recent clothbound editions of books by WCW published by New Directions.

Published May 31, 1963, at $4.00; 2904 copies printed by The Haddon Craftsmen, Scranton, Pa., from plates of the first edition. *On verso of title page:* "Revised edition"

Contents: "The Self" is substituted for "Turkey in the Straw," p. 204; "The Rose" section is bound in, pp. 233–245; and a section, beginning with "An Editorial Note" by John C. Thirlwall, is added, pp. 249–266: THE LOST POEMS (1944–1950): The Rare Gist—Death—To a Sparrow—To the Dean—At Kenneth Burke's Place—Sunflowers—Death by Radio (for F.D.R.)—East Coocoo—Rogation Sunday—The Marriage of Souls—Threnody—Translation (There is no distinction)—Period Piece: 1834—The Sale—The Counter—How Bad It Is to Say:—Christmas 1950.

Note on front flap of dust jacket: "(The poems written before 1940 will be found in *The Collected Earlier Poems of William Carlos Williams* . . . and those written since 1950 in *Pictures from Brueghel & Other Poems.*)"

70

f. Revised edition, second impression ([*1964*]):

Same as *e*, except for blue cloth boards lettered in gold on spine.

Published June, 1964, at $4.50; 2032 copies printed (plus 1500 sets of sheets for MacGibbon & Kee, London—see *g* below; 987 bound June, 1964; 1032 bound January, 1967). *On verso of title page:* "Revised Edition | Second Printing"

g. English issue (1965):

The Collected Later Poems of | WILLIAM | CARLOS | WIL-LIAMS | LONDON | MACGIBBON & KEE | 1965

Collation as in *e* and *f*. 8 3/16 × 5 5/16 inches. Brown paper boards stamped in gold on spine. Rose dust jacket printed in black and purple. Design matches other books by WCW published by MacGibbon & Kee.

Published May 31, 1965, at 25*s.*; 1500 copies printed by New Directions for MacGibbon & Kee; bound and jacketed in England. *On verso of title page:* "First published by New Directions, New York 1950; | Revised edition, 1963 | First published in the United Kingdom 1965 | Printed in the United States of America" *On back flap of dust jacket:* "Printed in Great Britain"

A32   MAKE LIGHT OF IT   [1950]

First edition:

[*Two pages, facing; on left page:*] MAKE LIGHT | OF IT | [*in gray:*] COLLECTED STORIES [*on right; author's name in gray:*] WILLIAM | CARLOS | WILLIAMS | RANDOM HOUSE · NEW YORK [*device*]

ix, 342 pp. 8 1/4 × 5 7/16 inches. Gray cloth boards stamped on cover and spine with black and white rectangular design; lettering and publisher's device stamped in gold and black on spine; end papers; top edges stained red. White dust jacket printed in gray, red, and black; Elliott Erwitt photograph of WCW and comments about the stories by Alfred Kazin, Ruth Lechlitner, Clifton Fadiman, Gorham Munson, N. L. Rothman, and others on the back. Book and jacket design by Maurice Kaplan.

Published November 30, 1950, at $3.50; 5000 copies printed by The Haddon Craftsmen, Scranton, Pa. *On verso of title page:* "First printing"

Contents: I. THE KNIFE OF THE TIMES: The Knife of the Times
—A Visit to the Fair—Hands Across the Sea—The Sailor's Son—An
Old Time Raid—The Buffalos—Mind and Body—The Colored Girls of
Passenack, Old and New—A Descendant of Kings—Pink and Blue—
Old Doc Rivers. II. LIFE ALONG THE PASSAIC RIVER: Life
Along the Passaic River—The Girl with a Pimply Face—The Use of
Force—A Night in June—The Dawn of Another Day—Jean Beicke—
A Face of Stone—To Fall Asleep—The Cold World—Four Bottles of
Beer—At the Front—The Right Thing—Second Marriage—A Difficult
Man—Danse Pseudomacabre—The Venus—The Accident—Under the
Greenwood Tree—World's End. III. BEER AND COLD CUTS: The
Burden of Loveliness—Above the River—No Place for a Woman—In
Northern Waters—The Paid Nurse—Frankie the Newspaper Man—
Ancient Gentility—The Final Embarrassment—The Round the World
Fliers—The Redhead—Verbal Transcription: 6 A.M.—The Insane—
The Good Old Days—A Good-Natured Slob—A Lucky Break—The
Pace That Kills—Lena—Country Rain—Inquest—Comedy Entombed—
The Zoo.

Notes: Dedication: "For our troops in Korea"

Many of the stories in the third section appeared first in periodicals:
C266, 273, 274, 276, 302, 319, 337, 384, 429, 439. "The Insane" appeared
after book publication in *The Literary Review,* I. 4 (Summer 1958) 505–
508. See A13, 19, 46 for other printings of the stories.

[*I Wanted,* p. 84:] "Whenever I have chosen a title it has interested me
to find one with more than one meaning. You remember my explanation
of *First Act* [A21b]. *Make Light of It* followed the disheartening Library
of Congress affair, could be saying, make light of the whole thing, or
perhaps: make *light* of it."

[Letter to Edith Heal, dated "Income Tax Day" [March 15, 1950],
The Literary Review (Autumn 1965) 116:] "Send Lena back—in the
two parts. She has to be dressed for a party: A book of short stories to
be brought out later on. . . . I do want Lena back, especially the first
part which is a unique copy, as quickly as possible. No matter who has
it, take it away and send it to me quickly if you can do so without too
much putting yourself out." Edith Heal comments [*I Wanted,* p. 84]:
"The story 'Lena' in Part III had never appeared in print. Dr. Williams
had finished it shortly before Random House arranged for the collected
stories. I had borrowed his only copy to show to a magazine editor in

New York. A special delivery letter arrived at my house saying: 'Send Lena back quick. She has to be dressed up for a party.' The party, of course, was the good news that Random House was publishing the stories."

A33   A BEGINNING ON THE SHORT STORY   1950

First (limited) edition:

[*The words, BEGINNING, SHORT STORY, and WILLIAM CARLOS WILLIAMS are printed in red, all else in black:*] A | BE-GINNING | on the | SHORT STORY | [Notes] | by | WILLIAM | CARLOS | WILLIAMS | [*device*] | 1950 | THE ALICAT BOOK-SHOP PRESS | YONKERS, NEW YORK [*On front cover:*] The Outcast Chapbooks | Number XVII

1 blank leaf, 23 pp., 1 blank leaf (the two blank leaves are yellow-orange). 8 5/16 × 5 7/16 or 8 3/16 × 5 7/16 inches. White or tan heavy paper covers printed in blue and red; stapled.

Published early December, 1950, at $1.00; 1000 copies printed. [Letter from Oscar Baron, the publisher, July 29, 1963:] "The W. C. Williams mss. was delivered by the doc about six weeks before he delivered the lecture (substance of the chapbook) to the U. of Washington students. I believed it was published in Dec. of 1950, and the variation in covers occurred because the printer ran out of the same stock. None preceded the other. We printed 1000, of which about 100 were sent to reviewers."

Colophon, on verso of title page: "Set up and printed in August, 1950, by David Zeitsoff for the Alicat Bookshop Press. This copy is one of 750 offered for sale, and type distributed."

Contents: [Note on verso of first printed leaf:] "The following is the substance of an address delivered in the fall of 1950 to students of the University of Washington, in Seattle, by Dr. Williams."

Notes: "A Beginning on the Short Story [Notes]" is dated December 15, 1949, at the top of the first page. In *SE*, with some changes.

An inscription in one copy is dated December 1, 1950.

[*I Wanted*, p. 83, comment by Edith Heal:] "Dr. Williams showed me a drastically penciled copy that he had done in preparation for the republication of the essay in the *Selected Essays* which Random House published in 1954. 'I certainly revised,' he said."

A34   PATERSON (BOOK FOUR)   [1951]

a. First (limited) edition:

PATERSON | (BOOK FOUR) | [*the following 4 lines within a border of 5 rules:*] A NEW | DIREC- | TIONS | BOOK | WILLIAM CARLOS | WILLIAMS [*Norfolk, Conn., James Laughlin*]

36 leaves, first three and last one blank, first and last pasted down as end papers. 9 7/16 × 6 1/4 inches. Tan cloth boards with PATERSON lettered in gold on front; lower two-thirds of title superimposed on narrow sienna rectangle stamped across front, spine, and back; fore and bottom edges untrimmed. Yellow-green dust jacket printed in sienna. Book and jacket design by George W. Van Vechten, Jr.

Published June 11, 1951, at $3.00; 995 copies bound. *Colophon, on verso of thirty-fifth leaf:* "Of this first edition of PATERSON: BOOK IV, one thousand copies have been printed for New Directions by Van Vechten Press, Inc., Metuchen, New Jersey. . . . The printing was completed in February, 1951."

Notes: [Letter to Kathleen Hoagland, from [Yaddo] Saratoga Springs, N.Y., July 26, 1950, *SL:*] "There is absolute silence here all day, from 9 to 4 in the afternoon. [¶]Everyone closely confines himself, writer, painter or composer, and slaves his head off. I too work every day consuming reams of paper trying to complete a first draft of *Paterson IV* before I leave. In a week I've blocked out Part 1 of the 3 parts. I won't finish but without this period of concentration I don't know how I should have been able to complete the task for another year."

[Letter to José García Villa, from Yaddo [Saratoga Springs, N.Y., 1950], *SL:*] "A cold east wind, today, that seems to blow from the other side of the world—at the same time to be blowing all poetry out of life. A man wonders why he bothers to continue to write. And yet it is precisely then that to write is most imperative for us. That, if I can do it, will be the end of *Paterson,* Book IV. The ocean of savage lusts in which the wounded shark gnashes at his own tail is not our home. [¶]It is the seed that floats to shore, one word, one tiny, even microscopic word, is that which can alone save us."

[*Autobiography,* p. 347:] "It was cold last August at Yaddo as I worked to finish *Paterson, Book IV* from my voluminous notes of at least a hundred and twenty-five pages, bringing them down to a scant twenty-two. . . . [¶]I worked steadily, seven days a week from right after

74

breakfast until noon, and from one to four P.M. without a break for two weeks. It was just about all I could do."

[From "A Statement by William Carlos Williams About the Poem *Paterson*," May 31, 1951 (D7):] "From the beginning I decided there would be four books following the course of the river whose life seemed more and more to resemble my own life as I more and more thought of it: the river above the Falls, the catastrophy [*sic*] of the falls itself, the river below the Falls and the entrance at the end into the great sea. [¶]There were a hundred modifications of this general plan as, following the theme rather than the river itself, I allowed myself to be drawn on. The noise of the Falls seemed to me to be a language which we were and are seeking and my search, as I looked about, became the struggle to interpret and use this language. This is the substance of the poem. But the poem is also the search of the poet for his language, his own language which I, quite apart from the material theme had to use to write at all."

For other editions, see descriptions below under *Paterson* [Collected] —A49.

A35   AUTOBIOGRAPHY   [1951]

a. First edition, first impression:

[*Two pages, facing, with the author's name in blue, all else in black; on left page:*] The Autobiography [*On right:*] of | William | Carlos | Williams | [RANDOM HOUSE · NEW YORK [*device*]
xiv, 402 pp. 8 7/16 × 5 9/16 inches. Blue cloth boards stamped in white and gold on front and spine; end papers; top edges stained pale blue. White dust jacket printed in gray-blue, black, and red. Photographs of author on front and back covers. Book and jacket design by Ernst Reichl.

Published September 17, 1951, on Williams' sixty-eighth birthday, at $3.75; 5000 copies printed by The Haddon Craftsmen, Scranton, Pa.; printing completed August 15, 1951. *On verso of title page:* "First Printing"

Contents: Foreword. PART ONE: First Memories—The Bagellon House—At the Shore—Pop and Mother—In My Early Teens—Sunday School—To Run—Switzerland—Paris—Back to School—Medicine—Ezra Pound—The Observatory—Dr. Henna—French Hospital—"The Wrath of God"—Hell's Kitchen—The First Book—Leipzig—Ezra in

London—Paris and Italy. PART TWO: First Years of Practice—Painters and Parties—Our Fishman—*The Waste Land*—Charles Demuth—*Sour Grapes*—The Baroness—New Faces—Pagany—A Sabbatical Year—Our Trip Abroad—Cousins—Paris Again—Good-bye, Paris—Home Again—A Maternity Case—Gertrude Stein—Christmas Day: Bronx Zoo—When a Man Goes Down—The End of the Middle. PART THREE: A Look Back—Of Medicine and Poetry—The City of the Hospital—*White Mule*—Storm—Lectures—The F.B.I. and Ezra Pound—Friendship—Projective Verse—Ezra Pound at St. Elizabeth's—Yaddo—Translations—The Practice—West: 1950—The College Life—The Ocean, the Orient—The Poem *Paterson*.

Notes: Acknowledgment on p. [vi]: "In June and August, 1948, and May, 1949, the magazine *Poetry* published an earlier version of the first twenty or thirty pages of this autobiography. I am grateful to them for the suggestion that the task be undertaken and for their kind permission to include much of this earlier material in the finished work." "Ezra Pound," "Hell's Kitchen," "Of Medicine and Poetry," and "Ezra Pound at St. Elizabeth's" are in *Reader*.

Dedication: "To F.H.W." [Florence Herman Williams]

[Letter to Ronald Lane Latimer, November 26, 1934, *SL:*] ". . . Yes, I doubt very much that I can really say anything to you about myself. . . . [¶]If only I could make a bolus of it of some sort, one grand pill, the whole mess of it squeezed into a lump and let you have it simply and quickly. But to have to tiresomely string it out—Nuts! I can't see what it could mean to you or anyone. I'm no journalist and autobiography doesn't mean a thing to me. All I'm interested in—or almost all—is impersonally, as impersonally as possible, to get the meaning over and see it flourish—and be left alone. That's bitter enough, I know that, but the early dreams of a communal life, of being important to my friends and neighbors, have almost evaporated forever. . . . [¶]But I'll try."

[Letter to Charles Henri Ford, March 30, 1938, *SL:*] ". . . not my autobiography just yet. That will have to be a monastic, brooding, gay sort of lonely thing that cannot be hurried—cannot even be put on the spot but will have to come about in the manner of the seasons. I don't feel up to it at present. There's too much to do before that."

[Letter to David McDowell, January 14, 1951, *SL:*] "You ain't never gonna see none of it until it's presented to you at Randam [*sic*] House,

Thursday, March 1 1951, at 9 A.M., finished. After that, if it's acceptable to you all, you can hire it out as you see fit but not until then. I now have it at 1,008 pages longhand with 200 to go outside of the fifty original pages already printed. That ought to hold you. 1,000 pages in 6 weeks, longhand, no dictaphone phonies permitted, is a record anybody can shoot at as wants to. But if they equal it I'll do 2,000 pages next time if I have to give half my time to it. [¶]My only worry now is the typing but I'll solve that too, right here in the suburbs. . . . [¶]Am reading Faulkner's *Light in August* as I go along with my biography. It's a good American language traveling companion. That's important. How could I do ANYthing if I had to read British as I went along?"

[Letter to David McDowell, March 13, 1951, *SL:*] "Been working hard at Part II. It needs it, as Part I needed it also—a close checking of all details. I was conscious of the defects but dumped it on you anyway to let you see what was going on. There's more to getting this script ready than meets the eye—but with patience we'll finally get it in order. . . . [¶]I think I have my title. It isn't spectacular but it describes the situation rather well:

ROOT, BRANCH & FLOWER:
The Autobiography
of
W.   C.   W."

[Letter to Norman Macleod, June 11, 1951, *SL:*] "My own autobiography is now being set up. I'll see galleys in a week or so—the lawyers have been holding us up a little in their search for possible libel. I don't think they'll find anything. . . . I hope the script will prove worth reading. I told it in the only way I could tell it, in a series of incidents as I lived them. I didn't say much of the lives of others except as they briefly knocked against mine. Thus many names have been left out. It isn't a story of the times during which I lived. It is as though I were a trout living in the water of my own stream, shut away in its waters, only rarely breaking the surface. I hope it will interest someone. I have no confidence that many will follow me into that world. But it was a good experience to put it down. I am most interested in the 3d part. I have not philosophized. Trivial incidents may seem just trivial. . . ."

[Letter to Marianne Moore, June 23, 1951, *SL:*] "Yes, when we are overactive, we suffer. I am glad you have learned that lesson even if it

77

cost you a bad time. It was from overwork on my *Autobiography* that I went under. I might have died. Poets seem to be tough (though they are left, sometimes, with the inability to hit the correct keys of their machines)."

[Unpublished letter, YALC, to Helen Russell, August 22, 1951:] "My autobiography, finished, arrived this morning in all the polish and shine of its dust covers. I can't look at it, no thrill at all, just threw it aside. In fact it doesn't mean a thing to me."

[*I Wanted,* pp. 85–86:] "With my sweet wife's consent I did not let her see this book until it was published. —'Which was a mistake,' both Mrs. Williams and many of his friends told him.—I decided if I was going to give an account of my feelings I wasn't going to let people tell me what to feel. If Flossie had seen it, the book never would have been written at all. I trusted to memory about too many things. I didn't make up any of it but I didn't edit—where in some cases I should have. There are also some inaccuracies about dates, places. The book made a lot of people mad. But it was good therapy for me. It got me back to the typewriter in high spirits."

b. First edition, second impression ([1951]):

Same as *a* except that "Second printing" is on verso of title page. Published September 20, 1951; 5000 copies printed.

In June, 1965, New Directions acquired the plates from Random House, together with 168 copies; a sticker printed "New Directions" is pasted on the title pages of these copies.

c. First edition, third impression—clothbound copies ([1967]):

THE AUTOBIOGRAPHY | OF WILLIAM CARLOS WILLIAMS | A NEW DIRECTIONS BOOK [*New York, James Laughlin*]

7 leaves, 3–402 pp., 1 blank leaf. 8 1/4 × 5 9/16 inches. Pale blue cloth boards stamped in blind with publisher's device on front and lettered in gold on spine; end papers. Blue, white, and black dust jacket. Design by Ernst Reichl matches other recent clothbound editions of books by WCW published by New Directions. The text is printed from the plates acquired from Random House; the table of Contents is reset, however, and the page numbers are deleted from the Foreword.

Published March 28, 1967, at $6.50; 915 copies bound.

d. Third impression—first paperbook printing ([1967]):

Title page and collation the same as *c.* 8 1/16 × 5 3/8 inches. Black and white paper covers, with Charles Sheeler photograph (1926) of WCW on front. Book design by Ernst Reichl.

Published simultaneously with the clothbound copies at $1.95; 4029 copies bound. *On verso of title page:* "First published as New Directions Paperbook 223 in 1967"

A36   THE COLLECTED EARLIER POEMS   [1951]

a. First edition, first impression:

The Collected Earlier Poems of | WILLIAM | CARLOS | WIL-LIAMS | A NEW DIRECTIONS BOOK [*Norfolk, Conn., James Laughlin*]

6 leaves, 3–482 pp., 2 blank leaves. 8 3/16 × 5 7/16 inches. Crimson cloth boards lettered in gold on spine; end papers. Yellow, white, black, and red dust jacket, with Charles Sheeler photograph of WCW on back. Book design by Maurice Serle Kaplan; jacket design after Peter Beilenson.

Published December 17, 1951, at $5.00; 5000 copies printed (2617 bound for the publication date; 1007 bound December 27, 1957; 1365 bound May, 1964) by The Haddon Craftsmen, Scranton, Pa.

Contents: SECTIONS: The Wanderer—The Tempers—March · History—History—Della Primavera Transportata [*sic*] Al Morale—An Early Martyr—Al Que Quiere (To Him Who Wants It)—Fish · Romance Moderne—Sour Grapes—Paterson · The Flower—Spring and All—Struggle of Wings—The Descent of Winter—Impromptu: The Suckers—Collected Poems 1934—An Elegy for D. H. Lawrence—Adam and Eve and the City—Morning · The Crimson Cyclamen—Recent Verse 1938—The Drunkard. POEMS IN SECTIONS: THE WANDERER: The Wanderer, A Rococo Study: Advent—Clarity—Broadway—The Strike—Abroad—Soothsay—St. James' Grove. THE TEMPERS: Peace on Earth—Postlude—First Praise—Homage—The Fool's Song—From "The Birth of Venus", Song—Immortal—Mezzo Forte—Crude Lament—An After Song—The Ordeal—Appeal—Fire Spirit—The Death of Franco of Cologne: His Prophecy of Beethoven—Portent—Ad Infinitum—Contemporania—Hic Jacet—Con Brio—To Wish Myself Courage—To Mark Anthony in Heaven—Transitional—Sicilian Emigrant's Song—Le Médecin

79

Malgré Lui—Man in a Room—A Coronal—The Revelation—Portrait of a Lady. MARCH · HISTORY: March, I–V. HISTORY: History, 1–5. DELLA PRIMAVERA TRANSPORTATA [*sic*] AL MORALE: Della Primavera Trasportata Al Morale—Full Moon—The Trees—The Wind Increases—The Bird's Companion—The House—The Sea-Elephant—Rain —Death—The Botticellian Trees. AN EARLY MARTYR: An Early Martyr—Flowers by the Sea—Wild Orchard—Winter—The Flowers Alone—Sea-Trout and Butterfish—A Portrait of the Times—The Locust Tree in Flower (Among/of/green)—The Locust Tree in Flower (Among/the leaves/bright)—Item—View of a Lake—To a Mexican Pig-Bank—To a Poor Old Woman—Late for Summer Weather—Proletarian Portrait—Tree and Sky—The Raper from Passenack—Invocation and Conclusion—The Yachts—Hymn to Love Ended—Sunday—The Catholic Bells—The Dead Baby—A Poem for Norman MacLeod. AL QUE QUIERE (To Him Who Wants It): Sub Terra—Spring Song—The Shadow—Pastoral (When I was younger)—Chicory and Daisies, I–II— Metric Figure (There is a bird in the poplars)—Pastoral (The little sparrows)—Love Song (Daisies are broken)—Gulls—Winter Sunset— In Harbor—Tract—Apology—Promenade, I–III—Libertad! Igualidad! [*sic*] Fraternidad!—Summer Song—The Young Housewife—Love Song (Sweep the house clean)—Dawn—Hero—Drink—El Hombre—Winter Quiet—A Prelude—Trees—Canthara—M. B.—Good Night—Keller Gegen Dom—Danse Russe—Mujer—Portrait of a Woman in Bed—Virtue —Smell!—The Ogre—Sympathetic Portrait of a Child—Riposte—K. McB.—The Old Men—Spring Strains—A Portrait in Greys—Pastoral (If I say I have heard voices)—January Morning, Suite: I–XV—To a Solitary Disciple—Ballet—Dedication for a Plot of Ground—Conquest— First Version: 1915—Love Song (I lie here thinking of you). FISH · ROMANCE MODERNE: Fish—Romance Moderne. SOUR GRAPES: The Late Singer—A Celebration—April (If you had come away with me)—At Night—Berket and the Stars—A Good Night—Overture to a Dance of Locomotives—The Desolate Field—Willow Poem—Approach of Winter—January—Blizzard—Complaint—To Waken An Old Lady —Winter Trees—The Dark Day—Spring Storm—Thursday—The Cold Night—To Be Closely Written On A Small Piece Of Paper Which Folded Into A Tight Lozenge Will Fit Any Girl's Locket—The Young Laundryman—Time The Hangman—To a Friend (Well, Lizzie Anderson!)—The Gentle Man—The Soughing Wind—Spring—Play—Lines

—The Poor (By constantly tormenting them)—Complete Destruction—
Memory of April—Daisy—Primrose—Queen-Ann's-Lace [*sic*]—Great
Mullen—Epitaph—Waiting—The Hunter—Arrival—To a Friend Con-
cerning Several Ladies—The Disputants—The Birds—Youth and Beauty
—The Thinker—The Tulip Bed—Spouts—The Widow's Lament in
Springtime—The Nightingales—Blueflags—Lighthearted William—The
Lonely Street—Portrait of the Author—The Great Figure. PATERSON
· THE FLOWER: Paterson—The Flower (A petal, colorless). SPRING
AND ALL: I. Spring and All–II. The Pot of Flowers–III. The Farmer–
IV. Flight to the City—V. The Black Winds—VI. To Have Done Noth-
ing—VII. The Rose (The rose is obsolete)—VIII. At the Faucet of June
—IX. Young Love—X. The Eyeglasses—XI. The Right of Way—XII.
Composition—XIII. The Agonized Spires—XIV. Death the Barber—
XV. Light Becomes Darkness—XVI. To an Old Jaundiced Woman—
XVII. Shoot it Jimmy!—XVIII. To Elsie—XIX. Horned Purple—XX.
The Sea—XXI. The Red Wheelbarrow—XXII. Quietness—XXIII. Riga-
marole—XXIV. The Avenue of Poplars—XXV. Rapid Transit—XXVI.
At the Ball Game—XXVII. The Hermaphroditic Telephones—XXVIII.
The Wildflower. STRUGGLE OF WINGS: Struggle of Wings. THE
DESCENT OF WINTER: The Descent of Winter: 9/29 (My bed is
narrow)—9/30 (There are no perfect waves)—10/9 (and there's a little
blackboy)—10/10 (Monday)—10/21 (In the dead weeds a rubbish heap)
—10/22 (that brilliant field)—10/28 (On hot days)—10/28 (in this
strong light)—10/29 (The justice of poverty)—10/30 (To freight cars
in the air)—11/1 (The moon, the dried weeds)—11/2 (Dahlias)—11/2
A Morning Imagination of Russia—11/7 (We must listen)—11/8 (O
river of my heart polluted)—11/10 (The shell flowers)—11/20 (Even
idiots grow old)—11/22 (and hunters still return)—11/28 (I make
really very little money)—12/15 (What an image in the face of Almighty
God is she). IMPROMPTU: THE SUCKERS: Impromptu: The Suck-
ers. COLLECTED POEMS 1934: All the Fancy Things—Hemmed-in
Males—Brilliant Sad Sun—It Is a Living Coral—To—This Florida: 1924
—Young Sycamore—The Cod Head—New England—The Bull—In the
'Sconset Bus—Poem (As the cat)—Sluggishly—The Jungle—Between
Walls—The Lily—On Gay Wallpaper—The Source, I–II—Nantucket—
The Winds—Lines on Receiving the Dial's Award: 1927—The Red Lily
—Interests of 1926—The Attic Which Is Desire—This Is Just to Say—
Birds and Flowers, I–III. AN ELEGY FOR D. H. LAWRENCE: An

Elegy for D. H. Lawrence. ADAM AND EVE AND THE CITY: To a Wood Thrush—Fine Work with Pitch and Copper—Young Woman at a Window—The Rose (First the warmth)—A Chinese Toy—La Belle Dame de Tous les Jours—Adam—Eve—St. Francis Einstein of the Daffodils—The Death of See—To an Elder Poet—Perpetuum Mobile: The City—Cancion. MORNING · THE CRIMSON CYCLAMEN: Morning—The Crimson Cyclamen. RECENT VERSE 1938: Classic Scene—Autumn—The Term—Weasel Snout—Advent of Today—The Sun—A Bastard Peace—The Poor—To a Dead Journalist—Africa—Lovely Ad—4th of July, I–III—The Defective Record—Middle—A Fond Farewell—The Unknown—Porous—The Petunia—The Graceful Bastion—The Return to Work—The Deceptrices—Detail (Her milk don't seem to . .) —Detail (Doc, I bin lookin' for you)—Detail (Hey!)—Detail (I had a misfortune in September)—Their Most Prized Possession—Unnamed (From "Paterson"): 1. Your lovely hands 2. When I saw 3. I bought a new 4. Better than flowers—At the Bar—Graph for Action—Breakfast —To Greet a Letter-Carrier—These. THE DRUNKARD: The Drunkard—Paterson: Episode 17—The Last Words of My English Grandmother (1920)—The Waitress—A Marriage Ritual—The Swaggering Gait—The Predicter of Famine—Illegitimate Things—The Province—The Brilliance—Fragment (My God, Bill, what have you done)—The Yellow Season—Mistrust of the Beloved—Passer Domesticus—The United States—The Sun Bathers—Sparrow Among Dry Leaves—The Men—Song (The black-winged gull)—Descent—You Have Pissed Your Life—Moon and Stars—The Girl (The wall, as I watched)—Simplex Sigilum Veri—The Phoenix and the Tortoise.

Notes: Inscription in Florence Williams' copy: "Dearest Floss—here is the early record—decipher it as you may—and best luck—with love. Bill —William Carlos Williams 11-13-51"

b. First edition, second impression ([*1966*]):

Title page and collation as in *a* above. 8 1/4 × 5 1/2 inches. Red cloth boards stamped in blind with publisher's device on front and lettered in gold on spine; end papers. Red, white, and black dust jacket. Design matches other recent clothbound editions of books by WCW published by New Directions.

Published July, 1966, at $5.00; 2475 copies bound (also 1500 sets of sheets printed for MacGibbon & Kee, London—see *c* below). *On verso of title page:* "Second Printing | Manufactured in the United States | New Directions books are published for James Laughlin by | New Directions Publishing Corporation, | 333 Sixth Avenue, New York 10014"

c. English issue (*[1967]*):

The Collected Earlier Poems of | WILLIAM | CARLOS | WILLIAMS | [*device*] | MACGIBBON & KEE [*London*]
Collation and size as in *b* above. Brown paper boards stamped in gold on spine; end papers. Pale green dust jacket printed in black and purple. Design matches other books by WCW issued by MacGibbon & Kee.

Published March 17, 1967, at 42*s.*; 1500 copies printed by New Directions for MacGibbon & Kee; bound and jacketed in England. *On verso of title page:* "Second Printing | Manufactured in the United States" *On back flap of dust jacket:* "Printed in Great Britain"

A37   THE BUILD-UP   [1952]

a. First edition:

[*Title is repeated fourteen times in vertical order on right half of page; all else is at the foot of the page:*] THE BUILD-UP | [*device*] | A Novel by | WILLIAM CARLOS WILLIAMS | [*heavy rule*] | RANDOM HOUSE NEW YORK
4 leaves, 3–335 pp., 1 blank leaf. 8 1/2 × 5 5/8 inches. Black cloth on spine and one-eighth of orange paper boards; front and spine stamped in royal blue; royal blue end papers; top edges stained dull blue. Light gray dust jacket printed in dark gray and crimson, with "Critical Comment on the Prose Works of William Carlos Williams" on the back. Book design by Merle Armitage.

Published October 17, 1952, at $3.50; 6000 copies printed. In June, 1965, New Directions acquired the plates from Random House together with 684 copies; a sticker printed "New Directions" is pasted on the title pages of these copies.

Contents: A continuation of *White Mule* (A18) and *In the Money* (A21), *The Build-Up* has 32 chapters, untitled.

Notes: Dedication: "For David McDowell"

[Acknowledgment, on verso of title page:] "An earlier version of chapter one first appeared in the 'Briarcliff Quarterly' and appears by courtesy of the editor, Norman Macleod"

[Letter to Norman Macleod, June 11, 1951, *SL*:] "Just the last few days I'm again in the clear. I'm going to stay that way for a while thinking up a novel which Random House has ordered. I have to do a lot of thinking about that. It's going to be a job for me. . . ."

[Letter to Kathleen Hoagland, from West Haven, Conn., July 23, 1951, *SL*:] ". . . I've done no writing myself. Floss and I did have one good talk last evening about her family life in preparation for what I intend to do in going on with the *White Mule* series but that is all."

[Letter to Robert Lowell, March 11, 1952, *SL*:] "I'm writing a novel; it's a novel, as usual, about my local scene (the scene is merely what I know). I want to write some prose fiction and not to tell anyone anything about today. I want to write it so that when I speak of a chair it will stand upon four legs in a room. And of course it will stand upon a four-legged sentence on a page at the same time."

[Letter to David McDowell, May 5, 1952, *SL*:] "I'm happy that the novel pleased you in the first part; let's hope the interest continues to rise, as it should to the end."

[*I Wanted*, pp. 86–87:] "When I wrote *White Mule* and *In the Money* I knew that I had enough material in Floss's family for possibly two more novels. The *Build-Up* showed the family at a later period. The texture of the novel was concerned with data of the town where the family lived, which was, of course, my own town, Rutherford. I had trouble. I found much of what I was writing was too personal. I had to change names, fictionalize situations, so that living persons would be protected. As in the case of the *Autobiography,* I was still in a hurry because I had the respect of any businessman for a contract."

b. English edition [scheduled for publication *1967–1968*]:

MacGibbon & Kee, London, has announced a forthcoming edition.

A38   THE DESERT MUSIC   [1954]

a. First edition, ordinary copies:

THE DESERT MUSIC | AND OTHER POEMS BY | WILLIAM CARLOS WILLIAMS | [*device*] | RANDOM HOUSE · NEW YORK

1 blank leaf, 5 leaves, [3]–90 pp., 2 blank leaves. 9 3/16 × 6 1/4 inches.

Yellow cloth boards stamped in crimson and black on front and downward on spine; gray end papers. Gray dust jacket printed in crimson and black.

Published March 25, 1954, at $3.00; 2532 copies printed by The Spiral Press, New York.

b. Signed copies:

Collation the same as *a*, except that another leaf, for the colophon, is tipped in after second leaf at the beginning. 9 7/16 × 6 5/16 inches. Olive green cloth on spine and one-eighth of gray-green paper boards; gray paper label, printed downward in crimson and black, pasted on spine; gray-green end papers. Glassine dust wrapper. Gray-green slipcase.

Published simultaneously, March 25, 1954, with the ordinary copies at $10.00; 111 copies printed. *Colophon, on recto of third printed leaf:* "This first edition of THE DESERT MUSIC AND OTHER POEMS is limited to 100 copies. It has been printed at The Spiral Press, New York, and is here signed by the author . . . [*signed*] William Carlos Williams | This copy is number . . ."

Contents: PART ONE: The Descent—To Daphne and Virginia—The Orchestra—For Eleanor and Bill Monahan—To a Dog Injured in the Street—The Yellow Flower—The Host—Deep Religious Faith—The Garden—The Artist—Work in Progress. PART TWO: Theocritus: Idyl I (A Version from the Greek). PART THREE: The Desert Music.

Notes: Dedication: "To Bill and Paul" [William Eric Williams and Paul Williams, Sr., sons of WCW]

All the poems are in *Pictures from Brueghel* (A48), except "Work in Progress," which is incorporated in "Asphodel, That Greeny Flower" in the *Journey to Love* section of *PB*.

[Letter to Louis Martz, May 27, 1951, *SL*:] "On June 18 I shall read a new 17-page poem at Harvard for the Phi Beta Kappa ceremonial at the Sanders Theatre. It is an important event for me. Since my illness I have been working on it. It has taken up most of my spare time. I wish you were going to be there to hear it, but if you can't make it I will send it to you later. Whether rightly or wrongly, I feel that many of my culminating ideas as to form have entered into this poem."

[Letter to Norman Macleod, June 11, 1951, *SL*:] ". . . I am going to Harvard at the invitation of Phi Beta Kappa to read a '15 minute' poem at their Annual Literary Celebration on June 18. It has taken me a month or more to write it, transcribe it, have it typed, correct it and polish. That took about all the drive I had."

[Letter to Srinivas Rayaprol, October 26, 1953, *SL:*] "The poem which I enclose is one of my recent ones. I expect to have a book of them published in February. All will be made after the same fashion, an assembly of three-line groups arranged after a pattern which offers the artist, with much freedom of movement, a certain regularity."

[*I Wanted,* pp. 88–89:] "There is something special about this book. Just before I had my cerebral accident, I had received an invitation to read a poem at Phi Beta Kappa exercises at Harvard. I had no poem to read them so I wrote one. I had just returned from a trip to the West and the picture of the desert country around El Paso was fresh in my mind. I'd crossed the desert and *seen* the desert. It is always important to me to be familiar with what I am writing about. I was honored by the invitation to read at Harvard (but was perhaps not so honored after I had read). The students were tickled to death but some of the gentlemen sitting on the platform disapproved. After all, it is a pretty shocking poem, speaking as it does of the whores of Juarez. [¶]When I recovered from the cerebral attack, I began to write again. My whole interest in poetry now was in developing the concept I had discovered—the variable foot—based on the model of the poem in *Paterson* Book Two, section three. Now, consciously, I knew what I wanted to do. I had a group of poems ready and Dave McDowell said, 'You also have the one you did for Harvard—that will make a book.' The other poems in *Desert Music* are more important than the title poem because they consciously use what I had discovered."

c. Readers' Subscription Club Edition ([*1955*]):

Same collation as *a.* 9 1/4 × 6 3/16 inches. Binding and dust jacket are similar to *a;* the cover is stamped in scarlet and black instead of crimson and black, and the spine of the dust jacket is printed in brown and black rather than crimson and black.

Published summer, 1955, at $2.50 (first announced by Readers' Subscription Club in its monthly magazine, *The Griffin,* I. 4, Jan. 1955); 1000 copies printed from the Random House plates. Changes in the text include: first line of "The Descent," p. 3, is set in small capitals rather than regular capitals and lower case; "I declare it boldly" is at the top of p. 20 rather than the foot of p. 19; other lines on p. 20 are in different order than the first printing. Inscription in Florence Williams' copy: "Darling, save as you will see by page 21, most of the errors have been corrected in this edition. Love, Bill Aug 11, 1955" The text on p. 21 is identical to the first printing.

In June, 1965, New Directions acquired the plates from Random House; all copies of the book had been sold.

For another edition, see description below under *Pictures from Brueghel* (A48).

Notes: "The Descent" is reprinted in *Poet's Choice,* edited by Paul Engle and Joseph Langland (New York: The Dial Press, 1962), pp. 3–4, together with a brief signed statement by WCW: "I write in the American idiom and for many years I have been using what I call the variable foot. 'The Descent' is the first poem in that medium that wholly satisfied me." The book contains poems and signed statements by 112 contemporary poets. A new edition was published by Time, Inc., in 1966 as one of the books of Time Reading Program.

A39 THE DOG AND THE FEVER [1954]

First edition:

[*On left half of page in large type:*] The Dog | & | the Fever [*on right half of page in smaller type:*] A Perambulatory Novella | by Don Francisco de Quevedo | who published under the name | of Pedro Espinosa | translated by | William Carlos Williams | and Raquel Hélène Williams | The Shoe String Press | Hamden, Connecticut [*Facing the title page is a drawing of a dog by Fernando Zobel*]

96 pp. 7 × 6 1/4 inches. Maroon cloth boards stamped in gold on front and downward on spine; maroon end papers. White dust jacket printed in black with Zobel drawing in maroon on front; comment by Norman Holmes Pearson on the front flap about the novella.

Published November, 1954, at $3.00; 1000 copies printed. *Colophon, on verso of title page:* "This book was composed by The Shoe String Press in 1954 on an IBM Executive typewriter in Bookface No. 1. It was printed by photo-offset lithography at Cushing-Malloy, Inc., Ann Arbor, Michigan, and bound by Van Rees Book Binding Corp., New York City. The drawing on the title page and jacket is by Fernando Zobel. The book was designed by Alvin Eisenman. . . ."

Contents: Brief note about the author of EL PERRO Y LA CALEN-
TURA.   Introduction by WCW, pp. 7–39, dated at end, Rutherford,
New Jersey, September, 1954.   Translation of brief introduction by
Quevedo, dated at end, San Lucar, October 15, 1625. Translation of the
novella, pp. 45–96.

Notes: [Letter to Ezra Pound, November 6, 1936, *SL*:] "Me Mother
is helping me translate an old book I think it was you left here once:
El Perro y la Calentura, by Quevedo."

[*Yes, Mrs. Williams,* pp. 37–38:] "It is an octavo of very much worn
brown leather, with the title in crooked gilt letters, all but completely
obliterated. The print is large, old fashioned, and irregularly spaced, and
the punctuation is to say the least individual. [¶]The various owners of
the book since 1700 have scribbled their names and a few faded notes
among the fly leaves at the front and back. A young librarian, a friend
of mine, on taking up the book discovered at once—a thing I hadn't
noticed—that two of the front (flyleaf) pages had been gummed together. He held them to the light and there was a name between them
—perhaps that of the original owner."

[Letter to James Laughlin, June 7, 1939, *SL*:] "By all means have Lorca
in the 1939 *N.D.* There's so much of the Spanish stuff that is unknown,
old and new. Geez, how I'd like you to use some of the *novella* by
Quevedo I've been translating, 1627 stuff, right on the ball. I could give
you anywhere from twenty to forty pages or more if you had room for
it. Maybe ten pages would be enough—the only difficulty being that
unless the whole business is offered, it might be too puzzling for the
ordinary reader to get the drift of it. I'm using the whole *novella* as a
framework to hang my mother's biography on."

[*I Wanted,* pp. 90–92:] "This book . . . offered a challenge to my
mother and myself. She was almost blind when we began to translate it.
We'd work out a few phrases, a couple of lines, fight over them, and
finally compromise. It was a funny and very scandalous book. Quevedo
wrote frankly. Sometimes we were absolutely defeated. We appealed
finally to a Professor of Spanish at Johns Hopkins and he simply sent
the book back, telling us it was in '15th century Madrid slang' that was
impossible to translate. The story appears to be an attack on a member
of the church hierarchy in Madrid, implying that some church dignitary
had been implicated in the seduction of a girl. To tell that story, to
have it accepted by a Spanish-Catholic audience, Quevedo had to write

cryptically—you can imagine the problem this was to the translator. Finally we succeeded in getting a translation. It lay there for years. Norman Pearson came to me in 1954, telling me about a group of men at Yale who had more or less sponsored a small offset printing firm. There was an opening for a book. Did I have anything? I fished out the Quevedo thing. It wasn't quite long enough. 'Can't you add an Introduction?' Pearson said. I looked through papers written twenty years ago and found an Introduction I'd started, stopped in the middle of a sentence. It needed more, so I wrote it. And the book, to be a book, still needed more. I had also found a piece about my mother, her childhood, so I made it into the true story of our work together on the translation. I was interested in this, didn't care anything about style. Perhaps this is the way to do certain things. Ezra Pound was tickled, thought it was the best piece of prose I'd ever written. [¶]Few people saw the book. But somehow I wasn't sad. It was a very special book, in the tradition of my early ones.

A40   SELECTED ESSAYS   [1954]

First edition:

[*Two pages, facing, with the author's name in green, all else in black; on left page:*] Selected Essays of [*On right:*] William Carlos Williams | Random House · New York | [*device*]

xviii, 342 pp. 8 1/2 × 5 1/2 inches. Green cloth boards stamped in white and gold on front and spine; gray end papers; top edges stained orange. Gray dust jacket printed in black, orange, and green. Book design by Ernst Reichl.

Published November 5, 1954, at $4.50; 3350 copies printed. *On verso of title page:* "First Printing"

In June, 1965, New Directions acquired the plates from Random House together with 992 copies; a sticker printed "New Directions" is pasted on the title pages of these copies.

Contents: Preface [dated June 17, 1954, at end]—Prologue to Kora in Hell (1920)—Comment (1921)—A Matisse (1921)—Yours, O Youth (1922)—The Writers of the American Revolution (1925)—Shakespeare (1927)—George Antheil and the Cantilene Critics (1927)—Notes in Diary Form (1927)—A Note on the Recent Work of James Joyce (1927) —A Point for American Criticism (1929)—The Simplicity of Disorder

(1929)—Caviar and Bread Again: A Warning to the New Writer (1930)—Excerpts from a Critical Sketch: A Draft of XXX Cantos by Ezra Pound (1931)—The Work of Gertrude Stein (1931)—Marianne Moore (1931)—Kenneth Burke (1931)—The American Background: America and Alfred Stieglitz (1934)—A 1 Pound Stein (1934)—Pound's Eleven New "Cantos" (1934)—An Incredible Neglect Redefined (1936)—The Basis of Faith in Art (1937?)—Against the Weather: A Study of the Artist (1939)—Federico García Lorca (1939)—Introduction to Charles Sheeler: Paintings, Drawings, Photographs (1939)—The Tortuous Straightness of Chas. Henri Ford (1939)—A Letter [*To Reed Whittemore*] (1940)—Midas: A Proposal for a Magazine (1941)—An Afternoon with Tchelitchew (1942)—Author's Introduction to The Wedge (1944)—Shapiro Is All Right (1946)—Lower Case Cummings (1946)—Revelation (1947)—Carl Sandburg's Complete Poems (1948)—The Poem as a Field of Action (1948)—Marianne Moore (1948)—A Beginning on the Short Story: Notes (1949)—Foreword to The Autobiography of William Carlos Williams (1951)—'Parade's End' (1951) —In a Mood of Tragedy: The Mills of the Kavanaughs (1951)—Dylan Thomas (1954)—Painting in the American Grain (1954)—On Measure: Statement for Cid Corman (1954).

Notes: Dedication: "To the memory of 'Uncle' Billy Abbott | the first English teacher | who ever gave me an | A"

The date given with some of the essays is imprecise: "Yours, O Youth" should be dated spring, 1921 (C61); "George Antheil and the Cantilene Critics" was published in 1928 (C118); "Kenneth Burke" was published first in January, 1929 (C127); "The American Background" was not in *Twice a Year* (B24); "A 1 Pound Stein" was published in 1935 (C219); "Pound's Eleven New 'Cantos' " was published in 1935 (C218); "An Afternoon with Tchelitchew" was published first in 1937 (C256); "Carl Sandburg's Complete Poems" was not published until 1951 (C462). The essays printed for the first time are: "The Writers of the American Revolution," "Shakespeare," "The Basis of Faith in Art," and "The Poem as a Field of Action." "Notes in Diary Form," marked "Not previously published," was printed in 1928 (C122).

[*I Wanted,* pp. 89–90:] "This book made me happy because it brought back into print some of the prose that I felt was significant in my development as a writer—the Prologue to *Kora in Hell,* for example, written in 1920 and seen by few other than my friends. I have mentioned in my account of *Kora in Hell* how often I myself have referred to the Prologue throughout the years. The followers of modern poetry may find the letter from Wallace Stevens interesting, and may disagree with my sentiments about T. S. Eliot. [¶] 'Comment,' the second piece I included in the book, is an answer to the criticisms of the first issue of *Contact* [should be *Contact II* in headnote to essay]. *Contact* was the magazine—a little one of course—that I was concerned with in 1921. . . . [¶]The other piece that I feel is important is the Introduction to *The Wedge*, 1944. I think it says what I feel I have learned about the writing of my kind of poetry."

A41   JOURNEY TO LOVE   [1955]

First edition:

JOURNEY TO LOVE | BY | WILLIAM CARLOS WILLIAMS | [*device*] | RANDOM HOUSE · NEW YORK

4 leaves, 87 pp. 9 1/4 × 6 inches. Tan cloth boards stamped in green and black on front and downward on spine; tan end papers; top edges stained charcoal. Tan dust jacket printed in black and green.

Published October 21, 1955, at $3.00; 3000 copies printed. In June, 1965, New Directions acquired the plates from Random House; all copies of the book had been sold.

Contents: A Negro Woman—The Ivy Crown—View by Color Photography on a Commercial Calendar—The Sparrow—The King—Tribute to the Painters—To a Man Dying on His Feet—The Pink Locust—Classic Picture—The Lady Speaks—Address—The Drunk and the Sailor—A Smiling Dane—Come On!—Shadows—Asphodel, that Greeny Flower.

Notes: Dedication: "For my wife" Inscription in Florence Williams' copy: "For Floss | with my love, | as it happens, | on my birthday | Sept 17 '55 | William Carlos Williams"

All the poems are in *Pictures from Brueghel.*

[On front flap of dust jacket:] "Dr. Williams considers this collection his best and most important book of poetry."

[Unpublished letter, YALC, to Kenneth and Libby Burke, May 11, 1954:] "*Poetry* has accepted the *Coda* of a long, 30 page, three part poem which will not be published till next year. . . . It's slow work but after all it's only to keep busy that I write at all so I have no kick—the panic occasionally comes over me that at any moment I may find myself with no more projects to occupy my seething brain and then—as in the past, all my life—I turn and look behind me to try and see how far the hounds are behind me."

[*I Wanted*, p. 92:] "My theory of the variable foot is explicit in the whole thing. I'm convinced it's a valid concept. It may not be for everyone, but it is a way of escaping the formlessness of free verse. The one poem 'Asphodel, that greeny flower' has been noticed and enjoyed by many people. The reviews of the book made me very happy."

[*I Wanted*, pp. 94–95:] ". . . the colleges and universities who have graciously invited me to read my poetry. . . . At Wellesley, once, they practically carried me off on their shoulders. I was speechless. You could hear a pin drop. A million girls were there...at least it looked that way. A bell kept ringing, it finally stopped. Floss had asked me to read the Coda to 'Asphodel'...I thought I didn't have time...but they stood on their heels and yelled...the girls...my god I was breathless, but I said do you really want more and they said yes so I read what Floss knew they would like. They were so adorable. I could have raped them all!"

For another edition, see description below under *Pictures from Brueghel*, A48.

A42 THE SELECTED LETTERS [1957]

a. First edition, ordinary copies:

[*Two pages, facing; on left page:*] The Selected Letters | Edited with an introduction by John C. Thirlwall [*On right:*] of | William | Carlos | Williams | MCDOWELL, OBOLENSKY—NEW YORK [*device*]

xix, 347, [1] pp. 8 7/16 × 5 5/8 inches. Maroon cloth boards stamped in gold on front and spine; buff end papers. Gray, white, and black dust jacket with Paul Bishop photograph of WCW on back. Book design by Kenneth Milford.

Published August 27, 1967, at $5.00; over 2000 copies printed by The Haddon Craftsmen, Scranton, Pa. *On verso of title page:* "Published in New York by McDowell, Obolensky, Inc., and simultaneously in the Dominion of Canada by George J. McLeod Limited, Toronto."

b. Signed copies:

Collation the same as *a*, except that another leaf, for the colophon, is tipped in after first leaf at the beginning. 8 7/16 × 5 11/16 inches. Tan cloth on spine and one-fourth of maroon cloth boards; stamped in gold and maroon on spine; tan end papers; top edges stained maroon. Mottled tan paper slipcase with white paper label printed in black and maroon.

Published simultaneously, August 27, 1957, with the unsigned copies. *Colophon, on recto of second leaf:* "Seventy-five copies of this book have been specially bound and signed by the author . . . [*signed*] William Carlos Williams | This is copy number . . ."

Contents: Introduction by John C. Thirlwall. THE SELECTED LETTERS: I. *College and Medicine: 1902–1913.* II. *The Apprentice Poet*—Imagism and the Little Magazine: *1914–1922.* III. *Poetic Experiment*—Free Verse and Objectivism: *1923–1942.* IV. *Poetic Mastery and Control*—The Relative Measure: *1943–1956.*

Notes: Dedication: "To Floss and Fuji" [Mrs. William Carlos Williams and Mrs. John C. Thirlwall]

[Letter to John Thirlwall, Introduction, *SL:*] ". . . you must let the letters speak for themselves. . . . It should really be a portrait of my gallery of friends."

A43   I WANTED TO WRITE A POEM   [1958]

a. First edition, first impression:

[*Title and subtitle in red, all else in black:*] I Wanted to Write a Poem | William Carlos Williams | The Autobiography of the Works of a Poet | Reported and Edited by Edith Heal | Beacon Press Beacon Hill Boston

ix pp., 1 leaf, 99 pp. 9 1/4 × 6 1/8 inches. Sienna cloth boards printed downward in white on spine; end papers. White dust jacket printed in black and red; comments about book by John Ciardi, Marianne Moore, Howard Mumford Jones, and others on front and back flaps and back. Text printed in red and black.

Published April 9, 1958, at $3.95; 3543 copies bound. [*From Introduction by Edith Heal, pp. v–vi:*] "For five months I met with the poet and his wife, the Bill and Floss you will hear talking in these pages. The interviewer seldom asked a question because the poet did his own searching. I simply took notes. And Floss's acute observations were an important part of these notes. [¶] There was no set plan other than collecting the bibliographical material chronologically from Mrs. Williams' complete collection of published pamphlets and books. As soon as the interviews began I saw that there was far more than the bare bones of bibliographical data waiting for me. The books themselves, with their tantalizing title pages naming publishers unknown to the contemporary 'fifties, promised a nostalgic review of the early twentieth-century literary world. The amazing change in the poetry offered an illuminating study of the poet's lifetime preoccupation with technique: starting with imitations of the classical, bludgeoning into free forms, arriving finally at the theory of the 'variable foot,' Williams' triumph in combining form and freedom."

b. Second impression—paper covers [*1967*]:

[*Black only:*] I Wanted to Write a Poem | William Carlos Williams | The Autobiography of the Works of a Poet | Reported and Edited by Edith Heal | Beacon Press | Boston
ix pp., 1 leaf, 100 pp. 8 × 5 3/8 inches. Black, white, and red paper covers similar in design to the dust jacket of the 1958 printing; comments by Howard Mumford Jones, John Ciardi, and Marianne Moore on back cover. Text printed in black only.

Published September 5, 1967, at $1.95; 5500 copies printed. *On verso of title page:* "First published as a Beacon Paperback in 1967 | Published simultaneously in Canada by Saunders of Toronto, Ltd. | Beacon Press books are published under the auspices of the Unitarian Universalist Association" *On back cover:* "Beacon Paperback No. 261" To the text of the first impression is added, pp. 99–100, a notice of the poet's death, March 4, 1963, and a list of his books published since 1958.

A44   PATERSON (BOOK FIVE)   [1958]

a. First edition:

PATERSON | (BOOK FIVE) | [*the following 4 lines within a border of 5 rules:*] A NEW | DIREC- | TIONS | BOOK | WILLIAM CARLOS | WILLIAMS [*Norfolk, Conn., James Laughlin*]
1 blank leaf, 21 leaves, 2 blank leaves. 9 3/8 × 6 7/16 inches. Tan cloth boards with PATERSON lettered in gold on front and lettering in gold

downward on spine (according to the publisher, 53 copies have "genuine gold stamping"); lower two-thirds of title on front superimposed on narrow orange rectangle stamped across front, spine, and back; end papers; fore edges untrimmed. Cream dust jacket with printing in red and drawing of WCW in black and white on front; comments about *Paterson* on front and back flaps; photograph by John D. Schiff and biographical note on back. *At foot of front flap of jacket:* "The drawing of William Carlos Williams is by his brother, Edgar I. Williams, the distinguished architect." Book design after George W. Van Vechten, Jr., who designed *Paterson (Book One)*; jacket design by Stefan Salter.

Published September 17, 1958, at $3.00; 3000 copies printed (1500 bound for publication date; 1480 bound December, 1958) by Walpole Printing Office, Mt. Vernon, N.Y.

Notes: Dedication: "To the Memory of Henri Toulouse Lautrec, *Painter*"

[Unpublished letter, YALC, to Allen Ginsberg, February 27, 1952:] "You shall be the *center* of my new poem—of which I shall tell you: the extension of *Paterson.*"

[Letter to Robert Lowell, March 11, 1952, *SL*:] "I've become interested in a young poet, Allen Ginsberg, of Paterson—who is coming to personify the place for me. Maybe there'll be a 5th book of Paterson embodying everything I've learned of 'the line' to date."

[John C. Thirlwall, *New Directions 17* (1961) 288–289:] "The immediate choice of Lautrec [for the dedication] was suggested by a 'popular account' Dr. and Mrs. Williams had been reading, but earlier he had been attracted to Lautrec by the painter's ability to turn the gross into beauty (*Paterson Book III,* Section I). More particularly Williams chose him because, as he explained to me on January 23, 1958: 'Toulouse-Lautrec was an unfortunate man of aristocratic blood, whose feelings were not of the common herd. He was inclined to praise woman, even if she was a whore. It was important to him that a whore took him in. That was uppermost in my mind when we were reading a popular account of him. He was amusing and tragic at the same time. The aristocrats had more than the commonalty of mankind has.' What Mr. Williams meant by 'aristocrats' may be gathered from a comment he made when we were discussing *Paterson V:* 'My mother had the aristocratic spirit; she would never do a low thing, and she taught me always to tell the truth.' "

[Note on dust jacket of *Paterson, Five:*] "In a letter to New Directions, Dr. Williams, now 75, commented on the making of *Paterson, Five,* as follows: 'Were I younger, needless to say, it would have been a different poem. But then it would not have been written at all. After *Paterson, Four,* ten years have elapsed. In that period I have come to understand not only that many changes have occurred in me and the world, but I have been forced to recognize that there can be no end to such a story I have envisioned with the terms which I had laid down for myself. I had to take the world of Paterson into a new dimension if I wanted to give it imaginative validity. Yet I wanted to keep it whole, as it is to me. As I mulled the thing over in my mind the composition began to assume a form which you see in the present poem, keeping, I fondly hope, a unity directly continuous with the Paterson of *Pat. 1 to 4. . . .*'"

For other editions, see descriptions below under *Paterson* [Collected] —A49.

A45   YES, MRS. WILLIAMS   [1959]

First edition:

[*Two pages, facing; on left page:*] A Personal Record [*On right:*] of My Mother | Yes, | Mrs. Williams [*On left:*] by William [*On right:*] Carlos Williams | MCDOWELL, OBOLENSKY / NEW YORK | [*device*]

1 blank leaf, 5 leaves, 3–143, [1] pp., 3 blank leaves. 8 7/16 × 5 3/4 inches. Pale violet cloth boards stamped in dark gray on cover and dark gray and red-orange downward on spine; orange end papers; top edges of leaves stained gray. Green and white dust jacket. Book design by Kenneth Milford.

Published June 16, 1959, at $3.50; printed by The Haddon Craftsmen, Scranton, Pa.

Contents: 1. Introduction. 2. Section similar to the Introduction to *The Dog & the Fever* (A39). 3. "An account taken from my mother's conversation while she was living with me at my home in Rutherford, New Jersey, during the years from 1924 to her death." [Compare C295 and C538.]

Notes: Dedication: "To her grandchildren"

[Letter to Wallace Stevens, July 24, 1944, *SL:*] "Your short note gave me, as my mother still says, 'a little moment of happiness.' I'm working

96

at my trade, of course, harder than ever, but also gradually maneuvering a mass of material I have been collecting for years into the Introduction (all there will be of it) to the impossible poem *Paterson*. [¶]Then I'll do the biography of Mother, then either break loose to play for the rest of my days or die in the interim."

[*Yes, Mrs. Williams*, pp. 37–38:] "EL PERRO Y LA CALENTURA, *Novella Peregrina*, etc....What in the world is that? The Dog and the Fever...As she would lean over, the large reading glass in her hand, studying some difficult word, the scheme of what I had in mind began to unfold and I could secretly, under guise of taking down the translation take down rather her own words. It is obvious that she could not have told me all that is to follow in that way—but she told me enough—as I began to draw her out and the scheme developed—to which I add the notes I have taken for many years out of interest in her phraseology and way of thinking. . . . [¶]Very seldom does a man get a chance to speak intimately of what has concerned him most in the past. This is about an old woman who had been young and to a degree beautiful a short number of years ago—this is as good a way as any to pay her my respects and to reassure her that she has not been forgotten." (See also *The Dog and the Fever*, A39, Notes.)

A46 THE FARMERS' DAUGHTERS [1961]

a. First edition—clothbound copies:

THE FARMERS' DAUGHTERS | THE COLLECTED STORIES OF WILLIAM CARLOS WILLIAMS | Introduction by Van Wyck Brooks | A NEW DIRECTIONS BOOK [*Norfolk, Conn., James Laughlin*]

xix, 374 pp., 1 leaf, 2 blank leaves. 8 1/4 × 5 7/16 inches. Green cloth boards lettered in gold on spine; end papers. Green and white dust jacket printed in blue and white. Book design after Maurice Serle Kaplan and jacket design after Peter Beilenson match recent clothbound editions of books by WCW published by New Directions.

Published September 22, 1961, at $4.50; 1500 copies printed (1420 bound) from the Random House plates of *Make Light of It*, with additions, by Quinn & Boden, Rahway, N.J. *On verso of title page:* "First published by New Directions 1961 | Published simultaneously in Canada" *b. Paperbook copies:*

[*Title page as in clothbound copies except for last line:*] A NEW DI-
RECTIONS PAPERBOOK

xix, 374 pp., 2 leaves, 1 blank leaf. 8 × 5 3/8 inches. Black and white
paper covers with photograph of WCW by Eve Arnold, Magnum, on
front. Cover design by Gilda Rosenblum [Kuhlman].

Published simultaneously with the clothbound copies at $1.95 in the
United States and $2.05 in Canada; 10,000 copies printed. *On spine:*
"ND Paperbook 106"

Contents: As in *Make Light of It* (A32) with the addition: IV. The
Farmers' Daughters.

Notes: Dedication: "To our Pets, Grandchildren and Pals!"

[*I Wanted,* p. 50:] "The story 'Four Bottles of Beer' from the collection
Life Along the Passaic River experimented with the paragraph technique,
trying to quicken the prose. It is the same technique used in the story I
have just finished—one I've been working on for over fifteen years trying to get it right: 'The Farmers' Daughters.' *The Hudson Review* has
accepted it for publication sometime in 1957 [C541]."

A47   MANY LOVES   [1961]

a. First edition—clothbound issue:

MANY LOVES AND OTHER PLAYS | THE COLLECTED
PLAYS OF | WILLIAM CARLOS WILLIAMS | A NEW DIREC-
TIONS BOOK [*Norfolk, Conn., James Laughlin*]

5 leaves, 437 pp. 8 1/4 × 5 1/2 inches. Blue cloth boards lettered in
gold on spine; end papers. White, blue, and purple dust jacket. Book
design after Maurice Serle Kaplan and jacket design after Peter Beilenson
match other recent clothbound editions of books by WCW published by
New Directions.

Published September 22, 1961, at $6.50; 4426 copies printed (1487
bound for publication date; 496 bound August, 1964; 2443 sets of sheets
bound in paper covers in 1965—see *b* below) by Quinn & Boden, Rahway,
N.J.

Contents: Many Loves—A Dream of Love—Tituba's Children—The
First President—The Cure. Notes on William Carlos Williams as Playwright by John C. Thirlwall.

Notes: Dedication: "To Harriet and Bill Gratwick"

Acknowledgments, on verso of title page: "*The First President* was originally published in 1936 in *The American Caravan* [*The New Caravan*, B26] and is reprinted by permission of W. W. Norton & Co. Inc. [¶]*Many Loves* was first published in the anthology *New Directions 7* in 1942 [C311]. [¶]*A Dream of Love* was first published by New Directions in 1948 as Number 6 in the Directions Series [A27]. [¶]The Publisher wishes to thank Dr. John C. Thirlwall for his notes on the plays and assistance in reading proofs."

b. First edition, paperbook issue ([*1965*]):

2 blank leaves, 5 leaves, 437 pp., 2 blank leaves. 8 × 5 3/8 inches. White paper covers printed in black on front and downward on spine. Design by David Ford.

Published April 5, 1965, at $2.75; 2443 copies bound from sets of sheets printed in 1961. *On back cover:* "A New Directions Paperbook NDP 191 $2.75

c. First edition, second impression ([*1966*]):

Title page, collation, binding, and text as in *b* above.

Published January 25, 1966, at $2.75; 3770 copies printed.

A48   PICTURES FROM BRUEGHEL   [1962]

a. First edition, first impression:

Pictures from Brueghel | and other poems by | William Carlos Williams | including | The Desert Music & Journey to Love | A New Directions Paperbook [*Norfolk, Conn., James Laughlin*]

4 leaves, 3–184 pp., 1 leaf. 7 7/8 × 5 3/8 inches. Black and white paper covers with photograph of a shock of grain on front and spine and comments about book on back. Book design after Maurice Searle Kaplan; jacket design by Gilda [Rosenblum] Kuhlman.

Published June 26, 1962, at $2.25; 7500 copies printed by Golden Eagle Press, Mount Vernon, N.Y. *On verso of title page:* "First published as ND Paperbook 118 in 1962. | First edition"

Contents: PICTURES FROM BRUEGHEL: Pictures from Brueghel: I. Self-Portrait II. Landscape with the Fall of Icarus III. The Hunters in the Snow IV. The Adoration of the Kings V. Peasant Wedding

VI. Haymaking VII. The Corn Harvest VIII. The Wedding Dance in the Open Air IX. The Parable of the Blind X. Children's Games, I–III—Exercise (Maybe it's his wife)—Song (beauty is a shell)—The Woodthrush—The Polar Bear—The Loving Dexterity—The Chrysanthemum—3 Stances: I. Elaine II. Erica III. Emily—Suzy, I–III—Paul, I–III—Fragment (as for him who)—To a Woodpecker—Song (I'd rather read an account)—The Children—The Painting—The Stone Crock—He Has Beaten about the Bush Long Enough—Iris—Song (you are forever April)—The Dance (When the snow falls)—Jersey Lyric—To the Ghost of Marjorie Kinnan Rawlings—To Be Recited to Flossie on Her Birthday—Metric Figure (gotta hold your nose)—The Intelligent Sheepman and the New Cars—The Italian Garden—Poem (The rose fades)—A Formal Design—Bird—The Gossips—Exercise No. 2—The World Contracted to a Recognizable Image—The Fruit—Short Poem—Poem (on getting a card)—To Flossie—Portrait of a Woman at Her Bath—Some Simple Measures in the American Idiom and the Variable Foot: I. Exercise in Timing II. Histology III. Perpetuum Mobile IV. The Blue Jay V. The Existentialist's Wife VI. A Salad for the Soul VII. Chloe VIII. The Cocktail Party IX. The Stolen Peonies—The High Bridge above the Tagus River at Toledo—15 Years Later—The Title—Mounted as an Amazon—The Snow Begins—Calypsos, I–III—An Exercise (Sick as I am)—Three Nahuatl Poems—Sonnet in Search of an Author—The Gift—The Turtle—Sappho, Be Comforted—To My Friend Ezra Pound—Tapiola—Poem (The plastic surgeon who has)—Heel & Toe to the End—The Rewaking. THE DESERT MUSIC AND OTHER POEMS (1954): [*The contents are as in the first publication of the book* (A38), *except for the omission of "Work in Progress," which is incorporated in "Asphodel, That Greeny Flower" in* Journey to Love]. JOURNEY TO LOVE (1955): [*The contents are as in the first publication of the book* (A41)]. "Ten Years of a New Rhythm," an essay by John C. Thirlwall, *pp. 183–184.*

Notes: The poem "Chloe," p. 50, is reprinted in English in *Dieci poeti americani, Litografie di Angelo Savelli*, Roma, a portfolio (17 1/2 × 13 5/8 inches) in slipcase, containing 13 unnumbered broadsheets folded vertically. Published gennaio, 1963; limited to 110 copies.

A: Books and Pamphlets

b. First edition, second impression—paperbook covers ([1963]):

Pictures from Brueghel | and other poems by | William Carlos Williams | including | The Desert Music & Journey to Love | New Directions

8 × 5 3/8 inches. "Pulitzer Prize in Poetry" is added to the front and back covers, and a note on the back cover states: *"Pictures from Brueghel was awarded the Pulitzer Prize in Poetry only two months after William Carlos Williams' death on March 4, 1963."* "First Edition" is deleted on verso of title page. The list of Williams' books on the back cover is revised. Otherwise, the second printing is the same as the first.

Published May, 1963, at $2.25; 6726 copies printed (plus 1500 sets of sheets for MacGibbon & Kee, London—see *c* below; 5063 bound May, 1963; 1663 bound December, 1965) by Golden Eagle Press, Mount Vernon, N.Y.

c. English issue (1963):

Pictures from Brueghel | and other poems by | William Carlos Williams | including | The Desert Music & Journey to Love | London | MacGibbon & Kee | 1963

4 leaves, 3–182 pp. 8 1/8 × 5 7/16 inches. Brown paper boards stamped in gold on spine; end papers. Yellow dust jacket printed in black and orange. Design matches other books by WCW issued by MacGibbon & Kee.

Published October 24, 1963, at 30s.; 1500 copies printed by New Directions for MacGibbon & Kee (950 copies bound); bound and jacketed in England. *On verso of title page:* "First published by New Directions, New York, 1962. | First published in the United Kingdom, 1963. | Printed in the United States of America." *On back flap of dust jacket:* "Printed in Great Britain"

Except for the printing on the first two leaves and the deletion of the last two leaves, the sheets are the same as the American edition.

d. Third impression—paperbook covers ([1966]):

Published May 16, 1966, at $2.25; 5134 copies bound.

e. Fourth impression—paperbook covers ([1967]):

Pictures from Brueghel | and other poems by | WILLIAM | CARLOS | WILLIAMS | Collected Poems 1950–1962 | A NEW DIRECTIONS BOOK [*New York, James Laughlin*]

8 1/16 × 5 7/16 inches. Collation as in *a* and *b*. Covers remain the same except for minor changes on the back.

Published May 29, 1967, at $2.25; 6129 copies bound (also 1000 sets of sheets printed for clothbound copies—see *f* below). *On verso of title page and on back cover:* "Fourth Printing"

f. Fourth impression—clothbound issue ([*1967*]):

Title page and collation as in *e*. 8 1/4 × 5 9/16 inches. Russet cloth boards lettered in gold on spine; end papers. White, olive green, and russet dust jacket. Design matches other recent clothbound editions of books by WCW published by New Directions.

Published August 15, 1967, at $5.00; 1013 copies bound (see *e* above). *On verso of title page:* "Fourth Printing"

A49   PATERSON [COLLECTED]   [1949–1963]

The first edition of the complete collected *Paterson,* containing Books One to Five and the first publication of notes for a projected Book Six, is described first, but it is designated by *g,* its chronological letter in the sequence of editions of collected *Paterson* published from 1949 to 1963, all of which were set in the same type face. For description of *Paterson (One),* 1946, see A24; for *Paterson (Two),* 1948, A25; for *Paterson (Three),* 1949, A30; for *Paterson (Four),* 1951, A34; and for *Paterson (Five),* 1958, A44.

g. Complete collected edition of Books 1–5, including notes for a projected Book 6, first impression ([*1963*]):

William Carlos Williams | PATERSON | New Directions [*New York, James Laughlin*]

287 pp. 8 × 5 3|8 inches. Black and white paper covers with a drawing by Earl Horter of the Passaic Falls on front and comments about *Paterson* on back. Book design by David Ford after Maurice Serle Kaplan. Reviewers' comments are on the first leaf.

Published October 17, 1963, at $1.85; 8598 copies printed (also 1500 sets of sheets for MacGibbon & Kee, London—see *h* below) by Vail-Ballou Press, Inc., Binghamton, N.Y. *On verso of title page:* "First published as ND Paperbook 152 in 1963"

A: Books and Pamphlets

The same plates are used for Books 1, 2, 3, and 4 as for the previous collected editions (*a–d* below), with some alterations, *e.g.,* in Book One, at the end of part II, "T.J." is changed to "E.D." The type of *Paterson* (*Five*), 1958, is entirely reset to match the collected *Paterson,* thus altering the visual pattern of Book 5. More than forty textual changes have been noted in Book 5; the first change, other than punctuation, is in the letter from A[llen]. G[insburg]., p. 248, where "whitmanic mania" is substituted for the "whitmanesque mania" of the first printing.

Note on p. [8]: "Toward the end of 1960 and in the early months of 1961, Dr. Williams was writing to the publisher of his plans for a sixth section, but illness prevented him from working on it. Four pages of notes and drafts for *Book 6* were found among the poet's papers after his death and these have been added as an appendix at the end of this edition." *Acknowledgment, on verso of title page:* ". . . to Donald C. Gallup, Curator, Collection of American Literature, Yale University Library, and to Hugh Kenner for assistance with the texts . . . ."

a. Collected edition of Books 1 & 2 ([*1949*]):

PATERSON | William Carlos Williams | The New Classics [*New Directions, Norfolk, Conn., James Laughlin*]
   4 leaves, [11]–113 pp. 7 3/16 × 4 7/8 inches. Orange cloth boards lettered in black downward on spine; end papers. White, gray, yellow, and black dust jacket; front flap has "Paterson Books 1 & 2" at the top; "NC26" [New Classics Series 26] on spine. Jacket design by Alvin Lustig.
   Published early 1949 at $1.50; 1577 copies printed (500 sets of sheets sold to Peter Owen, London—see *d* below) by Vail-Ballou Press, Inc., Binghamton, N.Y.
   Note on front flap of dust jacket of *Paterson (Three)*, 1949: "Because the first limited edition of *Paterson I* is exhausted and that of *Paterson II* nearly so, these first two books are being re-issued together in the New Classics Series, so that new readers may enjoy the full sweep of the poem thus far."

b. Collected edition of Books 1, 2 & 3 ([*1950*]):

Title page, size, binding, and design of dust jacket the same as *a* above. 4 leaves, [11]–173 pp., 2 blank leaves. Front flap of dust jacket has

"Paterson Books 1, 2 & 3" at the top and the announcement at the bottom that "The National Book Award for Poetry was won in 1950 by William Carlos Williams for *Paterson & Selected Poems*"; "NC26" on spine.

Published summer, 1950, at $1.50; 3507 copies printed (1507 bound for summer publication; 2000 sets of sheets used for *Paterson*, Books 1, 2, 3, & 4—see *d* below) by Vail-Ballou Press, Inc.

c. Collected edition of Books 1, 2, 3, & 4, first impression ([1951]):

Title page, size, binding, and design of dust jacket the same as *a* and *c* above. 4 leaves, [11]–238 pp. Front flap of dust jacket has "Paterson Books 1, 2, 3 & 4" at the top; "NC26" on spine.

Published November 12, 1951, at $1.50; 2000 copies printed (2000 sets of sheets of *c* above bound together with a new printing of *Paterson* (*Four*); 1000 bound for publication date; 1000 bound February 1, 1952) by Vail-Ballou Press, Inc.

d. English issue of collected edition of Books 1 & 2 ([1953]):

PATERSON | by | William Carlos | Williams | Peter Owen Limited | London

Collation, size, and binding the same as *a* above; buff dust jacket printed in purple; "William Carlos | Williams | Paterson | National Book Award | Winner in America" on front and "Paterson Books 1 and 2 8s. 6d." on front flap.

Published March 30, 1953, at 8s. 6d.; 500 sets of sheets of New Directions printing (*a* above) sold to Peter Owen, Ltd., January 12, 1953.

e. Collected edition of Books 1, 2, 3, & 4, second impression ([1955]):

1980 copies printed June 8, 1955; 1000 bound at once; 980 bound February 20, 1958.

f. Collected edition of Books 1, 2, 3, & 4, third impression ([1960]):

2000 copies printed August 5, 1960; 996 bound at once; 990 bound March 23, 1962.

g. Complete collected edition of Books 1–5, including notes for a projected Book 6, first impression ([1963]):

See the beginning of A49.

h. English issue (1964):

PATERSON | Books I-V | William Carlos Williams | London | MacGibbon & Kee | 1964

> 284 pp. 8 3/16 × 5 7/16 inches. Brown paper boards stamped in gold on spine; end papers. Pale blue dust jacket printed in black and red. Design matches other books by WCW issued by MacGibbon & Kee.
>
> Published August 31, 1964, at 30*s.;* 1500 copies printed by New Directions for MacGibbon & Kee; bound and jacketed in England. *On verso of title page:* "This edition was first published by New Directions, New York, 1963, and first published in the United Kingdom by MacGibbon & Kee, London, 1964." *On back flap of dust jacket:* "Printed in Great Britain"
>
> The sheets are the same as *g,* except the first three leaves and the deletion of three pages of advertising at the end.

i. Second impression ([1964]):

> Same as *g,* except "Second Printing" is on verso of title page and on back cover.
>
> Published October 23, 1964, at $1.85; 7493 copies bound.

j. Third impression ([1966]):

> "Third Printing" replaces "Second Printing" on verso of title page and on back cover.
>
> Published December 16, 1966, at $1.95; 8593 copies bound.

A50   THE WILLIAM CARLOS WILLIAMS   [1966] READER

a. First edition, first impression:

The William Carlos Williams Reader | edited with an introduction by | M. L. Rosenthal | A NEW DIRECTIONS BOOK [*New York, James Laughlin*]

> xxxvi, 412 pp. 8 1/4 × 5 5/8 inches. Yellow cloth boards stamped in blind with publisher's device on front and lettered in gold on spine; end papers. Red, white, and black dust jacket with Charles Sheeler photograph of WCW on front.
>
> Published September 1, 1966, at $7.50; 3000 copies printed (1937 bound

July, 1966; 909 bound November, 1966; also 2000 sets of sheets printed for MacGibbon & Kee, London—see *b* below). *On verso of title page:* "Published simultaneously in Canada by McClelland and Stewart, Ltd."

Contents: Introduction by M. L. Rosenthal. POEMS: Danse Russe—Tract—El Hombre—Sympathetic Portrait of a Child—Winter Quiet—January Morning—Waiting—Spouts—The Widow's Lament in Spring-time—The Lonely Street—Spring and All—The Rose (The rose is obsolete)—To Elsie—The Sea—The Red Wheelbarrow—At the Ball Game—Portrait of a Lady—The Trees—The Sea-Elephant—Death—The Botticellian Trees—The justice of poverty [The Descent of Winter 10/29]—This Is Just to Say—Flowers by the Sea—To a Poor Old Woman—Proletarian Portrait—The Raper from Passenack—The Yachts—The Catholic Bells—St. Francis Einstein of the Daffodils—The Term—Paterson: Episode 17—A Sort of a Song—The Dance (In Brueghel's great picture)—Sometimes It Turns Dry and the Leaves Fall before They Are Beautiful—The Night Rider—To Ford Madox Ford in Heaven—The Thing—When Structure Fails Rhyme Attempts to Come to the Rescue—The Horse Show—And Who Do You Think "They" Are?—The Centenarian—April Is the Saddest Month—A Note—The Sound of Waves—Impromptu: The Suckers—The Last Words of My English Grandmother—To a Dog Injured in the Street—Suzy—Asphodel, That Greeny Flower—*Paterson,* Book II, Part I: Sunday in the Park—*Paterson,* Book V, Part II. "IMPROVISATIONS": From *Kora in Hell: Improvisations* (I: 1-3—V:1—XIX:3—XXI:1-3, Coda—XXVII:1-3. From *The Great American Novel:* Chapter I, The Fog—Chapter II.—Chapter VI.—Chapter X.—Chapter XI. FICTION: From *A Voyage to Pagany:* Chapter III, Looking About—from Chapter V, The Supper. The Venus—Life Along the Passaic River—The Use of Force—A Night in June—Jean Beicke—A Face of Stone—The Burden of Loveliness—The Zoo. From *White Mule:* Chapter I, To Be—Chapter III, To Go on Being. From *In the Money:* from Chapter IX, The Four Leafed Clover—Chapter XIII, Hotel Room Symphony—Chapter XVII, Night. DRAMA: From *A Dream of Love:* Act I, Scene 1. AUTOBIOGRAPHY: From *The Autobiography:* from Chapter 12, Ezra Pound—Chapter 17, Hell's Kitchen—Chapter 43, Of Medicine and Poetry—Chapter 51, Ezra Pound at St. Elizabeth's. OTHER PROSE: From *Spring and All.* From *In the American Grain:* The Fountain of Eternal Youth—Sir Walter Raleigh—Voyage of the Mayflower—Jacataqua—from Edgar Allan Poe—Abraham Lincoln. A

Point for American Criticism—Marianne Moore—A Matisse—An Afternoon with Tchelitchew—Lower Case Cummings—On Measure: Statement for Cid Corman. Textual Note by Rosenthal.

b. English issue ([*1967*]):

The William Carlos Williams Reader | edited with an introduction
by | M. L. Rosenthal | [*device*] | [*rule*] | MacGibbon & Kee [*London*]
Collation as in *a*. 8 1/4 × 5 1/2 inches. Brown paper boards stamped
in gold on spine. Yellow dust jacket printed in yellow and red. Design
matches other books by WCW issued by MacGibbon & Kee.

Published March 20, 1967, at 42*s.;* 2000 copies printed by New Directions for MacGibbon & Kee; bound and jacketed in England. *On verso
of title page:* "First published in the U.S.A. by New Directions 1966 |
First published in Great Britain by MacGibbon & Kee Ltd 1966 | Printed
in the U.S.A." *On back flap of dust jacket:* "Printed in Great Britain"

c. First (American) edition, second impression ([*1967*]):

Published May, 1967, at $7.50; 5000 copies printed (1035 bound May,
1967; 4000 to be bound either in paper or cloth covers at a later date).

A. BOOKS AND PAMPHLETS
ADDENDA

B

BOOKS, PAMPHLETS, AND PORTFOLIOS WITH
CONTRIBUTIONS BY WILLIAM CARLOS WILLIAMS

Section B describes in detail first editions containing the first publication
in book form of contributions by Williams. The method of describing
collation is the same as in Section A.

THE 'SCOPE | BEING THE CLINICAL CHART OF NINE-
TEEN HUNDRED AND SIX MEDICAL OF | THE UNIVER-
SITY OF PENNSYLVANIA | [*device*] | ADMITTED . . . .
OCTOBER, 1902 | DISCHARGED . . . . JUNE, 1906 | [*rule*] |
BOARD OF EDITORS. | HERBERT CHARLES CLARK, EDI-
TOR-IN-CHIEF. WILLIAM PENN VAIL, BUSINESS MAN-
AGER. | JOHN C. DALLENBACH. WILLIAM RICHARD
BROWN, JR. | DAVID JOHN MOYLAN. GEORGE CARROLL
RHOADES. [*Press of The John C. Winston Company, 1006–1016*
Arch Street, Philadelphia]
   3 blank leaves, 174 pp., 3 blank leaves. 7 13/16 × 10 5/8 inches. Dark
blue cloth boards stamped in gold and crimson.
   Published late spring, 1906.
   Contains four line drawings signed "W. C. Williams": Design for
"Class History" (p. 21)—Design for "Societies" (p. 107)—Design for
"Fraternities" (p. 129)—Design for "The Southeastern Dispensary" (p.
141). The other drawings in the book are unsigned.
   William Carlos Williams is listed second in a group of "members of
the class who gave valuable assistance in preparing *The Scope*" (p. 9).
Photographs include the individual class photograph with biographical
note (p. 76), a group photograph of the Stillé Medical Society with
WCW seated first on the front row (p. 109), a photograph of "Billy"
Williams in fencer's uniform (p. 150), and a photograph of "Billy" Williams as "Polonius" (p. 155). Comment on p. 144: "William Carlos
Williams is our fencer. During the season of '04–05 he was a regular
member of the 'Varsity fencing team, and won considerable notice by
his brilliant work." On p. 154: "The year 1905 saw two more of our
men in the annual production [by the Mask and Wig Club], 'Mr.
Hamlet of Denmark.' W. C. Williams . . . was hidden behind a tre-
mendous beard in the part of Polonius."

B2   CATHOLIC ANTHOLOGY   1915

CATHOLIC | ANTHOLOGY | 1914–1915 | [*device*] | LONDON
| ELKIN MATHEWS, CORK STREET | 1915
   vii, 99, [1] pp. 7 11/16 × 5 3/16 inches. Gray paper boards printed in
black with design by "D.S." [Dorothy Shakespear Pound]; end papers.
   Published November, 1915, at 3*s.* 6*d;* 500 copies printed.

Edited by Ezra Pound. Donald Gallup notes in *A Bibliography of Ezra Pound*: "Shortly after publication, according to Ezra Pound, protests were received by Elkin Mathews from Francis Meynell and other Catholics because of the title of the anthology; but the book was not suppressed and was still in print in the original—and only—edition, at the published price, as late as April 1936."

Contains "In Harbour [C5]—The Wanderer [C4]" by WCW, pp. 70–85. This is the first book publication of these poems, which are in *CEP*. The anthology also contains poems by W. B. Yeats, T. S. Eliot, Alfred Kreymborg, Edgar Lee Masters, Carl Sandburg, Ezra Pound, and others.

B3   OTHERS   1916

OTHERS | AN ANTHOLOGY OF THE NEW VERSE | EDITED BY | ALFRED KREYMBORG | [*device*] | [*rule*] | NEW YORK | [*ornament*] ALFRED A KNOPF [*ornament*] MCMXVI

4 leaves, 152 pp. 8 1/4 × 5 1/4 inches. Brown paper boards printed in gold (or in red) on covers and spine; brown end papers. Orange dust jacket printed in red-orange.

Published March 25, 1916, at $1.50. *On verso of title page:* "Published March, 1916"

Contains "Pastoral (The little sparrows) [C9]—The Ogre [C9]—Pastoral (If I say I have heard voices) [C9]—Appeal [C9]—Tract [C10]—Touché [C10]—To a Solitary Disciple [C10]—*Stillness [C528]" by WCW, pp. 133–143. This is the first book publication of these poems, which are in *CEP,* except for "Stillness"; "Touché" is retitled "Sympathetic Portrait of a Child." The anthology also contains poems by Wallace Stevens, T. S. Eliot, and others.

B4   THE NEW POETRY   1917

THE NEW POETRY | AN ANTHOLOGY | EDITED BY | HARRIET MONROE | AND | ALICE CORBIN HENDERSON | EDITORS OF POETRY | New York | THE MACMILLAN COMPANY | 1917 | All rights reserved

xxxi pp., 1 leaf, 404 pp., 4 leaves, 1 blank leaf. 7 3/4 × 5 1/4 inches.

Green cloth boards stamped in blind and gold on front and in gold on spine; end papers. Dust jacket.

Published February 28, 1917, at $1.75; 4000 copies printed. *On verso of title page:* "Published February, 1917"

Contains "Sicilian Emigrant's Song [C2]—Peace on Earth [C2]—The Shadow [C7]—Metric Figure (There is a bird in the poplars) [C7] —Sub Terra [C7]—*Slow Movement [C7]—Postlude [C2]" by WCW, pp. 369–374. "Peace on Earth" and "Postlude" had appeared in *The Tempers* (1913) [A2], but this is the first book publication of the other poems. All are in *CEP* except "Slow Movement."

| B5 | OTHERS | 1917 |

OTHERS | AN ANTHOLOGY OF THE NEW VERSE | (1917) | EDITED BY ALFRED KREYMBORG | [*device*] | [*rule*] | NEW YORK [*ornament*] ALFRED A KNOPF [*ornament*] MCMXVII

120 pp. 7 13/16 × 5 3/16 inches. Orange paper boards printed in blue on covers and spine; end papers. Orange dust jacket printed in black.

Published October 31, 1917, at $1.50. *On verso of title page:* "Published, October, 1917"

Contains "Keller Gegen Dom—Spring Song—Spring Strains—El Hombre—New Prelude—Danse Russe—Ballet—Good-Night—Pastoral (When I was younger)" by WCW, pp. 112–120 [all in C15]. This is the first book publication of these poems, which are in *CEP;* "New Prelude" is retitled "A Prelude."

| B6 | ANTHOLOGY OF MAGAZINE VERSE | [1919] |
| | FOR 1919 | |

ANTHOLOGY | OF | MAGAZINE VERSE | FOR 1919 | AND YEAR BOOK OF | AMERICAN POETRY | EDITED BY | WIL-LIAM STANLEY BRAITHWAITE | [*device*] | BOSTON | SMALL, MAYNARD & COMPANY | PUBLISHERS

xiv, 320 pp., 1 blank leaf. 8 9/16 × 5 3/4 inches. Brown cloth on spine and one-eighth of brown paper boards with paper labels printed in black on front and spine; end papers.

Published December 15, 1919, at $2.25.

Contains "To Be Closely Written on a Small Piece of Paper Which Folded into a Tight Lozenge Will Fit any Girl's Locket—The Soughing Wind—Epitaph—Spring—*Stroller—Memory of April" by WCW, pp. 65–66 [all in C34]. This is the first book publication of these poems, which are in *CEP*, except for "Stroller."

B7   OTHERS FOR 1919   1920

[*Within single rule border:*] OTHERS FOR 1919 | An Anthology of the New Verse | Edited by Alfred Kreymborg | NICHOLAS L. BROWN | NEW YORK MCMXX

xiv, 190 pp., 2 leaves. 7 7/8 × 5 5/16 inches. Blue paper boards with yellow paper labels printed in brown on front and spine; end papers.

Published April 24, 1920, at $2.00.

Contains "Flowers of August: I. Daisy—II. Queenannslace [*sic*]—III. *Untitled (It is a small plant)—IV. *Healall—V. Great Mullen—VI. *Butterandeggs—VII. *Thistle" by WCW, pp. 183–190. This is the first publication of these poems. "Daisy," "Queen-Ann's-Lace [*sic*]," and "Great Mullen" are in *CEP*; the other four poems are not reprinted.

B8   CONTACT COLLECTION   [1925]

CONTACT COLLECTION OF | CONTEMPORARY WRITERS | Djuna Barnes | Bryher | Mary Butts | Norman Douglas | Havelock Ellis | F. M. Ford | Wallace Gould | Ernest Hemingway | Marsden Hartley | H. D. | John Herrman | James Joyce | Mina Loy | Robert McAlmon | Ezra Pound | Dorothy Richardson | May Sinclair | Edith Sitwell | Gertrude Stein | W. C. Williams [*Contact Editions, Three Mountains Press, Paris*]

2 blank leaves, 4 leaves, 338 pp., 1 leaf, 2 blank leaves. About 7 5/8 × 5 5/8 inches (size varies according to the trimming of the leaves). Gray paper covers printed in black on front and back and upward on spine, folded over side, top and bottom of first and last blank leaves. Glassine outer wrappers on some copies.

Published June, 1925, at $3.00; about 300 copies printed. *On p.* [*339*]: "Printed at Dijon by Maurice Darantière M. CM. XXV"

Contains "Marianne Moore," an essay, by WCW, pp. 326–338, which appeared also in *The Dial*, May, 1925 (C102), and *A Novelette*, 1932 (A12); in *SE* and *Reader*, in a shorter version. The collection, edited by Robert McAlmon and published jointly by McAlmon and William Bird, includes work in progress from Joyce's *Finnegans Wake*, Part One of Ford's *No More Parades*, Hemingway's "Soldier's Home," and "A Canto" by Ezra Pound.

B9   THE AMERICAN CARAVAN   [1927]

[*ornament*] | THE AMERICAN | CARAVAN | [*ornament*] | A YEARBOOK | OF AMERICAN LITERATURE | EDITED BY | VAN WYCK BROOKS   LEWIS MUMFORD | ALFRED KREYMBORG   PAUL ROSENFELD | [*ornament*] | NEW YORK | THE MACAULAY COMPANY

xvi, 1 leaf, 843 pp., 1 blank leaf. 9 9/16 × 6 7/16 inches. Green cloth boards stamped in gold on cover and spine; green end papers with drawings in gray. Orange dust jacket printed in black.

Published September 15, 1927, at $5.00.

Contains "From: A Folded Skyscraper: 1. [poem] Hemmed-in Males —2. *[prose] When I think about how my grandmother flirted with me . . . [a sketch of Emily Nolan at the shore]—3. [poem] The Winds —4. *[prose] Ezra Pound" by WCW, pp. 216–221. This is the first publication of the two poems, which are in *CEP*, and the only publication of the two prose pieces.

B10   THE SECOND AMERICAN CARAVAN   1928

[*Within a double rule border:*] THE SECOND | AMERICAN CARAVAN | [*rule*] | A YEARBOOK | OF AMERICAN | LITERATURE | EDITED BY | ALFRED KREYMBORG | LEWIS MUMFORD | PAUL ROSENFELD | [*ornament*] | [*rule*] | NEW YORK | THE MACAULAY COMPANY | MCMXXVIII

xii, 872 pp. 9 1/2 × 6/12 inches. Cream cloth boards stamped in blue and gold; end papers.

Published September 24, 1928, at $5.00.

Contains "The Atlantic City Convention, A Composition in Two Parts, Poem and Speech: 1. The Waitress—2. *The Conservation of the Human Sub-Species" by WCW, pp. 219–224. This is the first publication of "The Waitress," which is in *CEP,* and the only publication of the prose "Speech."

B11   OUR EXAGMINATION . . .   1929

OUR EXAGMINATION | ROUND HIS FACTIFICATION | FOR INCAMINATION | OF WORK IN PROGRESS | By | Samuel Beckett, Marcel Brion, Frank Budgen, | Stuart Gilbert, Eugene Jolas, Victor Llona, | Robert McAlmon, Thomas McGreevy, | Elliot Paul, John Rodker, Robert Sage, | William Carlos Williams. | with | Letters of Protest | By | G. V. L. Slingsby and Vladimir Dixon. | SHAKESPEARE AND COMPANY | SYLVIA BEACH | 12, Rue de l'Odéon—Paris | [*short rule*] | M CM XX IX [*Stamped in some copies:*] MADE IN | GREAT BRITAIN

1 or 2 blank leaves, 4 leaves, [3]–194 pp., 1 leaf, 1 blank leaf. About 7 7/8 × 5 3/4 inches (size varies according to the trimming of the leaves). Heavy buff paper covers printed in black with a circular design on front, printed upward on spine.

Published early summer, 1929. *Colophon, on p.* [*195*]: "96 copies of this book have been printed on Vergé d'Arches numbered 1–96" *On p.* [*196*]: "Chartres.—Imprimerie Durand, Rue Fulbert (5–1929)." Distributed in the United States by New Directions at $2.00.

The title of this collection of essays, which are mostly about *Finnegans Wake,* the "Work in Progress," is Joyce's; according to Sylvia Beach the book was referred to at Shakespeare and Company as " 'Our Exag' pour gagner du temps."

Contains "A Point for American Criticism" by WCW, pp. [171]–191. First periodical publication: C129. In *SE.*

A new edition of *Our Exagmination,* with a new introduction by Sylvia Beach, was published by Faber & Faber, London, 1936, at 6*s.,* and another edition by New Directions, Norfolk, Conn., 1962, at $5.00.

B12   ANTHOLOGY OF MAGAZINE VERSE   1929
                        FOR 1929

ANTHOLOGY OF | MAGAZINE VERSE | FOR 1929 | AND YEARBOOK OF | AMERICAN POETRY | EDITED BY | WIL-

LIAM STANLEY | BRAITHWAITE | NEW YORK | GEORGE
SULLY AND COMPANY, INC. | 1929
> 1 blank leaf, xxxix pp., 1 leaf, 677 pp., 1 blank leaf. 8 3/16 × 5 9/16
> inches. Crimson cloth boards stamped in gold on spine; end papers.
>
> Published October 29, 1929, at $4.00.
>
> Contains "The Source, I–III," by WCW, pp. 393–394. First periodical
> publication: C124. In *CEP;* some changes, including the division of the
> poem into two parts, rather than three.

B13   PRIZE POEMS 1913–1929   1930

PRIZE POEMS | [*star*] 1913 [*star*] 1929 [*star*] | EDITED BY |
CHARLES A WAGNER | WITH AN INTRODUCTION BY |
MARK VAN DOREN | 19 [*line drawing by Rockwell Kent*] 30 |
Charles Boni PAPERBACKS New York
> 1 blank leaf, 247 pp., 1 leaf, 2 blank leaves. 7 3/8 × 5 inches. White
> stiff paper covers printed in shades of blue and purple with design by
> Rockwell Kent, printed upward in white on spine; end papers printed
> in blue with decorative design of books and skyscrapers (or, with same
> title page, white linen boards stamped in black with design by Rock-
> well Kent, white paper label printed downward in black on spine).
>
> Published April 25, 1930, at 50¢ for paperbound copies, $1.50 for
> hardbound copies. *On verso of title page:* "Published April, 1930"
>
> Contains "Paterson" by WCW, pp. 203–206. See C108. In *CEP.*

B14   IMAGIST ANTHOLOGY   1930

[*Two pages, facing; on left page within single rule border:*] IMAG-
IST ANTHOLOGY 1930 | COVICI, FRIEDE [*star*] NEW YORK
[*on right within single rule border:*] NEW POETRY BY THE
IMAGISTS | RICHARD ALDINGTON | JOHN COURNOS
[*star*] H. D. [*star*] JOHN GOULD FLETCHER | F. S. FLINT
[*star*] FORD MADOX FORD [*star*] JAMES JOYCE | D. H. LAW-
RENCE [*star*] | WILLIAM CARLOS WILLIAMS | *Forewords by*
FORD MADOX FORD [*star*] GLENN HUGHES
> 229 pp., 1 leaf, 4 blank leaves. 8 3/8 × 5 5/8 inches. Blue cloth boards
> with yellow paper label printed in black on spine; end papers. Red,
> black, and white dust jacket.

Published May 10, 1930, at $3.50. *Colophon, on p.* [*231*]: "The first edition of this book consists of one thousand copies."

Books by WCW are listed on p. 229: "*Tempera* [*sic*], 1913 | *Kora in Hell,* 1920 | *Four* [*sic*] *Grapes,* 1921 | *In the American Grave* [*sic*], 1925"

Contains "Della Primaverra [*sic*] Transportata [*sic*] al Morale: (*incomplete*)—The Trees [C155]—The Wind Increases—Love in a Truck *or* The Sea–Elephant [C155]—Rain [C138]—The Flower [C143]" by WCW, pp. 197–226. The first poem is later spelled ". . . Primavera Trasportata . . ."; the version in this anthology is shorter than later versions, and the line "THIS IS MY PLATFORM" is printed as though it were the title of another poem. This is the first publication of the first four poems and the first book publication of all the poems. All are in *CEP.*

B15   AMERICAN CARAVAN IV   1931

[*Double rule on left side of page*] AMERICAN | CARAVAN | IV. | EDITED BY | ALFRED KREYMBORG | LEWIS MUMFORD | PAUL ROSENFELD | [*device*] | NEW YORK | THE MACAULAY COMPANY | 1931

viii, 579 pp., 3 blank leaves. 9 5/16 × 6 1/4 inches. Green cloth boards lettered in black; end papers. White dust jacket printed in orange, blue, gold, and black.

Published March 27, 1931, at $5.00.

Contains "Sunday—A Crystal Maze [C206]" by WCW, pp. 453–455. This is the first publication of these poems. "Sunday" is in *CEP,* "A Crystal Maze" in *CLP* as Part I of the poem with that title.

B16   READIES FOR BOB BROWN'S MACHINE   1931

READIES | for | Bob Brown's Machine | by | A. Lincoln Gillespie Jr. John A. Farrell | Alfred Kreymborg   John Banting | Axton Clark Kay Boyle | B. C. Hagglund   K. T. Young | Carlton Brown   Laurence Vail | Charles Beadle   Lloyd Stern | Clare L. Brackett   Manuel Komroff | Charles Henri Ford   Nancy Cunard | Daphne Carr Norman Macleod | Donal MacKenzie   Paul Bowles | Eugene Jolas Peter Neagoè | Ezra Pound   Richard Johns | Filippo Tommaso Marinetti   Robert McAlmon | George Kent   Rose Brown | Gertrude Stein   Rue Menken | Herman Spector   Samuel Putnam | Hilaire

Hiler   Sidney Hunt | Hiler, pere [*sic*]   Theodore Pratt | J. Jones
Walter Lowenfels | James T. Farrell   Wambly Bald | Jay du Von
William Carlos Williams | Roving Eye Press | Cagnes-sur-Mer (A.-M.)
| 1931

> 2 leaves, 2 leaves of coated paper (containing "Contents" and photograph
> of Bob Brown's reading machine), 5–208 pp. 8 1/2 × 5 3/8 inches. Green
> paper covers printed in black on front and upward on spine.
>
> Published late December, 1931.
>
> *From "Appendix" by Bob Brown, p. 177:* "The word 'readies' sug-
> gests to me a moving type spectacle, reading at the speed-rate of the
> present day with the aid of a machine, a method of enjoying literature
> in a manner as up to date as the lively talkies." *"Appendix," p. 195:* "The
> form of the Story To Be Read on A Reading Machine suggests the ab-
> breviated dispatches sent by foreign newspaper correspondents to cut
> down cable expense, it is not offered as a new literary style, it is merely
> given as an experiment in writing prose that might be rapidly readable
> when passing before the intelligent, experienced eye. New forms, styles
> and condensations will suggest themselves. The twenty-five words most
> used in English are left out entirely, sometimes to the loss and often to
> the gain of the text."
>
> Contains "Readie Pome" by WCW, p. 114. The "pome" follows in its
> entirety: "Grace - face: hot - pot: lank - spank: meat - eat: hash - cash:
> sell - well: old - sold: sink - wink: deep - sleep: come - numb: dum - rum:
> some - bum." The "pome" is not reprinted.

B17   PROFILE   1932

[*PROFILE is in red*] EZRA POUND | PROFILE | AN ANTHOL-
OGY COLLECTED IN MCMXXXI | MILAN MCMXXXII [*John
Scheiwiller*]

> 1 blank leaf, 3 leaves, 9–142 pp., 3 leaves. 8 3/16 × 6 3/16 inches. Gray-
> green paper wrappers printed in black on front and upward on spine,
> folded over stiff white blanks. Glassine outer wrapper.
>
> Published late May, 1932, at $3.00; 250 copies printed. *Colophon, on
> recto of last leaf:* "Edition privately printed for John Scheiwiller limited
> to 250 numbered copies. Copy N. [stamped number] Tipografia Card.
> Ferrari - Milano"
>
> Edited by Ezra Pound; *on recto of first printed leaf:* "A collection of

poems which have stuck in my memory and which may possibly define their epoch, or at least rectify current ideas of it in respect to at least one contour." The anthology includes poems by Ezra Pound, James Joyce, Ford Madox Ford, H. D., W. B. Yeats, T. S. Eliot, Marianne Moore, E. E. Cummings, Ernest Hemingway, Archibald MacLeish, Louis Zukofsky, and others.

Contains "Hic Jacet ('About 1910') [C1]—Postlude ('About 1912') [C2]—Portrait of a Woman in Bed ('About 1917') [C15]—The Botticellian Trees ('First published in *Poetry,* Chicago, 1931') [C158]" by "Carlos Williams," pp. 20, 37, 64–66, 128–129. The dates printed with the poems are evidently the author's attempt to report the year each poem was written. This is the first book publication of "The Botticellian Trees" only. All are in *CEP.*

The original typescript of "The Botticellian Trees" is reproduced in *Famous Verse | Manuscripts |* Facsimiles of | Original Manuscripts | as submitted to | Poetry | T. S. Eliot   Robert Frost   James Joyce   D. H. Lawrence | Vachel Lindsay   Louis MacNeice   Edgar Lee Masters   Marianne Moore   Ezra Pound   Carl Sandburg | William Carlos Williams | Prepared by the Editors of Poetry [under the direction of Karl Shapiro, Modern Poetry Association], Chicago, 1954. The manuscript facsimile, pp. 23–24, is signed by the author in three places and is dated February, 1931.

B18   AN "OBJECTIVISTS" ANTHOLOGY   [1932]

AN "OBJECTIVISTS" ANTHOLOGY | EDITED BY LOUIS ZUKOFSKY | TO, PUBLISHERS   MCMXXXII   [*Le Beausset, Var, France, and New York*]

1 blank leaf, 3 leaves, [9]–210 pp., 1 leaf. 8 15/16 × 5 9/16 inches. Tan heavy paper covers printed in black on front and upward on spine.

Published summer, 1932, at $1.25. *On recto of last leaf:* "Printed by Maurice Darantière at Dijon, France   M.CM.XXXII" The book was distributed in the United States by Bruce Humphries, Boston.

Contributors include Basil Bunting, Robert McAlmon, Carl Rakosi, Kenneth Rexroth, Charles Reznikoff, and Louis Zukofsky. Many of the poems appeared in the "Objectivists" number of *Poetry,* February, 1931, also edited by Zukofsky. However, the one poem by WCW in that issue, "The Botticellian Trees," is not reprinted here.

Contains by WCW "I. Untitled (I make very little money) [C122]—II. It Is a Living Coral [C95]—III. This Florida: 1924—IV. Downtown [C84]—V. Untitled (On hot days) [C122]—VI. Untitled (The pure products of America) [C97]—VII. A Morning Imagination of Russia [C122]," pp. 98-111, and "The Jungle [C70]—On Gay Wallpaper [C124]—Untitled (Nothing is lost! the white) [C145]—In the 'Sconset Bus [C179]—All the Fancy Things [C111]—The Red Lily [C174]—To—The Avenue of Poplars [A7]—To Mark Anthony in Heaven [C47]—Portrait of a Lady [C51]—Full Moon [C91]," pp. 173-182. This is the first publication of "This Florida: 1924" and "To" and the first book publication of everything except "The Avenue of Poplars"; "In the 'Sconset Bus" was published contemporaneously in *Hound and Horn* (July–Sept. 1932). All are in *CEP;* the first and fifth poems, untitled, are part of "The Descent of Winter: 11/28" and "10/28"; "Downtown" is retitled "New England"; the sixth poem is "To Elsie"; the other untitled poem (Nothing is lost!) is the third part of "Birds and Flowers"; "To Mark Anthony in Heaven" is retitled "Mark Anthony in Heaven."

B19   THE CANTOS OF EZRA POUND   [1933]

THE CANTOS | of | EZRA POUND | Some Testimonies by | ERNEST HEMINGWAY | FORD MADOX FORD | T. S. ELIOT | HUGH WALPOLE | ARCHIBALD MacLEISH | JAMES JOYCE | and OTHERS | FARRAR & RINEHART, Inc. [*device*] PUBLISHERS: NEW YORK
22, [2] pp. 7 7/8 x 5 1/8 inches. Unbound; stapled.
     Published early 1933; number of copies printed unknown.
     Contains letter by WCW, pp. 5-7, dated at end "18 Sept. 1932." This is the only publication of the letter.

B20   FIFTY POETS   [1933]

FIFTY POETS | An | AMERICAN | Auto-Anthology | [*line drawing of flowers*] | Edited by William Rose Benét | Duffield and Green | New York City
xii, 153 pp., 1 blank leaf. 8 3/4 × 5 9/16 inches. Green cloth boards stamped in gold and black on spine; end papers.

Published June 19, 1933, at $2.50.

Contains a brief statement by WCW, not published elsewhere, about "The Red Wheelbarrow" and the poem, pp. 60–61. Williams concludes, "in fact I find the poem quite perfect."

B21   ACTIVE ANTHOLOGY   [1933]

ACTIVE | ANTHOLOGY | EDITED BY | EZRA | POUND | LONDON | FABER AND FABER LTD | 24 RUSSELL SQUARE 255 pp. 7 9/16 × 5 inches. Sienna cloth boards stamped in blue downward on spine; end papers. Yellow dust jacket printed in black and red.

Published October 12, 1933, at 7s. 6d.; 1516 sets of sheets printed (750 were bombed during World War II). *On verso of title page:* "First published in October MCMXXXIII"

Note by Ezra Pound, p. [5]: "My anthology *Profile* was a critical narrative, that is I attempted to show by excerpt what had occurred during the past quarter of a century. In this volume I am presenting an assortment of writers, mostly ill known in England, in whose verse a development appears or in some case [*sic*] we may say 'still appears' to be taking place, in contradistinction to authors in whose work no such activity has occurred or seems likely to proceed any further." The writers include Louis Zukofsky, E. E. Cummings, Ernest Hemingway, Marianne Moore, T. S. Eliot, and Ezra Pound.

Contains "I. Untitled (The farmer) [C86]—II. Untitled (O tongue) [C73]—III. Untitled (Our orchestra) [C86]—All the Fancy Things [C111]—It Is a Living Coral [C95]—The Cod Head [C173]—To [B18]—Sluggishly—The Flowers Alone [C191]—The Red Wheelbarrow [A7]—Light Becomes Darkness [A7]—To Elsie [C97]—Death [C152] —In the 'Sconset Bus [C179]—Sea-Trout and Butterfish [C154]" by WCW, pp. 31–55. This is the first publication of "Sluggishly" and the first book publication of "Death" and "Sea-Trout and Butterfish"; "The Flowers Alone" was published contemporaneously in *Poetry* (Oct. 1933). All are in *CEP*; the first three are titled "The Farmer—To an Old Jaundiced Woman—Shoot it Jimmy!"

B22   GALAXY   1934

GALAXY | AN ANTHOLOGY | Compiled by | BEATRIX REYNOLDS | and JAMES GABELLE | 1934 | [*ornament*] | Lino-

leum Cuts by | LEANDER LEITNER | THE GAYREN PRESS |
RIDGEWOOD, N. J.

    2 leaves, 274 pp. 8 9/16 × 5 3/4 inches. Silver cloth on spine and one-
fifth of black cloth boards, lettered in white on front; silver end papers.

    Contains two poems, "To a Mexican Pig-bank [C211]—Study for a
Figure Representing Modern Culture [C223]," by WCW, pp. 97–98.
Both in *CEP*; the second poem is retitled "Proletarian Portrait."

B23   MODERN THINGS   [1934]

MODERN THINGS— | [*double rule*] | EDITED BY | PARKER
TYLER | [*device*] | NEW YORK | THE GALLEON PRESS

    92 pp., 2 blank leaves. 8 13/16 × 5 1/2 inches. White cloth on spine
and one-fifth of violet cloth boards, lettered in white on front; end
papers. Gray dust jacket printed in black and violet.

    Published September, 1934, at $2.00.

    On front flap of dust jacket: "This collection of the newer poems (the
majority here for the first time published) of first-class modern poets
means an indispensable volume is ready for all serious readers of poetry
as well as for the large public which is still to be persuaded of the popular virtues of modernist work."

    Contains "An Occasional Poem: St. Francis Einstein of the Daffodils
[C64]—Tree and Sky [C191]—Flowers by the Sea [C154]—Simplex
Sigilum Veri [C137]—Wedded Are the River and the Sky [C150]—
The Death of See—The Locust Tree in Flower (Among/of/green)
[C474]" by WCW, pp. 30–36. This is the first publication of "The
Death of See" and of this version of "The Locust Tree in Flower" (See
C474a for a note by WCW about the poem) and the first book publica-
tion of all the poems. All are in *CEP*; "An Occasional Poem . . ." is
retitled "St. Francis Einstein . . ."; "Wedded are the River and the
Sky" is retitled "A Marriage Ritual" and has other changes; "The Death
of See" has some changes.

B24   AMERICA & ALFRED STIEGLITZ   [1934]

AMERICA & | ALFRED STIEGLITZ | A Collective Portrait |
Edited by Waldo Frank · Lewis | Mumford · Dorothy Norman |
Paul Rosenfeld & Harold | Rugg · With 120 Illustrations | THE

LITERARY GUILD · NEW YORK | [*ornament*] [*Doubleday, Doran & Company, Inc.*]

1 blank leaf, 6 leaves, 3–339 pp., and 34 coated leaves, 32 with illustrations, bound in between pp. 308 and [309]. 9 1/2 × 6 5/16 inches. Black cloth boards stamped in blind on front and in silver on spine; end papers. White, black, gray, and silver dust jacket.

December 3, 1934, Literary Guild selection. *On verso of title page:* "First edition" Doubleday also published a regular trade edition December 3, 1934, at $3.50; number of copies printed not available.

Contributors include the editors, John Marin, Marsden Hartley, Charles Demuth, Gertrude Stein, Sherwood Anderson.

Contains an essay, "The American Background," by WCW, pp. 9–32. This is the only publication of this essay until it was reprinted in *SE*.

B25 TRIAL BALANCES 1935

[*Double rule*] | [*rule*] | TRIAL BALANCES | Edited by | Ann Winslow | NEW YORK | THE MACMILLAN COMPANY | 1935 [*rule*] | [*double rule*]

xvi pp., 1 leaf, 225 pp., 2 blank leaves. 8 3/4 × 5 7/8 inches. Dark blue cloth boards stamped on front and spine in silver; end papers. Silver dust jacket printed in blue.

Published October 8, 1935, at $2.00; 2500 copies printed.

Contains a commentary by WCW, pp. 196–197, on James McQuail's poem, "Tea Time Tales." This is the only publication of the statement.

B26 THE NEW CARAVAN [1936]

THE NEW | CARAVAN | EDITED BY Alfred Kreymborg | Lewis Mumford, Paul Rosenfeld | W · W · NORTON & COMPANY, INC · | PUBLISHERS · NEW YORK

ix pp., 1 leaf, 663 pp. 8 3/4 × 5 3/4 inches. Off-white cloth boards stamped in crimson on spine; end papers. White, black, and orange dust jacket.

Published November 2, 1936, at $3.95; 1350 copies printed.

Contains "THE FIRST PRESIDENT, Libretto for an Opera (and Ballet) in Three Acts: 1. Introduction for the Composer: An Occasion for Music 2. Opera Libretto" by WCW, pp. 563–602. This is the first publication of *The First President*, which is in *Many Loves* (A47).

B27   WILLIAM ZORACH | TWO DRAWINGS   1937
WILLIAM CARLOS WILLIAMS | TWO POEMS

[*Artist's and poet's names in red*] WILLIAM ZORACH | TWO DRAWINGS | WILLIAM CARLOS WILLIAMS | TWO POEMS | [*device*] | THE STOVEPIPE PRESS | 1937

4 leaves. 8 1/4 × 5 5/16 inches. Slate green heavy paper covers with white label printed in red pasted on front and publisher's device printed in black in lower right of front cover; fore edges of leaves untrimmed; tied with white silk string in holes stabbed in fold.

Colophon, on verso of last leaf: "Pamphlet Number One. Five hundred copies of this pamphlet have been handset and printed by the Stovepipe Press, of which four hundred and thirty are for sale at twenty-five cents a copy."

Contents: [Zorach drawing]—Advent of To-day—[Zorach drawing] —The Girl.

Notes: The first poem, with some changes, is in *CEP*; the second [C246] is in *CLP*.

[*I Wanted*, p. 59:] "William Zorach, today a well-known sculptor, and I were together in a play by Alfred Kreymborg produced at the Provincetown Theatre on McDougal Street in the Village—the theatre where Eugene O'Neill's plays were being given. The play was called *Lima Beans*. Zorach was the huckster, Mina Loy and I were the lovers. It ran for several nights. That's all it was: we were theatre pals, and somehow it came about that we combined our work, his two drawings, nudes, and my two poems "Advent of Today" and "The Girl."

B28   AND SPAIN SINGS   1937

. . . and | Spain sings | Fifty Loyalist Ballads | Adapted by American Poets | Edited by M. J. Benardete and | Rolfe Humphries | The Vanguard Press | New York · 1937

xx, 123 pp. 7 11/16 × 5 1/4 inches. Red paper boards lettered in black on cover and downward on spine; end papers. Red and white dust jacket printed in black.

Published September 29, 1937, at $1.00. Copyright date: July 29, 1937. Contains an adaption by WCW of a ballad by Miguel Hernández, "Wind of the Village," pp. 14–16. This is the only publication of Williams' translation.

B29   CHRISTOPHER COLUMBUS   [1937]

CHRISTOPHER COLUMBUS | and Other Poems | By | Sydney Salt | With an Introduction by | William Carlos Williams | [*device*] | Boston | Bruce Humphries, Inc. | Publishers

80 pp., 1 leaf. 8 3/16 × 5 11/16 inches. Blue linen on spine and one-sixth of tan cloth boards with buff paper label printed downward in blue on spine; end papers. Blue and gray dust jacket printed in black.

Published late December, 1937, at $2.00; 500 copies printed. *Colophon, on recto of last leaf:* "This first edition of *Christopher Columbus and Other Poems* . . . is limited to 500 copies. Finished printing December, 1937. This is number . . . [signed] Sidney Salt"

Contains "Introduction" by WCW, pp. 7–10.

B30   THE GARDEN OF DISORDER   [1938]

English edition:

THE | GARDEN OF DISORDER | AND OTHER POEMS | BY | CHARLES HENRI FORD | WITH AN INTRODUCTION BY | WILLIAM CARLOS WILLIAMS | AND A FRONTISPIECE BY | PAVEL TCHELITCHEW | LONDON | EUROPA PRESS | 7 Great Ormond Street, W. C. 1

78 pp., 1 leaf, and frontispiece leaf of coated paper. 8 13/16 × 5 11/16 inches. Green cloth boards stamped in yellow downward on spine; end papers; white dust jacket printed in black. Signed copies are bound in Cockerell's hand-marbled cover paper. Copies A to K, not for sale, are bound in white cloth on spine and one-sixth of paper boards, lettered in green downward on spine; end papers; fuchsia dust jacket printed in black with frontispiece drawing by Tchelitchew on front.

Published January, 1938, at 5*s*. or $1.50 for ordinary copies and 12*s*. 6*d*. or $3.50 for signed copies; 500 copies printed by Temple Press, Letchworth, England. Some of these were distributed by New Directions with a different title page and dust jacket (see below). *Colophon, on verso of title page:* "Europa Poets VI | This, the first edition of *The Garden of Disorder,* is limited to 500 numbered copies, of which those numbered I to XXX are signed by the Author. Copies A to K are not for sale, and are reserved for the Author and Publisher. Copies 41 to 500 constitute the ordinary edition. This is number . . ."

Contains Introduction, "The Tortuous Straightness of Charles Henri Ford," by WCW, pp. 9–11. The Introduction is dated "5th June 1937" at end—in *SE* it is misdated 1939.

American edition:

THE | GARDEN OF DISORDER | AND OTHER POEMS | BY | CHARLES HENRI FORD | WITH AN INTRODUCTION BY | WILLIAM CARLOS WILLIAMS | AND A FRONTISPIECE BY | PAVEL TCHELITCHEW | NEW DIRECTIONS | NORFOLK, CONN. [*James Laughlin*]
Collation, size, and binding the same as English edition. Tan dust jacket printed in blue.

Published June, 1938, at $2.00.

B31   SONNETS FROM NEW DIRECTIONS   1938

Sonnets From | New Directions | Merrill Moore | For Dudley Fitts | New Directions | Norfolk, Connecticut | 1938 [*Pamphlet Series, Number Two, edited by James Laughlin*]
23 unnumbered leaves, I blank leaf. About 7 × 5 1/16 inches. Blue paper covers printed in sienna; stapled.

Published April 4, 1938, at 75¢; 1000 copies printed. *Colophon, on verso of title page:* "One thousand copies printed in February 1938 by the Otter Valley Press in Middlebury, Vermont"

Contains a foreword, "Merrill Moore's Sonnets | Present total, steadily mounting, 50,000," by WCW, third leaf, pp. [5–6]; an excerpt from the introduction is printed on the back cover.

The foreword (or excerpts from it) is reprinted at least four times: (1) on the inside back cover of *The Noise that Time Makes* | *A First Volume of 101 Sonnets* by Merrill Moore (with a Foreword by John Crowe Ransom and Some Reviews of This Book), probably published in Boston, 1938; this is a new edition of *The Noise that Time Makes,* with reviews of the first edition, which was published in 1929 by Harcourt, Brace and Company, New York; (2) on last leaf, pp. [1016–1017] of M | *One Thousand Autobiographical Sonnets* by Merrill Moore, Harcourt, Brace and Company, 1938, which was in the press at the time of publication of *Sonnets from New Directions;* (3) excerpt only, on the back flap of the dust jacket of Moore's *Case-Record from a Sonnetorium,* 1951 (B59); (4) excerpt only, on broadsheet—see D6.

Merrill Moore wrote an average of five sonnets each day from his eighteenth year.

B32   A POET'S LIFE   1938

[*Within rectangular border of two thick and one thin rules:*] A | POET'S LIFE | Seventy Years | in a Changing World | BY | HARRIET MONROE | [*ornament*] | NEW YORK | THE MACMILLAN COMPANY | 1938

1 blank leaf, viii pp., 2 leaves, 488 pp., 1 blank leaf, and 17 coated leaves of illustrations tipped in passim. 9 7/16 × 6 3/16 inches. Green cloth boards stamped in green on front and in green and blind on spine; end papers. Tan dust jacket printed in black and red.

Published March 8, 1938, at $5.00; 2500 copies printed. *On verso of title page:* "Set up and printed. Published March, 1938. First Printing"

Contains letters and excerpts from letters by WCW to Harriet Monroe: long letter, March 5, 1913, pp. 270–271 (in *SL*)—note, undated [probably April, 1913], p. 272—brief letter, June, 1913, p. 272—letter, October 14, 1913, p. 272 (in *SL*)—two excerpts, undated [probably 1917], p. 389. The letters are about poems sent to *Poetry* and reviews published in *Poetry.*

B33   WRITERS TAKE SIDES   [1938]

WRITERS TAKE SIDES | LETTERS ABOUT THE WAR IN SPAIN | FROM 418 AMERICAN AUTHORS | Published by | THE LEAGUE OF AMERICAN WRITERS | 381 FOURTH AVENUE, NEW YORK CITY

4 leaves, 82 pp., 2 leaves, 1 blank leaf. 7 1/8 × 5 9/16 inches. Blue paper covers printed in white and black.

Published May, 1938, at 15¢.

Contains a statement by WCW, in answer to a questionnaire, supporting "the legal government and the people of Republican Spain," pp. 64–65. A similar book was published in England in 1937, *Authors Take Sides on the Spanish War,* Left Review, 2 Parton Street, London.

B34   THE OXFORD ANTHOLOGY   1938

THE | OXFORD ANTHOLOGY | OF | AMERICAN LITER-ATURE | CHOSEN AND EDITED BY | WILLIAM ROSE BENÉT | AND | NORMAN HOLMES PEARSON | New York | OXFORD UNIVERSITY PRESS | 1938

xxx, 1705 pp. 9 7/16 × 6 7/16 inches. Blue cloth boards lettered in gold on spine; end papers. Trade edition bound in maroon cloth boards lettered in gold on spine; end papers. Blue dust jacket printed in maroon.

Published October 27, 1938, at $4.50; trade edition published November, 1938. *On verso of title page:* "First edition"

Contains "A Note on Poetry" by WCW, pp. 1313–1314. This is the only publication of the Note. This is not the first book publication of the poems (Peace on Earth—The Bull—The Red Wheelbarrow—The Sea-Elephant—Rain—The Botticellian Trees—Nantucket—The Red Lily—This Is Just to Say—The Yachts—Fine Work with Pitch and Copper).

B35   CHARLES SHEELER . . .   1939

CHARLES SHEELER | paintings | drawings | photographs | WITH AN INTRODUCTION BY | WILLIAM CARLOS WILLIAMS | THE MUSEUM OF MODERN ART · NEW YORK · 1939

1 blank leaf, 53, [1] pp., including illustrations. 10 3/16 × 7 5/8 inches. Gray paper boards printed in charcoal on front and downward on spine.

Published October, 1939, at $1.00. *Colophon, on verso of p. 53:* "Five thousand five hundred copies of this catalog have been printed for the Trustees of the Museum of Modern Art at The Spiral Press, New York. Of the edition, four thousand copies have been reserved for members of the Museum."

Contains "Introduction" by WCW, pp. 6–9. In *SE.* Compare B65.

B36 WE MODERNS [1939]

[Within white space imposed on Carl Van Vechten's photograph of a painting by Ruth Bower:] WE MODERNS | GOTHAM BOOK MART | 1920–1940 | *[in white rectangle at bottom:]* The Life of the Party at FINNEGANS WAKE in our Garden | on Publication Day | Painting by Ruth Bower Photograph by Carl Van Vechten *[Catalogue No. 42, Gotham Book Mart, New York]*

Cover-title, 3–88, [2] pp. 8 × 5 7/16 inches. Heavy white paper covers printed in black; stabbed.

Distributed December, 1939, gratis; 5000 copies printed. Also 500 copies printed on coated paper, with stiff white paper covers and spiral loose-leaf binding, were issued simultaneously at $1.00. *Note on inside front cover of both bindings:* "For those desiring to keep this catalogue up to date, we have issued a limited quantity in loose-leaf binding . . . which will also provide space for several introductions expected from abroad unavoidably delayed because of war conditions."

Contains foreword to *We Moderns* by WCW, p. 9. The catalogue, compiled by Frances Steloff and Kay Steele to commemorate the twentieth anniversary of Frances Steloff's Gotham Book Mart, groups the titles of books by each author with a brief introductory note about each author by another writer.

B37 CALENDAR: [1940]
AN ANTHOLOGY OF 1940 POETRY

[In red:] Calendar: | an anthology of 1940 poetry | edited by Norman Macleod | Sponsored by The Poetry Center of the | Young Men's Hebrew Association | Lexington Avenue at 92nd Street, New York | The Press of James A. Decker | Prairie City, Illinois *[ornament at each corner of the page]*

1 blank leaf, 4 leaves, 7–63 pp., 1 blank leaf. 9 5/16 × 6 1/16 inches. Blue imitation leather boards stamped in silver on front and downward on spine; end papers. Also in gray paper wrappers folded over blank cardboard covers, printed in red and black; stapled.

Published late 1940 at 50¢ for paperbound edition.

Contains "Writer's Prologue: to a Play in Verse" by WCW, pp. 7–12. This is the first publication of this poem, which is in *CLP*.

B38   NEW POEMS: 1940   1941

[*Six thin rules*] | NEW POEMS: | 1940 | An Anthology of British and American Verse | Edited by Oscar Williams [*ornament*] A Living Age Book | The Yardstick Press [*ornament*] New York [*ornament*] 1941 | [*six thin rules*]

> 5 leaves, 9–276 pp., 1 blank leaf. 8 1/4 × 5 5/8 inches. Ivory-green cloth boards stamped in red and gold on spine; end papers. Red, black, and ivory dust jacket.
>
> Published April 17, 1941, at $2.50. *On verso of title page:* "First printing"
>
> Contains "The Forgotten City" by WCW, pp. 239–240 [C282]. In *CLP*.

B39   CALENDAR: [1941]
AN ANTHOLOGY OF 1941 POETRY

CALENDAR: | an anthology of 1941 poetry | edited by | NORMAN MACLEOD | Sponsored by The Poetry Center of the Young Men's Hebrew Association | Lexington Avenue at 92nd Street, New York | THE PRESS OF JAMES A. DECKER | PRAIRIE CITY, ILLINOIS

> 55 pp. 8 7/8 × 5 7/8 inches. Maroon cloth boards stamped in gold; end papers. Also in stiff yellow paper covers printed in brown; spiral binding.
>
> Published late 1941 at $1.00 for spiral edition.
>
> Contains "The Yellow Season" by WCW, p. 31. This is the first publication of this poem, which is in *CEP*.

B40   THIS IS MY BEST   1942

America's 93 Greatest Living Authors Present | This Is My Best | [*ornament*] OVER 150 SELF-CHOSEN AND | COMPLETE MASTERPIECES, TOGETHER WITH | THEIR REASONS FOR THEIR SELECTIONS | [*device*] Edited by Whit Burnett | Burton C. Hoffman   THE DIAL PRESS   New York, 1942

> xiv, 1180 pp., 2 blank leaves. 8 3/4 × 6 inches. Tan cloth boards stamped in gold on front and in blue-green and gold on spine; end papers. Tan dust jacket printed in black, white, and crimson.
>
> Published October 13, 1942, at $3.50; 70,000 copies printed.

Contains a statement, "Why He Selected Some Flower Studies," by WCW, pp. 641–644, to accompany "Daisy—Primrose—Queen-Ann's-Lace [*sic*]." This is the only publication of the statement, which is dated June 14, 1942, at the end, but is not the first book publication of the poems—see B7 and A5.

B41   CALENDAR: AN ANTHOLOGY OF 1942   [1942]
                       POETRY

[*In blue:*] AN ANTHOLOGY OF 1942 POETRY [*ornament*] EDITED BY NORMAN MACLEOD | [*in black:*] William Carlos Williams   André Spire   Hugh Mac- | Diarmid   Louis Zukofsky R. P. Blackmur   Denis | Devlin   Norman Rosten   Frederick Mortimer Clapp | Norman Macleod   Harvey Breit   Norman McCaig | [*white letters on rectangular background of blue and white squares:*] CALENDAR | [*in black:*] RUTHVEN TODD   J. F. HENDRY GLYN JONES   ALAN | SWALLOW   ALAIN BOSQUET LYNETTE ROBERTS   ERIN | CROMARTY   ARTHUR BLAIR ROBERT MCALMON   CRIEFF | WILLIAMSON   FRANK JONES   V. WATKINS   JOHN PRICHARD | [*in blue:*] SPONSORED BY THE POETRY CENTER OF THE YOUNG MEN'S HEBREW | ASSOCIATION, LEXINGTON AVENUE AT 92ND STREET, NEW YORK CITY | THE PRESS OF JAMES A. DECKER   PRAIRIE CITY, ILLINOIS

72 pp., 2 leaves. 8 3/16 × 5 7/16 inches. Gray paper wrappers flapped at sides over heavy buff blank covers; sewn, signatures visible at spine; printed in black and blue like title page.

Published late 1942 at $1.00.

Contains "Three Sonnets" by WCW, pp. 12–14. This is the first publication of this poem, which is in *CLP*, with some changes.

B42   TWENTIETH CENTURY AUTHORS   1942

TWENTIETH CENTURY | AUTHORS | A Biographical Dictionary of Modern Literature | Edited by | STANLEY J. KUNITZ | and | HOWARD HAYCRAFT | COMPLETE IN ONE VOLUME WITH | 1850 BIOGRAPHIES AND | 1700 PORTRAITS | [*device*] | NEW YORK | THE H. W. WILSON COMPANY | NINETEEN HUNDRED FORTY-TWO

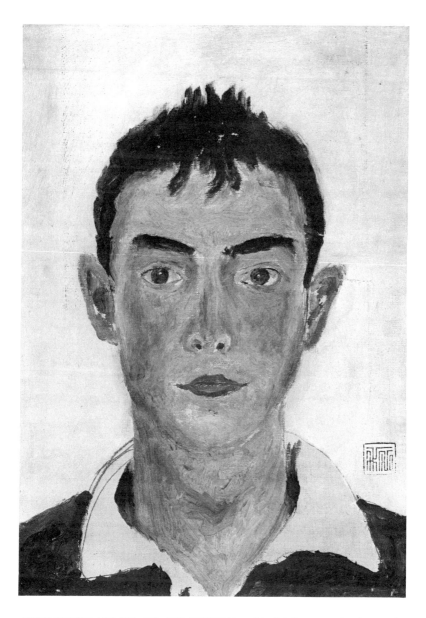

SELF-PORTRAIT IN OIL BY WILLIAM CARLOS WILLIAMS, 1914
Reproduced by permission of the University of Pennsylvania Library
from the original, a gift of Mrs. William Carlos Williams.

vii, 1577 pp., 2 blank leaves. 10 1/4 × 6 7/8 inches. Green cloth boards stamped in gold on spine; end papers.

Published December 1, 1942, at $8.50; 57,600 copies printed. *On verso of title page:* "Set up and published at the press of the H. W. Wilson Company November 1942"

The entry under William Carlos Williams includes at the end a biographical statement by WCW of approximately 600 words, pp. 1525–1526.

B43   AMERICAN DECADE   [1943]

AMERICAN DECADE | 68 POEMS FOR THE FIRST TIME IN AN ANTHOLOGY | BY | ELIZABETH BISHOP, R. P. BLACKMUR, TOM BOGGS, | MYRON H. BROOMELL, JOHN CIARDI, ROBERT CLAIRMONT, | MALCOLM COWLEY, E. E. CUMMINGS, REUEL DENNEY, | THOMAS W. DUNCAN, KENNETH FEARING, THOMAS HORNSBY FERRIL, | LLOYD FRANKENBERG, ROBERT FROST, CLIFFORD | GESSLER, W. W. GIBSON, HORACE GREGORY, LANGSTON | HUGHES, ROBINSON JEFFERS, WELDON KEES, E. I. MAYO, | JOSEPHINE MILES, SAMUEL FRENCH MORSE, MURIEL | RUKEYSER, CARL SANDBURG, WINFIELD TOWNLEY SCOTT, | KARL JAY SHAPIRO, THEODORE SPENCER, WALLACE | STEVENS, MARK VAN DOREN, EDWARD WEISMILLER, | JOHN WHEELWRIGHT, WILLIAM CARLOS WILLIAMS | [*design*] | EDITED BY TOM BOGGS | *And star-dials pointed to morn.* –Poe | [*design*] | THE CUMMINGTON PRESS, Publishers

93, [1] pp., 1 leaf. 9 11/16 × 6 3/8 inches. Blue cloth boards stamped in white downward on spine; end papers. White dust jacket printed in blue. Also in blue, white, and black paper boards with linen back and white paper label printed downward on spine; bound by hand.

Published June 24, 1943, at $3.50 for ordinary copies, $7.50 for handbound copies; 475 copies printed. *Colophon, p.* [*96*]: ". . . Four-hundred-seventy-five copies, of which fifty are not for sale, are on Andria paper, and twenty-five, especially bound by hand and numbered 1 to 25, on Sterling Laid . . . ."

Contains "In Chains" by WCW, p. 93 [C282]. In *CLP.*

B44   THE POETS SPEAK   1943

THE POETS SPEAK | TWELVE POEMS FROM A SERIES OF
READINGS AT | THE NEW YORK PUBLIC LIBRARY | OC-
TOBER AND NOVEMBER, 1943 | WITH AN INTRODUCTION
BY | MAY SARTON | [*device*] | NEW YORK | THE NEW
YORK PUBLIC LIBRARY | 1943

    1 blank leaf, 22 pp., 2 blank leaves. 10 × 7 1/16 inches. Blue paper
covers printed in black on front; stapled.

    Published November, 1943, at 25¢; 600 copies printed. *On verso of title
page:* "Reprinted from The Bulletin of the New York Public Library
of November 1943, printed at the New York Public Library."

    Contains "The Dance (In Breughel's great picture, The Kermess)"
by WCW, p. 21, with acknowledgment to *Palisade* (C327).

    The readings were given, the first on October 19 and the last on
November 23, in the auditorium of the New York Public Library.

B45   JEAN SANS TERRE | LANDLESS JOHN   1944

[*In orange:*] JEAN SANS TERRE | BY YVAN GOLL [*in green:*]
LANDLESS JOHN | [*The large first L of* LANDLESS *encloses the
following in black:*] TRANSLATED BY | LIONEL ABEL | WIL-
LIAM CARLOS WILLIAMS | CLARK MILLS | JOHN GOULD
FLETCHER | PREFACE BY ALLEN TATE | WITH TWO
ORIGINAL DRAWINGS | BY EUGENE BERMAN | THE
GRABHORN PRESS | SAN FRANCISCO | MCMXLIV

    4 blank leaves, leaf with drawing, 2 leaves, 28, [1] pp., leaf with draw-
ing, 4 blank leaves, the first and last leaves pasted down as end papers;
pages are numbered in duplicate, French in red and English in black
on facing pages. 15 7/16 × 11 3/16 inches. Marbled yellow, green, and
tan paper boards; spine covered in dark green cloth with yellow paper
label printed downward in red.

    Published early 1944. *Colophon, on verso of p.* [*28*]: "One hundred
and seventy-five copies of this edition have been printed at the Grabhorn
Press of San Francisco September, 1943 . . . February 1944"

    Contains translations "Jean sans terre fait sept fois le tour de la terre—
Landless John Circles the Earth Seven Times," pp. 2-3; "Jean sans terre
conduit la caravane—Landless John Leads the Caravan," pp. 7-8; "Jean

sans terre aborde au dernier port | à Claire sans Lune—Landless John at the Final Port | to Claire sans Lune," p. 27, by WCW. These translations are reprinted, with three new ones, in *Jean Sans Terre*, 1958 (B76). Periodical publications: C301; C511.

B46   THE HAPPY ROCK   [1945]

THE HAPPY ROCK | [*line drawing of Henry Miller*] | A | Book | About | Henry Miller [*Packard Press, Berkeley, Bern Porter*]
  1 blank leaf, 1 leaf, 1 blank leaf, 4 leaves, 157 pp., 2 leaves. 10 1/2 × 7 1/16 inches. Gray cloth on spine and one-sixth of gray paper boards, printed in red and black on front; end papers of same gray paper as binding. White dust jacket printed in black on front like title page. Colored leaves of green, deep yellow, pale yellow, blue, pink, orange, white.
  Published early 1945 at $5.00; 3000 copies printed. *Colophon, on verso of title page:* "Of the three thousand copies printed for Bern Porter by the Packard Press at Berkeley, seven hundred and fifty were bound for distribution during 1945."
  Contains "To the Dean" by WCW, p. 97 [C341]. In *CLP*².

B47   YANKEE DOODLE   1945

YANKEE DOODLE | A DRAMA OF THE AMERICAN REVO-LUTION | by | Coley Taylor | [*Benson J. Lossing's drawing of a device on the sword presented by the Continental Congress to Lafayette*] | With a Foreword by | William Carlos Williams | New York | The Devin-Adair Company | 23 East 26th Street, at Madison Square | 1945
  vii pp., 1 leaf, 161, [1] pp., 2 blank leaves. 8 1/4 × 5 1/2 inches. Green cloth boards stamped in gold on front and downward on spine; gray end papers. Gray dust jacket printed in sienna and blue-green.
  Published 1945 at $2.50
  Contains "An Introductory Note" by WCW, pp. vii–[viii].

B48   NORTH, EAST, SOUTH, WEST   [1945]

[*Within ornamental border of black and red; in black:*] NORTH, EAST, | SOUTH, WEST | [*in red:*] A Regional Anthology | of

American Writing | [*in black:*] General Editor: Charles Lee | New England: Sarah Cleghorn | Middle Atlantic: Edwin Seaver | Middle West: A. C. Spectorsky | The West: Joseph Henry Jackson | The South: Struthers Burt | Howell, Soskin, Publishers [*New York*]

xv, 558 pp., 4 leaves. 9 × 6 inches. Blue cloth boards lettered in gold on spine; end papers.

Published December, 1945, at $3.75.

Contains "Complaint" by WCW, p. 202, and a brief statement by WCW in a biographical note, p. 554. This is the first publication of both; the poem is in *CEP*.

B49   TRANSFIGURED NIGHT   1946

TRANSFIGURED NIGHT | POEMS BY | BYRON VAZAKAS | THE MACMILLAN COMPANY · NEW YORK | 1946

xvi, 77 pp., 1 blank leaf. 8 9/16 × 5 3/4 inches. Dark blue cloth boards stamped in orange on front and downward on spine; end papers. Dark blue, white, and orange dust jacket.

Published October 1, 1946, at $2.00; 2000 copies printed.

Contains foreword by WCW, pp. ix–xiv. Note at end of essay: "Acknowledgment is made to the Editor of the Quarterly Review of Literature for permission to reprint this Introductory Essay [originally published as a prepublication review, C361]."

B50   SPEARHEAD   [1947]

[*Line drawing of a spearhead on left side of page*] SPEARHEAD | 10 YEARS' EXPERIMENTAL | WRITING IN AMERICA | A NEW DIRECTIONS BOOK [*New York, James Laughlin*]

3 leaves, 9–604 pp. 9 1/4 × 6 1/16 inches. Tan cloth boards stamped in black on spine; end papers. White dust jacket printed in gray, yellow, and black.

Published November 10, 1947, at $5.00; 4965 copies printed (of which 999 were distributed in England by the Falcon Press).

Spearhead was published "to commemorate, and celebrate, the first ten years' activity of New Directions by reprinting some of the best work that was published in the annual volumes *New Directions in Prose & Poetry*" and "to present an impartial historical survey of the significant *experimental* and *advance guard* writing in the United States during the past decade" [*"Editorial Notes," James Laughlin, p. 9*]; also contains previously unpublished writing.

Contains by WCW: (1) "From Paterson (There is no direction. . . . it drives in among the rocks fitfully)," pp. 525–531; (2) TEN LITTLE POEMS: The Locust Tree in Flower (Among/of/green)—Poem (As the cat)—Young Woman at a Window—Between Walls—Poem (so much depends) [The Red Wheelbarrow]—A Chinese Toy—This Is Just to Say—Proletarian Portrait—Complete Destruction—The Great Figure," pp. 532–533; (3) "Night" [a chapter from *In the Money*, A21], pp. 534–540; (4) "Perpetuum Mobile: The City," pp. 541–546.

This is the first publication of two poems, "Between Walls" and "The Great Figure," but is not the first book publication of the other items. The last poem is reprinted from *New Directions in Prose & Poetry;* the others are from books published by New Directions. "Ten Little Poems" are reprinted as a group in *Perspectives U.S.A.*, Fall, 1952. "From Paterson" is in *Paterson, One*, II, 28–37, and all the other poems are in *CEP.* "Night" is in *Reader.*

B51   WOMEN   [1948]

[*The W of Women is in black, the other letters in gray:*] WOMEN | [*in black:*] A COLLABORATION OF ARTISTS AND WRITERS | [*in gray:*] SAMUEL M KOOTZ EDITIONS | NEW YORK
15 × 11 3/16 inches. 12 broadsheets folded vertically, each in a different color. Cardboard portfolio covered with pink and gray paper, with flaps pasted down at sides over white lining paper; title printed in black on front. Cellophane dust wrapper. Black and white reproduction of a painting pasted on the first page of each broadsheet and an essay printed on the two inside pages.

Published 1948 at $2.95.

The artists and writers are: Pablo Picasso and Lewis Galantière—Georges Braque and Benjamin Péret—Fernand Léger and Clement Greenberg—William Baziotes and Harold Rosenberg—Romare Bearden and William Carlos Williams—Byron Browne and Barry Ulanov—Adolph Gottlieb and Victor Wolfson—David Hare and Jean-Paul Sartre—Hans Hofmann and Tennessee Williams—Carl Holty and Paul Goodman—Robert Motherwell and Weldon Kees.

From the Preface by Samuel M. Kootz: "The idea for an exhibition of paintings of 'Women' came into being in February, 1947, with my acquisition from Picasso of his savage 'Woman in Green Costume' (which aroused such violent controversy in the great London show in 1945). I began to compare this picture with the paintings of women done in the French tradition, which reached its sensuous culmination in the work of Renoir and Bonnard. And I thought of all the modern artists who have painted women: how different their points-of-view from the Renoir tradition, yet how inevitable their return to and concern with this same subject-matter. [¶] So, with the Picasso to start with, I consulted the other artists associated with the gallery about a special show to be devoted to 'Women.' Their response was immediate, enthusiastic. And, when in September the show was finally on the walls, came the additional thought: to preserve this exhibit in book-form, and to ask modern poets and writers to collaborate. No restrictions were imposed on the writers."

Contains essay, "Woman as Operator" by WCW, with painting, "Women with an Oracle (1947)" by Romare Bearden, on pale blue broadsheet.

B52   POETS AT WORK   [1948]

POETS AT WORK | ESSAYS BASED ON THE MODERN POETRY | COLLECTION AT THE LOCKWOOD MEMORIAL | LIBRARY, UNIVERSITY OF BUFFALO, BY | RUDOLPH ARN-HEIM | W. H. AUDEN | KARL SHAPIRO | DONALD A. STAUFFER | INTRODUCTION BY CHARLES D. ABBOTT | NEW YORK | HARCOURT, BRACE AND COMPANY

ix, 186 pp. 8 3/16 × 5 7/16 inches. Maroon cloth boards stamped in black and gold on spine; end papers. White dust jacket printed in black, gray, and maroon

Published January 22, 1948, at $2.75; 4000 copies printed.

Contains "Philomena Andronico" by WCW in an essay, "Study of 'Philomena Andronico,'" by Karl Shapiro, pp. 105–111, with reproduction of "worksheets" of poem, p. 84. The beginning of the essay states, "The following poem has never appeared in a book." It is in *The Clouds,* published in the summer of 1948 (A26), and *CLP.*

138

B53   THE CASE OF EZRA POUND   1948

THE CASE OF | EZRA POUND | BY | CHARLES NORMAN |
THE BODLEY PRESS | NEW YORK 1948 [*Subtitle on front
cover:*] with opinions by Conrad Aiken   E. E. Cummings   F. O.
Matthiessen   William Carlos Williams   Louis Zukofsky
    71 pp. 7 × 5 inches. Stiff blue paper covers printed in black on front,
back, and spine; end papers.
      Published October 1, 1948, at $1.50.
    From Charles Norman's "Foreword," pp. 12–13: "The article on
Pound appeared in *PM,* Sunday, November 25, 1945. To bring it up to
date, I have added the findings of the psychiatrists appointed by the District
Court of the United States, the federal jury's verdict, and a section
dealing with Pound's latest *Cantos.*"
    Contains statement by WCW, pp. 47–54.

B54   ENGLISH INSTITUTE ESSAYS, 1947   1948

ENGLISH INSTITUTE | ESSAYS [*ornament*] 1947 | New York
· Columbia University Press · 1948
    1 blank leaf, 6 leaves, [3]–202 pp., 1 blank leaf. 7 11/16 × 5 1/8 inches.
Gray cloth boards stamped in blind on front and in gold and sienna on
spine; end papers. Dust jacket in dark gray and light gray.
    Published October 21, 1948, at $2.50; 800 copies printed. *On verso of
title page:* "Copyright 1948 | Columbia University Press, New York |
Published in Great Britain and India by | Geoffrey Cumberlege | Oxford
University Press, London and Bombay | Manufactured in the United
States of America"
    Contains "An Approach to the Poem" by WCW, pp. 50–75. This is
the only publication of this essay.

B55   100 MODERN POEMS   1949

[*On top half of page is a single rule square; above square:*] 100 [*on
left side of square, printed upward:*] MODERN [*on right side of
square, printed downward:*] POEMS [*inside square:*] selected | with
an introduction | by | Selden Rodman | [*rule beneath square*] |
PELLEGRINI & CUDAHY | 1949

xxx pp., 2 leaves, 3–191 pp. 8 5/16 × 5 9/16 inches. Dark blue cloth boards lettered in silver downward on spine; end papers. Tan dust jacket printed in white and blue.

Published November, 1949, at $2.75.

Contains "Sir Walter Raleigh—Spring and All (Part XVIII)" by WCW, pp. 94–98 and pp. 153–155. This is the first publication of a chapter from *In the American Grain* (see A9) as a poem. The section from "Spring and All" is titled "To Elsie" in *CEP*.

A new edition was published March, 1951, as a Mentor paperbook, The New American Library of World Literature, Inc., New York, at 35¢.

B56   TRANSITION WORKSHOP   [1949]

TRANSITION WORKSHOP | EDITED BY EUGENE JOLAS | [*printed vertically:*] NEW YORK   THE VANGUARD PRESS, INC. | [*ornament*]

1 leaf of black and white striped paper, 413 pp. 9 7/16 × 6 3/8 inches. Gray and charcoal cloth boards lettered in black; black end papers. Black and red dust jacket.

Published November 29, 1949, at $6.00; 3500 copies printed. *On verso of title page:* "Published simultaneously in Canada by the Copp Clark Company, Ltd., Toronto."

Contains an improvisation, *"Theessentialroar," pp. 168–169, and two poems, "The Dead Baby" and "Winter," pp. 268–270, by WCW. This is the only book publication of the improvisation [C116]. The two poems had previously been published in books and are in *CEP*.

B57   WILLIAM CARLOS WILLIAMS   [1950]

[*Line drawing of a hand holding a pen*] William Carlos Williams | BY VIVIENNE KOCH | THE MAKERS OF MODERN LITERATURE | New Directions Books – Norfolk, Connecticut [*James Laughlin*]

x, 278 pp. and frontispiece photograph by Charles Sheeler, 1926, on coated paper. 7 3/16 × 4 13/16 inches. Tan cloth boards lettered in black downward on spine; end papers. White dust jacket printed in black and green.

Published January, 1950, at $2.00; 2721 copies printed.

A "critical estimate" [Preface, p. ix] of Williams' writing to 1949; Contents: Preface—I. The Poems—II. The Plays—III. The Novels and Short Stories—IV. Prose Other than Fiction—Bibliography—Index.

Contains quotations from unpublished manuscripts and notes by WCW, passim.

B58   MODERN AMERICAN POETRY   [1950]

MODERN | AMERICAN POETRY | EDITED BY B. RAJAN | [*names of contributors enclosed in single rule rectangle:*] FRED- ERICK BRANTLEY | DAVID DAICHES | VIVIENNE KOCH | JAMES LAUGHLIN | ROBERT LOWELL | ARCHIBALD MAC- LEISH | NORMAN MACLEOD | LOUIS L. MARTZ | MARI- ANNE MOORE | EZRA POUND | B. RAJAN | THEODORE SPENCER | WALLACE STEVENS | JOSÉ GARCIA VILLA | ROBERT PENN WARREN | WILLIAM CARLOS WILLIAMS | YVOR WINTERS | [*device*] | London: Dennis Dobson Ltd [*Half title on recto of first leaf:*] FOCUS FIVE

190 pp., 1 leaf. 8 5/8 × 5 1/2 inches. Green cloth boards stamped in black on spine; end papers. Green dust jacket printed in dark green and red.

Published May, 1950, at 8s. 6d.; 1500 copies printed.

Contains "Perpetuum Mobile: The City [C238]—The Pink Church [C374]—The Sea Farer [C396]—The Sound of Waves [C396]" by WCW, pp. 178–179, and WCW's reply, pp. 187–190, to four questions, "American and English Poetry: A Questionnaire." This is the first book publication of "The Sea Farer" and "The Sound of Waves" and the only publication of the answers to the questionnaire. The first poem is in *CEP*; the others are in *CLP* where "The Pink Church" is retitled "Choral: The Pink Church," and "The Sea Farer" is retitled "Seafarer."

B59   CASE-RECORD FROM A SONNETORIUM [1951]

[*Two pages, facing; on left page:*] CASE [*on right:*] RECORD FROM [*on left:*] A [*on right:*] SONNETORIUM [*on left a list of books by Merrill Moore; on right:*] *Cartoons by* Edward St. John Gorey | *Illustrated with Poems by* Merrill Moore | *Consultants:* Louis

Untermeyer, *Esq.* | *Professor* John Crowe Ransom | Henry W. Wells, *Ph.D.* | William Carlos Williams, *M.D.* | TWAYNE PUBLISHERS, New York

32 unnumbered leaves. 9 1/4 × 6 1/16 inches. Gray cloth boards stamped in crimson on cover (Gorey cartoons on cover) and downward on spine; end papers. Black, yellow-orange, and white dust jacket; back flap contains excerpt from Williams' Introduction to Moore's *Sonnets from New Directions*, 1938 (B31).

Published 1951 at $1.50; 2000 copies printed.

Contains "Discharge Note" by WCW, p. [63]. The first part of this is reprinted in *Merrill Moore and the American Sonnet*, illustrated by Edward St. John Gorey (Christchurch, New Zealand: The Pegasus Press, January, 1954), p. [31], on recto of last leaf of book.

B60   THE AUTHOR LOOKS AT FORMAT   [1951]

[*Two leaves, facing; on left page:*] The Author [*on right:*] Looks at Format | COMMENTS BY | [*on left page a long brace to enclose the names on the right page:*] VAN WYCK BROOKS | PEARL S. BUCK | ERSKINE CALDWELL | DOROTHY CANFIELD | JOHN DOS PASSOS | JOHN HERSEY | JOHN STEINBECK | LIONEL TRILLING | THORNTON WILDER | WILLIAM CARLOS WILLIAMS [*on left:*] Edited by Ray Freiman, Chairman, | The Trade Book Clinic · 1950–1951 [*on right:*] [*device*] A. I. G. A.

1 blank leaf, 3 leaves, 9–58 pp., 1 blank leaf. 6 1/2 × 3 7/8 inches. Black and red paper covers flapped at side over first and last blank leaves; printed in black; stapled.

On verso of title page: "Copyright 1951, by The American Institute of Graphic Arts, Inc."

Contains "No Pretense Anywhere" by WCW, pp. 39–40, the only publication of this essay about the format of books, which WCW prefers to be without "cheap finery of any sort."

B61   MODERN POETRY,   [1951]
          AMERICAN AND BRITISH

Modern Poetry | AMERICAN | AND | BRITISH | [*ornament*] | EDITED BY | KIMON FRIAR | AND | JOHN MALCOLM

B: Books, Pamphlets, and Portfolios

BRINNIN | [*device*] | New York | APPLETON-CENTURY-CROFTS, Inc.

xviii pp., 1 leaf, 580 pp., 4 blank leaves. 8 11/16 × 5 3/8 inches. Blue cloth (or red cloth) boards stamped in silver on cover, and in black and silver on spine; end papers. Dust jacket.

Published February 27, 1951, at $4.25.

Contains brief notes by WCW about "Our language in the United States" and about four of his five poems reprinted in the volume, "The Clouds, I–IV—The Monstrous Marriage—Burning the Christmas Greens—St. Francis Einstein of the Daffodils," pp. 545–546; there is no note for the fifth poem, "The Yachts." This is the only publication of the notes, but is not the first book publication of the poems.

B62   7 ARTS   [1953]

7 ARTS | Selected and edited by | FERNANDO PUMA | [*line drawing*] | PERMABOOKS, | a division of | Doubleday & Company, Inc., Garden City, New York

xii pp., 1 leaf, 210 pp., and 48 pages of reproductions bound in between pp. 114 and 115. 7 1/8 × 4 1/4 inches. White heavy paper covers printed in black, sienna, green, blue, and pink.

Published March 2, 1953, at 50¢ (60¢ in Canada).

The seven arts listed on the front cover are "PAINTING | SCULPTURE · MUSIC | DANCE · THEATRE | LITERATURE | ARCHITECTURE," with "articles by: | Thomas Mann | J. B. Priestly | José Limon | Frank Lloyd Wright | Aaron Copland | William Carlos Williams | Henri Cartier-Bresson | works of art by: | Rouault, Picasso, | Matisse, Modigliani, | Dufy, Klee, Marin, | Lipchitz, Moore, others"

From the Foreword by Fernando Puma, pp. xi–xii: "The policy of 7 ARTS is— . . . To create a publication in which each art will benefit by close association with the other."

Contains "The Present Relationship of Prose to Verse" by WCW, pp. 140–149. This is the only publication of this essay.

B63   THE FLOWERS OF FRIENDSHIP   1953

THE | FLOWERS OF FRIENDSHIP | Letters written to | GERTRUDE STEIN | Edited by Donald Gallup | Before the Flowers of

Friendship Faded Friendship Faded | (Title of a book by Gertrude Stein) | [*device*] 1953 | ALFRED A. KNOPF · NEW YORK
  1 blank leaf, xxvi pp., 2 leaves, [3]–403 pp., xiii, [1] pp. 8 9/16 × 5 13/16 inches. Blue cloth boards stamped in gold on cover and spine; end papers. Black, violet and white dust jacket with photographs of Gertrude Stein on front and back.
    Published August 17, 1953, at $5.00; 4500 copies printed.
    Contains letter from WCW to Gertrude Stein, dated September 16, 1933, pp. 266–267. In *SL*.

B64   NEW POEMS BY AMERICAN POETS   1953

NEW | POEMS | By American Poets | [*thin rule*] | Edited by ROLFE HUMPHRIES | BALLANTINE BOOKS · NEW YORK · 1953
  10 leaves, 179, [1] pp. 8 × 5 5/16 inches. Green paper boards printed in yellow on front and downward on spine; end papers. White, blue, yellow, and black dust jacket. Also in paper covers similar to the dust jacket of the hardbound copies.
    Published September 21, 1953, at $2.00 for hardbound copies, 35¢ for paperbound copies; 3000 hardbound and 100,000 paperbound copies printed.
    Contains "To a Dog Injured in the Street" by WCW, pp. 165–166 In *DM*.

B65   CHARLES SHEELER | A RETROSPECTIVE   1954
EXHIBITION

CHARLES SHEELER | A Retrospective Exhibition | with a foreword by | WILLIAM CARLOS WILLIAMS | essays by | BARTLETT H. HAYES, JR. | FREDERICK S. WIGHT | organized by the | ART GALLERIES, UNIVERSITY OF CALIFORNIA, LOS ANGELES | M. H. DE YOUNG MEMORIAL MUSEUM, SAN FRANCISCO | FORT WORTH ART CENTER | MUNSON-WILLIAMS-PROCTOR INSTITUTE, UTICA | PENNSYLVANIA ACADEMY OF THE FINE ARTS, PHILADELPHIA | SAN DIEGO FINE ARTS GALLERY | Sponsored by the Fine Arts Production Committee, University of California, Los Angeles | Published by the Art Galleries, October, 1954

47 pp. 11 1/8 × 8 1/4 inches. Glossy black paper covers with a black and white reproduction of a painting by Charles Sheeler. Plates include a photograph of WCW

> Published October 11, 1954, at $1.25; 2500 copies printed.

> Contains "foreword" by WCW, pp. 3–4. Published the same month in *Art in America,* October, 1954, with the title "Postscript by a Poet" (C500). Compare B35.

B66   LEAVES OF GRASS ONE HUNDRED   1955
                    YEARS AFTER

LEAVES OF GRASS | ONE HUNDRED YEARS AFTER | NEW ESSAYS BY | WILLIAM CARLOS WILLIAMS, RICHARD CHASE | LESLIE A. FIEDLER, KENNETH BURKE | DAVID DAICHES, AND J. MIDDLETON MURRY | EDITED AND WITH AN INTRODUCTION BY | MILTON HINDUS | [*green device*] | STANFORD UNIVERSITY PRESS | STANFORD, CALIFORNIA | LONDON: GEOFFREY CUMBERLEGE | OXFORD UNIVERSITY PRESS | 1955

> 1 blank leaf, 4 leaves, 3–149 pp., 1 blank leaf. 9 9/16 × 6 1/16 inches. Dark green cloth boards stamped in gilt downward on spine; end papers. Cream dust jacket printed in black over photograph in pale green of Whitman on front; black and white photographs of contributors on back.

> Published January 3, 1955, at $5.00; 2500 copies printed (reissued September, 1966, with an initial printing of 500 clothbound copies and 3000 paperbound copies).

> Contains "An Essay on *Leaves of Grass*" by WCW, pp. 22–31. The essay is reprinted in *Whitman, A Collection of Critical Essays,* edited by Roy Harvey Pearce (Englewood Cliffs, N.J.: Prentice-Hall, Inc., 1962), pp. 146–154.

B67   JOHN MARIN MEMORIAL EXHIBITION   1955

JOHN | MARIN | MEMORIAL | EXHIBITION | with a foreword by *Duncan Phillips* / appreciations by | *William Carlos Williams* and *Dorothy Norman* / | Conclusion to a Biography by *MacKinley Helm* / John | Marin—Frontiersman by *Frederick S. Wight* | or-

ganized by the Art Galleries, University of California, | Los Angeles /
Cleveland Museum of Art / Minneapolis Insti- | tute of Arts / Mu-
seum of Fine Arts, Boston / Phillips Gallery, | Washington, D. C. /
San Francisco Museum of Art | sponsored by the Fine Arts Produc-
tions Committee, University of California, Los Angeles / published
by the Art Galleries, | University of California, Los Angeles, February
1955 / designed by Sherman Rifkin

> 36 leaves of coated paper, with reproductions. 10 11/16 × 8 5/16 inches.
> Glossy white paper covers with color reproduction of a watercolor by
> Marin, "Boat and Sea—Deer Isle, Maine, Series No. 27," 1927.
>
> Published February 25, 1955, at $1.40; 3500 copies printed.
>
> Contains an "Appreciation" by WCW on recto of fourth leaf.

Issued in hard covers, 1956.

JOHN | [The M is in red:] MARIN | Tributes by William Carlos
Williams / Duncan Phillips / Dorothy Norman | Conclusion to a
Biography by MacKinley Helm | John Marin—Frontiersman by
Frederick S. Wight | University of California Press, Berkeley and Los
Angeles, 1956

> 40 unnumbered leaves. 10 15/16 × 8 7/16 inches. Beige cloth boards
> stamped in blind on front and in green downward on spine; end papers.
> Dust jacket similar to paper covers of first issue.
>
> Contains "Tribute" (same text as "Appreciation" of first printing) by
> WCW on recto of fourth leaf.

B68   THE WRITER OBSERVED   [1956]

HARVEY BREIT | THE WRITER OBSERVED | [*device*] | THE
WORLD PUBLISHING COMPANY | CLEVELAND AND NEW
YORK

> 286 pp., 1 leaf. 8 9/16 × 5 3/4 inches. Crimson cloth boards with black
> rectangle on cover and spine stamped in gold. Dust jacket in tan, sienna,
> yellow, and black.
>
> Published January, 1956, at $3.75; 6000 copies printed.
>
> Contains "William Carlos Williams," pp. 99–101, an essay by Harvey
> Breit that includes statements by WCW. The essay is dated January 15,
> 1950 (C443).

A new edition was published by Collier Book, New York, 1961, at 95¢.

B69   HYPNOS WAKING   [1956]

Hypnos Waking | Poems and Prose | by René Char | SELECTED AND TRANSLATED BY | JACKSON MATHEWS | With the collaboration of William Carlos Williams, | Richard Wilbur, William Jay Smith, Barbara Howes, | W. S. Merwin and James Wright. | RANDOM HOUSE | New York [*device*]

viii, 279, [1] pp. 7 5/8 × 4 9/16 inches. White cloth on spine and one-eighth of yellow-green paper boards; design printed in black on front and stamped in blue-green and black downward on spine; yellow-green end papers. Blue-green dust jacket printed in white and black.

Published June, 1956, at $5.00; 1500 copies printed.

Contains two translations by WCW (French and English on facing pages): [prose] "Madeleine Qui Veillait || Magdalene Waiting," pp. 242–249, and [poem] "Vers L'Arbre-Frère Aux Jours Comptés || To Friend-Tree of Counted Days," pp. 252–253. This is the only publication of these translations.

B70   THE IMPROVED BINOCULARS   1956

[*Two pages, facing; in the center of each page is a rough circle in red with* IRVING *within the left circle and* LAYTON *within the right circle, printed in black; on right at top of page:*] Selected Poems, with an Introduction by | William Carlos Williams [*on left:*] the | improved [*on right:*] binoculars [*on left:*] IRVING [*on right:*] LAYTON [*on left:*] JONATHAN WILLIAMS [*ornament*] PUBLISHER [*on right:*] HIGHLANDS [*ornament*] 1956

1 blank leaf, 5 leaves, 13–106 pp., 1 blank leaf, 2 leaves. 8 15/16 × 6 inches. Stiff white blanks covered by yellow paper wrappers, side flaps pasted to blanks, with photograph of author on front, and printed in blue and black on front and downward on spine.

Published autumn, 1956, at $2.50; 500 copies printed. *Colophon, on verso of last leaf:* "First Edition of 500 copies | printed by Stephens Press, Asheville, North Carolina, | Autumn 1956 | Distribution: in Canada,

Contact Press (Toronto) | in England, Migrant Books (Worcester) | Designed and published by | Jonathan Williams, Highlands, North Carolina, | as Jargon 18"

Contains Introduction, "A Note on Layton," by WCW, fourth leaf.

Second edition published winter, 1957, at $3.00; in stiffer covers printed in black and red, with different photograph on cover and thirty additional poems inside (1 blank leaf, 5 leaves, 13–139 pp., 2 leaves). *Colophon, on verso of last leaf:* "Second Edition of 100 copies . . . Winter 1957"

B71   HOWL AND OTHER POEMS   [1956]

HOWL | AND OTHER POEMS | BY | ALLEN GINSBERG | 'Unscrew the locks from the doors! | Unscrew the doors themselves from their jambs!' | THE POCKET POETS SERIES: Number Four | The City Lights Pocket Bookshop | San Francisco [*On front cover:*] THE POCKET POETS SERIES | HOWL | AND OTHER POEMS | ALLEN GINSBERG | Introduction by | William Carlos Williams | NUMBER FOUR

44 pp. 6 3/16 × 4 15/16 inches. Heavy black paper covers printed in gray, with large white paper rectangle printed in black pasted from front to back cover; stapled at spine.

Published October, 1956, at 75¢; 2000 copies printed. At least seventeen impressions, in black and white paper covers similar to first impression, have been published since 1956, making a total of over 120,000 copies.

Contains Introduction, "Howl for Carl Solomon," by WCW, pp. 7–8.

B72   THE DANCE OF DEATH   [1957]

[*In white on a black rectangle beneath a black and white reproduction of a woodcut:*] the dance of | death in the | twentieth century | POEMS BY Merrill Moore | Illustrations by Hans Holbein [*I. E. Rubin, Brooklyn, N.Y.*]

95 pp. 9 1/4 × 6 1/4 inches. Red cloth boards lettered in black on front and downward on spine; buff end papers.

Published 1957 at $3.00.

Contains foreword by WCW, p. 7.

B73   HOT AFTERNOONS HAVE BEEN   1957
IN MONTANA

HOT | AFTERNOONS | HAVE BEEN IN | MONTANA: |
POEMS | BY ELI SIEGEL | WITH A LETTER BY WILLIAM
CARLOS WILLIAMS | [*rule*] | New York · Definition Press ·
1957

    1 blank leaf, xviii, 107, [1] pp. 8 7/8 × 5 7/8 inches. Sienna cloth
boards stamped downward in gold on spine; end papers. Gray dust jacket
printed in sienna. Also in paper covers, 8 9/16 × 5 5/8 inches, of the
same gray paper as the dust jacket of the cloth edition; stiff end papers;
back cover contains excerpts from the flaps of the jacket of the cloth
edition.

    Published May 31, 1957, at $3.25 for hardbound copies, $1.65 for paper-
bound copies; 500 hardbound and 1000 paperbound copies printed. *On
p. [108]:* "Designed by David J. Way and printed by Clarke & Way,
Inc. at The Thistle Press, May 1957."

    Contains as a foreword a letter from WCW to Martha Baird, No-
vember 3, 1951, pp. xv–xviii. Excerpts from the letter are printed on the
front and front flap of the dust jacket. *On p. [v]:* "William Carlos Williams' letter was printed for the first time in its entirety in the October–
December 1956 issue of *Poetry Public* [C524], edited by Lawrence
Richard Holmes. Portions of it were quoted previously in an article by
Nat Herz in *Poetry*, August, 1952." Compare B94.

    A second impression was published February, 1958; 1000 hardbound
and 2000 paperbound copies printed. Identical with the first impression
except for correction of a spacing error in the Notes on p. 106.

B74   PILGRIM'S TERRACE   1957

PILGRIM'S | TERRACE | POEMS AMERICAN WEST IN-
DIAN | TRAM COMBS | Editorial La Nueva Salamanca | San
Germán, Puerto Rico | 1957 [*Dust jacket:*] pilgrim's | terrace |
[*drawing*] | poems american west indian | tram combs | forewords
by | William Carlos Williams & Kenneth Rexroth

    1 blank leaf, 2 leaves, 7–86, [1] pp. 8 7/8 × 5 13/16 inches. White
heavy paper covers printed in black on cover and upward on spine.
White dust jacket printed in brown, dark brown, pink, and black.

Published October 15, 1957, at $2.00 (later $2.50); 1000 copies printed. Contains "foreword" by WCW, pp. 7–8. A quotation from the foreword is printed on the front flap of the dust jacket. See also G12.

Tram Combs is the pen name of Elisha Trammell Combs, Jr.

B75   POEMS IN FOLIO   [1957]

Portfolio, 19 × 13 inches, with dark red cloth on spine and one-fourth of red cloth boards; stamped in black on front with drawing of a harp; pale blue lining paper and pale blue paper wrappers folded over the contents. The editors were Stanley Kunitz, Henry Rago, and Richard Wilbur. A letter inside the portfolio explains: "Each month we issue one poem by an outstanding American or English poet, designed and printed by one of a selection of America's fine presses, and accompanied by a smaller sheet of notes . . . . At the end of the year, we shall issue a 12 inch LP high fidelity recording of the year's poems read by the poets themselves."

Published 1957 at 75¢ for a single poem, $7.50 for ordinary portfolio (described above) with all 12 poems, $30.00 for signed copies of the poems in an "imported folio" with the recording.

Folio poem by WCW:

SAPPHO | A TRANSLATION BY WILLIAM CARLOS WILLIAMS [*Poems in Folio, Box 448, San Francisco*]
Broadsheet, 18 × 12 inches, printed in red and black on one side, accompanied by broadsheet, 10 × 7 1/4 inches, printed on one side, containing a statement by WCW about the translation.

Published December, 1957. *Colophon at foot of smaller broadsheet:* "Printed at the Grabhorn Press, San Francisco, from Lutetia types, designed by Jan Van Krimpen, and cast by Johann Enschede en Zonen, Haarlem, Holland, in an edition of 1150 copies of which 150 are on Millbourn handmade paper, signed and numbered by the poet."

Notes: Periodical publication of the poem: C535. In *Paterson, Five,* II, 253.

[From the notes on the smaller broadsheet:] ". . . as far as I have been able to do I have been as accurate as the meaning of the words permitted—always with a sense of our own American idiom to instruct me.

B: Books, Pamphlets, and Portfolios

[*New Directions 17* (1961) 291–292, as reported by John C. Thirlwall:] "I am particularly interested in the sound of words in Sappho, for the beauty must inhere in the words. I'm going to exhaust every possible way of knowing how she got her effects. As you know, I'm not even a heathen. If there is any possibility of reproduction in another world, it must consist in refinement as of a poet. The conventional terms of heaven and hell don't mean a damn thing. That's why I want to dig around and find the concentration of everything that Sappho had to give. If we can recover one complete poem, it will be worthwhile. I'm always looking for a concentrate in one poem."

[*I Wanted*, pp. 92–93:] "My purpose was to speak as I thought this remarkable woman meant to speak—not what the classic English students had done to her in their stilted translations. I had the poem read aloud to me, over and over, in the original Greek by scholars who knew how the words should sound so that I might catch the rise and fall of the beat."

B76   JEAN SANS TERRE   [1958]

[*Two pages, facing; on left:*] JEAN SANS TERRE | by YVAN GOLL | preface by W. H. AUDEN | drawings by EUGENE BERMAN | MARC CHAGALL | SALVADOR DALI | [*ornament*] | New York · THOMAS YOSELOFF · London [*on right:*] critical notes by LOUISE BOGAN | CLARK MILLS | JULES ROMAINS | ALLEN TATE | translations of the Poems by | LIONEL ABEL · LÉONIE ADAMS · JOHN PEALE BISHOP · | LOUISE BOGAN · BABETTE DEUTSCH · JOHN GOULD FLETCHER | · ISABELLA GARDNER · CLAIRE AND YVAN GOLL · PAUL | GOODMAN · GALWAY KINNELL · W. S. MERWIN · CLARK MILLS · | ROBERT NURENBERG · KENNETH PATCHEN · GEORGE REAVEY | · KENNETH REXROTH · ERIC SELLIN · WILLIAM JAY | SMITH · ROBERT WERNICK · WLLLIAM CARLOS WILLIAMS

190 pp., 1 blank leaf. 8 7/16 × 5 9/16 inches. Brown cloth boards lettered in blue and silver downward on cover; end papers. White dust jacket printed in brown, tan, and white.

Published November 14, 1958, at $5.00; 3000 copies printed.

Contains "Jean Sans Terre Reviews the Fathers," pp. 89–90, "Jean

Sans Terre Leads the Caravan," pp. 126–127, "Jean Sans Terre Circles the Earth Seven Times," pp. 148–149, "Jean Sans Terre Discovers the West Pole," pp. 170–171, "Jean Sans Terre at the Final Port (First Version)," p. 175, and "Jean Sans Terre at the Final Port (Fifth Version)," p. 181, translated by WCW. This is the first book publication of the first, fourth, and last translations by WCW. See B45 for prior book publication of the others.

B77   SPRINGTIME TWO   [1958]

SPRINGTIME TWO | an anthology of current | trends in literature | edited by | Peter Owen | and | Wendy Owen | PETER OWEN: LONDON
126 pp., 1 blank leaf. 8 9/16 × 5 5/8 inches. Yellow cloth boards stamped in blue-green downward on spine; blue-green end papers. Yellow and blue-green dust jacket printed in black.

Published May 23, 1958, at 21s.; 1000 copies printed.

Contains "The Gift" by WCW, pp. 30–35. Prior publications: C526 (periodical); D16, 17 (Christmas cards). In *PB*.

B78   LUNAR BAEDEKER & TIME TABLES   1958

[*Two pages, facing, with a line drawing of a bird with outspread wings printed in orange-brown covering background of both pages; all else in black; on left page:*] LUNAR | [*on right:*] BAEDEKER [*on left:*] & | [*on right:*] TIME-TABLES | [*on left:*] SELECTED POEMS | [*on right:*] MINA LOY | JONATHAN WILLIAMS · PUBLISHER | HIGHLANDS 1958 [*North Carolina*]
3 blank leaves, 8 leaves, 19–82 pp., 1 leaf, 2 blank leaves, the first and last leaves pasted down as end papers. *Regular Edition:* 9 3/4 × 5 5/8 inches. Glossy paper covers with side flaps pasted over the first and last blank leaves, printed in orange, black, and sienna. *Author's Edition:* 9 15/16 × 5 7/8 inches. Gray silk boards with white paper label printed in orange-brown on spine. Cellophane wrapper.

Published summer, 1958, at $3.50 for Regular Edition, $10.00 for Author's Edition; 500 copies printed. *Colophon, on verso of last printed leaf:* "Regular Edition of 450 by Heritage Printers, Charlotte, North Carolina, summer 1958. Designed & published by Jonathan Williams,

Highlands, North Carolina, as *Jargon 23*" or "Author's Edition of 50 . . ." continued as in regular edition, and with signature of Mina Loy and number of book at top of page.

Contains foreword, "Mina Loy," by WCW on both sides of fourth printed leaf and recto of fifth printed leaf. Also contains forewords by Kenneth Rexroth and Denise Levertov.

Lunar Baedeker was first published in 1923 by Contact Publishing Company, Paris, but without the three forewords.

B79   DOCTORS AND PATIENTS   1959

DOCTORS AND PATIENTS | STORIES BY LEADING AMER-ICAN PHYSICIANS | Edited by | Noah D. Fabricant, M.D. | [*device*] Grune & Stratton 1959 | New York London
  xiii, 204 pp., 3 blank leaves. 9 1/4 × 6 1/16 inches. Blue-green cloth on spine and one-sixth of mottled gray paper boards, stamped downward in black on spine; end papers. Blue, white, black, and gray dust jacket.
  Published 1959 at $5.25; 3500 copies printed.
  Contains "An Incident" by WCW, pp. 86–87, a story about a difficult birth. This is the only publication of the story.

B80   WATERMELONS   [1959]

WATERMELONS | RON | LOEWINSOHN | totem press | NEW YORK [*on back cover:*] INTRODUCTION by | ALLEN GINS-BERG | LETTER by | WILLIAM CARLOS WILLIAMS | $1.00
  2 leaves, 3–29, [1] pp. 8 7/16 × 5 1/2 inches. Heavy white paper covers printed in black and red, designed by Basil King; stapled.
  Published spring, 1959, at $1.00; 1000 copies printed. *Colophon, on p.* [*30*]: "This edition of WATERMELONS is limited to 1000 copies published by the TOTEM PRESS, 402 W. 20th St. NYC. Printed at the Troubador Press, San Francisco." *On verso of title page:* "© 1959 by LeRoi Jones"
  Contains as foreword a letter, p. [2], from WCW to Ron Loewinsohn, dated April 8, 1958.

B81 ROBERT McALMON 1959

Second edition:

ROBERT E. KNOLL | Robert McAlmon | Expatriate Publisher and Writer | university of nebraska press: lincoln: 1959
[*On front cover:*] ROBERT McALMON | Expatriate Publisher and Writer | ROBERT E. KNOLL | Foreword by William Carlos Williams | NEBRASKA PAPERBACK [*device*] $1.50

1 blank leaf, xiii, 96 pp. 9 × 6 inches. Black and white paper covers; the front cover is divided diagonally into white with black printing and black with white printing.

Published August 1, 1959, at $1.50; 500 copies printed. *On verso of title page:* "This work was first published in a series sponsored by the Senate Committee on University Studies (University of Nebraska Studies: New Series No. 18)."

Contains "Foreword" by WCW, pp. vii–ix. The first edition of the book, with red, white, and black paper covers, was published August, 1957, without the Foreword by WCW. Compare review by WCW, C559.

B82 POETS AND THE PAST [1959]

POETS AND THE PAST | AN ANTHOLOGY OF POEMS, AND OBJECTS OF ART OF THE PRE-COLUMBIAN PAST | EDITED BY DORE ASHTON | PHOTOGRAPHS BY LEE BOLTIN | [*device*] ANDRÉ EMMERICH GALLERY | NEW YORK

63, [1] pp., 2 leaves. 9 11/16 × 6 15/16 inches. Rough white cloth on spine and one-sixth of black cloth boards, lettered in black downward on spine; gray end papers. Signed copies in green leather, stamped in gold.

Published November 30, 1959, at $5.00; 1500 copies printed. *Colophon, on recto of last leaf:* "Of this volume fifteen hundred copies have been made. The first fifty copies, containing autographs of contributing poets, have been especially bound and are numbered I through L."

On page 8: "The title of this collection was suggested to the poets as a limitation. It was intended that everything should be as elusive, as elastic as possible. If the 'grand themes' remain the same always, their expression in art is phenomenally varied. Within the compass of this book the vast distances and the intimate details covered by both ancient and contemporary artists are astonishing."

Contains "Portrait of a Woman at Her Bath" by WCW, facing photograph labeled "Girl and Obsidian Mirror, *Tlatilco* 1000 B.C." Prior publication (titled "View of a Woman at Her Bath"): C536. In *PB*.

B83   "A" 1–12   1959

["A" *in red, all else in black:*] LOUIS ZUKOFSKY | "A" | 1–12 | with an essay on Poetry by the author | and a final note by William Carlos Williams | ORIGIN PRESS 1959 [*Cid Corman*]
296 pp., 1 blank leaf, 2 leaves. 7 3/8 × 5 3/16 inches. Red cloth boards stamped in gold; end papers. Glassine dust jacket.

Published December 25, 1959, at $5.00; 200 copies printed. *Colophon, on recto of last leaf:* "This first edition is limited to 200 copies printed by the Genichido Printing Company in Kyoto, Japan, December 1959."

Contains an essay, "Zukofsky," by WCW, pp. 291–296, dated "Rutherford, New Jersey, 1957." The essay is reprinted in *Agenda*, London, III. 6, Special issue edited by Charles Tomlinson (Dec. 1964) 1–4, with note: "Printed by kind permission of Florence Williams and Louis Zukofsky, with acknowledgements to Cid Corman and Origin Press."

B84   THE COMPLETE WORKS OF FRANÇOIS   [1960]
                     VILLON

THE COMPLETE WORKS | OF | FRANÇOIS VILLON | Translated, | with a biography and notes by | ANTHONY BONNER | With an introduction by | WILLIAM CARLOS WILLIAMS | [*device*] | BANTAM BOOKS/NEW YORK
xxvi, 228 pp., 1 leaf. 7 × 4 1/4 inches. Silver-gray paper covers printed in black, red, yellow, blue, and white. *On p.* [*229*]: "The art work on the cover of this Bantam Classic reproduces with color a pen and India ink drawing by Alex Tsao."

Published February, 1960, at 50¢; 80,000 copies printed.

Contains "introduction" by WCW, pp. ix–xv.

Edition in hard covers [*1960*]:

THE COMPLETE WORKS | OF | FRANÇOIS VILLON |
Translated, | with a biography and notes by | Anthony Bonner |
With an introduction by | William Carlos Williams | David McKay
Company, Inc. | New York

> xxvi, 228 pp. 8 1/4 × 5 7/16 inches. Blue cloth boards stamped in gold;
> end papers. Dust jacket similar to covers of Bantam paperback edition.
> Published August 26, 1960, at $3.95; 5000 copies printed by photo-
> offset from the Bantam edition, but enlarged in size.

B85   THE ROMAN SONNETS OF G. G. BELLI   1960

[*Two pages, facing; the lower half is a collage drawing in sienna by
Jean-Jacques Leble, after prints by Pinelli, of people around a priest
with St. Peter's Cathedral in the distance; across the two pages:*] THE
ROMAN SONNETS OF | [*on right:*] G. G. BELLI [*on left:*]
TRANSLATED BY HAROLD NORSE | PREFACE BY WIL-
LIAM CARLOS WILLIAMS | INTRODUCTION BY ALBERTO
MORAVIA | JONATHAN WILLIAMS: HIGHLANDS: 1960
> 1 blank leaf, 36 unnumbered leaves. 8 1/4 × 5 5/16 inches. Stiff paper
> covers with photograph on front in black and white, with green overlay,
> of a papal procession; lettering in black; on back is photograph of transla-
> tor Harold Norse with a brief biography. Cover design by Ray Johnson.
> Published March, 1960, at $1.95; 2000 copies printed. *On recto of last
> leaf:* ". . . published at Highlands, North Carolina, March, 1960, as
> Jargon 38. . . . A cloth-bound 'Roma Edition' has been signed by the
> translator and writers of the preface and the introduction and carries an
> appropriate colophon." A signed edition (to consist of 100 copies at
> $10.00, containing a slip bearing the signatures of William Carlos Wil-
> liams, Harold Norse, and Alberto Moravia) is planned for publication.
> Contains "Preface" by WCW, dated February, 1956, on fifth leaf.
> G[iuseppe]. G[ioachino]. Belli lived from 1791 to 1863.

B86   EZRA POUND   1960

EZRA POUND | by | CHARLES NORMAN | THE MACMIL-
LAN COMPANY | New York 1960

xvi pp., 1 leaf, 493 pp., and 5 leaves of photographs on coated paper, including frontispiece. 8 7/16 × 5 3/4 inches. Sienna cloth boards stamped in gold on front and in dark brown and gold on spine; end papers. White dust jacket printed in orange and brown, with Alvin Langdon Coburn's frontispiece photograph of Ezra Pound on front.

Published October 31, 1960, at $6.95; 7567 copies printed. *On verso of title page:* "First Printing"

Contains quotations from WCW's conversation with Charles Norman, passim.

B87   THE LOVER AND OTHER POEMS   [1961]

[*White on black:*] the lover and other poems | by Mimi Goldberg | introduction by William | Carlos | Williams [*Printed for the author by Kraft Printing Company, Philadelphia*]

vi pp., 1 leaf, 54 pp., 1 blank leaf. 8 7/8 × 5 7/8 inches. Glossy white stiff paper covers printed in black on front and back and downward on spine; end papers.

Published May 17, 1961, at $1.25; 1000 copies printed.

Contains "introduction" by WCW, pp. iv–vi.

B88   EMPTY MIRROR   [1961]

EMPTY MIRROR | EARLY POEMS BY | ALLEN GINSBERG | Introduction by William Carlos Williams | Totem Press | in association with | CORINTH BOOKS | 32 West Eighth Street | New York 11, New York

47, [1] pp. 8 × 5 5/16 inches. White stiff paper covers printed in black.

Published September 5, 1961, at $1.25; 3000 copies printed (also 1675 copies printed in 1963; 1834 copies printed in 1965).

Contains "Introduction" by WCW, dated 1952 at end, pp. 5–6. *On verso of title page:* "Black Mountain Review #7 (Williams' Note)" [C543].

B89   POESIE   [1961]

WILLIAM CARLOS WILLIAMS | POESIE | TRADOTTE E
PRESENTATE | DA CRISTINA CAMPO E VITTORIO SERENI
| GIULIO EINAUDI EDITORE [Torino]
  1 blank leaf, 2 leaves, 7–318 pp., 1 leaf, 2 blank leaves. 8 9/16 × 6 1/4
  inches. Ivory paper covers printed in black; leaves untrimmed on top
  and fore edges. Cellophane dust wrapper. Crimson paper band folded
  about book, printed in white: "Il piu 'americano' dei poeti d'oggi nella
  versione di Vittorio Sereni e Cristina Campo." Loose slip (5 3/4 ×
  3 1/4 inches) inserted inside book contains photograph of Williams and
  biographical and critical comment about Williams in Italian.
    Published 1961 at L.2000.
    Contains the first book publication (English and Italian on facing
  pages) of one poem, "The World Contracted to a Recognizable Image,"
  pp. 302–303. In *PB*. Also contains the only publication of a comment by
  WCW about the poem in an unpublished letter (2 ottobre 1959) to
  Cristina Campo, Italian only, Notes, p. 311. For other contents of book,
  see T39.
    A second impression of this book was published early in 1967 at L.2500.
  Same title page and collation. Charles Sheeler photograph of Williams
  on front cover.

B90   DUST AND DESIRE   1962

Second edition:

DUST AND DESIRE | BY | RONALD H. BAYES | with an in-
troduction to the second edition | by William Carlos Williams | "To
be able to take the near for analogy, that may be called | the square
of humanitas, and that's that." | The Confucian Analects | (*tr.* Ezra
Pound) | 1962 | Arthur H. Stockwell Limited | Elms Court · Ilfra-
combe | Devon
  47 pp. 7 1/4 × 4 7/8 inches. Pale blue paper covers printed in black.
    Published December 10, 1962, at 3*s*. 6*d*.; 1000 copies printed.
    Contains "Introduction to the Second Edition: A Note to the Author

by William Carlos Williams," p. 6. The Introduction is dated June, 1960, at the end.

B91   POETRY IN CRYSTAL   1963

[*design*] | POETRY IN CRYSTAL | BY STEUBEN GLASS | [*design*]

86 pp., 1 leaf. 10 11/16 × 7 1/8 inches. Maroon cloth boards lettered in gold on front and downward on spine; maroon end papers. Glassine wrapper.

Published April 18, 1963, at $5.00; 5000 copies printed (also 5000 copies printed March 25, 1964; 5000 copies printed March, 1965). *On p.* [2]: "Interpretations in crystal of thirty-one new poems by contemporary American poets." *On verso of title page:* "First Edition | © Steuben Glass, A Division of Corning Glass Works, 1963" *On verso of last leaf:* "Steuben Glass Fifth Avenue at Fifty-sixth Street | New York 22, New York"

From "The Nature of the Collection" by John Monteith Gates," p. 9: "In the Spring of 1961 the [Poetry] Society [of America], in cooperation with Steuben, invited a number of distinguished American poets to submit new, hitherto-unpublished poems from which our glass designers and artist associates might derive themes for designs in crystal. There were two specifications only: that the poems not concern crystal or glass and that they be no fewer than eight nor more than forty lines in length."

Contains "Bird Song" by WCW, p. 72. (The glass design is by George Thompson, the engraving design by Alexander Seidel.) This is the only book publication of this poem. See D22.

B92   SYLVIA BEACH   1963

SYLVIA BEACH | (1887–1962) | [*device*] | MERCURE DE FRANCE | MCMLXIII

1 blank leaf, 3 leaves, [8]–174 pp., 1 leaf, and 12 coated leaves with photographs. 8 1/8 × 5 1/2 inches. Glossy, yellow stiff paper covers printed in red and black on front and upward on spine; photograph of Sylvia Beach on front.

Published December, 1963, at "18,00 F + T.L. (18,50 F [T.L.I.])."

On recto of last leaf: "Achevé d'imprimer le 26 novembre 1963 par Firmin-Didot et Cie Mesnil-sur-l'Estrée (Eure)"

Contains letter from WCW to Sylvia Beach, dated June 24, 1928, pp. 114–116. A French translation by Roger Giroux follows, pp. 116–118. This is the only publication of this letter; part of it is quoted in A10n.

B93   THE POEMS OF WILLIAM CARLOS   [1964]
WILLIAMS
A CRITICAL STUDY

THE POEMS OF | William Carlos Williams | [*long rule*] | A CRITICAL STUDY BY | LINDA WELSHIMER WAGNER | [*encircled:*] WCW | Wesleyan University Press: Middletown, Connecticut

6 leaves, [3]–169 pp., 2 blank leaves. 8 3/4 × 5 15/16 inches. Dark blue cloth boards stamped in gold on front and spine. White, dark blue, and pink dust jacket.

Published August 27, 1964, at $6.50; 2054 copies printed (also a second impression of 1000 copies, 500 bound January, 1966). *On verso of title page:* "First Edition"

Contains many quotations from unpublished material by WCW, passim, and the first book publication of his essay, "How to Write," pp. [145]–147 (Appendix). The essay is reprinted from the first number of *New Directions in Prose and Poetry* (C237).

B94   WILLIAMS' POETRY TALKED ABOUT . . .   1964

WILLIAMS' POETRY TALKED ABOUT | BY ELI SIEGEL | AND WILLIAM CARLOS WILLIAMS TALKING: 1952 | Selections from Recording of | "Williams' Poetry Looked At: A Critical Poem" | By Eli Siegel, March 5, 1952, with | William Carlos Williams Present and Talking in Return | Introduction and Comments by Martha Baird | Secretary, Society for Aesthetic Realism | Presented at the Terrain Gallery | 39 Grove Street, New York City | October 17, 1964 | © 1964 by Eli Siegel

Title leaf, ii–viii, 29 pp. 11 × 8 1/2 inches. White and blue stiff paper covers printed in blue and white; narrow blue tape covers spine and staples on spine edge. First eight leaves and last leaf of yellow paper.

Published October 17, 1964, at $1.50; 150 copies mimeographed (cover is offset). New and enlarged edition scheduled for publication November, 1968, at $1.75.

Contains letter from WCW to Martha Baird, pp. iii–vi, and comments by WCW, pp. 16–28. See C524 and B73 for previous publications of the letter. This is the only publication of the comments.

B95   ENCYCLOPEDIA OF POETRY AND POETICS   1965

ENCYCLOPEDIA | OF POETRY | AND POETICS | ALEX PREMINGER | EDITOR | FRANK J. WARNKE AND O. B. HARDISON, JR. | ASSOCIATE EDITORS | PRINCETON, NEW JERSEY | PRINCETON UNIVERSITY PRESS | 1965
xxiv, 906 pp., 1 blank leaf. 9 1/2 × 6 1/4 inches. Dark blue cloth boards lettered in gold on spine; gray end papers. White dust jacket printed in gray and blue-green.

Published April 13, 1965, at $25.00 (£10 in U.K.).

Contains a statement about "Free Verse," pp. 288–290, of about 1500 words, and a statement about "Objectivism," p. 582, of about 150 words, by WCW. This is the only publication of these statements.

B96   MY, THIS MUST HAVE BEEN A BEAUTIFUL   1965
PLACE WHEN IT WAS KEPT UP

[*Photograph of dancers outdoors on right side of page with* "1925" *beneath it; on left:*] MY, THIS MUST HAVE BEEN | A BEAUTI-FUL PLACE WHEN | IT WAS KEPT UP. | As documented in the year 1965 by | WILLIAM GRATWICK [*Pavilion, New York*]
36 leaves. 8 1/2 × 10 7/8 inches. Orange stiff paper covers printed in black downward on spine, and white paper label, 3 9/16 × 8 inches, printed in black pasted on front; map of Gratwick Highlands on back; yellow end papers.

Published December, 1965, at $5.00. *Colophon, on verso of front cover:* "One thousand copies of this book have been printed, of which two hundred are numbered and signed by the author."

Contains poem, "The Yellow Tree Peony," by WCW on p. [39]. *Comment by William Gratwick on p.* [*38*], *facing the poem and a photograph of a sculpture:* "One summer when Bill Williams was here he watched me working on the plant form allegory shown on the opposite page. He wrote this poem, printed here for the first time with the permission of his wife and Buffalo's Lockwood Library. . . ."

B97 HARVARD ADVOCATE CENTENNIAL [1966] ANTHOLOGY

HARVARD ADVOCATE | CENTENNIAL | ANTHOLOGY | edited by Jonathan D. Culler | SCHENKMAN PUBLISHING CO., INC. | Cambridge, Massachusetts

xxxi pp., 1 leaf, 460 pp. 9 1/2 × 6 9/16 inches. Crimson cloth boards stamped in black and gold on spine; end papers. White dust jacket printed in crimson, purple, green, and black.

Published March 17, 1966, at $7.95; 5000 copies printed.

Contains by WCW an untitled statement about T. S. Eliot [C265]— a poem, "From a Play" [C320]—an essay, "The Element of Time, Advice to a Young Writer" [C196]—an untitled statement about Wallace Stevens [C300]—a short story, "A Face of Stone" [C236], pp. 73, 195–207. This is the first book publication of all items except the short story.

B98 POEMS AND ANTIPOEMS [1967]

Nicanor Parra | POEMS AND ANTIPOEMS | Edited by Miller Williams | A New Directions Book [*New York, James Laughlin*]

ix, 149 pp. 8 1/4 × 5 1/2 inches. Olive green cloth on spine and one third of rose–red paper boards. Lettered in gold downward on spine; end papers. Rose–red, white, and olive green dust jacket. Also in black and white paper covers (8 × 5 3/8 inches; "A New Directions Paperbook NDP242").

Published October 16, 1967, at $5.50 for cloth covers; $1.95 for paper covers; 1003 hardbound and 5167 paperbook copies printed. *On verso of title page:* "Published simultaneously in Canada by McClelland and Stewart, Ltd."

Contains translation by WCW (Spanish and English on facing pages) of one poem, "Solo de Piano || Piano Solo," pp. 32–33. Periodical publication: C564.

B. BOOKS, PAMPHLETS, AND PORTFOLIOS
ADDENDA

B. BOOKS, PAMPHLETS, AND PORTFOLIOS
ADDENDA

C

CONTRIBUTIONS BY WILLIAM CARLOS WILLIAMS
TO PERIODICALS

Williams' contributions to periodicals are arranged chronologically by date of first periodical publication; subsequent periodical publications of an item are listed with the entry of its first publication. After the date of first book publication of an item, periodical publications are listed only in cases of special interest.

Poem and prose titles of a first periodical publication are set in all capitals; a previously published title appearing in a group of new contributions is given within square brackets with the number of prior publication and with only initial capitals, e.g., [C6: Peace]

All changes in titles are noted. For untitled poems and improvisations and for different poems with the same title, the first line is given within parentheses. First and last lines are supplied for fragments of a poem.

Significant cross references and the major or most accessible book in which an item may be found are given in abbreviated form. An asterisk marks those items not reprinted in the major collections of Williams' work listed on page 3 with their abbreviations.

The place of publication of a periodical is given only with the first mention of the periodical (and in the index), unless the periodical changed its place of publication, in which case the place is given with the first mention of each separate issue of the periodical.

Several items published in Bengali, French, Italian, Japanese, and Spanish periodicals before they appeared in English or American periodicals are included in this section, but other translations into foreign languages are listed only in the translations section (T).

C1 [Seven poems] "A Selection from *The Tempers*. By William Carlos Williams. With Introductory Note by Ezra Pound." *The Poetry Review*, London, I. 10 (Oct. 1912) 481–484.

FROM "THE BIRTH OF VENUS," SONG—HOMAGE—*A MAN TO A WOMAN—AN AFTER-SONG—*IN SAN MARCO, VENEZIA—THE FOOL'S SONG—HIC JACET.

In *CEP*, except for the starred poems.

1913

C2 [Four poems] *Poetry*, Chicago, II. 3 (June 1913) 93–96.

PEACE ON EARTH—SICILIAN EMIGRANT'S SONG: IN NEW YORK HARBOUR—POSTLUDE—PROOF OF IMMORTALITY.

In *CEP*; PROOF OF IMMORTALITY is retitled IMMORTAL. POSTLUDE is also in *The New Freewoman*, London, I. 6 (Sept. 1, 1913) 114, and *The Glebe*, Ridgefield, N.J., I. 5 (Feb. 1914) 39. Part of this impression of *The Glebe*, including POSTLUDE, is in *Des Imagistes, An Anthology*, edited by Ezra Pound (New York: Albert and Charles Boni, 1914); for description and notes, see Donald Gallup's *A Bibliography of Ezra Pound* (London: Rupert Hart-Davis, 1963), pp. 139–142. The first book publication of POSTLUDE is *The Tempers*, 1913 (A2).

C3 [Poem in letter to the editor, Harriet Monroe] *Poetry*, II. 3 (June 1913) 114–115.

*ON FIRST OPENING *THE LYRIC YEAR*.

The brief letter is not reprinted, but the poem is in *New Directions 16* (1957) 9.

[Medical article in *Archives of Pediatrics* (Aug. 1913). See H1.]

1914

C4 [Poem] *The Egoist*, London, I. 6 (March 16, 1914) 109–111.

THE WANDERER: A ROCOCO STUDY.

In *CEP*.

C5 [Nine poems] "Invocations." *The Egoist*, I. 16 (Aug. 15, 1914) 307–308.

*AT DAWN—*RENDEZVOUS—(My townspeople, beyond in the

great world)—*TO THE OUTER WORLD—*LA FLOR (For
E. P.)—*OFFERING—*A LA LUNE—IN HARBOUR—THE
REVELATION.

In *CEP;* the untitled poem is titled GULLS and IN HARBOUR
is spelled IN HARBOR. All the starred poems, except AT DAWN,
are reprinted in *New Directions 16* (1957) 9–12.

C6 [Five poems] *The Egoist,* I. 23 (Dec. 1, 1914) 444.

*WOMAN WALKING — TRANSITIONAL — *INVITATION
(We live in this flat blue basin)—*AUX IMAGISTES—*PEACE.

TRANSITIONAL is in *CEP.* WOMAN WALKING is in *Al Que
Quiere!* (A3) and is reprinted with the other starred poems in *New
Directions 16* (1957) 12–14.

1915

C7 [Five poems] "Root Buds." *Poetry,* VI. 2 (May 1915) 62–66.

THE SHADOW—METRIC FIGURE (There is a bird in the
poplars)—SUB TERRA—*SLOW MOVEMENT (For E. P.)—*A
CONFIDENCE.

The first three poems are in *CEP.* SLOW MOVEMENT is in *The
New Poetry* (B4) and is reprinted with A CONFIDENCE in *New
Directions 16* (1957) 14–15.

C8 [Poem] *Rogue,* New York, I. 6 (June 15, 1915) 18.

LYRIC.

In *CEP;* retitled CHICORY AND DAISIES; other changes.

C9 [Four poems] *Others,* Grantwood, N.J., I. 2 (Aug. 1915) 23–25.

PASTORAL (The little sparrows)—PASTORAL (If I say I have
heard voices)—THE OGRE—APPEAL.

In *CEP.*

1916

C10 [Five poems] *Others,* II. 2 (Feb. 1916) 139–147.

*METRIC FIGURE (Veils of clarity)—TRACT—TOUCHÉ—TO
A SOLITARY DISCIPLE—*EPIGRAMME.

In *CEP;* the 145 short lines of TRACT in *Others* are printed as 70
long lines in *CEP;* TOUCHÉ is retitled SYMPATHETIC POR-

TRAIT OF A CHILD. The starred poems are reprinted in *New Directions 16* (1957) 17–18.

C11 [Poem] *Others*, III. 1 (July 1916) 30.

DRINK.

In *CEP*.

C11a [Translations by William George Williams] *Others*, III. 2 (Aug. 1916) 35–42 [entire issue].

Translations from the Spanish of R. Arévalo Martínez, José Santos Chocano, Alfonso Guillén Zelaya, Luis C. López, Juan Julian Lastra, Leopold Díaz, José Asunción Silva by William George Williams, WCW's father. WCW probably assisted his father in translating and in editing the translations for publication in this periodical. See also C31 and C40.

C12 [Letter to the editor, Harriet Shaw Weaver] *The Egoist*, III. 9 (Sept. 1916) 137.

THE GREAT OPPORTUNITY.

In *SL*, pp. 30–33 [dated 1915].

C13 [Poem] *The Egoist*, III. 10 (Oct. 1916) 148–149.

MARCH.

In *CEP*.

C14 [Six poems] "New Verse." *Poetry*, IX. 2 (Nov. 1916) 81–86.

LOVE SONG (What have I to say to you)—*NAKED—*MARRIAGE—APOLOGY—SUMMER SONG—*THE OLD WORSHIPPER.

In *CEP;* LOVE SONG is retitled FIRST VERSION: 1915. The starred poems are reprinted in *New Directions 16* (1957) 15–17.

C15 [Sixteen poems] *Others*, III. 4 (Dec. 1916) 15–31.

KELLER GEGEN DOM—LOVE SONG (Daisies are broken)—THE OLD MEN—THE YOUNG HOUSEWIFE—PORTRAIT OF A WOMAN IN BED—MUJER—K. McD.—SPRING STRAINS—EL HOMBRE—NEW PRELUDE—DANSE RUSSE—BALLET—GOOD-NIGHT—SPRING SONG—FIRE SPIRIT—PASTORAL (When I was younger).

In CEP; K. McD. is titled K. McB.; the form of EL HOMBRE is different in *CEP* and in Wallace Stevens' *Harmonium* (1923) where Stevens uses it as the first verse for "Nuances of a Theme by Williams"; NEW PRELUDE is retitled A PRELUDE; DANSE RUSSE

169

was set to music by Irwin Heilner with the title SECOND RHAP-
SODY and is reprinted with the music in *New Music,* San Francisco,
VIII, 4 (July 1935) 12–15 [see also E1]. GOOD-NIGHT is not the
same poem as A GOOD NIGHT, both in *CEP.*

C16 [Three poems] *The Poetry Journal,* Boston (Dec. 1916) 45–47.
  M. B.—*NIGHT—TREES
  In *CEP;* TREES is not the same as THE TREES, also in *CEP.*

1917

C17 [Two poems] *The Masses,* New York, IX. 3, Issue 67 (Jan. 1917) 42.
  *SICK AFRICAN—*CHINESE NIGHTINGALE.
  In correspondence section of magazine and signed "W. C. Williams,
  Rutherford, N. J."
C18 [Letter to the editor, Harriet Shaw Weaver] *The Egoist,* IV. 3
  (April 1917) 46.
  *THE GREAT SEX SPIRAL, A CRITICISM OF MISS [Dora]
  MARSDEN'S "LINGUAL PSYCHOLOGY," CHAPTER 1.
  Discussion continued in issue of August, 1917.
C19 [Letter to the editor] *The Rutherford Republican and Rutherford
  American,* Rutherford, N.J., XXVIII. 9 (Sat., May 12, 1917) 1.
  *Letter refutes local accusations that he is pro-German, but extends
  sympathy to "German-Americans among my friends who are quite
  as honest as I am."
C20 [Two poems] *Poetry,* X. 4 (July 1917) 194–196.
  HISTORY, I–III—SMELL!
  In *CEP;* HISTORY is revised. SMELL! is reprinted in *Perspec-
  tives U.S.A.,* New York, No. 1 (Fall 1952) 25.
C21 [Letter to the editor, Harriet Shaw Weaver] *The Egoist,* IV. 7 (Aug.
  1917) 110–111.
  *THE GREAT SEX SPIRAL, A CRITICISM OF MISS [Dora]
  MARSDEN'S "LINGUAL PSYCHOLOGY."
  Discussion continued from issue of April, 1917.
C22 [Improvisations] *The Little Review,* Chicago, IV. 6 (Oct. 1917) 19.
  I. Fools have big wombs—II. For what it's worth—III. Talk as you
  will.
  In *Kora in Hell* (A4) and *Reader* (A50).
C23 [Improvisation] *The Egoist,* IV. 9 (Oct. 1917) 137.

*THE DELICACIES.
In *Sour Grapes* (A5) as a prose poem.
C24 [Essay] *The Poetry Journal*, VIII. 1 (Nov. 1917) 27–36.
*AMERICA, WHITMAN, AND THE ART OF POETRY.

1918

C25 [Improvisations] *The Little Review*, V. 9 [*sic*; should be numbered
IV. 9] (Jan. 1918) 3–9.
I: 1. So far away August green as it yet is—2. My wife's uncle went
to school with Amundsen—3. What can it mean to you that a child
wears pretty clothes II: 1. Mamselle Day—2. How smoothly the
car runs—3. The frontispiece is her portrait. III: 1. Beautiful white
corpse of night actually!—2. It is the water we drink—3. Marry in
middle life and take the young thing home. IV: 1. Of course history
is an attempt to make the past seem stable—2. Quarrel with a purple
hanging—3. Think of some lady better than Rackham draws them.
V: 1. It is still warm enough to slip from weeds—2. The little
Polish Father of Kingstand—3. What I like best's the long unbroken
line of hills there. Coda. VI: 1. Some fifteen years we'll say—2. You
speak of the enormity of her disease—3. Hercules is in Hacketstown
doing farm labor.
In *Kora in Hell* (A4). "Beautiful white corpse of night" is in
Reader (A50), p. 105.
C26 [Poem] *The Egoist*, V. 5 (May 1918) 73–74.
A CELEBRATION.
In *CEP*.
C27 [Essay] *The Little Review*, VI. 2 [*sic*; should be numbered V. 2],
American Number (June 1918) 5–10.
*PROSE ABOUT LOVE.
C28 [Poem] *The Little Review*, VI. 2 [*sic*; should be numbered V. 2],
American Number (June 1918) 11.
*LOVE SONG (He: You have come between me and the terrify-
ing presence/of the moon, the stars).
C29 [Poem] *Poetry*, XII. 4 (July 1918) 192–193.
LE MÉDECIN MALGRÉ LUI.
In *CEP*.
C30 [Improvisation] *The Little Review*, V. 8 (Dec. 1918) 39–40.

*THE IDEAL QUARREL.

C31 [Translated short story] *The Little Review*, V. 8 (Dec. 1918) 42–53.
*THE MAN WHO RESEMBLED A HORSE.

Translated from the Spanish of Rafael Arévalo Martínez. WCW was assisted by his father, William George Williams. At end of story: "Guatemala, Oct., 1914." Reprinted in *New Directions 8* (1944) 309–319.

1919

C32 [Poem] *Others*, V. 3 (Feb. 1919) 22–25.
ROMANCE MODERNE.
In *CEP*.

C33 [Improvisations] "Three Professional Studies." *The Little Review*, V. 10–11 (Feb.–March 1919) 36–44.
1. *THE DOCTOR—2. *MRS. M——3. *SOMETHING.

C34 [Eighteen poems] "Broken Windows." *Poetry*, XIII. 6 (March 1919) 300–305.

BERKET AND THE STARS—THE YOUNG LAUNDRYMAN —TIME THE HANGMAN—COMPLETE DESTRUCTION— THE POOR (By constantly tormenting them)—A FRIEND OF MINE—THE GENTLE MAN—FOR ANY GIRL'S LOCKET— THE SOUGHING WIND—EPITAPH—SPRING—*STROLLER —MEMORY OF APRIL—PLAY—LINES—THE DARK DAY— THURSDAY—MAN IN A ROOM.

In *CEP*, except for STROLLER; A FRIEND OF MINE is retitled TO A FRIEND; FOR ANY GIRL'S LOCKET is retitled TO BE CLOSELY WRITTEN ON A SMALL PIECE OF PAPER WHICH FOLDED INTO A TIGHT LOZENGE WILL FIT ANY GIRL'S LOCKET. COMPLETE DESTRUCTION is reprinted in *Perspectives U.S.A.*, No. 1 (Fall 1952) 40. STROLLER is reprinted in *New Directions 16* (1957) 19. See *Anthology of Magazine Verse for 1919* (B6).

C35 [Essay] *The Little Review*, V. 12 (April 1919) 1–10.
PROLOGUE: THE RETURN OF THE SUN.

This is the first part of the Prologue to *Kora in Hell* (A4), ending with a letter from Wallace Stevens; also in *SE*. See C37.

C36 [Play] *Others*, V. 5 (April–May 1919) 1–16.

*THE COMIC LIFE OF ELIA BROBITZA.

A comedy with an incident based on "The Reeve's Tale" by Chaucer.

C37 [Essay] *The Little Review*, VI. 1 (May 1919) 74–80.

PROLOGUE TO A BOOK OF IMPROVISATIONS, KORA IN HELL, NOW BEING PUBLISHED BY THE FOUR SEAS COMPANY.

Second part of the Prologue to *Kora*; also in *SE*. See C35.

C38 [Improvisations] *The Little Review*, VI. 2 (June 1919) 52–59.

I: 1. Throw that flower in the waste basket—2. The time never was when he could play more than a mattress—3. One has emotions about the strangest things. II: 1. If I could clap this in a cage and let that out—2. You would learn—if you knew even one city—3. Truth's a wonder. III: 1. The brutal lord of all will rip us from each other—2. To you! whoever you are, wherever you are!—3. It's all one! Richard worked years.

In *Kora in Hell* (A4).

C39 [Poem] *The Egoist*, VI. 3 (July 1919) 38.

THE LATE SINGER.

In *CEP*.

C40 [Essay] *Others*, V. 6 (July 1919) 3–4.

*GLORIA!

An editorial criticizing *Others;* edited and copyrighted by WCW, this is the last issue.

C41 [Essay] *Others*, V. 6 (July 1919) 25–32.

*BELLY MUSIC.

About American poetry criticism.

C42 [Essay] *Poetry*, XIV. 4 (July 1919) 211–216.

*NOTES FROM A TALK ON POETRY.

C43 [Essay] *The Little Review*, VI. 4 (Aug. 1919) 37–39.

*A MAKER.

In praise of Wallace Gould's poetry, then unpublished except in *Others* and *The Little Review*. See C128.

C44 [Essay] *The Little Review*, VI. 5 (Sept. 1919) 36–39.

*FOUR FOREIGNERS.

About Richard Aldington, D. H. Lawrence, James Joyce, and Dorothy Richardson.

C45 [Essay] *The Little Review*, VI. 6 (Oct. 1919) 29–30.

*MORE SWILL.

About American criticism.

C46 [Poem] *The Egoist*, VI. 5 (Dec. 1919) 73.

CHICAGO.

In *CEP*; retitled APRIL and in present rather than past tense.

1920

C47 [Six poems] *The Little Review*, VI. 9 (Jan. 1920) 49–52.

A CORONAL—WAITING—THE HUNTER—ARRIVAL—
MARK ANTHONY IN HEAVEN—TO A FRIEND CONCERN-
ING SEVERAL LADIES.

In *CEP*; MARK ANTHONY IN HEAVEN is retitled TO MARK
ANTHONY IN HEAVEN.

C48 [Short story] *The Little Review*, VII. 1 (May–June 1920) 46–49.

DANSE PSEUDOMACABRE

In *FD*.

C49 [Poem in letter to the editor, Harriet Monroe] *Poetry*, XVI. 3 (June
1920) 173.

The poem in the *letter is *SPIRIT OF '76.

C50 [Essay] *The Freeman*, New York, I. 15 (June 23, 1920) 348–349.

*A MAN VERSUS THE LAW.

About John Coffey, a young radical who was sent without trial to
a hospital for the criminally insane to prevent his testifying in court
that he stole furs from exclusive stores to feed the poor because the
city was doing nothing for them. The title poem of *An Early Martyr*
(A16) is about the same subject and the book is dedicated "To John
Coffee" (WCW spelled the name both ways). Florence Williams "re-
called that *The Freeman* bought the poem, paid for it, but lost their
nerve and didn't publish it" [*I Wanted*, p. 56].

C51 [Six poems] *The Dial*, New York, LXIX, 2 (Aug. 1920) 162–165.

PORTRAIT OF A LADY—TO WAKEN AN OLD LADY—
THE DESOLATE FIELD—WILLOW POEM—BLIZZARD—
SPRING STORM.

In *CEP*. TO WAKEN AN OLD LADY is reprinted in *Perspec-
tives U.S.A.*, No. 1 (Fall 1952) 23–24, and in *Chelsea Twelve*, New
York (Sept. 1962) 122–123, with an Italian translation by Vittorio
Sereni.

C52 [Essay] *Contact,* New York [No. 1] (Dec. 1920) 1.
*Unsigned editorial describing the policy of *Contact* in regard to contributors.
WCW was co-editor of *Contact* with Robert McAlmon.

C53 [Poem] *Contact* [No. 1] (Dec. 1920) 4.
*MARIANNE MOORE.

1921

C54 [Essay] *Contact* [No. 2] (Jan. 1921) [1].
*Introduction to two poems by Marianne Moore, "Those Various Scalpels" and "In the Days of Prismatic Color," which were reprinted from *The Bryn Mawr Lantern,* Bryn Mawr, Pa.

C55 [Essay] *Contact* [No. 2] (Jan. 1921) [7].
A MATISSE.
In *SE* and *Reader.*

C56 [Essay] *Contact* [No. 2] (Jan. 1921) [11–12].
COMMENT.
In *SE.*

C57 [Poem] *Poetry,* XVII. 4 (Jan. 1921) 182–184.
A GOODNIGHT.
In *CEP*; spelled A GOOD NIGHT; not the same poem as GOOD NIGHT, also in *CEP.*

C58 [Three poems] *The Dial,* LXX. 1 (Jan. 1921) 63–64.
JANUARY—APPROACH OF WINTER—WINTER TREES.
In *CEP.*

C59 [Letter to the editors, Francis Neilson and Albert Jay Nock] *The Freeman,* II. 45 (Jan. 19, 1921) 449.
*WHAT EVERY ARTIST KNOWS.

C60 [Poem] *Contact* [No. 3] [Spring 1921] 12.
PORTRAIT OF THE AUTHOR.
In *CEP.*

C61 [Essay] *Contact* [No. 3] [Spring 1921] 14–16.
YOURS, O YOUTH.
In *SE.*

C62 [Short story] *Contact* [No. 3] [Spring 1921] 18–19.
THE ACCIDENT.
In *FD.*

C63 [Poem with letter to the editor, O. Davis Keep] *The Rutherfordian*, Rutherford, N.J. (March 1921) 32.

   THE LONELY STREET.

   The *letter offering the poem to the Rutherford High School publication is addressed to "Davis" and dated January 5, 1921. In *CEP*. Reprinted in *Poetry*, XIX. 4 (Jan. 1922) 201, and *Chelsea Twelve*, No. 10 (Sept. 1961) 58.

C64 [Poem] *Contact*, No. 4 [Summer 1921] 2–4.

   ST. FRANCIS EINSTEIN OF THE DAFFODILS.

   In *CEP*. A revised version is in *Literary America*, New York, I. 3 (July 1934) 11–12, and the version in *CEP* has other changes. Subtitle of poem: "On the first visit of Professor Einstein to the United States in the spring of 1921."

C65 [Short story] *Contact*, No. 4 [Summer 1921] 10–13.

   *SAMPLE PROSE PIECE: THE THREE LETTERS.

   Preliminary sketch for a chapter of *A Voyage to Pagany* (A10).

C66 [Essay] *Contact*, No. 4 [Summer 1921] 18–19.

   *SAMPLE CRITICAL STATEMENT. COMMENT.

   Editorial about *Contact* and American art.

C67 [Two poems] *The Dial*, LXXI. 1 (July 1921) 69.

   THE BIRDS—YOUTH AND BEAUTY.

   In *CEP*.

1922

C68 [Four poems] *Poetry*, XIX. 4 (Jan. 1922) 200–202.

   WILD ORCHARD—[C63: The Lonely Street]—SPOUTS—THE WIDOW'S LAMENT IN SPRINGTIME.

   In *CEP*. THE WIDOW'S LAMENT is reprinted in *Perspectives U.S.A.*, No. 1 (Fall 1952) 22–26.

C69 [Two poems] *Manuscripts*, New York, No. 1 (Feb. 1922) 15.

   Untitled (1. *Picture showing—2. *My luv).

C70 [Two poems] *The Dial*, LXXII. 2 (Feb. 1922) 156–157.

   THE BULL—THE JUNGLE.

   In *CEP*.

C71 [Poem] *Broom*, Rome, II. 1 (April 1922) 55–58.

   FISH.

   In *CEP* with some changes.

C72 [Poem] *Broom*, Rome, III. 1 (Aug. 1922) 55.
*HULA-HULA.

C73 [Poem] *Secession*, Reutte (Tirol), Austria, No. 3 (Aug. 1922) 5.
THE ATTEMPT.
In *CEP*; retitled TO AN OLD JAUNDICED WOMAN.

C74 [Essay] *The Little Review*, IX. 3 [*sic;* should be numbered IX. 1],
Stella Number (Autumn 1922) 59–60.
*READER CRITIC.
Praise of *The Little Review*.

C75 [Poem] *Forum*, New York, LXVIII. 9 (Sept. 1922) 783.
*VIEW.

1923

C76 [Poem] *Secession*, Brooklyn, No. 4 (Jan. 1923) 21.
THE HOTHOUSE PLANT (Dedicated to Charles Demuth).
In *CEP*; retitled THE POT OF FLOWERS.

C77 [Essay] *Broom*, Berlin, IV. 2 (Jan. 1922 [*sic*—should be 1923]) 112–
120.
THE DESTRUCTION OF TENOCHTITLAN.
In *AG*. Reprinted in *Perspectives U.S.A.*, No. 1 (Fall 1952) 11–21
[published also in German and Italian editions].

C78 [Essay] *Broom*, Berlin, IV. 3 (Feb. 1923) 182–186.
THE DISCOVERERS: I. RED ERIC.
In *AG*; retitled RED ERIC.

C79 [Essay] *Broom*, Berlin, IV. 4 (March 1923) 252–260.
THE DISCOVERY OF THE INDIES.
In *AG*, with many changes.

C80 [Poem] *The Chapbook*, London, No. 36 (April 1923) 5.
CORNUCOPIA.
In *CEP*; retitled FLIGHT TO THE CITY.
The poems for this issue were collected by Alfred Kreymborg.

C81 [Poem] *Rhythmus*, New York, I. 4–5 (April–May 1923) 109.
*FROM A BOOK.
Reprinted in *New Directions 16* (1957) 19–20.

C82 [Poem] *The Dial*, LXXIV. 6 (June 1923) 562.
Untitled (By the road to the contagious hospital).
In *CEP*; titled SPRING AND ALL. Reprinted without title in
Broom, New York, V. 4 (Nov. 1923) 208–210, and with title in

Chelsea Twelve (Sept. 1962) 124–125, with an Italian translation by Cristina Campo.

C83 [Essay] *Contact*, No. 5 (June 1923) [1–5].
   *GLORIOUS WEATHER.
   Unsigned editorial about "the object of writing is to celebrate the triumph of sense," and "sense is in the form."

C84 [Poem] *Contact*, No. 5 (June 1923) [11].
   NEW ENGLAND.
   In *CEP*; some revisions. In *CP* (A15) and in *New Directions 16* (1957) 24, titled DOWN–TOWN.

C85 [Essay] *Contact*, No. 5 (June 1923) [12].
   *CRITICAL NOTE.
   Unsigned editorial about the poems in *Contact*, No. 5.

C86 [Three poems] *The Dial*, LXXV. 2 (Aug. 1923) 170–172.
   Untitled (I. The farmer in deep thought—II. Our orchestra—III. The crowd at the ball game).
   In *CEP*; titled THE FARMER—SHOOT IT JIMMY!—AT THE BALL GAME. The poems were published contemporaneously in *Spring and All* (A7). The second poem, with title, is reprinted in *The Bookman*, New York, LVIII. 3 (Nov. 1923) 318.

C87 [Essay] *Broom*, New York, V. 2 (Sept. 1923) 73–77.
   THE FOUNTAIN OF ETERNAL YOUTH.
   In *AG* and *Reader*.

C88 [Essay] *Broom*, New York, V. 3 (Oct. 1923) 167–176.
   SOTO [*sic*] AND THE NEW WORLD.
   In *AG*.

C89 [Four poems] *Broom*, New York, V. 4 (Nov. 1923) 208–210.
   Untitled (1. *The new cathedral overlooking the park—2. The stars, that are small lights—3. [C82: Spring and All]—4. *How has the way been found?).
   The first and last poems are reprinted in *New Directions 16* (1957) 20. The first poem is printed as a prose paragraph in *Spring and All* (A7), p. 8. The second poem is in *CEP* with the title AT NIGHT and other changes.

1924

C90 [Essay] *Broom*, New York, VI. 1 (Jan. 1924) 23–25.
   SIR WALTER RALEIGH.

In *AG* and *Reader*.

C91 [Poem] *The Dial*, LXXVI. 1 (Jan. 1924) 48.
FULL MOON.
In *CEP*.

C92 [Poem] *the transatlantic review*, Paris, I. 3 (March 1924) 28–30.
LAST WORDS OF MY GRANDMOTHER.
In *CEP*; titled THE LAST WORDS OF MY ENGLISH GRAND-
MOTHER and the first 44 lines omitted. Reprinted, with the title
LAST WORDS OF MY ENGLISH GRANDMOTHER and the
first 44 lines omitted, in *Furioso*, New Haven, I. 1 (Summer 1939)
7–8. An early prose version of this poem is in *The Great American
Novel* (A6), p. 66.

C93 [Letter to the editor, Ford Madox Ford] *the transatlantic review*,
I. 5 (May 1924) 361–364.
*ROBERT McALMON'S PROSE.
About McAlmon's *A Hasty Bunch*.

C94 [Essay] *the transatlantic review*, II. 1 (Aug. 1924) 46–51.
VOYAGE OF THE MAYFLOWER.
In *AG* and *Reader*.

C95 [Poem] *The Arts*, Brooklyn, VI. 2 (Aug. 1924) 91–92.
IT IS A LIVING CORAL.
In *CEP*; shorter version.

C96 [Letter to the editor, Ford Madox Ford] *the transatlantic review*,
II. 2 (Aug. 1924) 215–217.
*ROBERT McALMON'S PROSE.
About McAlmon's *A Companion Volume* and *Post Adolescence*.

C97 [Two poems] *Der Querschnitt*, Berlin, IV. 4 (Herbst 1924) 197–198.
Untitled (The pure products of America)—THE VERITABLE
NIGHT.
In *CEP* titled TO ELSIE and RIGAMAROLE.

C98 [Essay] *1924*, Woodstock, N.Y., No. 4 (Dec. 1924) 143–145.
*PORTRAIT OF A GENERATION.
Review of Robert McAlmon's *Portrait of a Generation*.

C99 [Improvisations] *1924*, No. 4 (Dec. 1924) 124–126.
*GOODBYEVIENNA—*REALLYTHESOUND.

1925

C100 [Letter to the editor, Walter S. Hankel] *Aesthete 1925*, New York, I. 1 (Feb. 1925) 9–10.

*Criticism of H. L. Mencken, written in response to Ernest Boyd's essay, "Aesthete: Model 1924," in *The American Mercury*, New York, I. 1 (Jan. 1924) 51–56.

C101 [Essay] *This Quarter*, Paris, I. 1 (Spring 1925) 173–175.

*AN ESSAY ON VIRGINIA [the state].

In *A Novelette* (A12).

C102 [Essay] *The Dial*, LXXVIII. 5 (May 1925) 393–401.

MARIANNE MOORE.

Review of Marianne Moore's *Observations*. Published contemporaneously in *Contact Collection* (B8), reprinted in *A Novelette*, and with some deletions, in *SE*, pp. 121–131, and *Reader*.

C103 [Essay] *This Quarter*, Milan, I. 2 ([Autumn–Winter] 1925–1926) 182–194.

JACATAQUA.

In *AG* and *Reader*. Reprinted in *The New English Weekly*, London, VI. 12 (Thurs., Jan. 3, 1935) 251–253.

1926

C104 [Three poems, essay, and improvisation] "Interests of 1926." *The Little Review*, New York, XII. 1 (Spring-Summer 1926) 10–12.

[Poems:] INSANITY OR GENIUS—TWO FUGITIVE POEMS (1910): *MARTIN AND KATHERINE—*MISERICORDIA.

[Essay:] *POEM: DANIEL BOONE.

[Improvisation:] *STOLEN LETTER (DEAR AUNT N.).

INSANITY OR GENIUS is retitled INTERESTS OF 1926 in *CEP*. MARTIN AND KATHERINE, retitled THE WARTBURG, and MISERICORDIA are reprinted in *New Directions 16* (1957) 6.

C105 [Short story] *New Masses*, New York, I. 1 (May 1926) 19, 29.

*THE FIVE DOLLAR GUY.

C106 [Poem] *The Dial*, LXXXI. 1 (July 1926) 22–24.

STRUGGLE OF WINGS.

The text ends with "[Incomplete]," but the same text without additions is in *CEP*.

1927

C107 [Poem] *The Dial*, LXXXII. 1 (Jan. 1927) 7.
*TREE.

C108 [Poem] *The Dial*, LXXXII. 2 (Feb. 1927) 91–93.
PATERSON
Parts of this poem are scattered throughout *Paterson (One)*. The complete poem is in *CEP*. In *Prize Poems 1913–1929* (B13).

C109 [Three poems] *The Dial*, LXXXII. 3 (March 1927) 210–211.
*MARCH IS A LIGHT—YOUNG SYCAMORE—LINES ON RECEIVING THE DIAL'S AWARD.
In *CEP*.

C110 [Poem] *transition*, Paris, No. 2 (May 1927) 118.
THE DEAD BABY.
In *CEP*.

C111 [Two poems and improvisation] *The Dial*, LXXXII. 6 (June 1927) 476–478.
[Poems:] ALL THE FANCY THINGS—BRILLIANT SAD SUN.
[Improvisation:] *A MEMORY OF TROPICAL FRUIT.
The poems are in *CEP*, the improvisation in *A Novelette* (A12).

C112 [Two chapters for a novel] *transition*, No. 7 (Oct. 1927) 9–17.
A NEW PLACE TO MEET—REITSCHULE.
In *A Voyage to Pagany* (A10). REITSCHULE is reprinted in *The Massachusetts Review*, Amherst, III. 2 (Winter 1962) 325–327.

C113 [Essay] *transition*, No. 8 (Nov. 1927) 149–154.
A NOTE ON THE RECENT WORK OF JAMES JOYCE.
In *A Novelette* (A12) and *SE*.

C114 [Poem] *transition*, No. 9 (Dec. 1927) 129.
WINTER.
In *CEP*.

1928

C115 [Letter to the editors, Elliot Paul and Eugene Jolas] *transition*, No. 10 (Jan. 1928) 145–146.
*About Laura Riding's criticism, "Jamais Plus," of WCW's essay on Edgar Allan Poe in *In the American Grain*.

C116 [Improvisation] *transition*, No. 10 (Jan. 1928) 49–50.
*THEESSENTIALROAR.
In *Transition Workshop* (B56).

C117 [Improvisations] *transition*, No. 13, American Number (Summer 1928) 55–58.
*THAT POEM JAYJAY—*WELLROUNDEDTHIGHS—*THE DEAD GROW.

C118 [Essay] *transition*, No. 13, American Number (Summer 1928) 237–240.
GEORGE ANTHEIL AND THE CANTILENE CRITICS: A NOTE ON THE FIRST PERFORMANCE OF ANTHEIL'S MUSIC IN NYC; APRIL 10, 1927.
In *A Novelette* (A12) and *SE*.

C119 [Five chapters for a novel] *The Dial*, LXXXIV. 6 (June 1928) 456–462.
THE VOYAGE—CARCASSONNE—THE ARNO—NAPLES—THE TYROL.
In *A Voyage to Pagany* (A10); THE VOYAGE is part of the chapter OUTWARD BOUND; NAPLES is part of SOUTH TO NAPLES AND RETURN; THE TYROL is part of THE MOUNTAINS.

C120 [Poem] *The Dial*, LXXXIV. 6 (June 1928) 463.
THE MEN.
In *CEP*. Reprinted in *City Lights Journal*, San Francisco, No. 1 (1963) 5.

C121 [Short story] *The Dial*, LXXXV. 1 (July 1928) 21–28.
THE VENUS.
Written originally as a chapter of *A Voyage to Pagany* (See A10, Notes), but not published in the novel, THE VENUS is in *A Novelette, FD*, and *Reader*.

C122 [Twenty-one poems and eighteen prose pieces] "The Descent of Winter." *The Exile*, New York, No. 4 (Autumn 1928) 30–69. [Edited by Ezra Pound.]
*9/27 [poem] What are these elations I have—9/29 [poem] My bed is narrow—9/30 [poem] There are no perfect waves—10/9 [poem] and there's a little blackboy—10/10 [poem] Monday/the canna flaunts—*10/13 [prose] a beard...not of stone—10/21 [poem] In the dead weeds a rubbish heap—10/22 [poem] that

brilliant field—10/23 [prose] I will make a big, serious portrait—10/27 [prose] And Coolidge said—10/28 [prose] born, September 15, 1927, 2nd child—10/28 [poem] On hot days—10/28 [prose] a flash of juncos—10/28 [poem] in this strong light—10/29 [poem] The justice of poverty—10/30 [poem] To freight cars in the air—11/1 [prose] INTRODUCTION (in almost all verse you read)—11/1 [poem preceded by prose sentence] The moon, the dried weeds —11/2 [poem] Dahlias—11/2 [poem] A MORNING IMAGINA-TION OF RUSSIA—*11/6 [prose] Russia is every country, here he must live—11/7 [poem followed by prose sentence] We must listen. Before—11/8 [poem] O river of my heart polluted—11/8 [prose] Out of her childhood—11/10 [poem] The shell flowers—11/11 [prose] A cat licking herself solves most—11/13 [prose] SHAKE-SPEARE—11/16 [prose] The art of writing is all but lost—*11/13 [prose] TRAVELLING IN FAST COMPANY—11/20 [poem] Even idiots grow old—11/22 [poem] and hunters still return—11/24 [prose] If genius is profuse—11/28 [poem] I make really very little money—12/2 [prose] The first snow—12/9 [prose] Imagine a family of four grown men—12/15 [poem] What an image in the face of Almighty God is she—12/18 [prose] Here by the watertank and the stone.

All the poems are in *CEP,* except the first one; poem 9/30 is shortened. All the prose is in *SE,* grouped under the title "Notes in Diary Form," except 10/13, 11/6, and 11/13 TRAVELLING IN FAST COMPANY; changes include the omission of one line from 10/23, and the inclusion of the prose sentence following the poem of 11/7 with the prose sentence preceding the poem of 11/1. "The Descent of Winter" was begun on board the *S. S. Pennland* in the fall of 1927 when WCW was returning alone to Rutherford, having left his wife in Europe to care for their two sons who were attending school in Switzerland for a year.

C123 [Essay] *The Bookman,* LXVIII. 1 (Sept. 1928) 27.
      *STATEMENTS OF BELIEF.
      About the relative significance of literature, science, and philosophy in the twentieth century. In *A Novelette* (A12), titled STATE-MENT.

C124 [Three poems] *The Dial,* LXXXV. 5 (Nov. 1928) 391-394.
      ON GAY WALLPAPER—THE LILY—THE SOURCE, 1-3.

In *CEP*; some changes in THE SOURCE, including the division of the poem into two parts, rather than three. (A pencil sketch of WCW by Eva Herrmann is reproduced on unnumbered leaf between pp. 396 and 397 in this issue of *The Dial*.)

C125 [Essay] *The Dial*, LXXXV. 5 (Nov. 1928) 431–432.
*IMPASSE AND IMAGERY.
Review of Paul Rosenfeld's *The Boy in the Sun*.

1929

C126 [Answer to a questionnaire] *New Masses*, IV. 8 (Jan. 1929) 6.
*[*In its entirety:*] "*Question:* What's wrong with American literature? *Answer:* You ask me? How much do I get?"

C127 [Essay] *The Dial*, LXXXVI. 1 (Jan. 1929) 6–7.
KENNETH BURKE.
In *A Novelette* (A12) and *SE*.

C128 [Essay] *The Dial*, LXXXVI. 1 (Jan. 1929) 66–67.
*FROM QUEENS TO CATS.
Review of Wallace Gould's *Aphrodite and Other Poems*. See C43.

C129 [Essay] *transition*, No. 15 (Feb. 1929) 157–166.
A POINT FOR AMERICAN CRITICISM.
In *SE, Reader,* and *Our Exagmination Round His Factification* (B11).

C130 [Essay] *The Dial*, LXXXVI. 3 (March 1929) 250–251.
*GOOD . . . FOR WHAT?
Review of Carl Sandburg's *Good Morning, America*.

C131 [Essay] *Blues*, Columbus, Miss., I. 2 (March 1929) 30–32.
*FOR A NEW MAGAZINE.
WCW was a contributing editor of *Blues*.

C132 [Essay] *Blues*, I. 4 (May 1929) 77–79.
*A NOTE ON THE ART OF POETRY.

C133 [Answers to a questionnaire] *The Little Review*, Paris, XII. 2, Last Issue (May 1929) 87–88.
*The questions include: "What should you most like to do, to know, to be? (In case you are not satisfied.)"
A photograph of WCW sitting on a tree stump holding some kittens is on p. 87. This is probably the same photograph, borrowed

from Sylvia Beach, that appeared in *transition*, No. 14 (Fall 1928), facing p. 86.

C134 [Essay] *The Little Review*, Paris, XII. 2, Last Issue (May 1929) 95–98.
*A TENTATIVE STATEMENT.
About Ezra Pound's *Cantos*.

C135 [Essay (in French)] *Bifur*, Paris, No. 2 (25 juillet 1929) 95–103.
*L'ILLÉGALITÉ AUX ÉTATS-UNIS.
About a speech by President Hoover concerning Americans who break the law, translated into French by Georgette Camille.

C136 [Essay] *Blues*, No. 7 (Fall 1929) 3.
*INTRODUCTION TO A COLLECTION OF MODERN WRITINGS.
Introduction to the writings in this issue of *Blues*.

C137 [Poem] *Blues*, No. 7 (Fall 1929) 9–10.
SIMPLEX SIGILUM VERI: A CATALOGUE.
In *CEP*.

C138 [Poem] *Hound and Horn*, Cambridge, Mass., III. 1 (Oct.–Dec. 1929) 78–81.
RAIN.
In *CEP*.

C139 [Answer to a questionnaire] *Tambour*, Paris, No. 5 (Nov. 1929) 34.
*ANATOLE FRANCE, A POST-MORTEM FIVE YEARS LATER.
WCW's answer begins, "Since I have never read anything that Anatole France has written I cannot answer your questions," but explains why he has not "felt impelled to read Anatole France."

C140 [Essay] *transition*, No. 18 (Nov. 1929) 147–151.
*THE SOMNAMBULISTS.
Review of Kay Boyle's *Short Stories*. In *A Novelette* (A12).

1930

C141 [Essay] *Pagany*, Boston, I. 1 (Winter [Jan.–March] 1930) 1.
*MANIFESTO.

C142 [Essay] *Pagany*, I. 1 (Winter [Jan.–March] 1930) 41–46.
THE WORK OF GERTRUDE STEIN.

In *A Novelette* (A12) and *SE.*

C143 [Poem] *U.S.A.*, Philadelphia, [No. 1] (Spring 1930) 31.
THE FLOWER (A petal, colorless).
In *CEP.*

C144 [Two poems] *Blues*, No. 8 (Spring 1930) 20–21.
THE ATTIC WHICH IS DESIRE—*THE MOON.
The first poem is in *CEP* with some changes. THE MOON is reprinted only in *New Directions 16* (1957) 21.

C145 [Poem] *The Miscellany*, New York, I. 1 (March 1930) 8–10.
BIRDS AND FLOWERS, I–II.
In *CEP* with many changes. Part III of *CEP* version is in *An "Objectivists" Anthology* (B18) without a title.

C146 [Poem] *This Quarter*, Milan, II. 4 (April–June 1930) 685–686.
*CHILD AND VEGETABLES.
Reprinted in *New Directions 16* (1957) 21–22.

C147 [Short story] *Pagany*, I. 2 (Spring 1930) 38–42.
FOUR BOTTLES OF BEER.
In *FD.*

C148 [Chapter for a novel] *Pagany*, I. 3 (Summer 1930) 4–10.
WHITE MULE—A Novel. Chapter 1 [TO BE].
In *White Mule* and *Reader.*

C149 [Chapters for a "Novelette"] *transition*, Nos. 19–20 (June 1930) 279–286.
I. THE SIMPLICITY OF DISORDER—II. A BEAUTIFUL IDEA—III. CONVERSATION AS DESIGN.
A note at the beginning says, "These fragments have been extracted from *January: A Novelette* which is to appear in New York soon." Also in *SE.*

C150 [Poem] *Scribner's Magazine*, New York, LXXXVIII. 1 (July 1930) 59.
WEDDED ARE THE RIVER AND THE SKY.
In *CEP* retitled A MARRIAGE RITUAL, and with other changes.

C151 [Two poems] *Poetry*, XXXVI. 4 (July 1930) 194–195.
THE UNFROCKED PRIEST—POEM (As the cat).
THE UNFROCKED PRIEST is in *CLP*. POEM is in *CEP* and is reprinted in *Perspectives U.S.A.*, No. 1 (Fall 1952) 38.

C152 [Poem] *Blues*, No. 9 (Fall 1930) 22–23.
DEATH

A shorter version is in *CEP*.

C153 [Essay] *Blues*, No. 9 (Fall 1930) 46–47.
CAVIAR AND BREAD AGAIN | A WARNING TO THE NEW WRITER.
In *SE*.

C154 [Two poems] *Pagany*, I. 4 (Fall 1930) 5–6.
FLOWERS BY THE SEA—SEA-TROUT AND BUTTER-FISH.
In *CEP*; the second poem is reprinted in *Poetry*, XLIII. 1 (Oct. 1933) 7, in a shorter version like the one in *CEP*.

C155 [Two poems] *The Miscellany*, I. 5 (Nov. 1930) 14–18.
LOVE IN A TRUCK *or* THE SEA-ELEPHANT—THE TREES.
In *CEP*; the first poem is titled THE SEA ELEPHANT; the second has many revisions and is not the same poem as TREES, also in *CEP*.

1931

C156 [Chapter for a novel] *Pagany*, II. 1 (Winter [Jan.–March] 1931) 48–58.
WHITE MULE, II: [A Flower from the Park].
In *White Mule* (A18).

C157 [Letter to the editors, Lincoln Kirstein and Bernard Bandler II] *Hound and Horn*, IV. 2 (Jan.–March 1931) 277.
*About a review, "Cinque Cento Charles IV," by John Wheelwright in the previous issue.

C158 [Poem] *Poetry*, XXXVII. 5 (Feb. 1931) 266–267.
THE BOTTICELLIAN TREES.
In *CEP*. This issue of *Poetry* was edited by Louis Zukofsky. See *Profile* and *Famous Verse Manuscripts* (B17).

C159 [Poem] *Front*, The Hague, I. 2 (Feb. 1931) 113.
THE HOUSE.
In *CEP*

C160 [Chapter for a novel] *Pagany*, II. 2 (Spring 1931) 80–95.
WHITE MULE, III: [To Go on Being].
In *White Mule* and *Reader*.

C161 [Essay] *The Symposium*, Concord, N.H., II. 2 (April 1931) 257–263.

EXCERPTS FROM A CRITICAL SKETCH: THE XXX CANTOS OF EZRA POUND.
In *SE.*

C162 [Chapter for a novel] *Pagany,* II. 3 (Summer 1931) 127–135.
WHITE MULE, IV: To Start Again Once More.
In *White Mule* (A18).

C163 [Chapter for a novel] *Pagany,* II. 4 (Autumn 1931) 133–136.
WHITE MULE, V: The Boundaries of Thought.
In *White Mule* (A18).

C164 [Short story] *Clay,* Albuquerque, N.M., No. 2 (Winter 1931–32) 37–38.
SECOND MARRIAGE.
In *FD.*

1932

C165 [Chapter for a novel] *Pagany,* III. 1 (Winter 1932) 151–157.
WHITE MULE, VI: [Summer Days].
In *White Mule* (A18).

C166 [Letter to the editor, Wayne Andrews] *Demain,* Lawrenceville, N.J., II. 14 (Feb. 10, 1932) [3].
[Title of letter on cover of *Demain:*] LA POÉSIE FRANÇAISE ET MON OEUVRE.
The letter, partially in French, is dated March 10, 1932 [*sic*]. In *SL. Demain,* III. 1 (Nov. 15, 1932) [2], reprinted a section of *Kora in Hell* (A4), translated into French by J. Douglas Peck, titled VIVRE D'ERREURS ET DE PARFUMS: [first and last lines:] "Ce que j'ai le plus combattu . . . . la dernière couche est enfreinte." [*Kora,* XVII, 2].

C167 [Essay] *Contact,* New York, I. 1 (Feb. 1932) 7–9.
*COMMENT.
Editorial about writing. WCW was the editor of this issue and the two that followed; associate editors were Robert McAlmon and Nathanael West. COMMENT was reprinted in *Contact,* San Francisco, I. 1 (1959)—C550.

C168 [Short story] *Contact,* I. 1 (Feb. 1932) 55–63.
THE COLORED GIRLS OF PASSENACK, OLD AND NEW.
In *FD.* Reprinted in *Negro Anthology Made by Nancy Cunard*

1931–1933 (London: Wishart & Co., 1934), a book published entirely at Miss Cunard's expense; WCW's story, pp. 93–96, appeared first in book form in his *The Knife of the Times*, 1932 (A13).

C169 [Essay] *Contact*, I. 1 (Feb. 1932) 86–90.
   *THE ADVANCE GUARD MAGAZINE.

C170 [Short story] *Story, Vienna*, I. 6 (March–April 1932) 55–60.
   A DIFFICULT MAN
   In *FD*.

C171 [Chapter for a novel] *Pagany*, III. 2 (Spring 1932) 143–152.
   WHITE MULE, VII: Conflict
   In *White Mule* (A18).

C172 [Essay] *Contempo*, Chapel Hill, N.C., I. 21 (April 1, 1932) 1.
   *VIVA: E. E. CUMMINGS.
   Review of Cummings' *Viva*.

C173 [Poem] *Contempo*, I. 21 (April 1, 1932) 4.
   THE COD HEAD.
   See A14; also in *Contact*, I. 2 (May 1932) 38–39. These versions and the one in *CEP* are each slightly different.

C174 [Two poems] *Contact*, I. 2 (May 1932) 37–39.
   THE CANADA LILY—[C173: The Cod Head].
   In *CEP*; THE CANADA LILY is retitled THE RED LILY.

C175 [Essay] *Contact*, I. 2 (May 1932) 109–110.
   *COMMENT.
   Editorial about writing.

C176 [Chapter for a novel] *Pagany*, III. 3 (Summer 1932) 123–132.
   WHITE MULE, VIII: Men.
   In *White Mule* (A18).

C177 [Essay] *Contempo*, II. 4 (July 5, 1932) 1, 4.
   *HART CRANE (1899–1932).
   Review of Crane's *White Buildings* (1926).

C178 [Letter to the editor, Gorham Munson] *The New English Weekly*, I. 14 (Thurs., July 21, 1932) 331.
   *About Anglo-American literary relationships.

C179 [Poem] *Hound and Horn*, V. 4 (July–Sept. 1932) 540–541.
   IN THE 'SCONSET BUS.
   In *CEP*.

C180 [Short story] *The New English Weekly*, I. 17 (Thurs., Aug. 11, 1932) 400–401.

UNDER THE GREENWOOD TREE.

In *FD*.

C181 [Short story] *Contact*, I. 3 (Oct. 1932) 22–34.

*FOR BILL BIRD.

C182 [Essay] *Contact*, I. 3 (Oct. 1932) 131–132.

*COMMENT.

Editorial about poetry.

C183 [Two chapters for a novel] *Pagany*, III. 4 (Fall [Oct.–Dec.]–Winter [Jan.–March] 1932–1933) 108–124.

WHITE MULE, X: Strike! XI: The Giveaway.

In *White Mule* (A18), renumbered IX and X.

C184 [Letter to the editor, Gorham Munson] *The New English Weekly*, II. 4 (Thurs., Nov. 10, 1932) 90–91.

*In reply to Austin Warren's criticism of WCW in the October 6, 1932, issue.

1933

C185 [Essay] *The Symposium*, IV. 1 (Jan. 1933) 114–116.

*Review of *An "Objectivists" Anthology* edited by Louis Zukofsky (B18).

C186 [Poem] *The New English Weekly*, III. 13 (Thurs., July 13, 1933) 309.

*OUR (AMERICAN) RAGCADEMICIANS.

C187 [Essay] *Contempo*, III. 2 (July 25, 1933) 5, 8.

*SORDID? GOOD GOD!

Review of Nathanael West's *Miss Lonelyhearts*.

C188 [Poem] *The Westminster Magazine*, Oglethorpe University, Ga., XXII. 3 (Autumn 1933) 48–49.

*THE LOBSTER.

[Subtitle:] "Rhymed address to Carl Rakosi acknowledging (with thanks) the excellence of his poem."

C189 [Short story] *Blast, A Magazine of Proletarian Short Stories*, New York, I. 1 (Sept.–Oct. 1933) 3–6.

JEAN BEICKE.

In *FD* and *Reader*. WCW was Advisory Editor of *Blast*.

C190 [Translated short story] *Blast*, I. 1 (Sept.–Oct. 1933) 30–32.

*CAGE.

Authorized translation from the French of E. C. Fabre.

C191 [Eight poems] "That's the American Style." *Poetry*, XLIII. 1 (Oct. 1933) 1–8.

THE FLOWERS ALONE—THE LOCUST TREE IN FLOWER(Among/the leaves/bright)—TREE AND SKY—THE CENTENARIAN—4TH OF JULY, I–III—[154: Sea-Trout and Butterfish]—AN OLD SONG (The black-winged gull)—*A FOOT-NOTE.

In *CEP* or *CLP*; AN OLD SONG is retitled SONG in *CEP*, but is in *The Literary Digest*, New York, CXVI. 17 (Oct. 21, 1933) 32, with the original title.

C192 [Short story] *Blast*, I. 2 (Nov.–Dec. 1933) 17–18.

THE USE OF FORCE.

In *FD* and *Reader*.

1934

C193 [Essay] *The Literary Workshop*, New York, I. 2 (1934) 50–53.

*SEQUENCE AND CHANGE.

Comments on poems by five students in the previous issue of the magazine.

C194 [Short story] *The Magazine*, Beverly Hills, Calif., I. 2 (Jan. 1934) 47–51.

LIFE ALONG THE PASSAIC RIVER.

In *FD* and *Reader*.

C195 [Short story] *Blast*, I. 3 (Jan.–Feb. 1934) 3–8.

THE DAWN OF ANOTHER DAY.

In *FD*.

C196 [Essay] *The Harvard Advocate*, Cambridge, Mass., CXX. 4 (Feb. 1934) 10.

*THE ELEMENT OF TIME, Advice to a Young Writer.

Reprinted in *Harvard Advocate Centennial Anthology* (B97).

C197 [Chapter for a novel] *The Magazine*, I. 4 (March 1934) 135–142.

WHITE MULE, XI: Ständchen.

In *White Mule* (A18).

C198 [Poem] *Smoke*, Providence, R.I., III. 2 (Spring 1934).

AN EARLY MARTYR.

In *CEP*. Reprinted in *Bozart-Westminster*, Oglethorpe University,

Ga., IX. 1 (Spring–Summer 1935) 36–37 [this issue also titled *The Westminster*, XXIV. 1].

C199 [Contributions to a symposium] *A Year Magazine*, Philadelphia, No. 2 (April 1934) 133–134.
THE STATUS OF RADICAL WRITING.
In *SL.*

C200 [Chapter for a novel] *The Magazine*, I. 5 (April 1934) 173–180.
WHITE MULE, XII: A Visit.
In *White Mule* (A18).

C201 [Chapter for a novel] *The Magazine*, I. 6 (May 1934) 209–214.
WHITE MULE, XIII: The Flirtation.
In *White Mule* (A18).

C202 [Short story] *Blast*, I. 4 (May–June 1934) 15–20.
THE GIRL WITH A PIMPLY FACE.
In *FD*.

C203 [Letter to the editor, Harriet Monroe] *Poetry*, XLIV. 3 (June 1934) 174–175.
*DR. WILLIAMS AND THE ENGLISH ATTITUDE.
Reply to critical comments by F. R. Leavis in the previous issue of *Poetry*.

C204 [Essay] *Poetry*, XLIV. 4 (July 1934) 220–225.
*THE NEW POETICAL ECONOMY.
Review of George Oppen's *Discrete Series*, a book of poems with a preface by Ezra Pound.

C205 [Chapter for a novel] *The Magazine*, II. 1 (July–Aug. 1934) 44–52.
WHITE MULE, XIV: Gurlie & the Jewess.
In *White Mule* (A18).

C206 [Three poems] *The Westminster Magazine*, XXIII. 3 (Autumn 1934) 183–184.
A CRYSTAL MAZE—*YOUNG WOMAN AT A WINDOW (While she sits)—YOUNG WOMAN AT A WINDOW (She sits with).
A CRYSTAL MAZE is in *CLP* as part II of the poem with that title. The second version of YOUNG WOMAN AT A WINDOW is in *CEP* and in *Perspectives U.S.A.*, I. 1 (Fall 1952) 38.

C207 [Poem] *Smoke*, III. 4 (Autumn 1934) [8].
TO A POOR OLD WOMAN
"Relieved" in line 12 is inked out by the editors. In *CEP*.

C208 [Essay] *Direction*, Peoria, Ill., I. 1 (Autumn 1934) 27–28.
　　*REPLY TO A YOUNG SCIENTIST BERATING ME BE-
CAUSE OF MY DEVOTION TO A MATTER OF WORDS.

C209 [Chapter for a novel] *The Magazine*, II. 2 (Sept.–Oct. 1934) 101–
106.
　　WHITE MULE, XV: One Year Old.
　　In *White Mule* (A18).

C210 [Answer to "An Inquiry"] *New Verse*, London, No. 11 (Oct. 1934)
16.
　　*About poetry.

C211 [Poem] *The New Tide*, Hollywood, Calif., I. 1 (Oct.–Nov. 1934)
19.
　　TO A MEXICAN PIG-BANK.
　　Published contemporaneously in *Galaxy, An Anthology* (B22),
and reprinted in *Programme*, Oxford, No. 9 (Oct. 23, 1935) [15–16]
with the title POEM (To a Mexican pig-bank). In *CEP*.

C212 [Short story] *Blast*, I. 5 (Oct.–Nov. 1934) 2–4.
　　A NIGHT IN JUNE.
　　In *FD* and *Reader*.

C213 [Essay] *Mosaic*, New York, I. 1 (Nov.–Dec. 1934) 27–28.
　　*NOTES ON NORMAN MACLEOD.
　　Review of Macleod's *Horizons of Death*.

C214 [Chapter for a novel] *The Magazine*, II. 3 (Nov.–Dec. 1934) 145–
152.
　　WHITE MULE, XVI: The Second Year.
　　In *White Mule* (A18), retitled "Flight."

C215 [Essay] *The New English Weekly*, VI. 9 (Thurs., Dec. 13, 1934)
193–194.
　　GEORGE WASHINGTON.
　　In *AG*.

1935

C216 [Two poems] *Alcestis*, New York, I. 2 (Jan. 1935) [2–4].
　　HYMN TO LOVE ENDED (IMAGINARY TRANSLATION
FROM THE SPANISH)—THE RAPER FROM HACKENSACK.
　　In *CEP*; the second poem is retitled THE RAPER FROM
PASSENACK.

C217 [Chapter for a novel] *The Magazine*, II. 4 (Jan.–Feb. 1935) 198–206.
WHITE MULE, XVII: The Country.
In *White Mule* (A18).

C218 [Essay] *New Democracy*, New York, III. 10–11 (Jan. 15–Feb. 1, 1935) 191–192.
POUND'S ELEVEN NEW CANTOS.
In *SE.*

C219 [Essay] *The Rocking Horse*, Madison, Wis., II. 3 (Spring 1935) 3–5.
A 1 POUND STEIN.
In *SE.*

C220 [Three poems] *Bozart-Westminster*, IX. 1 (Spring–Summer 1935) 36–37. [This issue also titled *The Westminster*, XXIV. 1].
LATE FOR SUMMER WEATHER—[C198: An Early Martyr]—INVOCATION AND CONCLUSION.
In *CEP.*

C221 [Poem] *Poetry*, XLV. 6 (March 1935) 311–315.
AN ELEGY FOR D. H. LAWRENCE.
In *CEP.*

C222 [Chapter for a novel] *The Magazine*, II. 5 (March–April 1935) 253–260.
WHITE MULE, XVIII: The Payson Place.
In *White Mule* (A18).

C223 [Poem] *Direction*, I. 3 (April–June 1935) 145.
PROLETARIAN PORTRAIT.
First titled STUDY FOR A FIGURE REPRESENTING MODERN CULTURE in *Galaxy, An Anthology* (B22). In *CEP.* Reprinted in *Perspectives U.S.A.*, No. 1 (Fall 1952) 39.

C224 [Poem] *Artists' and Writers' Chap Book*, White Plains, N.Y., "issued on the occasion of the Beaux Arts Marionette Costume Ball," Westchester County Center (May 3, 1935) 28.
VIEW OF A LAKE.
In *CEP.*

C225 [Poem] *The New Republic*, Washington, D.C., LXXXII. 1066 (May 8, 1935) 364.
THE YACHTS.

In *CEP*. Reprinted in *Perspectives U.S.A.*, No. 1 (Fall 1932) 25–26.

C226 [Poem] *Programme*, No. 5 (May 17, 1935) [2].
*GENESIS.
In *An Early Martyr* (A16).

C227 [Essay] *Fantasy*, Pittsburgh, Pa., V. 1 (Summer 1935) 12–14.
*TO WRITE AMERICAN POETRY.

C228 [Chapter for a novel] *The Magazine*, II. 6 (May–June 1935) 299–310.
WHITE MULE, XIX: Country Rain.
In *White Mule* (A18).

C229 [Poem] *Poetry*, XLVI. 3 (June 1935) 134.
ITEM.
In *CEP*.

C230 [Poem] *Alcestis*, I. 4 (July 1935) [15].
FINE WORK WITH PITCH AND COPPER.
In *CEP*.

C231 [Poem] *The New Republic*, LXXXIII. 1078 (July 31, 1935) 328.
TO A DEAD JOURNALIST.
In *CEP*.

C232 [Two poems] *Smoke*, IV. 4 (Autumn 1935).
TO A WOOD THRUSH—ANTIQUE ENGINE.
In *CEP;* ANTIQUE ENGINE is retitled A CHINESE TOY and, with that title, is in *Perspectives U.S.A.*, No. 1 (Fall 1952) 41.

C233 [Poem] *Caravel*, Majorca, Spain, No. 4 ([Fall] 1935) 1.
THE ROSE (First the warmth).
In *CEP*.

C234 [Essay] *New Democracy*, V. 4 (Oct. 15, 1935) 61–62.
*JEFFERSON AND/OR MUSSOLINI.
Review of Ezra Pound's book of that title.

C235 [Essay] *New Democracy*, V. 5 (Nov. 1, 1935) 81–83.
*NEW DIRECTION IN THE NOVEL.
Review of John Hargrave's *Summertime Ends*.

C236 [Short story] *The Harvard Advocate*, CXXII. 3 (Dec. 1935) 19–23.
A FACE OF STONE.
In *FD* and *Reader*. Reprinted in *New Directions*, Norfolk, Conn., [No. 1] (1936) [68–77], and in *Harvard Advocate Centennial Anthology* (B97).

1936

C237 [Essay] *New Directions in Prose and Poetry* [No. 1] (1936).
*HOW TO WRITE.
See B93 for first book publication of this essay.

C238 [Poem] *New Directions* [No. 1] (1936).
PERPETUUM MOBILE: THE CITY.
In *CEP*. Also in *New Democracy*, VI. 2 (April 1936) 35–36.

C239 [Essay] *Poetry*, XLVII. 4 (Jan. 1936) 227–229.
*A TWENTIETH CENTURY AMERICAN.
Review of four pamphlets by H. H. Lewis: *Thinking of Russia*,
1932; *Red Renaissance*, 1930; *Salvation*, 1934; *Road to Utterly*,
1935. Compare C255

C240 [Two poems] *New Democracy*, VI. 2 (April 1936) 35–36.
[C238: Perpetuum Mobile: The City]—LA BELLE DAME DE
TOUS LES JOURS.
In *CEP*.

C241 [Essay] *New Democracy*, VI. 2 (April 1936) 26–27.
*A SOCIAL DIAGNOSIS FOR SURGERY.
"A Poet-Physician on the Money-Cancer."

C242 [Contribution to a symposium] *Partisan Review and Anvil*, New
York, III. 3 (April 1936) 13–14.
WHAT IS AMERICANISM? A SYMPOSIUM ON MARXISM
AND THE AMERICAN TRADITION.
In *SL*.

C243 [Essay] *The North American Review*, New York, CCXLII. 1
(Autumn 1936) 181–184.
Review of H. L. Mencken's *The American Language*.
In *SE*.

C244 [Poem] *Poetry*, XLIX. 2 (Nov. 1936) 69.
TO AN ELDER POET.
In *CEP*.

1937

C245 [Poem] *New Directions 2* (1937).
PATTERSON [*sic*]: *EPISODE* 17.

In *CEP*, spelled PATERSON; parts of this poem are scattered throughout *Paterson, Three*, 1.

C246 [Essay with poem] *The Patroon*, Teaneck, N.J., I. 1 (May 1937) 1–2, 36–40.

[essay:] *THE SO-CALLED SO-CALLED.

[poem:] THE GIRL (with big breasts).

Essay about poetry. Poem is in *CLP*, with some revisions. See *William Zorach | Two Drawings | William Carlos Williams | Two Poems* (B27).

C247 [Poem] *The New Republic*, LXXXXI. 1171 (May 12, 1937) 10.

CLASSIC SCENE.

In *CEP*.

C248 [Poem] *Life and Letters Today*, London, XVI. 8 (Summer 1937) 49–50.

THE SUN.

In *CEP*.

C249 [Essay] *The Writer*, Boston, L. 8 (Aug. 1937) 243–245.

WHITE MULE VERSUS POETRY.

About genesis and history of *White Mule*.

C250 [Essay] *The Nation*, New York, CXLV. 11 (Sept. 11, 1937) 268.

*A GOOD DOCTOR'S STORY.

Review of A. J. Cronin's *The Citadel*.

C251 [Three poems] *Poetry*, LI. 1, 25th Anniversary Number (Oct. 1937) 4–6.

AUTUMN—AFRICA—WEASEL SNOUT.

In *CEP*.

C252 [Essay] *The Columbia Review*, New York, XIX. 1 (Nov. 1937) 3–5.

*POETRY.

C253 [Poem] *Barometer*, Paterson, N.J., I. 1 (Nov.–Dec. 1937) 9.

*SHE WHO TURNS HER HEAD.

C254 [Essay] *The New Republic*, LXXXXIII. 1198 (Nov. 17, 1937) 50.

*Review of Wallace Stevens' *The Man with the Blue Guitar and Other Poems*.

C255 [Essay] *New Masses*, XXV. 9 (Nov. 23, 1937) 17–18.

*AN AMERICAN POET.

[Subtitle:] "H. H. Lewis, Missouri dirt farmer and song maker,

evaluated as an instigator to thought about what poetry can and
cannot do."

Review of Lewis' *Red Renaissance, Thinking of Russia, Salvation,*
and *The Road to Utterly.* Compare C239.

C256 [Essay] *Life and Letters Today,* XVII. 10 (Winter 1937) 55–58.
AN AFTERNOON WITH TCHELITCHEW.
In *SE* and *Reader.* Compare C321.

C257 [Poem] *The New Republic,* LXXXXIII. 1200 (Dec. 1, 1937) 92.
THE TERM.
In *CEP.*

1938

C258 [Essay] *The New Republic,* LXXXXIV. 1214 (March 9, 1938)
141–142.
*MURIEL RUKEYSER'S *US1.*
Review of Miss Rukeyser's poems.

C259 [Poem] *Forum,* XCIX. 4 (April 1938) 217.
*MAN AND NATURE.
Reprinted in *New Directions 16* (1957) 27.

C260 [Essay] *The New Republic,* LXXXXIV. 1221 (April 27, 1938)
375–376.
*HARRIET MONROE.
Review of Harriet Monroe's *A Poet's Life: Seventy Years in a
Changing World.*

C261 [Poem] *The New Republic,* LXXXXV. 1228 (June 15, 1938) 155.
THE POOR (It's the anarchy of poverty).
In *CEP.*

C262 [Essay] *New Masses,* XXVIII. 8 (Aug. 16, 1938) 23–25.
*IMAGE AND PURPOSE.
Review of S. Funaroff's *The Spider and the Clock.*

C263 [Answers to a questionnaire] *Twentieth Century Verse,* London,
Nos. 12–13, American Number (Sept.–Oct. 1938) 109.
*About American poetry.
Mark Van Doren, Marianne Moore, Wallace Stevens, and Allen
Tate also answered the three questions.

C264 [Essay] *The New Republic,* LXXXXVI. 1244 [*sic,* should be 1245]
(Oct. 12, 1938) 282–283.

*Review of Walker Evans' *American Photographs* (New York, Museum of Modern Art).

C265 [Contribution to a symposium] *The Harvard Advocate*, CXXV. 3, T. S. Eliot issue (Dec. 1938) 42.

*HOMAGE TO T. S. ELIOT.

Reprinted in *Harvard Advocate Centennial Anthology* (B97).

C266 [Short story] *The Nation*, CXLVII. 24 (Dec. 10, 1938) 623–624.

ABOVE THE RIVER.

In *FD*.

C267 [Letter to the editor] *The New York Times*, LXXXVIII. 29545 (Thurs., Dec. 15, 1938) 26.

*SPECIAL HIGHWAYS FOR FREIGHT.

Letter is dated December 12, 1938.

1939

C268 [Prose descriptions] *New Directions 4* (1939) 243–251.

*THE DRILL SERGEANT—*A BOY IN THE FAMILY— *THE PLUMBER AND THE MINISTER—*THE OFFICIAL DISCLAIMER.

A typed sheet by WCW, YALC, lists "Four Pictures (ND39)," under "LATER STORIES."

C269 [Letter to the editors, Bruce Bliven, Malcolm Cowley, and others] *The New Republic*, LXXXXVII. 1258 (Jan. 11, 1939) 289.

*ON THE SPOT.

About Philip Horton's review of WCW's *The Complete Collected Poems 1906–1938* in *The New Republic* (Dec. 21, 1938).

C270 [Essay] *The Kenyon Review*, Gambier, Ohio, I. 2 (Spring 1939) 148–158.

FEDERICO GARCIA LORCA.

In *SE*.

C271 [Chapter for a novel] *Partisan Review*, New York, VI. 3 (Spring 1939) 92–99.

BACK TO THE CITY.

Chapter 2 of *In the Money* (A21).

C272 [Essay] *Twice a Year*, New York, No. 2 (Spring–Summer 1939) 53–78.

AGAINST THE WEATHER: A STUDY OF THE ARTIST.

In *SE*.

C273 [Short story] *The New Anvil*, Chicago, I.1 (March 1939) 5–8.
THE PAID NURSE.
In *FD*

C274 [Short story] *The New Anvil*, I. 2 (April–May 1939) 16–17.
A LUCKY BREAK.
In *FD*.

C275 [Three poems] *Furioso*, I. 1 (Summer 1939) 7–8.
THE CURE—[C92: Last Words of My English Grandmother]—
IN SISTERLY FASHION.
In *CLP*; THE CURE has some revisions.

C276 [Short story] *Creative Writing*, Chicago, I. 7 (Summer 1939) 3–4.
ANCIENT GENTILITY.
In *FD*.

C277 [Answers to a questionnaire] *Partisan Review*, VI. 4 (Summer
1939) 41–44.
*WILLIAM CARLOS WILLIAMS' REPLY TO "THE SITUA-
TION IN AMERICAN WRITING: SEVEN QUESTIONS."

C278 [Answer to a questionnaire] *The New Republic*, LXXXXIX. 1282
(June 28, 1939) 209.
*AMERICA AND THE NEXT WAR: III.
About American foreign policy.

C279 [Essay] *The New Republic*, LXXXXIX. 1282 (June 28, 1939)
229–230.
*PENNY WISE, POUND FOOLISH.
A review of Ezra Pound's *Culture*.

C280 [Poem] *The New Republic*, LXXXXIX. 1283 (July 5, 1939) 246.
THE SWAGGERING GAIT.
In *CEP*.

C281 [Poem] *Poetry World*, New York (July–Aug. 1939) 8.
THE THOUGHTFUL LOVER.
In *CLP*.

C282 [Six poems] *Poetry*, LIV. 7 (Sept. 1939) 295–301.
ILLEGITIMATE THINGS—*THE POET AND HIS POEMS,
I–II—*DEFIANCE TO CUPID—A COLD FRONT—THE FOR-
GOTTEN CITY—IN CHAINS.
The first poem is in *CEP*, the last three in *CLP*. ILLEGITIMATE
THINGS is reprinted in *Kavita*, Calcutta, XVI. 1 (Dec. 1950) 42–
43, English and Bengali (by Buddhadeva Bose) on facing pages.

Eleven lines, with some changes, of THE POET AND HIS POEMS are in *CLP* with the title THE POEM (It's all in the sound). DEFIANCE TO CUPID is reprinted in *New Directions 16* (1957) 31.

C283 [Poem] *The University Review*, Kansas City, Mo., VI. 1 (Oct. 1939) 40.
*TAILPIECE.
Reprinted in *New Directions 16* (1957) 33.

C284 [Poem] *Matrix*, Philadelphia, II. 1 (Oct. 1939) 24.
FIGUERAS CASTLE.
In *CLP*.

1940

C285 "LETTER TO REED WHITTEMORE [editor]." *Furioso*, I. 2, New Year Issue (1940) 21–23.
In *SE*.

C286 [Poem] *Fantasy*, VI. 4 (1940) 3.
PERFECTION.
In *CLP*.

C287 [Poem] *Compass*, Prairie City, Ill., II. 2–3, Issue 6 (Feb. 1940) 13.
A PORTRAIT OF THE TIMES.
In *CEP*.

C288 [Poem] *The Nation*, CL. 6, Seventy-fifth Anniversary Issue (Feb. 10, 1940) 200.
A VISION OF LABOR.
In *CLP;* titled A VISION OF LABOR: 1931.

C289 [Poem] *Furioso*, I. 3 (Spring 1940) 4–5.
TO FORD MADOX FORD IN HEAVEN.
In *CLP*.

C290 [Poem] *Poetry*, LVI. 2 (May 1940) 69.
RALEIGH WAS RIGHT.
In *CLP*.

C291 [Short story] *Hika*, Gambier, Ohio, VI. 7, Guest Contributor Issue (May 1940) 5.
*JEW.
"Rejected fragment from a recently completed novel, *In the Money* . . ."

C292 [Letter to the editors] *Partisan Review*, VII. 3 (May–June 1940) 247–248.

*POETS AND CRITICS.

Criticism of Randall Jarrell's review of Kenneth Patchen's verse.

C293 [Poem] *The New Republic*, CIII. 8, Issue 1342 (Aug. 19, 1940) 243.

RUMBA! RUMBA!

In *CLP*.

C294 [Poem] *The New Yorker*, New York, XVI. 28 (Aug. 24, 1940) 45.

THE GRACEFUL BASTION.

In *CEP*.

C295 [Essay] *Twice a Year*, Nos. 5–6 (Fall–Winter 1940—Spring–Summer 1941) 402–412.

RAQUEL HÉLÈNE ROSE. "A biography, gathered and roughly assembled from my mother's conversation, followed by a selection from her more recent letters together with the translation of an early 17th century Spanish novel by Quevedo interpolated through the text: 'Qui n'entend qu'un cloche, n'entend qu'un son.' "

Much of the same material as in *The Dog and the Fever* (A39) and *Yes, Mrs. Williams* (A45). Compare C538.

C296 [Essay] *View*, New York, I. 2 (Oct. 1940) 2, 5.

*A NEW BOOK OF THE DEAD.

Review of Norman Macleod's *You Get What You Ask For*. See D1.

C297 [Poem] *Diogenes*, Madison, Wis., I. 1 (Oct.–Nov. 1940) [2].

*THE SLEEPING BRUTE.

C298 [Seven poems] *Poetry*, LVII. 2 (Nov. 1940) 125–129.

THE OBSERVER—*FROM A WINDOW—*RIVER RHYME (The rumpled river)—THE WORLD NARROWED TO A POINT —A FOND FAREWELL—FERTILE—THE UNKNOWN.

A FOND FAREWELL and THE UNKNOWN are in *CEP*. The others are in *CLP* except for the starred poems, which are in *New Directions 16* (1957) 31–32.

C299 [Four poems] *Matrix*, II. 6 (Nov.–Dec. 1940) 20–21.

*SKETCH FOR A PORTRAIT OF HENRY FORD—*AN INFORMATIVE OBJECT—*TO A WOMAN SEEN ONCE— *THE NEW CLOUDS.

C300 [Contribution to a symposium] *The Harvard Advocate*, CXXVII. 3, Wallace Stevens issue (Dec. 1940) 32.

*STATEMENTS ABOUT WALLACE STEVENS.

Reprinted, untitled, in *Harvard Advocate Centennial Anthology* (B97).

1941

C301 [Translated poem] *The Nation*, CLII. 1 (Jan. 4, 1941) 23–24.
*JOHN LANDLESS AT THE FINAL PORT.
Translated from the French of Yvan Goll. See B45.

C302 [Short story] *Decision*, New York, I. 2 (Feb. 1941) 21–27.
THE ZOO.
In *FD* and *Reader*.

C303 [Letter to the editor, George Dillon] *Poetry*, LVIII. 2 (May 1941) 112.
*A WARM WORD FOR [David] DAICHES.

C304 [Poem] *The Providence Sunday Journal*, Providence, R.I. (May 4, 1941) Section VI, Feature Section, 2.
*DEFENSE.
Reprinted in *New Directions 16* (1957) 33–34.

C305 [Poem] *Partisan Review*, VIII. 4 (July–Aug. 1941) 311–312.
*AN EXULTATION.
A prose footnote by WCW follows the poem.

C306 [Essay] *Now*, New York, I. 1 (Aug. 1941) 18–24.
MIDAS: A PROPOSAL FOR A MAGAZINE.
"This article was to preface a new magazine which failed to appear due to lack of funds." In *SE*.

C307 [Essay] *The Columbia Review*, XXIII (Autumn 1941) 1–5.
*THE POET IN TIME OF CONFUSION.
About the utility of art.

C308 [Essay] *Decision*, II. 3 (Sept. 1941) 16–24.
*EZRA POUND: LORD GA-GA!

C309 [Poem] *The New Yorker*, XVII. 37 (Oct. 25, 1941) 41.
THE HOUNDED LOVERS.
In *CLP*.

1942

C310 [Essay] *Fantasy*, X. 26 (1942) 102–107.
[Title on cover of *Fantasy*:] *A COUNSEL OF MADNESS.
Review of Kenneth Patchen's *The Journal of Albion Moonlight*.

C311 [Play] *New Directions 7* (1942) 233–305.
TRIAL HORSE NO. 1 (MANY LOVES): AN ENTERTAINMENT IN THREE ACTS AND SIX SCENES.

Retitled simply MANY LOVES in *Many Loves and Other Plays* (A47). Reprinted with the title MANY LOVES and some changes in *Theatre Arts,* New York, XLVI. 2 (Feb. 1962) [25]–56.

C312 [Essay] *New Directions 7* (1942) 413–414.
*A GROUP OF POEMS BY MARCIA NARDI: INTRODUC-TION BY WILLIAM CARLOS WILLIAMS WHO DISCOV-ERED HER.

C313 [Essay] *New Directions 7* (1942) 429–436.
*MEN . . . HAVE NO TENDERNESS.
Review of Anais Nin's *Winter of Artifice.*

C314 [Contribution to a symposium] *New Directions 7* (1942) 490–491.
*HOMAGE TO FORD MADOX FORD—A SYMPOSIUM.

C315 [Contribution to a symposium] *Trend,* Chicago, I. 1 (Jan. 1942) 3–5.
*THE INVISIBLE UNIVERSITY. THE POET, THE TEACHER, AND THE STUDENT: A SYMPOSIUM.

C316 [Letter to Dwight Macdonald, editor] *Partisan Review,* IX. 1 (Jan.–Feb. 1942) 39.
*ON THE "BROOKS-MACLEISH THESIS."
About Van Wyck Brooks's theory of modern literature, as discussed in Macdonald's "Kulturbolschewismus Is Here" in *Partisan Review,* VIII. 6 (Nov.–Dec. 1941) 442–451.

C317 [Answers to a questionnaire] *View,* I. 11–12 (Feb.–March 1942) 10.
*TOWARD THE UNKNOWN.
The questions are: "1. What do you see in the stars? 2. What is the disappearing point of the unconscious? 3. What value does death give to life?"

C318 [Poem] *Harper's Bazaar,* New York, No. 2762, 75th Year (March 1, 1942) 49.
*WAR THE DESTROYER! (For Martha Graham).
Reprinted in *New Directions 16* (1957) 36–37.

C319 [Short story] *Trend,* I. 4 (April 1942) 4–7, 25.
COMEDY ENTOMBED.
Reprinted in *New Directions 9* (1946) 315–323, and, with the title COMEDY ENTOMBED: 1930, in *Perspectives U.S.A.,* No. 1 (Fall 1952) 27–36 [published also in French, German, and Italian editions].

C: Periodicals

In *FD*.

C320 [Two poems] *The Harvard Advocate,* CXXVIII. 4, 75th Anniversary Issue (April 1942) 43.

    I. *PASSAIC, N. J.—II. *FROM A PLAY.

    FROM A PLAY is reprinted in *Harvard Advocate Centennial Anthology* (B97).

C321 [Essay] *View,* II, 2 (May 1942) [17–18].

    *CACHE CACHE.

    About Tchelitchew; dated at end of essay, "Easter Day, 1942." *SE* mistakenly gives *View* as the first printing of "An Afternoon with Tchelitchew"—see C256.

C322 [Letter to Charles Henri Ford, editor] *View,* II, 2 (May 1942) [19].

    *SURREALISM AND THE MOMENT.

C323 [Poem] *VVV,* New York, No. 1 (June 1942) 3.

    CATASTROPHIC BIRTH.

    Dated at end, "April 22, 1942." In *CLP*.

C324 [Essay] *Poetry,* LX. 6 (Sept. 1942) 338–340.

    *AN EXTRAORDINARY SENSITIVITY.

    Review of Louis Zukofsky's *55 Poems.*

C325 [Essay] *View,* II. 3 (Oct. 1942) 23.

    *ADVICE TO THE YOUNG POET.

C326 ["Translated" poem] *American Prefaces,* Iowa City, Iowa, VII. 2 (Winter 1942) 155–157.

    *PRELUDE IN BORICUA. [Boricua is a corruption of the old native name for Puerto Rico.]

    Interpreted from the Spanish of Luis Pales Matos. Introductory note by WCW: "This not-to-be-called translation of Matos' introductory poem from the collection *Tuntun de Pasa y Griferia* is offered with profound apologies to the poet. It is no more than an approximate translation which makes no attempt to give the musical sense of the original. Some of the words cannot be rendered in English at all. . . . *Poemas Afroantillanos* [poem as one word] is what Matos calls them. . . ."

    Reprinted, with changes, in *Upstate,* Buffalo, N.Y., III. 3 (Autumn 1943) 26.

C327 [Poem] *Palisade,* Indianola, Iowa, I. 4 (Winter 1942) 66.

    THE DANCE (In Breughel's great picture, The Kermess).

In *CLP*. Reprinted in *The Bulletin of the New York Public Library*, XLVII. 11 (Nov. 1943) 826, with acknowledgment to *Palisade*. See B44.

1943

C328 [Poem] *Partisan Review*, X. 1 (Jan.–Feb. 1943) 58–59.
THE SEMBLABLES.
In *CLP*.

C329 [Essay] *Retort*, Bearsville, N. Y., I. 4 (Spring 1943) 56–58.
*RETORTING.
Unsigned editorial defending the magazine's criticism of Marxism; attributed to WCW by Vivienne Koch in *William Carlos Williams* (B57), p. 270.

C330 [Poem] *View*, III. 1 (April 1943) 19.
PATERSON: THE FALLS.
In *CLP*, but not in *Paterson*.

C331 [Poem] *The Old Line*, College Park, Md., XII. 6, International Literary Issue (April 1943) 19.
A POSSIBLE SORT OF SONG.
In *CLP;* retitled A SORT OF A SONG, with other changes. Reprinted in *The University Review*, X. 3 (Spring 1944) 200–201, with the latter title.

C332 [Poem] *Hemispheres*, French American Quarterly, Brooklyn, N.Y., No. 1 (Summer 1943) 29.
THE CLOUDS, I.
This is the first section only of THE CLOUDS in *CLP*.

C333 [Three poems] *American Prefaces*, VIII. 4 (Summer 1943) 295–296.
*GOTHIC CANDOR—THE YELLOW CHIMNEY—*LILLIAN (Wandering among the chimneys).
GOTHIC CANDOR is reprinted in *New Directions 16* (1957) 23. LILLIAN is in a slightly different version in *The Wedge* (A23), where it is titled THE GENTLE NEGRESS; this poem in *The Wedge* is not the same poem as THE GENTLE NEGRESS which appeared in *Palisade* (C340), but the subject is the same. THE YELLOW CHIMNEY is in *CLP*. In a letter to Reed Whittemore, 1939, Williams wrote: "The Lilian [*sic*] piece is a parody of Yeats' 'Down by the Salley Gardens'" [quoted by John Thirlwall in *New Directions 17* (1961) 264].

C334 [Two poems] *Palisade*, II. 2 (Summer 1943) 23–24.
I. STORM—II. AN ADDRESS.
In *CLP*; STORM titled THE STORM. AN ADDRESS is not the
same poem as ADDRESS which appeared in *The Quarterly Review
of Literature* (C352).

C335 [Poem] *The New Republic*, CIX. 8, Issue 1499 (Aug. 23, 1943) 251.
THE MONSTROUS MARRIAGE.
In *CLP*.

C336 [Letter to the editor] *The New Republic*, CIX. 8, Issue 1499 (Aug.
23, 1943) 256.
*PAPER SHORTAGE, POETS AND POSTAL RATES.

C337 [Short story] *Matrix*, No. 1 (Fall 1943) 40–47.
THE BURDEN OF LOVELINESS.
In *FD* and *Reader*.

C338 [Letter to the editors] *Partisan Review*, X. 5 (Sept.–Oct. 1943) 466–
468.
*A FAULT OF LEARNING: A COMMUNICATION.
This is followed by a disapproving editorial note titled "The
Politics of W. C. Williams."

C339 [Poem] *The New Yorker*, XIX. 40 (Nov. 20, 1943) 69.
THE END OF THE PARADE.
In *CLP*.

C340 [Poem] *Palisade*, II. 4 (Winter 1943) 81.
*THE GENTLE NEGRESS (No other such luxuriance).
Reprinted in *New Directions 16* (1957) 37. See C333.

1944

C341 [Poem] *Circle*, Berkeley, I. 2 (1944) [32].
TO THE DEAN.
"Written in tribute to Henry Miller for the compendium of Mil-
lerana being gathered by Bern Porter for publication this fall"
(B46). In *CLP²*. Reprinted in *New Directions 16* (1957) 40.

C342 [Poem] *New Directions 8* (1944) 66–70.
TO ALL GENTLENESS.
In *CLP*.

C343 [Poem] *Partisan Review*, XI. 1 (Winter [Jan.] 1944) 42.
THESE PURISTS.
In *CLP*.

C344 [Poem] *Rocky Mountain Review*, Murray, Utah, VIII. 2 (Winter [Jan.] 1944) 23.
THE PROVINCE.
In *CEP* and *CLP*.

C345 [Poem] *Poetry*, LXIII. 4 (Jan. 1944) 207–209.
BURNING THE CHRISTMAS GREENS.
In *CLP*.

C346 [Essay] *The University Review*, Kansas City, Mo., X. 3 (Spring 1944) 198–199.
INTRODUCTION.
Brief biographical note by WCW on p. 224. The INTRODUC-TION was written for *The Wedge* (A23) and is also in *SE*.

C347 [Five poems] *The University Review*, X. 3 (Spring 1944) 200–201.
[C331: A Sort of a Song]—*THE VIRTUOUS AGENT—A FLOWING RIVER—THE AFTERMATH—THE BARE TREE.
In *CLP*.

C348 [Poem] *Experiment*, Salt Lake City, Utah, I. 1 (April 1944) 11.
*THINKING BACK TOWARD CHRISTMAS: A STATE-MENT FOR THE VIRGIN.

C349 [Contribution to a symposium] *View*, IV. 2 (Summer 1944) 61–62.
*HERBERT READ'S "POLITICS OF THE UNPOLITICAL."
The contributors are listed as Nicolas Calas, Nicola Chiarmonte, Parker Tyler, and "Thug" Williams.

C350 [One-act play] *The University of Kansas City Review*, XI. 1 (Autumn 1944) 26–28.
*UNDER THE STARS.
Dialogue between Washington and Lafayette after the battle of Monmouth about the conduct of General Charles Lee. Lee's behavior is also the subject of Act II, Scene 1, of *The First President*, first published in 1936 (B26) and reprinted in *Many Loves* (A47). See D20.

C351 [Poem] *Orígenes*, Revista de Arte y Literatura, Habana, Cuba, I. 3 (otoño 1944) 22–23.
THE BITTER WORLD OF SPRING || EL MUNDO AMARGO DE LA PRIMAVERA.
English and Spanish on facing pages; translation by José Rodríguez Feo. In *CLP*. Reprinted in *The Quarterly Review of Literature*, New Haven, II. 2 ([1945]) 90.

1945

C352 [Fifteen poems] "Summary of a Year's Verse." *The Quarterly Review of Literature*, II. 2 ([1945]) 89–99.

THE WORDS LYING IDLE—[C351: The Bitter World of Spring]—LAMENT—TO A LOVELY OLD BITCH—THE DISH OF FRUIT—A HISTORY OF LOVE, 1–3—THE GOAT—SUNFLOWERS—ADDRESS—THE MIRRORS—THRENODY—THE RARE GIST—THE CLOUDS, II—THE CLOUDS, III—THE CLOUDS, IV.

In *CLP;* ADDRESS is retitled THE HURRICANE; SUNFLOWERS, THRENODY, and THE RARE GIST are in *CLP²* and are reprinted in *New Directions 16* (1957) 38–39. THE DISH OF FRUIT is reprinted in *The General Magazine and Historical Chronicle,* Philadelphia, XLVII. 4 (Summer 1945) 220–221.

C353 [Essay] *The Quarterly Review of Literature,* New Haven, II. 2 [1945] 125–126.

*THE FATAL BLUNDER.

About T. S. Eliot.

C354 [Essay] *The Quarterly Review of Literature,* II. 2 [1945] 145–149.

*IN PRAISE OF MARRIAGE.

Review of Kenneth Rexroth's *The Phoenix and the Turtle.* See C358.

C355 [Poem] *Tomorrow,* New York, IV. 7 (March 1945) 45.

TO A SPARROW.

In *CLP².*

C356 [Three poems] *The General Magazine and Historical Chronicle,* Philadelphia, XLVII. 4 (Summer 1945) 220–221.

THE STATUE—APRIL 6—[C352: The Dish of Fruit].

In *CLP;* THE STATUE is retitled HARD TIMES; APRIL 6 is retitled AIGELTINGER—in this first version the spelling is Aegeltinger throughout the poem.

C357 [Poem] *Briarcliff Quarterly,* Briarcliff Manor, N.Y., II. 6 (July 1945) 98.

FRANKLIN SQUARE.

In *CLP.*

C358 [Poem] *Pacific,* Oakland, Calif., I. 1 (Nov. 1945) 47–48.

THE PHOENIX AND THE TORTOISE.

In *CEP.* See C354.

C359 [Contribution to a symposium] *PM*, New York, VI. 138 (Sun., Nov. 25, 1945), Magazine Section, 16.

*THE CASE FOR AND AGAINST EZRA POUND.

See *The Case of Ezra Pound* (B53).

1946

C360 [Translated poems] "Translations of Paul Eluard—Poet of France." *New Directions* 9 (1946) 343–345.

*A WOLF (The good snow the sky black)—*A WOLF (The day astonishes and the night fills me with fear)—*UNCERTAIN OF THE CRIME—*CURFEW—*FROM THE OUTSIDE— *FROM THE INSIDE.

C361 [Essay] *The Quarterly Review of Literature*, New Haven, II. 4 ([1946]) 346–349.

*PREFACE.

Prepublication review of Byron Vazakas' *Transfigured Night;* reprinted as Introduction to *Transfigured Night* (B49).

C362 [Poem] *Yale Poetry Review*, New Haven, I. 3 (Spring 1946) 19.

CHANSON.

In *CLP*.

C363 [Poem] *Arizona Quarterly*, Tucson, Ariz., II. 1 (Spring 1946) 4.

THE HORSE.

In *CLP*.

C364 [Essay] *The Harvard Wake*, Cambridge, No. 5, Special E. E. Cummings Issue with José García Villa as Guest Editor (Spring 1946) 20–23.

LOWER CASE CUMMINGS.

In *SE* and *Reader*.

C365 [Nine poems] "The Peacock's Eyes." *The Harvard Wake*, No. 5 (Spring 1946) 80–82.

1. THE MANOEUVRE—2. THE BANNER BEARER—3. THE THING—4. THE ACT—5. *HEY RED!—6. THE NIGHT RIDER—7. THE BRILLIANCE—8. DEATH BY RADIO (For F. D. R.)—9. THE BIRDSONG.

THE BRILLIANCE is in both *CEP* and *CLP*. DEATH BY RADIO is in *CLP²*, and is reprinted in *New Directions 16* (1957) 38. The other unstarred poems are in *CLP*.

C366 [Poem] *Contemporary Poetry*, Baltimore, VI. 1 (Spring 1946) 6–7.
THE MIND'S GAMES.
In *CLP*.

C367 [Essay] *Accent*, Urbana, Ill., VI. 3 (Spring 1946) 203–206.
*Review of Parker Tyler's *The Granite Butterfly*.

C368 [Poem] *Briarcliff Quarterly*, III. 9 (April 1946) 1–2.
THE VISIT.
In *CLP*.

C369 [Poem] *The New Republic*, CXIV. 17, Issue 1639 (April 29, 1946) 615.
RUSSIA.
In *CLP*.

C370 [Four poems] *Yale Poetry Review*, II. 1 (Summer 1946) 19–22.
EAST COOCOO—OL' BUNK'S BAND—THE SAVAGE BEAST—AT KENNETH BURKE'S PLACE.
In *CLP*; EAST COOCOO and AT KENNETH BURKE'S PLACE are in *CLP²*, and are reprinted in *New Directions 16* (1957) 40–42.

C371 [Poem] *The Nation*, CLXII. (June 22, 1946) 751–752.
THE INJURY.
In *CLP*

C372 [Poem] *Poetry*, The Australian International Quarterly of Verse, Lucindale, South Australia, No. 19 (June 30, 1946) 22.
*" · THE ROCK-OLD DOGMA · "

C373 [Essay] *View*, VII. 1 (Fall 1946) 43–47.
*THE GENIUS OF FRANCE.
Review of André Breton's *Young Cherry Trees Secured against Hares*.

C374 [Poem] *Briarcliff Quarterly*, III. 11 (Oct. 1946) William Carlos Williams issue, 165–168.
CHORAL: THE PINK CHURCH.
Celia Thaew (Mrs. Louis Zukofsky) set the poem to music, which is printed on two coated leaves inserted between pp. 192 and 193. In *CLP*. See *The Pink Church* (A29).
This issue of *Briarcliff Quarterly* contains, in addition to the items listed below, many photographs of WCW and his family and a reproduction of the Stuart Davis drawing that was used as the frontispiece to *Kora in Hell* (A4).

C375 [Poem] *Briarcliff Quarterly,* III. 11 (Oct. 1946) 175.
APPROACH TO A CITY.
In *CLP.* Reprinted in *Chelsea Twelve* (Sept. 1962) 126–127, with an Italian translation by Vittorio Sereni.

C376 [Chapter for a novel] *Briarcliff Quarterly,* III. 11 (Oct. 1946) 176–184.
THE BUILD-UP. 1.

C377 [Poem] *Briarcliff Quarterly,* III. 11 (Oct. 1946) 185.
FOR A LOW VOICE.
In *CLP.*

C378 [Letter] *Briarcliff Quarterly,* III. 11 (Oct. 1946) 205–208.
*LETTER TO AN AUSTRALIAN EDITOR.
About Ezra Pound. The Australian editor is Flexmore Hudson, who reprinted the letter in *Poetry,* The Australian International Quarterly of Verse, No. 25 (Dec. 10, 1947) 7–12.

C379 [Poem] *Harper's Bazaar,* No. 2819, 80th Year (Nov. 1946) 391.
*THE USURERS OF HEAVEN.

C380 [Poem] *The Kenyon Review,* VIII. 1 (Winter 1946) [55]–58.
A PLACE (ANY PLACE) TO TRANSCEND ALL PLACES.
In *CLP.*

C381 [Essay] *The Kenyon Review,* VIII. 1 (Winter 1946) 123–126.
SHAPIRO IS ALL RIGHT.
Review of Karl Shapiro's *Essay on Rime.* In *SE.*

C382 [Poem] *The Nation,* CLXIII. 23 (Dec. 7, 1946) 649.
A UNISON.
In *CLP.*

1947

C383 [Poem] *The Nation,* CLXIV. 8 (Feb. 22, 1947) 240.
LABRADOR.
In *CLP.*

C384 [Short story] *The Ark,* San Francisco (Spring 1947) 55–58.
INQUEST.
In *FD.*

C385 [Three poems] *The New Leader,* New York, XXX. 9 (March 1, 1947) 12.
HIS DAUGHTER—THE RED-WING BLACKBIRD—PICTURES OF A NUDE IN A MACHINE SHOP.

In *CLP*.

C386 [Poem] *Partisan Review*, XIV. 3 (May–June 1947) 296.
THE APPARITION.
In *CLP*.

C387 [Essay] *Yale Poetry Review*, No. 7 ([Summer] 1947) 11–13.
REVELATION.
In *SE*.

C388 [Poem] *Cronos*, Columbus, Ohio, I. 3 (Fall 1947) 36.
LUSTSPIEL.
In *CLP* with some changes.

C389 [Poem] *Poetry*, LXXI. 1, 35th Anniversary Number (Oct. 1947) 30.
FROM "PATERSON: BOOK II."
[First and last lines:] America the golden! . . . and take our
hats/in hand. In *Paterson, Two*, II, 85.

C390 [Three poems] *Accent*, VII. 2 (Winter 1947) 84–85.
THE MOTOR-BARGE—THE UNITED STATES—*THE RE-
SEMBLANCE.
The first is in *CLP*, the second in *CEP*.

C391 [Two poems] *Contemporary Poetry*, VI. 4 (Winter 1947) 3–4.
RAINDROPS ON A BRIAR—THE LIGHT SHALL NOT
ENTER.
In *CLP*.

C392 [Essay] *The New Quarterly of Poetry*, New York, II. 2 (Winter
1947–1948) 8–16.
*A NEW LINE IS A NEW MEASURE.
Review of Louis Zukofsky's *Anew*, a book of poems published in
1946. See G11.

1948

C393 [Essay] *The Quarterly Review of Literature*, Annandale-on-Hudson,
N.Y., IV. 2, Marianne Moore Issue ([1948]) 125–126.
MARIANNE MOORE.
In *SE*, pp. 292–294.

C394 [Three poems] *Yale Poetry Review*, No. 8 (1948) 4–5.
NAVAJO—THE GRAPH—A WOMAN IN FRONT OF A
BANK.
In *CLP*; THE GRAPH is titled simply GRAPH.

C395 [Poem] *Botteghe Oscure,* Rome, Quaderno II (MCMXLVIII) 300–302.

THE BIRTH OF VENUS.

In *CLP.*

C396 [Two poems] *Interim,* Seattle, Wash., III. 3 (1948) 20–21.

THE SEA FARER—THE SOUND OF WAVES.

In *CLP*; THE SEA FARER is titled simply SEAFARER.

C397 [Essay] *Touchstone,* New York, I. 3 (Jan. 1948) 2–7.

*VS.

About the need for a new prosody; similar to a talk given early in the same month at New York University.

C398 [Three poems] *Partisan Review,* XV. 2 (Feb. 1948) 213–216.

FROM "PATERSON: BOOK II.

[First and last lines:] I. Signs everywhere of birds nesting, while . . . . He is led forward by their announcing wings. II. The descent beckons . . . . endless and indestructible. III. On this most voluptuous night of the year . . . . and nothing disturb the full octave of its run.

I is in *Paterson, Two,* I, 61–63. II is in *DM,* 3–4, where it is titled THE DESCENT, and *Paterson, Two,* III, 96–97. III is in *Paterson, Two,* III, 105.

C399 [Essay] *Four Pages,* Galveston, Texas, No. 2 (Feb. 1948) 1–4.

*WITH FORCED FINGERS RUDE.

About T. S. Eliot.

C400 [Four poems] *Wake, Cambridge,* No. 6 (Spring 1948) 50–52.

THE MIND HESITANT—THE COUNTER—TRAGIC DETAIL—MISTS OVER THE RIVER.

In *CLP*; THE COUNTER is in *CLP²*.

C401 [Poem] *Cronos,* II. 4 (March 1948) 33.

PERIOD PIECE: 1834.

In *CLP².*

C402 [Poem] *The Tiger's Eye,* Westport, Conn., I. 3 (March 15, 1948) 80–81.

THE OLD HOUSE.

In *CLP.*

C403 [Essay] *Poetry,* LXXII. 1 (April 1948) 38–41.

*THE STEEPLE'S EYE.

Review of Robert Frost's *A Masque of Mercy.*

C404 [Poem] *Poetry*, LXXII. 2 (May 1948) 59–60.
LEAR.
In *CLP.*

C405 [Two poems] *The General Magazine and Historical Chronicle,*
L. 4 (Summer 1948) 210.
THE PAUSE—BRAHMS FIRST PIANO CONCERTO.
In *CLP*; the second poem is retitled NOTE TO MUSIC:
BRAHMS 1ST PIANO CONCERTO. See D4.

C406 [Essay] *The General Magazine and Historical Chronicle,* L. 4
(Summer 1948) 211–213.
SOMETHING FOR A BIOGRAPHY.
About Ezra Pound, activities at the University of Pennsylvania,
and writing, this essay with revisions is part of Chapter 12 in *The
Autobiography* (A35). See D4. Compare C410, 414, 427.

C407 [Poem] *The Golden Goose,* Columbus, Ohio, No. 1 (Summer
1948) 5.
NEW MEXICO.
In *CLP.*

C408 [Two poems] "Two Deliberate Exercises." *The Kenyon Review,*
X. 3 (Summer 1948) 427–429.
I. LESSON FROM A PUPILS' [*sic*] RECITAL (For Agnes)—
II. VOYAGES.
In *CLP*; the poems are indexed under the single title TWO DE-
LIBERATE EXERCISES.

C409 [Two poems] *Imagi,* Baltimore, IV. 2 (Summer–Fall 1948) 1–2.
APRIL IS THE SADDEST MONTH—SONG (If I could count
the silence).
In *CLP.*

C410 "SOME NOTES TOWARD AN AUTOBIOGRAPHY." *Poetry,*
LXXII. 3 (June 1948) 147–155.
THE CHILDISH BACKGROUND, I.
Similar to the first three chapters of *The Autobiography* (A35).
Compare C406, 414, 427.

C411 [Letter] *The Tiger's Eye,* I. 4 (June 15, 1948) 29–31.
*A LETTER, TOUCHING THE COMINTERN, UPON CEN-
SORSHIP IN THE ARTS.
Also the "Tale of the Contents," p. 70, contains by WCW a brief
statement that accompanied "A Letter."

C412 [Poem] *Harper's Magazine,* New York, CXCVII. 1178 (July 1948) 62.

THE WELL DISCIPLINED BARGEMAN.

In *CLP.*

C413 [Poem] *Harper's Magazine,* CXCVII. 1179 (Aug. 1948) 58.

FOR G.B.S., OLD.

In *CLP.*

C414 "SOME NOTES TOWARD AN AUTOBIOGRAPHY." *Poetry,* LXXII. 5 (Aug. 1948) 264–270.

THE CHILDISH BACKGROUND, II.

Expanded and differently organized in *The Autobiography* (A35). Compare C406, 410, 427.

C415 [Essay] *Four Pages,* No. 8 (Aug. 1948) 3.

*ON BASIL BUNTING'S POEM IN *FOUR PAGES.*

Bunting's poem was in issue No. 5 (May 1948) 3.

C416 [Three poems] *The Golden Goose,* Columbus, Ohio, I. 2 (Autumn 1948) 30–31.

*THE MODEST ACHIEVEMENT—*NO GOOD TOO—MAMA.

The last poem is in *CLP.*

C417 [Poem] *Partisan Review,* XV. 10 (Oct. 1948) 1101.

THE TESTAMENT OF PERPETUAL CHANGE.

In *CLP.*

C418 [Essay] *The Nation,* CLXVII. 18 (Oct. 30, 1948) 498–499.

* EAT ROCKS.

Review of Emery Neff's *Edwin Arlington Robinson,* a critical biography in The American Men of Letters Series.

C419 [Essay] *The New York Times Book Review,* LIII. 47 (Sun., Nov. 21, 1948) 50.

*POETRY WITH AN IMPRESSIVE HUMAN SPEECH.

Review of David Ignatow's *Poems.*

C420 [Poem] *Partisan Review,* XV. 12 (Dec. 1948) 1308–1309.

THE LION, 1–2.

In *CLP.*

1949

C421 "FOURTEEN NEW POEMS." *New Directions 11* (1949) 355–364.

MAY 1ST TOMORROW—APRÈS LE BAIN—SPRING IS

HERE AGAIN, SIR—THE HARD CORE OF BEAUTY—TOL-STOY—CUCHULAIN—TWELVE LINE POEM—NUN'S SONG—ANOTHER OLD WOMAN—WIDE AWAKE, FULL OF LOVE—SONG (Pluck the florets)—SONG (Russia! Russia!)—TRANSLATION—CONVIVO.

IN *CLP*; TRANSLATION is in *CLP*². MAY 1ST TOMORROW is reprinted in *Poetry Ireland*, Cork, Ireland, No. 7, An American Issue (Oct. 1949) 20. WIDE AWAKE, FULL OF LOVE is reprinted in *The Quarterly Review of Literature*, IV. 4 [1949] 358–359. SONG (Russia! Russia!) is retitled NO SONG in *Wake*, New York, No. 8 (Autumn 1949) 96–97, and has other changes. TRANSLATION is retitled IMITATION OF A TRANSLATION in *Wake*, No. 8 (Autumn 1949) 95; "Chloe" in the first line is changed to "Sweet" in *Wake* and *CLP*².

C422 [Three poems] *The Quarterly Review of Literature*, Annandale-on-Hudson, N.Y., IV. 4 ([1949]) 356–359.

THE RAT—THE HORSE SHOW—[C421: Wide Awake, Full of Love].

In *CLP*.

C423 [Two poems] "Two Pendants (for the ears)." *Botteghe Oscure*, Quaderno IV (MCMXLIX) 340–355.

I. THE PARTICULARS OF MORNING ARE BETTER THAN NIGHT'S VAGUE IMAGES—II. ELENA.

In *CLP*; some changes; indexed with the title TWO PENDANTS: FOR THE EARS.

C424 [Poem] *Interim*, III. 4 (1949–1950) 20.

THE SALE.

In *CLP*².

C425 [Essay] *Imagi*, Allentown, Pa., IV. 4 (Spring 1949) 10–11.

*THE FISTULA OF THE LAW

Review of Ezra Pound's *The Pisan Cantos*, which won for Pound in February, 1949, the first $1000 Bollingen poetry award.

C426 [Poem] *Zero*, Paris, No. 1 (Spring 1949) 63–65.

ALL THAT IS PERFECT IN WOMAN.

In *CLP*.

C427 "NOTES TOWARD AN AUTOBIOGRAPHY." *Poetry*, LXXIV. 2 (May 1949) 94–111.

THE CHILDISH BACKGROUND.

Expanded and differently organized in *The Autobiography* (A35).
Compare C406, 410, 414.

C428 [Poem] *Gale,* Arroyo Hondo, N.M., I. 2 (May 1949) 15.
SONG, FROM PATTERSON [*sic*] III. [First and last lines:]
The birds in winter . . . . with the rose.
In *Paterson, Three,* III, 168–169.

C429 [Short story] *Zero,* Tangier, Morocco, No. 2 (Summer 1949) 85–96.
COUNTRY RAIN.
In *FD.*

C430 [Essay] *The Golden Goose,* Columbus, Ohio, No. 3 (June 1949)
29–30.
*NOTE ON UNIVERSITY INSTRUCTION IN THE NA-
TURE OF THE POEM.
Probably based on a talk given by WCW at the University of
Washington, May 16, 1948.

C431 [Poem] *The Tiger's Eye,* I. 8 (June 15, 1949) 1–4.
PART OF PATERSON III. [First and last lines:] With due
ceremony a hut would be constructed . . . . Unabashed. So be it.
In *Paterson, Three,* II, 138–142.

C432 [Three poems] *Wake,* New York, No. 8 (Autumn 1949) 95–97.
[C421: Imitation of a Translation]—AN ETERNITY—[C421:
No Song (Russia! Russia!)].
AN ETERNITY has some revisions in *CLP.*

C433 [Poem] *Poetry,* LXXV. 3 (Nov. 1949) 88.
THE THREE GRACES.
In *CLP.*

C434 [Poem] *12th Street,* New York, III. 1, Poetry Issue (Dec. 1949)
9–11.
PATERSON: BOOK III | PREFACE. [First and last lines:]
Blow! So be it. Bring down! So be it. Consume . . . . So be it. So
be it. So be it.]
In *Paterson, Three,* I. 120, with some changes.

C435 [Essay] *12th Street,* III. 1, Poetry Issue (Dec. 1949) 27.
*BRIEF NOTE ON A RECENT TALK.
About the American language. The "recent talk" was probably
the one given by WCW at Brandeis University, November 2, 1949.

C436 [Poem] *Glass Hill,* Buffalo, N.Y., No. 2 (Dec. 1949) [7].

3 A.M. | THE GIRL WITH THE HONEY COLORED HAIR
(For C.A.).
In *CLP* the dedication is omitted.

1950

C437 [Poem] *New Directions 12* (1950) 422.
THE SELF.
In *CLP²*.

C438 [Poem] *Poetry New York*, New York, No. 3 (1950) 24–25.
MONEY, FROM PATERSON, BOOK IV. [First and last lines:]
MONEY : JOKE (i.e., crime . . . . to be wiped out sooner or later
at a stroke/of thought.
In *Paterson, Four*, II, 214–215, with some changes.

C439 [Short story] *Wake*, New York, No. 9 (1950) 22–25.
THE ROUND THE WORLD FLIERS.
In *FD*.

C440 [Poem] *Wake*, No. 9 (1950) 67.
SONG: FROM PATERSON IV. [First and last lines:] You
dreamy/Communist . . . . together.
In *Paterson, Four*, I, 189–190.

C441 [Letter to the editor, Theodore Weiss] *The Quarterly Review of
Literature*, Annandale-on-Hudson, N.Y., V. 3 ([1950]) 301.
*In praise of the Ezra Pound issue of the magazine.

C442 [Two poems] *Imagi*, Baltimore, Md., V. 2, Issue 13 (1950) 19.
MOON AND STARS—THE GIRL (The wall, as I watched,
came neck-high).
In *CEP*. Reprinted in *New Directions 16* (1957) 43–44.

C443 [Interview] *The New York Times Book Review*, LV. 3 (Sun., Jan.
15, 1950) 18.
TALK WITH W. C. WILLIAMS BY HARVEY BREIT.
See B68.

C444 [Poem] *Gale*, II. 1 (Feb. 1950) 4.
*POEM (Looking up, of a sudden).

C445 [Essay] *The New York Times Book Review*, LV. 11 (Sun., March
12, 1950) 14.
*DIAMONDS IN BLUE CLAY.

Review of Peter Viereck's *Strike through the Mask*.

C446 [Essay] *The New York Post* (Sun., March 12, 1950).
*IT'S ABOUT "YOUR LIFE AND MINE, DARLING."
Review of T. S. Eliot's *The Cocktail Party*.

C447 [Poem] *Janus*, Paris, No. 2 (Avril 1950) 30.
AND WHO DO YOU THINK "THEY" ARE?
In *CLP*.

C448 [Interview] *Paterson Morning Call*, Paterson, N.J. (Thurs., May 4, 1950) 12.
*POET-PEDIATRICIAN TELLS WHY HE CHOSE TO WRITE ABOUT PATERSON.
WCW interviewed by Staff Correspondent.

C449 [Essay] *The General Magazine and Historical Chronicle*, LIII. 1 (Autumn 1950) 40–41.
*PICASSO BREAKS FACES.
First printed on a broadsheet announcing a Picasso show at a New York art gallery (D5) with the title *PICASSO STICKS OUT AN INVESTED WORLD and a different beginning.

C450 [Letter to the editor, Richard Rubenstein] *Gryphon*, San Francisco, No. 2 (Fall 1950) 32.
*About "the poem IS stronger than stupidity."

C451 [Two poems] *Kavita*, Calcutta, XVI. 1, Series 67, Special Bilingual Issue (Dec. 1950) 4, 42–43.
SONNET IN SEARCH OF AN AUTHOR—[C282: Illegitimate Things].
Bengali by Buddhadeva Bose. In *PB* and in Horace Mann School Edition of *CLP*, signed copies only (A31d). SONNET is reprinted in *The Nation*, CLXXXII. 15 (April 14, 1956) 313, and in *New Directions 16* (1957) 7.

1951

C452 [Poem] *The Quarterly Review of Literature*, Annandale-on-Hudson, N.Y., VI. 1 ([1951]) 50–52.
PATERSON, BOOK IV: (PART 2) [*sic*]—END OF PART 2.
[First and last lines:] You were not more than 12, my son . . . . international acclaim (a drug) *and* Money : Joke . . . . scants our lives.

In *Paterson, Four,* II, 201–202, 217–218, with some changes.

C453 [Poem] *Botteghe Oscure,* Quaderno VIII (MCMLI) 310–322.
THE DESERT MUSIC.
[Note in *DM:*] "Poem given at the Harvard Assembly in June, 1951, subsequent to which Dr. Williams was awarded an honorary Phi Beta Kappa membership."
In *DM*. Reprinted in *Origin,* Dorchester, Mass., I. 6 (Summer 1952) 65–75.

C454 [Essay] *The New York Times Book Review,* LVI. 4 (Sun., Jan. 28, 1951) 5.
*VERSE WITH A JOLT TO IT.
Review of Kenneth Rexroth's *Beyond the Mountains,* a book of his translations into English of *Phaedra, Iphegenia, Hermaios,* and *Berenike.*

C455 [Poem] *The Beloit Poetry Journal,* Beloit, Wis., I. 3 (Spring 1951) 9.
THE DRUNKARD.
In *CEP* with some revisions in the prose letter that precedes the poem.

C456 [Poem] *Spearhead,* Martinsville, Va., II. 2 (Spring 1951) 18.
*JUNE 9.
Reprinted in *Shenandoah,* Lexington, Va., II. 2 (Summer 1951) 10–11.

C457 "LETTER TO [Robert] CREELEY." *Origin,* Dorchester, Mass., I. 1 (Spring 1951) 34.
*About writing, dated March 3, 1950. (An excerpt from another letter from WCW to Creeley, August 9, 1954, is quoted in a footnote to Creeley's essay "A Character for Love" in *William Carlos Williams: A Collection of Critical Essays,* edited by J. Hillis Miller (Englewood Cliffs, N.J.: Prentice-Hall, 1966), p. 160; this excerpt is about Creeley's essay.)

C458 [Essay] *The New York Times Book Review,* LVI. 6 (Sun., April 22, 1951) 6.
IN A MOOD OF TRAGEDY.
Review of Robert Lowell's *The Mills of the Kavanaughs.* In *SE.*

C459 [Two poems] *Shenandoah,* Lexington, Va., II. 2 (Summer 1951) 10–11.
[C456: *June 9]—*STILL LIFE.

C460 [Contribution to a symposium] *The Golden Goose,* Columbus, Ohio, III. 2 (Autumn 1951) 89–96.
*SYMPOSIUM ON WRITING.
Partial transcription of a program prepared by Richard Wirtz Emerson and broadcast October 7, 1950, on Station WOSU, Columbus, Ohio. The other contributors to the symposium were Charles Olson, Kenneth Patchen, Leslie Woolf Hedley, and Henry Rago.

C461 [Essay] *Kirgo's,* "a catalog-magazine," New Haven, No. 3 (Aug. 1951) 20–21.
FOREWORD.
First publication of the Foreword to *The Autobiography of William Carlos Williams* (A35).

C462 [Essay] *Poetry,* LXXVIII. 6 (Sept. 1951) 345–351.
CARL SANDBURG'S COMPLETE POEMS.
In *SE.*

C463 [Front-page feature article] *The Rutherford Republican,* Rutherford, N.J., LX. 20 (Thurs., Nov. 15, 1951) 1, 4.
*UNITE FOR FREEDOM, WRITTEN FOR RUTHERFORD PUBLIC SCHOOLS, NATIONAL EDUCATION WEEK.

C464 [Essay] *The Sewanee Review,* Sewanee, Tenn., LIX. 1 (Winter 1951) 154–161.
PARADE'S END.
Review of Ford Madox Ford's *Parade's End.* In *SE.*

C465 [Poem] *What's New,* Chicago (Christmas 1951) [51].
*DECEMBER.
"Written especially for *What's New.*" Reprinted in *The Abbott Christmas Book* (Doubleday and Co., 1960) 37.

1952

C466 [Presentation speech] *Proceedings of the American Academy of Arts and Letters and the National Institute of Arts and Letters,* New York, Second Series, No. 2 (1952) 13–14.
*PRESENTATION TO JOHN CROWE RANSOM OF THE RUSSELL LOINES AWARD FOR POETRY.
Speech given at the Joint Ceremonial of the AAAL and NIAL, May 25, 1951.

C467 [Essay] *Proceedings of the American Academy of Arts and Letters* and the *National Institute of Arts and Letters,* Second Series, No. 2 (1952) 51–59.

*THE AMERICAN SPIRIT IN ART.

Speech given at the Dinner Meeting of the NIAL, December 18, 1951.

C468 [Essay] *University of Buffalo Studies,* Buffalo, N.Y. XIX. 4 (Feb. 1952) 10–12.

*THE FUTURE OF THE CREATIVE ARTS.

C469 [Poem] *The Golden Goose,* Columbus, Ohio, III. 4 (May 1952) 159.

A POEM FOR NORMAN MACLEOD.

In *CEP.*

C470 [Essay] *The Golden Goose,* III. 4 (May 1952) 172.

*A NOTE ON "PURE AS NOWHERE."

Review of the poems by Norman Macleod in this issue of the magazine.

C471 [Essay] *Inferno,* San Francisco, Nos. 6–7 ([May–July] 1952) 67–73.

*KENNETH LAWRENCE BEAUDOIN.

C472 [Poem] *Quarto,* New York, III. 2 (Summer 1952) 63.

*THE WRONG DOOR.

C473 [Five poems] *Perspectives U.S.A.,* New York, I. 1 (Fall 1952) 22–26 [published also in French, German, and Italian editions].

[A20: These]—[C51: To Waken an Old Lady]—[C68: The Widow's Lament in Springtime]—[C20: Smell!]—[C225: The Yachts].

C474 [Ten poems] *Perspectives U.S.A.,* I. 1 (Fall 1952) 36–42 [published also in French, German, and Italian editions].

[B23: The Locust Tree in Flower (Among/of/green)]—[C151: Poem (As the cat)]—[C206: Young Woman at a Window]—[A20: Between Walls]—[C223: Proletarian Portrait]—[C34: Complete Destruction]—[A5: The Great Figure]—[A7: Poem (So much depends)]—[C232: A Chinese Toy]—[A15: This Is Just to Say].

In *CEP.* These ten poems first appeared as a group in *Spearhead,* 1947 (B50).

C474a [Statement about poem] *More Power, Report of the Newark Public Library, 1946–1952* ([Fall–Winter] 1952) 7–8.

THE LOCUST TREE IN FLOWER is reprinted, both the early version (Among/the leaves/bright [C191]) and the second shorter version, with a *statement WCW made in response to a Newark

Public Library patron who had read the second version in *Perspectives U.S.A.* (C474, above), liked it, but did not understand it. WCW's reply: "It's . . . the whole history of May. It was first written in full and published . . . . Then I cut out everything except the essential words to leave the thing as simple as possible and to make the reader concentrate as much as he can. Could anything be plainer?"

C475 [Two letters] *The Golden Goose*, Sausalito, Calif., IV. 5 (Oct. 1952) 29–32.

*To Robert Lawrence Beum, Jan. 5, 1950, and Jan. 9, 1950.

About prosody; edited by Richard Wirtz Emerson. A full page photograph of WCW by Emerson is on p. 28.

C476 [Poem] *Poetry*, LXXXI. 1 (Oct. 1952) 89–90.

PATERSON, BOOK V: THE RIVER OF HEAVEN.

Not in *Paterson* (*Five*), this is an early version of the first 24 lines of ASPHODEL, THAT GREENY FLOWER, which is printed in *DM* as WORK IN PROGRESS, and in *JL,* with changes. Compare C486.

C477 [Interview] *A.D. 1952*, New York, III. 1 (Winter 1952) 5, 7–8, 10–11, 13–14.

*THE EDITORS MEET WILLIAM CARLOS WILLIAMS.

The interview was conducted by Dorothy Tooker.

C478 [Self-portrait] *A.D. 1952, III.* 1 (Winter 1952) 9.

Black and white reproduction of a self-portrait in oil painted *c.* 1914 by WCW. Reproduced also in *The Massachusetts Review*, III. 2, A Gathering for William Carlos Williams (Winter 1962) 309.

C479 [Poem] *Poetry*, LXXXI. 3 (Dec. 1952) 159–162.

THE ORCHESTRA.

In *DM*. Reprinted in *College Music Symposium*, Winston–Salem, N.C., I. (Fall 1961) 7–9.

1953

C480 [Poem] *Imagi*, Baltimore, Md., VI. 2, Issue for William Carlos Williams in His 70th Year (1953) [1–2].

THE YELLOW FLOWER.

In *D.M.*

C481 [Improvisation] *New Directions 14* (1953) 345.

*EXULTATION (the first day at the lake cottage in the summer).

C482 [Poem] *Botteghe Oscure,* Quaderno XI (MCMLIII) 367–371.
TO DAPHNE AND VIRGINIA.
In *DM.*

C483 [Poem] *Poetry,* LXXXII. 2 (May 1953) 82–85.
FOR ELEANOR AND BILL MONOHAN.
In *DM;* MONOHAN spelled MONAHAN.

C484 [Poem] *The Kenyon Review,* XV. 3 (Summer 1953) 404–407.
THE HOST.
In *DM.*

C485 [Poem] *Origin,* I. 10 (Summer 1953) 71–72.
*THE PROBLEM.

C486 [Poem] *Perspective,* St. Louis, VI. 4, William Carlos Williams Issue
(Autumn–Winter 1953) 175–176.
WORK IN PROGRESS (PATERSON V) [First and last lines:]
What power has love but forgiveness? . . . to think well of me.
"(Paterson V)" is inked out in a copy of *Perspective* signed "William Carlos Williams" on title page. Not in *Paterson (Five),* but in
JL as first section of Book 3 of ASPHODEL, THAT GREENY
FLOWER. All of Book 3 (*JL* 68–87) appeared in *The Kenyon Review* (Summer 1955). See C509.

C487 [Poem] *The New Yorker,* XXIX. 41 (Nov. 28, 1953) 75.
THE ARTIST.
In *DM.* Reprinted in *The Saturday Review,* New York, XLI. 41
(Oct. 11, 1958) 38.

1954

C488 [Poem] *New World Writing,* New York, No. 5 [1954] 94–96.
WORK IN PROGRESS. [First and last lines:] Of asphodel, that
greeny flower . . . . when it puts all flowers/to shame.
In *DM* (45–49); in *JL* it is the first part of Book 1 of ASPHODEL,
THAT GREENY FLOWER (*JL* 43–47). Compare C476.

C489 [Contribution to a symposium] *The Quarterly Review of Literature,*
Annandale-on-Hudson, N.Y., VII. 3 ([1954]) 171–175.
*EXPERIMENTAL AND FORMAL VERSE: SOME HINTS
TOWARD THE ENJOYMENT OF MODERN VERSE.

Three poets, WCW, Louise Bogan, and Richard Wilbur, contributed essays which were "the consequence of a poetry conference on 'Experimental and Formal Verse' held some years ago at Bard College."

C490 [Poem] *The Quarterly Review of Literature*, Annandale-on-Hudson, N.Y., VII. 4 ([1954]) 255–260.
DACTYLS FROM THEOCRITUS.
In *DM*, titled THEOCRITUS, IDYL I (A VERSION FROM THE GREEK).

C491 [Essay] *Origin*, I. 12 (Spring 1954) 194–199.
ON MEASURE—STATEMENT FOR CID CORMAN.
In *SE* and *Reader*.

C492 [Poem] *Chicago Review*, Chicago, VIII. 2 (Spring–Summer 1954) 40–41.
VIEW BY COLOR-PHOTOGRAPHY ON A COMMERCIAL CALENDAR.
In *JL*.

C493 [Seven letters] *The Golden Goose*, Sausalito, Calif., No. 7 (April 1954) 124–132.
THE LETTERS OF WILLIAM CARLOS WILLIAMS.
To Marianne Moore, March 23, 1921, and May 2, 1934.
To Kenneth Burke, Jan. 26, 1921[?] and Jan. 26, 1933.
*To Norman Macleod, Nov. 29 [1950].
To Harriet Monroe, Oct. 26, 1916, and May 22, 1914.
Edited by John C. Thirlwall. In *SL*, except for starred letter.

C494 [Essay] *The Trinity Review*, Hartford, Conn., VIII. 3 (May 1954) 10–11.
*WALLACE STEVENS.

C495 [Essay] *Art News*, New York, LIII. 4 (June–Aug., 1954) 20–23, 62, 78.
PAINTING IN THE AMERICAN GRAIN.
In *SE*.

C496 [Essay] *New Ventures*, Philadelphia, No. 1 ([June] 1954) 4–11.
*THE FUNCTION OF LITERATURE: A LECTURE GIVEN TO JUNIOR EXECUTIVES.

C497 [Poem] *New Ventures*, No. 1 ([June] 1954) 12.
TO A MAN DYING ON HIS FEET.
In *JL*.

C498 [Poem] *Poetry,* LXXXIV. 5 (Aug. 1954) 249–254.
OF ASPHODEL: CODA.
In *JL.*

C499 [Poem] *The Beloit Poetry Journal,* V.1, Chapbook No. 3 ([Fall] 1954) 33–36.
THE IVY CROWN.
Also printed in *The Times Literary Supplement,* London, No. 2746, 53rd Year (Sept. 17, 1954) 588.
In *JL.*

C500 [Essay] *Art in America,* Cannondale, Conn., XLII. 3 (Oct. 1954) 214–215.
*POSTSCRIPT BY A POET.
About paintings by Charles Sheeler. See *Charles Sheeler, A Retrospective Exhibition* (B65).

C501 [Essay] *The Yale Literary Magazine,* New Haven, CXXII. 2, Dylan Thomas Issue (Nov. 1954) 21–22.
DYLAN THOMAS.
Published contemporaneously in *SE.*

C502 [Essay] *Holiday,* Philadelphia, XVI. 5 (Nov. 1954) 54–55, 78.
*SEVENTY YEARS DEEP.
About being a poet and a doctor in Rutherford, N.J. Material from this essay was used, with the permission of WCW and the Curtis Publishing Company, in a Voice of America broadcast, July, 1955 (F17).

C503 [Essay] *Arts Digest,* New York, XXIX. 5 (Dec. 1, 1954) 7–8.
*E. E. CUMMINGS' POEMS AND PAINTINGS.
Illustrated with reproductions of three paintings by Cummings.

1955

C504 [Poem] *Pennsylvania Literary Review,* Philadelphia, V. 2 (1955) 3–5.
SHADOWS.
In *JL.*

C505 [Poem] *New World Writing,* No. 8 [1955] 165–167.
TRIBUTE TO THE PAINTERS.
In *JL.* Reprinted with the title THE SATYRS, six more lines at the beginning, fifteen lines less at the end, in *The Nation,* CLXXX. 22 (May 3, 1958) 498–499; the version in *Paterson, Five,* II, 258–261,

is like the latter, beginning ". . or the Satyrs" and ending "the blameless beasts."

C506 [Poem] *Folio,* Bloomington, Ind., XX. 2 (Spring 1955) 24–25.
CLASSIC PICTURE.

On cover of the issue: "A New Poem by William Carlos Williams." In *JL.*

C507 [Poem] *Poetry,* LXXXVI. 2 (May 1955) 99–107.
OF ASPHODEL: BOOK 2. [First and last lines:] Approaching death . . . . it brought us together.

In *JL;* titled ASPHODEL, THAT GREENY FLOWER, Book 2. Published contemporaneously with *JL* in *Platform,* London, No. 4 (Autumn 1955) 3–8.

C508 [Poem (in Italian)] *La fiera letteraria,* Rome, X. 26 (domenica, 26 giugno 1950) 1–2.
WORK IN PROGRESS.

All of Book 1 of ASPHODEL, THAT GREENY FLOWER, (*JL*), translated into Italian by Roberto Sanesi. See C488.

C509 [Poem] *The Kenyon Review,* XVII. 3 (Summer 1955) 371–382.
OF ASPHODEL. [First and last lines:] What power has love but forgiveness? . . . forever more.

In *JL,* with title ASPHODEL, THAT GREENY FLOWER, Book 3. The first forty lines of this section of the poem were printed first in *Perspective* (Autumn–Winter 1953)—C486. The entire poem was reprinted after its book publication, 1955, in *Agenda,* London, III. 2 (Oct.–Nov. 1963) 1–24, with acknowledgment to Random House and New Directions.

C510 [Essay] *El Crepusculo,* Taos, N. M., VIII. 31, Section One (Aug. 4, 1955) 9.
*PATROCINIO BARELA.

Review of Barela's sculpture. Reprinted in *Poetry Taos,* Ranche of Taos, N.M., No. 1 (1957) [9].

C511 [Two translated poems] *Accent,* XV. 4 (Autumn 1955) 255–258.
*LANDLESS JOHN CIRCLES THE EARTH SEVEN TIMES
—*LANDLESS JOHN LEADS THE CARAVAN.
Translation from the French of Yvan Goll. See B45.

[Essay and letter in *The Pound Newsletter* (Oct. 1955). See D10 and 11.]

WILLIAM CARLOS WILLIAMS *(aet. 43)*
Photograph by Charles Sheeler, 1926.
Reproduced by permission of Mrs. William Carlos Williams.

C512 [Essay] *The New Republic*, CXXXIII. 18, Issue 2136 (Oct. 31, 1955) 16–17.
*POETRY AND THE MAKING OF THE LANGUAGE: HOW VERSE FORMS CREATE SOMETHING NEW.
With photograph of WCW.

C513 [Essay] *Arts*, New York, XXX. 2 (Nov. 1955) 21–25.
*BRANCUSI.

1956

C514 [Poem] *Neon*, Brooklyn, N. Y., No. 2 [1956] 8.
TO MY FRIEND EZRA POUND.
In *PB*.

C515 [Essay] *Poetry*, LXXXVII. 4 (Jan. 1956) 234–239.
*COMMENT: WALLACE STEVENS.
Tribute to Stevens after his death.

C516 [Letter] *Four Quarters*, Philadelphia, V. 2 (Jan. 1956) 17.
*A FURTHER VIEW—II.
Excerpt from a letter WCW wrote in answer to the question, "Why do not Catholic colleges and universities in the United States produce an adequate supply of Catholic writers?"

C517 [Letter to Srinivas Rayaprol, editor] *East and West*, Secunderabad, India, I. 1 (Spring 1956) 45–47.
*Letter dated May 29, 1951.

C518 [Essay] *The New York Times Book Review*, LXI. 12 (Sun., March 18, 1956) 37.
*RESTLESS POET.
Review of James Schevill's *The Right to Greet*. Compare C519.

C519 [Essay] *The Western Review*, Iowa City, Iowa, XX. 4 (Summer 1956) 325–326.
*THE SPEED OF POETRY.
Review of James Schevill's *The Right to Greet*. Compare C518.

C520 [Poem] *East and West*, I. Nos. 2–3 (Summer–Autumn 1956) 28.
SAPPHO, BE COMFORTED.
In *PB*.

C521 [Poem] *The Atlantic Monthly*, Boston, CXCVIII. 3 (Sept. 1956) 89.
THE TURTLE (For My Grandson).
In *PB*.

C522 [Essay] *The New Republic,* CXXXV. 12, Issue 2181 (Sept. 17, 1956) 18.

    *A POET WHO CANNOT PAUSE.

    Review of Rene Char's *Hypnos Waking.* See B69.

C523 [Poem] *Edge,* Melbourne, Australia, No. 1 (Oct. 1956) [17].

    THE HIGH BRIDGE ABOVE THE TAGUS RIVER AT TOLEDO.

    In *PB.* Reprinted in *The Quartely Review of Literature,* Annandale-on-Hudson, N.Y., IX. 1 ([1957]) 24; *Spectrum,* Santa Barbara, Calif., I. 1 (Winter [Jan.] 1957) 53; *Evergreen Review,* New York, I. 3 ([Fall] 1957) 56; and *The Massachusetts Review,* III. 2 (Winter 1962) 279. Compare prose description in *The Autobiography,* p. 123.

C524 [Letter to Martha Baird] *Poetry Public,* Hastings, Neb., IV. 4 (Oct.–Dec. 1956) 1–3.

    Dated November 3, 1951, the letter thanks Martha Baird for a copy of Eli Siegel's *Hot Afternoons Have Been in Montana* (B73); about sixty words of this letter had been quoted by Nat Herz in *Poetry,* Chicago, LXXX. V (Aug. 1952) 303–306. See B94.

C525 [Poem] *Prairie Schooner,* Lincoln, Neb., XXX. 4, Thirtieth Anniversary Issue (Winter 1956) 350.

    *BALLAD.

    Reprinted in *The Poet,* Glasgow, Scotland, No. 15, Final Issue ([Summer 1957]) [21].

C526 [Three poems] *The Hudson Review,* New York, IX. 4 (Winter 1956–1957) 485–487.

    THE GIFT—CALYPSO—THE TITLE.

    In *PB;* CALYPSO is the third section of CALYPSOS. THE TITLE is reprinted in *The Poet,* No. 15, Final Issue [Summer 1957] [20]. See D16 and 17.

C527 [Poem] *Colorado Review,* Fort Collins, Colo., I. 1 (Winter 1956–1957) 39.

    TO FLOSSIE.

    In *PB.*

1957

C528 [Sixty-three poems] "The Lost Poems of William Carlos Williams or The Past Recaptured" by John C. Thirlwall. *New Directions 16* (1957) 3–45.

*THE USES OF POETRY (for H. D.) [A1]—[*C104: Misericordia]—[*THE WARTBURG, same as *C104: Martin and Katherine]—[C451: Sonnet in Search of an Author]—[*C3: On First Opening the Lyric Year]—[*C5: Rendezvous]—[*C5: To the Outer World]—[*C5: La Flor (for E. P.)]—[*C5: Offering]—[*C5: A La Lune]—[*C6: Woman Walking]—[*C6: Invitation (We live in this flat blue basin)]—[*C6: Aux Imagistes]—[*C6: Peace]—[*C7: A Confidence]—[*C7: Slow Movement (for E. P.)]—[*C14: Naked]—[*C14: Marriage]—[*C14: The Old Worshipper (For Jim Hyslop)]—[*C10: Metric Figure (Veils of clarity)]—[*C10: Epigramme]—[*B3: Stillness]—[*A3: Invitation (You who had the sense)]—[*C34: Stroller]—[*C81: From a Book]—[*C89: The new cathedral overlooking the park]—[*C89: How has the way been found?]—*A LOVE POEM (Basic hatred) — [*C144: The Moon]—[*C146: Child and Vegetables]—*COMFORT—*THE HALF WORLD—[*C333: Gothic Candor]—[Down-Town, same as C84: New England]—*ROAR AND CLATTER—[*C259: Man and Nature]—*FLATTERY (For. F. W.)—*PIGHEADED POET —*THE GENIUS—*THE APPROACHING HOUR—*DETAILS FOR PATERSON—[*C282: Defiance to Cupid]—[*C298: From a Window]—*RIVER RHYME II—[*C298: River Rhyme]—[*C283: Tailpiece]—[*C304: Defense]—[A22: Love, the Tragedian] —*THE UNITED FRONT—*TO A CHINESE WOMAN—*THE FIGHT—[*C318: War the Destroyer (For Martha Graham)] —[*C340: The Gentle Negress (No other such luxuriance)]—[C365: Death by Radio (For F. D. R.)]—[C352: Sunflowers]—[C352: Threnody]—[C352: The Rare Gist]—[C341: To the Dean] —[C370: East Coocoo]—[C370: At Kenneth Burke's Place]—[D3: Rogation Sunday]—[C442: Moon and Stars]—[C442: The Girl (The wall, as I watched)].

Fourteen of these poems are not published in any other periodical or in book form. SONNET IN SEARCH OF AN AUTHOR is in *PB.* DOWN-TOWN is in *CEP,* but is titled NEW ENGLAND. LOVE THE TRAGEDIAN is in *CLP,* but is titled SOMETIMES IT TURNS DRY . . . . DEATH BY RADIO, SUNFLOWERS, THRENODY, THE RARE GIST, TO THE DEAN, EAST COOCOO, AT KENNETH BURKE'S PLACE, and ROGATION SUNDAY are in *CLP².* *MOON AND STARS* and *THE GIRL* are in

CEP. For other printings of ROGATION SUNDAY, see D3 and E3.

C529 [Essay] *The New Republic*, CXXXVI. 3, Issue 2199 (Jan. 21, 1957) 20.

*FIVE TO THE FIFTH POWER.

Review of Charles G. Bell's *Delta Return*. See G5.

C530 [Essay] *Arizona Quarterly*, XIII. 1 (Spring 1957) 89.

*THE GREENHOUSE IN THE GARDEN.

Review of Charles Edward Eaton's *The Greenhouse in the Garden*.

C531 [Letter to the editor, James Land Jones] *Nimrod*, Tulsa, Okla., I. 3 (Spring 1957) [7].

*Praise of a poem by W. W. Pemble that had been published in the previous issue of *Nimrod*.

C532 [Essay] *The Trinity Review*, XI. 3 (Spring–Summer 1957) 24.

*MARIANNE MOORE.

C533 [Poem] *The Beloit Poetry Journal* [VII. 4], Chapbook No. Five, Robert Frost Issue ([Summer] 1957) 48.

*THIS IS PIONEER WEATHER.

C534 [Essay] *Poetry*, XC. 3 (June 1957) 180–190.

*TWO NEW BOOKS BY KENNETH REXROTH.

Review of Rexroth's *In Defense of the Earth* and *One Hundred Poems from the Chinese*.

C535 [Translated poem] *Spectrum*, I. 3 (Fall 1957) 57.

TRANSLATION FROM SAPPHO.

Note with poem: "Why the poem ends as it does ["I am another person"] no one seems to know. It seems reasonable to believe that the poem is not complete as recorded and the little tab at the end is put there merely to continue the poet's thought, not her words—but we cannot be sure of this."

In *Paterson, Five*, II, 253, the last line is omitted. Reprinted, as it is in *Spectrum*, in *Evergreen Review*, I. 3 ([Fall] 1957) 57, with the title SAPPHO. See B75.

C536 [Three poems] *Evergreen Review*, I. 3 ([Fall] 1957) 56–58.

[C523: The High Bridge]—[C535: Sappho]—VIEW OF A WOMAN AT HER BATH.

The last poem is printed a second time in *Evergreen Review*, V. 17 (March–April 1961) 64, but with the title PORTRAIT OF A

WOMAN AT HER BATH, as in *PB,* and acknowledgment is made to André Emmerich Gallery—see B82.

C537 [Essay] *The American Scholar,* Washington, XXVI. 4 (Autumn 1957) 453–457.

*FAITHS FOR A COMPLEX WORLD.

One of ten essays in this issue grouped under the above title, WCW's essay is a shortened version of a typescript, YALC, headed "What has sustained me and made me feel in the face of the troubles of our time that it was worthwhile going on."

C538 [Essay] *The Literary Review,* Teaneck, N.J., I. 1 (Autumn 1957) 5–12.

FROM MY NOTES ABOUT MY MOTHER.

Some of these notes are in *Yes, Mrs. Williams* (A45). Compare C295. A cartoon by Edgar I. Williams titled "A Poem Is Born" is reproduced on p. 7.

C539 [Seven letters] *The Literary Review,* I. 1 (Autumn 1957) 13–28.

WILLIAM CARLOS WILLIAMS AS CORRESPONDENT.

*To James Laughlin, Sept. 18, 1942.

*To Horace Gregory, May 3, 1944.

To Srinivas Rayaprol, May 24, 1950.

To Richard Eberhart, Oct. 22, 1953.

To John Thirlwall, Nov. 30, 1954.

*To Ruth A. Jackson, Jan. 15, 1957.

*To Naomi Hunter, Jan. 19, 1957.

Edited by John C. Thirlwall. In *SL,* except for starred letters.

C540 "TWO SENTIMENTAL LITTLE POEMS." *The Literary Review,* I. 1 (Autumn 1957) 28.

Untitled (1. The flower—2. *At the brink of winter).

The first poem is titled THE LOVING DEXTERITY in *PB* and has some changes.

C541 [Short story] *The Hudson Review,* X. 3 (Autumn 1957) 329–352.

THE FARMERS' DAUGHTERS.

In *FD.*

C542 [Two essays] "Two Pieces." *The Black Mountain Review,* Black Mountain, N.C., 7 (Autumn 1957) 164–168.

*1. BEGINNINGS: MARSDEN HARTLEY—*2. LES AMIS DE FORD MADOX FORD.

C543 [Essay] *The Black Mountain Review*, 7 (Autumn 1957) 238–240.
EMPTY MIRROR.
Preface to Allen Ginsberg's *Empty Mirror*, unpublished until 1961; see B88.

C544 [Essay] *The New York Times Book Review*, LXII. 33 (Sun., Aug. 18, 1957) 6.
*POET OF A STEADFAST PATTERN.
Review of Wallace Stevens' *Opus Posthumous*.

C545 [Poem] *The New Yorker*, XXXIII. 30 (Sept. 14, 1957) 85.
PUERTO RICO SONG.
In *PB*; titled CALYPSOS I–II.

[Photographs of WCW: *Coronet*, New York, XLII, 252 (Oct. 1957) 42–51. Photographs by Eve Arnold with commentary by Gerold Frank in picture essay, "A Rich, a Full Life."]

[Photographs of WCW: *Friends*, Detroit (Oct. 1957) 6–7. Photographs by Carroll Seghers II, titled "The Doctor Who Became a Poet."]

C546 [Essay] *Poetry*, XCI. 1 (Oct. 1957) 60–64.
*CHAPMAN STILL HEARD.
Review of *Chapman's Homer: The Iliad and The Odyssey* (two volumes), edited, with introductions by Allardyce Nicoll. Reprinted as part of a long essay, "Measure—a loosely assembled essay on poetic measure" (C573).

C547 [Interview] *The New York Post* (Fri., Oct. 18, 1957) 46.
MIKE WALLACE ASKS WILLIAM CARLOS WILLIAMS: IS POETRY A DEAD DUCK?
In *Paterson, Five*, II, 261–262.

C548 [Poem] *The Grecourt Review*, Northampton, Mass., I. 2 (Dec. 1957) 14.
THE SWIVELHIPPED AMAZON.
In *PB*; retitled MOUNTED AS AN AMAZON. See also D13.

C549 [Letter to the editor, Edmund L. Epstein] *The James Joyce Review*, New York, I. 4 (Dec. 15, 1957) 1–2.
*About contemporary literature, dated Jan. 6/58 [*sic*].

1958

C550 [Essay] *Contact,* San Francisco, No. 1, Issue dedicated to William
Carlos Williams (1958) 75–78.

    *THE CONTACT STORY.

    Includes "Comment" from earlier *Contact,* New York, I. 1 (Feb.
1932) 7–9 (C167). Full-page photograph of WCW on verso of front
cover.

C551 [Essay] *The Nation,* CLXXXVI. 8 (Feb. 22, 1958) 171.

    *LEIF ERICSON'S VIOLENT DAUGHTER.

    Review of Winfield Townley Scott's *The Dark Sister.*

C552 [Poem] *Art News,* LVII. 3 (May 1958) 28.

    TAPESTRIES AT THE CLOISTERS. [First and last lines:]
The figures/are of heroic size. . . . out of it if you call yourself a
woman.

    In *Paterson, Five,* III, 273–276.

C553 [Four poems] "Poems from Paterson V." *The Nation,* CLXXXVI.
22 (May 31, 1958) 498–499.

    1. A WOMAN—2. THE SATYRS [Cf. C505]—3. A BRUE-
GHEL NATIVITY—4. THE MEASURE [First and last lines:]
1. There is a woman in our town . . . . or the birds. 2. . . . or the
Satyrs, a/pre-tragic play . . . . the blameless beasts 3. Peter Brueghel,
the elder, painted . . . . and he served/dispassionately 4. —learning
with age to sleep my life away . . . . Satyrically, the tragic foot.

    In *Paterson, Five*: (1) II, 255–257; (2) II, 258–261; (3) III,
263–265; (4) III, 277–278. A WOMAN is reprinted from *Spectrum,*
II. 1 (Winter [Jan.] 1958) 32–34, where it is titled FROM 'PAT-
TERSON 5' [*sic*] BOOK 2.

C554 [Poem] *Audience,* Cambridge, Mass., V. 3 (Summer 1958) 120–121.

    TAPIOLA (SECOND VERSION).

    Reprinted, with changes, in *Neon* 4 (1959) [24], and titled simply
TAPIOLA; the latter like the version in *PB.*

C555. [Essay] *Prairie Schooner,* XXXII. 3 (Fall 1958) 157–158.

    *BY THE AUTHOR OF *BOTTOM DOGS.*

    Review of Edward Dahlberg's *The Sorrows of Priapus,* illustrated
by Ben Shahn.

C556 [Essay] *Forum,* Houston, Texas, II. 3 (Fall 1958) 15–19.

*AND MANY AND MANY A TIME.

About WCW's method of work. Parts of this essay are similar to parts of *I Wanted* (A43).

C557 [Essay] *Spectrum*, II. 3 (Fall 1958) 189–191.

*SEEING IS BELIEVING.

Review of Charles Tomlinson's *Seeing Is Believing*.

C558 [Poem] *Poetry*, XCII. 6 (Sept. 1958) 341–345.

FROM 'PATERSON V.' [First and last lines:] Paterson has grown older . . . . among the oak trees.

In *Paterson, Five*, III, 268–273. A section of this, beginning "A flight of birds, all together," and ending "all together for his purposes," is reprinted in *Harvard Medical Alumni Bulletin*, Boston, XXXIV. 3 (April 1960) 34.

C559 [Essay] *College English*, Champaign, Ill., XX. 1 (Oct. 1958) 55–56.

*Review of Robert E. Knoll's *Robert McAlmon: Expatriate Publisher and Writer*. See B81.

C560 [Translated poem] *Delta*, Montreal (Oct. 1958) 13.

*SPRING SONG (A young lass).

Translated from the Chinese of Li Po by David Rafael Wang and WCW. Reprinted in *The Beloit Poetry Journal*, IX. 3 (Spring 1959) 17, and in *New Directions 19* (1966) 218–219.

C561 [Poem] *The Nation*, CLXXXVII. 14 (Nov. 1, 1958) 310.

POEM (The rose fades).

In *PB*.

C562 [Poem] *San Francisco Review*, San Francisco, I. 1 [Winter 1958] 71.

AN EXERCISE (Sick as I am).

In *PB*.

C563 [Essay] *The Hanover Forum*, Hanover, Ind., V. 1 (Winter 1958–1959) 60–63.

A NOTE ON THE TURN OF THE VIEW TOWARD POETIC TECHNIQUE.

Similar to letter of Jan. 13, 1955, *SL*. See D15.

C564 [Five translated poems] *New World Writing*, No. 14 (Dec. 1958) 92, 93, 94, 97–98, 99–101.

*GREEN EYES [Alí Chumacero]—*NAKED [Alvaro Figueredo]—*PIANO SOLO [Nicanor Parra]—*THE INFINITE HORSES [Silvina Ocampo]—*ODE TO LAZINESS [Pablo Neruda].

Translated from the Spanish; part of a selection of twenty Spanish writers titled "New Writing from Latin America, with an Introduction by José Vázquez-Amaral and Francisco Aguilera," pp. 86–181. PIANO SOLO is reprinted in Parra's *Poems and Antipoems*, B98.

1959

C565 [Two poems] *Chicago Review*, XIII. 1 (Winter–Spring 1959) 25–26.
BIRD—THE FRUIT.
In *PB*.

[Excerpts from letters, *Poetry Pilot*, New York (Jan. 1, 1959) 14.
*Selections from letters by WCW to *Poetry Pilot*. WCW was poetry editor of this issue.]

C566 [Two translated poems] *The Beloit Poetry Journal*, IX. 3 (Spring 1959) 17.
*THE NEWLYWED'S CUISINE—[*C560: Spring Song].
Translated from the Chinese of Wang Chien by David Rafael Wang and WCW. Reprinted in *New Directions 19* (1966) 227.

C567 [Poem] *Monmouth Letters*, West Long Branch, N.J., II. 2 (Spring 1959) [2].
THE SNOW BEGINS.
In *PB*. Reprinted in *Genesis*, West Long Branch, N.J., I. 1 (Spring 1962) 15.

C568 [Contribution to a symposium] *Wagner* [formerly *Nimbus*], Staten Island, N.Y. (Spring 1959) 24–25.
*THE BEAT POETS.

C569 [Nine poems] "Some Simple Measures in the American Idiom and the Variable Foot." *Poetry*, XCIII. 6 (March 1959) 386–391.
EXERCISE IN TIMING—HISTOLOGY—PERPETUUM MOBILE—THE BLUE JAY—THE EXISTENTIALIST'S WIFE—A SALAD FOR THE SOUL—CHLOE—THE COCKTAIL PARTY—THE STOLEN PEONIES.
In *PB*; the first line of A SALAD TO THE SOUL has "pleasant soul" rather than "peasant soul," as in *Poetry*. On p. 416 is a brief note by WCW about "Some Simple Measures."

C570 [Manuscript notes] *Today's Japan*, Tokyo, IV. 3 (March 1959) 65–70.

THE GENESIS OF THE EPIC "PATERSON."

This article by John C. Thirlwall contains quotations from unpublished material by WCW. Also see C598.

C571 [Statement] *Bulletin of the Bergen County Medical Society*, Hackensack, N.J., XXXI. 8 (April 1959) 29.

*Statement accepting honorary membership in the Bergen County Medical Society.

C572 [Poem] *East and West*, No. 5 (Autumn 1959) 2.

*AN OLD-FASHIONED GERMAN CHRISTMAS CARD.

C573 [Essay] *Spectrum*, III. 3 (Fall 1959) 131–157.

*MEASURE—A LOOSELY ASSEMBLED ESSAY ON POETIC MEASURE.

Reprinted in *Cambridge Opinion*, Cambridge, England, 41 (Oct. 1965) 4–14; textual corrections by Martin Wright and Michael Weaver. Part of the essay had appeared in *Poetry* (C546).

C574 [Poem] *The Massachusetts Review*, I. 1 (Oct. 1959) 39.

15 YEARS LATER.

In *PB*.

C575 [Two translated poems] *Evergreen Review*, II. 7 (Winter 1959) 59–61.

*WIDOWER'S MONOLOGUE—*THE WANDERINGS OF THE TRIBE.

Translated from the Spanish of the Mexican poet Alí Chumacero.

C576 [Essay] *Evergreen Review*, II. 7 (Winter 1959) 214–216.

*E. E. CUMMINGS.

Review of Cummings' *95 Poems*.

C577 [Poem] *The Galley Sail Review*, San Francisco, II. 1 (Winter 1959–1960) 17.

SUZY.

Reprinted in *The Hudson Review*, XIII. 3 (Autumn 1960) 429–430; first stanza the same but parts II and III have many changes. In *PB*; the latter version.

C578 [Poem] *Yūgen*, New York, 5 ([1959 or 1960]) 2.

A FORMAL DESIGN.

In *PB*. Reprinted in *The Massachusetts Review*, III. 2, A Gathering for William Carlos Williams (Winter 1962) 283.

C: Periodicals

1960

C579 [Essay] *Fresco,* Detroit, I. 1 (1960) 15–16.
  *THE AMERICAN IDIOM.
  Reprinted in *Agenda,* II. 1 (Sept. 1960) 8–9; *Poetry Dial,* South
  Bend, Ind., I. 1 (Wintertime 1960) 48–49; *New Directions 17* (1961)
  250–251; *Between Worlds,* Boulder, Colo., and San Germán, Puerto
  Rico, I. 2 (Spring–Summer 1961) 234–235.
C580 [Ten poems] "Pictures from Brueghel." *The Hudson Review,* XIII.
  1 (Spring 1960) 11–20.
  SELF-PORTRAIT: THE OLD SHEPHERD—BRUEGHEL: 1
  (According to Brueghel)—BRUEGHEL: 2 (The overall picture is
  winter)—BRUEGHEL: 3 (From the Nativity)—BRUEGHEL: 4
  (Pour the wine bridegroom)—BRUEGHEL: 5 (The living quality)
  —BRUEGHEL: 6 (Summer!)—BRUEGHEL: 7 (Disciplined by
  the artist)—BRUEGHEL: 8 (The parable of the blind)—BRUE-
  GHEL: 9 CHILDREN'S GAMES
    In *PB* with minor changes; titles: I. SELF-PORTRAIT—II.
  LANDSCAPE WITH THE FALL OF ICARUS—III. THE
  HUNTERS IN THE SNOW—IV. THE ADORATION OF THE
  KINGS—V. PEASANT WEDDING—VI. HAYMAKING—VII.
  THE CORN HARVEST—VIII. THE WEDDING DANCE IN
  THE OPEN AIR—IX. THE PARABLE OF THE BLIND—X.
  CHILDREN'S GAMES, I–III.
C581 [Translated poem] *Approach,* Rosemont, Pa., No. 35 (Spring
  1960) 2.
  *SUMMER SONG (The Mirror Lake).
  Translated from the Chinese of Li Po by David Rafael Wang and
  WCW. Reprinted in *New Directions 19* (1966) 219.
C582 [Poem] *The Transatlantic Review,* New York and London, No. 3
  (Spring 1960) 19.
  TO A WOODPECKER.
  In *PB.*
C583 [Poem] *Selection,* Chico, Calif., No. 1 (Spring 1960) 3.
  THE GOSSIPS.
  In *PB.*
C584 [Three poems] "3 Stances." *Poetry,* XCV. 6 (March 1960) 325–327

ELAINE—ERICA—EMILY.
In *PB*.

C585 [Poem] *Agenda*, No. 10 (April 1960) 1.
THE PAINTING.
In *PB*.

C586 [Statement] *Harvard Medical Alumni Bulletin*, XXXIV. 3 (April 1960) 34.
About maintaining an "equal interest in medicine and the poem," with photograph of WCW and a reprinting of part of *Paterson, Five* (See C558).

C587 [Poem] *Prairie Schooner*, XXXIV. 2 (Summer 1960) 134.
*MIDWINTER.

C588 [Poem] *Contact*, II. 5 (June 1960) 39–41.
THE ITALIAN GARDEN.
In *PB*. Reprinted in *Contact*, IV. 1 (July 1962) 43.

C589 [Two poems] *The Hudson Review*, XIII. 3 (Autumn 1960) 429–430.
PAUL—[C577: Suzy].
In *PB*.

C590 [Poem] *The Virginia Quarterly Review*, Charlottesville, XXXVI. 4 (Autumn 1960) 579–580.
TO THE GHOST OF MARJORIE KINNAN RAWLINGS.
In *PB*.

C591 [Poem] *Now*, Teaneck, N.J., I. 1 (Fall 1960) 5.
THE CHRYSANTHEMUM
In *PB*.

C592 [Poem] *The Minnesota Review*, Minneapolis, I. 1 (Oct. 1960) 59.
FRAGMENT (As for him who/finds fault).
In *PB*.

C593 [Poem] *Folio*, XXV. 1 (Winter 1960) 2.
POEM (on getting a card).
The card was from E. E. Cummings. In *PB*.

C594 [Poem] *Inscape*, Albuquerque, N.M., No. 6 (Winter 1960–1961) 1.
TO BE RECITED TO FLOSSIE ON HER BIRTHDAY.
In *PB*. See D18.

C595 [Poem] *The Hasty Papers*, New York, "A One-Shot Review" [I. 1] (Dec. 1960) 45.

THE WORLD CONTRACTED TO A RECOGNIZABLE
IMAGE.
In *PB*. See B89 and T39 for first book publication.

C596 [Translated poem] *San Francisco Review*, I. 7 (Dec. 1960) 32.
*PROFILE OF A LADY.
Translated from the Chinese of Tu Fu by David Rafael Wang
and WCW. Reprinted in *New Directions 19* (1966) 224–225.

C597 [Three poems] *The National Review*, New York, IX. 22 (Dec. 3,
1960) 348.
SONG (you are forever April)—THE STONE CROCK—SONG
(beauty is a shell).
In *PB*. The second SONG is reprinted in *Agenda*, III. 1 (Aug.–
Sept. 1963) 7.

1961

C598 [Manuscript notes] *New Directions 17* (1961) 252–310.
*WILLIAM CARLOS WILLIAMS' "PATERSON": The Search
for the Redeeming Language—A Personal Epic in Five Parts.
By John C. Thirlwall, the article contains quotations both from
unpublished material by WCW and from material by WCW previously published in another essay by Thirlwall (C570).

C599 [Poem] *Inland* [formerly *Interim*], Seattle (March 1961), IV.
EXERCISE (Maybe it's his wife).
In *PB*.

C600 [Interview] *The Minnesota Review*, I. 3 (April 1961) 309–324.
*A VISIT WITH WILLIAM CARLOS WILLIAMS.
The interview was conducted by Walter Sutton.

C601 [Poem] *Sparrow*, West Lafayette, Ind., No. 15 (April 1961) 12.
*CONSTRUCTION.
Reprinted in *Agenda*, II. 7–8 (May–June 1962) 11.

C602. [Poem] *The Nation*, CXCII. 19 (May 13, 1961) 416.
*CEZANNE.
Reprinted in *Poetry*, CIII. 4 (Jan. 1964) 253.

C603 [Two poems] *Harper's Magazine*, CCXXII. 1333 (June 1961) 85.
SONG (I'd rather read an account)—THE CHILDREN.
In *PB*.

C604 "A VISIT TO WCW: SEPTEMBER, 1958." *Mica 3,* Santa Barbara, Calif. (June 1961) 16–22.

*"A Visit . . . from the diary of Gael Turnbull" contains remembered conversation with WCW. Reprinted in *The Massachusetts Review,* III. 2 (Winter 1962) 297–300.

C605 [Poem] *The Saturday Review,* XLIV. 27 (July 8, 1961) 31.
HEEL & TOE TO THE END
In *PB.*

C606 [Poem] *College Music Symposium,* I (Fall 1961) 109.
THE REWAKING.

[Note at end of poem:] "Composed April 10, 1961, expressly for the first issue of *Symposium.*" In *PB.* See also C479.

C607 [Poem] *Epoch,* Ithaca, N.Y., XI. 1 (Winter 1961) 22.
IRIS
In *PB.* Reprinted in *Agenda,* III. 1 (Aug.–Sept. 1963) 6.

C608 [Poem] *The New England Galaxy,* Sturbridge, Mass., II. 3 (Winter 1961) 27.
THE POLAR BEAR.
In *PB.*

C609 [Four poems] *The Hudson Review,* XIV. 4 (Winter 1961–1962) 527–529.

THE DANCE (When the snow falls)—JERSEY LYRIC—THE WOODTHRUSH—HE HAS BEATEN ABOUT THE BUSH LONG ENOUGH.
In *PB.*

C610 [Letter to the Editor, Shiro Murano] *Mugen,* Quarterly Magazine of Poetry, Tokyo, IX ([Dec. 1] 1961) 56.

Reproduction of *undated letter, signed "William Carlos Williams," expressing pleasure that *Mugen* is to have a special issue dedicated to him. The rest of the periodical is in Japanese (T67–70).

1962

C611 [Poem] *Focus / Midwest,* St. Louis, I. 4 (Sept. 1962) 16.
*THE ORCHARD.

C612 [Poem] *Poetry,* CI. 1–2 (Oct.–Nov. 1962) 141.
*STORMY.

C613 [Essay] *The Harvard Advocate,* CXLV. Special Supplement (Nov. 1962) 12.

> *ROBERT LOWELL'S VERSE TRANSLATION INTO THE AMERICAN IDIOM.

> Review of Lowell's *Imitations.*

C614 [Four poems] "Some Recent Poems." *The Massachusetts Review,* III. 2, A Gathering for William Carlos Williams (Winter 1962) 279–283.

> [C523: The High Bridge]—*THE BIRTH—THREE NAHUATL POEMS—[C578: A Formal Design].

> In *PB.* "A Gathering for William Carlos Williams" contains, in addition to the items listed below, several photographs of WCW and a self–portrait (see C478).

C615 "FOUR UNPUBLISHED LETTERS." *The Massachusetts Review,* III. 2 (Winter 1962) 292–296.

> *To James Laughlin, Jan. 6, 1941, and Nov. 15, 1943.

> *To John C. Thirlwall, March 12, 1956.

> *To Miss Robinson, March 20, 1957.

> John C. Thirlwall, who supplies notes for these letters, writes of the last one, "The letter to the poetess (name changed) . . . ."

C616 [Fragment of poem] *The Massachusetts Review,* III. 2 (Winter 1962) 307.

> A reproduction of a manuscript page, titled INTRODUCTION, of a poem written in imitation of Keats's "Endymion" when WCW was a medical student, late 1905 or early 1906.

C617 [Poem] *The Massachusetts Review,* III. 2 (Winter 1962) 311.

> *THE END OF THE ROPE.

> Note introducing the poem: "Worn out after receiving an honorary degree in 1950, WCW called on Ben Shahn in Roosevelt, N.J., leaving some lines as 'payment' for an hour's sleep."

C618 [Poem] *The Massachusetts Review,* III. 2 (Winter 1962) 324.

> *MIN SCHLEPPNER.

> Note at end of the poem: "This poem was recently called to WCW's attention by his brother, the architect Edgar I. Williams, to whom he sent it in 1910. Written in Leipzig, it shows Williams still using conventional rhyme."

C619 [Fragments from a play] *The Massachusetts Review,* III. 2 (Winter 1962) 331, 334, 342.

Reproduction of two manuscript pages from "The Awakening," an unpublished dramatic fragment of approximately 40 pages, written probably in 1929. Also reproduced is a WCW prescription blank containing a note for "The Awakening."

1963

C620 [Poem] *The New York Review of Books,* Special Issue of Spring and Summer Books [preceding I. 1] (May 20, 1963) 47.
  *CHERRY BLOSSOMS AT EVENING.
  Quoted in essay, "William Carlos Williams, 1883–1963," by Kenneth Burke.

C621 "FOUR LAST POEMS." *The Hudson Review,* XVI. 4 (Winter 1963–1964) 515–516.
  *THE ART—*GREETING FOR OLD AGE—*STILL LIFES —*TRALA TRALA TRALA LA-LE-LA.
  Note on p. [486:] "The poems in this issue by William Carlos Williams were among the last he wrote, and were found among his papers after his death."

C622 [Quotations] *Roche Medical Image,* New York, V. 6 (Dec. 1963) 10–13.
  *FOCUS ON WILLIAM CARLOS WILLIAMS, M.D.
  Article contains comments by WCW about being a doctor and poet; with photographs.

1964

C623 [Two poems] *Poetry,* CIII. 4 (Jan. 1964) 253–254.
  [C602: *Cezanne]—*THE MORAL.

C624 "SOME UNPUBLISHED MANUSCRIPT NOTES." *Niagara Frontier Review,* Buffalo, N.Y. (Summer 1964) 62–70.
  The twenty-nine fragments selected by David Posner from "the prescription sheets, advertisements, notepaper scraps which William Carlos Williams jotted on and gave to the Lockwood Library Poetry Collection" are described by Posner as "intriguing epiphanies, phrases overheard, sentences for essays, stanzas for poems, dialogues for plays," with the "rough date" for most of the selections of May 15, 1939.

C625 [Interview] *The Paris Review,* Paris and New York, 32 (Summer-Fall 1964) 110–151.

    *THE ART OF POETRY.

    The interview was conducted by Stanley Koehler in April, 1962. Mrs. Williams contributed many comments. Photograph of manuscript page by WCW relating to *Paterson (One)* is on p. 109.

C626 [Letter] *Island,* Toronto, No. 1 (Sept. 17, 1964) 47.

    *To Raymond Souster, June 28, 1952.

    About the technique of poetry.

C627 "A Williams Memoir," *Prairie Schooner,* XXXVIII. 4, American Classics Issue (Winter 1964–1965) 299–305.

    Reminiscences by Charles Angoff, including *conversation and *correspondence with WCW.

1965

C628 [Poem] *The Literary Review,* IX. 1 (Autumn 1965) 4.

    *ON ST. VALENTINE'S DAY

    The poem was found by Mrs. Williams in November, 1964, folded inside a book.

C629 [Three letters] *The Literary Review,* IX. 1 (Autumn 1965) 116, 118, 119.

    *To Edith Heal, Income Tax Day [March 15, 1950].

    *To Steve Berrien, Sept. 8, 1956.

    *To Edith Heal, Nov. 4, 1957.

    The three letters are reproduced in an article, "A Poet's Integrity," by Edith Heal (Mrs. Stephen Berrien), pp. 115–119.

C630 [Excerpts from letters] *Texas Studies in Literature and Language,* Austin, VI. 4 (Winter 1965) 487, 508.

    *To Hart Crane, Nov. 15, 1916.

    *To Hart Crane, April 19, 1917.

    *To Louis Zukofsky, Dec. 2, 1928.

    *To Guy Rhodes, Oct. 15, 1946.

    Excerpts from unpublished letters in an article, "William Carlos Williams, Hart Crane and the Virtue of History," by Joseph Evans Slate, pp. 486–511.

1966

C631 [Thirty-seven translated poems] "The Cassia Tree." *New Directions 19* (1966) 211–230.

POPULAR T'ANG AND SUNG POEMS: I. *In spring you sleep [Meng Hao-Chuan]—II. *Spotting the moonlight [Li Po]—III. *The birds have flown away [Liu Chung-Yuan]—IV. *Returning after I left my home [Ho Chi-Chong]—V. *Steering my little boat [Meng Hao-Chuan]—VI. *Alighting from my horse [Wang Wei]—VII. *Silently I ascend [Li Yu]—*THE MAID [Ancient folk poem]—*LAMENT OF A GRAYING WOMAN [Cho Wen-Chun]—SOCIETY OF POETS: I. *TO LI PO [Tu Fu]—II. *TO MENG HAO-CHUAN [Li Po]—III. *TO WANG WEI [Meng Hao-Chuan]—*AFTER THE PARTY [Meng Hao-Chuan]—*LATE SPRING [Meng Hao-Chuan]—*CE-LIA THE IMMORTAL BEAUTY [Wang Wei]—*THE PEERLESS LADY [Wang Wei]—*A LETTER [Li Po]—[C560: *Spring Song]—[C581: *Summer Song]—*IN THE WINESHOP OF CHINLING [Li Po]—*SOLO [Li Po]—*THE YOUTH ON HORSEBACK [Li Po]—*THE KNIGHT [Li Po]—*DRINKING TOGETHER [Li Po]—*THE MARCH [Li Po]—*LONG BANISTER LANE [Li Po]—*THE VISITOR [Adaptation of Li Po]—[C596: *Profile of a Lady]—*VISIT [Tu Fu]—*CHANT OF THE FRONTIERS-MAN [Wang Ch'ang-Ling]—[C566: *The Newlywed's Cuisine]—BELLA DONNA IU [Li Yu]—*IN DREAM'S WAKE [Li Ts'un-Hsu]—*from PHOENIX UNDYING [Kuo Mo-Jo]—*SPRING IN THE SNOW-DRENCHED GARDEN [Mao Tse-Tung]—*THE OLD MAN AND THE CHILD [Ping Hsin]—*THREE GENERATIONS [Tsong Kuh-Chia].

Translated from the Chinese by David Rafael Wang and WCW.

C632 [Letter] *Origin,* Kyoto, Japan, III. 1 (April 1966) 10.

*To Cid Corman, Sept. 29, 1953.

This letter, which originally was sent with the manuscript of the essay "On Measure" (C491), here precedes letters on measure by Corman.

C633 [Manuscript notes] *The Literary Review,* IX. 4 (Summer 1966) 502, 504, 506, 507.

Quotations from unpublished material by WCW in an article,

"William Carlos Williams' Bibliography," by Emily Wallace, pp. 501–512.

C634 [Essay] *Form,* Cambridge, England, I. 2 (Sept. 1, 1966) 22, 24–25. *Emanuel Romano.

Introduced and edited by Michael Weaver, the essay, written in 1951 (see D8), is accompanied by black and white reproductions of an oil portrait (1951) and two pen drawings (1951 and 1957) of WCW by Romano.

1967

C635 [Poem] *Rutgers Review,* Rutgers, I. 2 (Spring 1967) 24–25. *TRIBUTE TO NERUDA THE POET COLLECTOR OF SEA-SHELLS.

Printed version is accompanied by reproduction of WCW's signed typescript of the poem, which was probably written early in 1960, according to José Vázquez-Amaral's Introduction, "Williams' Poem to Neruda," p. 23.

C. PERIODICALS
ADDENDA

D–H

MISCELLANEA

D. BROADSHEETS AND LEAFLETS, INCLUDING THEATER PROGRAMS, GREETING CARDS, ANNOUNCEMENTS OF ART EXHIBITIONS, AND OFFPRINTS

E. MUSICAL SETTINGS

F. RECORDINGS AND RADIO SCRIPTS OR TRANSCRIPTS

G. BRIEF STATEMENTS ON BOOK AND PERIODICAL COVERS AND IN ADVERTISEMENTS

H. MEDICAL ARTICLE IN MEDICAL JOURNAL

D. BROADSHEETS AND LEAFLETS, INCLUDING
THEATER PROGRAMS ET CETERA

D1 *Essay, A NEW BOOK OF THE DEAD!, about Norman Macleod's *You Get What You Ask For,* published by Harrison-Hilton
Books, Inc., New York, 1939.
> Broadsheet, 8 1/2 × 7 3/8 inches, printed on both sides.
> Published also in periodical, C296.

D2 *Statement, untitled, for catalog of paintings (1940): WEINGAERT-
NER | [*drawing*] | Weingaertner's Home Gallery | 312 Lake Avenue
| Lyndhurst, New Jersey | April 14, 1940.
> Broadsheet folded vertically and horizontally. [4] pp. 10 × 7 inches.
> Coated paper.
> [1:] *Title.* [2–3:] *Catalog of paintings by Hans Weingaertner.*
> [4:] *Statement by WCW about the paintings.*

D3 Poem, ROGATION SUNDAY, in bulletin (1947): Rural Life Sun-
day | May 18th, 1947, 7:30 p.m. | Livingston County Pomona
Grange | Third Annual Service | The Avon Methodist Church |
Avon, N.Y.
> Broadsheet folded vertically. [4] pp. 8 1/2 × 5 1/2 inches. Mimeo-
> graphed.
> [1:] *Title.* [2–3:] *Program of service.* [4:] ROGATION SUN-
> DAY, *dated* March 4, 1947, *written at Harriet Gratwick's request
> especially for the Linwood Grange Agricultural Chorus, which read it
> at the May 18 meeting.*
> Set to music by Thomas S. Canning in 1950 (E3). The poem is in
> *CLP²*; periodical publication, C528.

D4 Off-print of poems, THE PAUSE and BRAHMS FIRST PIANO
CONCERTO, and essay, SOMETHING FOR A BIOGRAPHY
(1948): Reprinted from | The General MAGAZINE | AND | His-
torical Chronicle | [*double rule*] | VOL. L—NO. IV PHILADEL-
PHIA SUMMER 1948 | [*rule*] | UNIVERSITY | OF | PENN-
SYLVANIA | THE | General Alumni Society. | [*device*] | [*rule*] |
SOMETIME | Printed and Sold by B. FRANKLIN. | 1741.
> 6 pp. numbered 209–214, as in first printing, with heavy blue
> paper covers printed in black on front; stapled. 9 1/2 × 6 1/4 inches.
> [Cover:] *Title.* [1:] *Printed material.* [2:] THE PAUSE—
> BRAHMS FIRST PIANO CONCERTO *by WCW.* [3–5:] SOME-
> THING FOR A BIOGRAPHY *by WCW.* [6:] *Printed material.*

First publication, C405, C406. The poems are in *CLP;* second poem retitled NOTE TO MUSIC: BRAHMS 1ST PIANO CONCERTO. The essay was revised for inclusion in Chapter 12 of *The Auto-biography* (A35).

D5   *Essay for announcement of art exhibition (1950): PICASSO | The Figure | NOVEMBER 6, 1939 – MAY 4, 1944 | JANUARY 9 – FEBRUARY 9, 1950 | LOUIS CARRÉ GALLERY | 712 Fifth Avenue, New York [*on back, p.* [4]:] GALERIE LOUIS CARRÉ | 10, Avenue de Messine, Paris.

Broadsheet of buff paper folded vertically. [4] pp. 9 7/8 × 6 1/2 inches; paper folded again (horizontally) to fit white envelope.

[1, 4:] *Title.* [2–3:] *Essay:* PICASSO STICKS OUT | AN IN-VESTED WORLD | "Nuts" says Spanish Painter in Effect to Forces of | Evil at Current Show From Inside | Louis Carré Gallery | By William Carlos Williams | Rutherford, N. J., 12/25/49.

Essay is prefaced by a brief account of an interview with WCW by "roving reporter" Jerome Mellquist, in which a statement by WCW is quoted.

Issued gratis January 9–February 9, 1950; 2,000 copies printed.

Reprinted in periodical, C449; retitled PICASSO BREAKS FACES, prefatory remarks about interview omitted, and first sentence of essay changed.

D6   *Statement about Merrill Moore's sonnets.

Yellow broadsheet printed in red. 11 × 8 1/2 inches. Issued gratis 1951 by Twayne Publishers, Inc., New York, to advertise Moore's *Clinical Sonnets* (1949), *Illegitimate Sonnets* (1950), and *Case Record from a Sonnetorium* (1951).

The statement is an excerpt from the foreword by WCW to Merrill Moore's *Sonnets from New Directions,* B31.

D7   *A STATEMENT BY WILLIAM CARLOS WILLIAMS | ABOUT THE POEM *PATERSON*: News from New Directions | for immedi-ate release | May 31, 1951.

3 pp. 14 13/16 × 8 11/16 inches. Mimeographed.

Statement of about 700 words about "the total poem," written by WCW shortly before the publication of *Paterson* (*Four*).

D8   *Statement, untitled, for catalog of paintings (1951): Emanuel | Romano | [Georgette] PASSEDOIT GALLERY | 121 EAST 57 ST., N.Y. | DECEMBER 3 – 22, 1951.

Broadsheet folded vertically. [4] pp. 9 × 6 inches.

[1:] *Title.* [2:] *Statement by WCW about Emanuel Romano's paintings.* [3:] *Catalog of paintings.* [4:] *Blank.*

Issued gratis December 3-22, 1951; 500 copies printed.

WCW's statement is four paragraphs of an essay completed November, 1951; the complete essay, edited by Michael Weaver, is published in *Form,* C634.

D9 *Letter in theater program ([1952]): THE LIVING THEATRE | [*line drawing*] | STEIN | PICASSO | ELIOT [*New York*]

16 pp. with dark brown paper covers printed in black; stapled at fold. 8 9/16 × 6 3/16 inches.

WCW's letter, pp. 5 and 7, titled "Reply," undated, is addressed "Dear X" and is about poetry and prose "X" had sent to WCW for comment.

The three plays listed in this program, Gertrude Stein's *Ladies' Voices,* Picasso's *Desire* (*Trapped by the Tail*), and T. S. Eliot's *Sweeney Agonistes,* opened March 2, 1952.

D9a *Statement, untitled, on theater handbill ([1952]).

Broadsheet. 13 1/4 × 6 7/8 inches. White paper into which red straws were matted; untrimmed, printed on one side in black.

Mailed to subscribers of The Living Theatre, the handbill announces the opening of Paul Goodman's *Faustina,* Sunday evening, May 25, [1952].

Statement by WCW is about the three plays presented by The Living Theatre listed above, D9.

D10 Essay, *THE AMERICAN LANGUAGE—AGAIN: *The Pound Newsletter,* Berkeley, Calif., No. 8 (Oct. 1955) 2-7.

35 pp. 11 × 8 1/2 inches. Mimeographed. Stapled at top left corner. Copies were available upon request.

D11 Letter to Babette Deutsch: *The Pound Newsletter,* No. 8 (Oct. 1955) 22-23. See D10 above. Dated January 18, 1943, the letter, which has some deletions, is preceded by a brief note by John C. Thirlwall. In *SL* without deletions.

D12 *Statement for catalog of paintings (1957): [*Reproduction of painting*] | #1 | HENRY NIESE | JANUARY 8 through FEBRUARY 2, 1957 | G Gallery [*large, square G with Gallery set into lower right corner*] | 200 East 59th Street New York 22, N.Y.

Broadsheet folded vertically and horizontally. [4] pp. 8 3/4 × 5 3/4 inches. Coated paper.

[1:] *Title*. [2:] *Statement by WCW about Henry Niese's paintings; reproduction of painting #12*. [3:] *Reproduction of painting #13; catalog of paintings*. [4:] *List of gallery artists*.

Issued gratis January 8–February 2, 1957; 2000 copies printed.

WCW's statement was written probably in November, 1956.

[*The Grecourt Review*, Northampton, Mass., December, 1957].

[4] pp. with buff blank paper covers; stapled at fold. 9 × 6 1/16 inches.

[1:] THE SWIVELHIPPED AMAZON *by WCW*. [All other pages are blank.]

First publication, C547. In *PB* retitled MOUNTED AS AN AMAZON.

D14 Poem, SAPPHO, on broadsheet ([1957]): See B75.

D15 Off-print of essay, A NOTE ON THE TURN OF THE VIEW TOWARD POETIC TECHNIQUE ([1958]): Reprinted from | THE HANOVER FORUM | Hanover, Indiana | Vol. V, No. 1 [Winter 1958–1959].

[8] pp. Stapled at fold. 9 × 6 1/16 inches.

Periodical publication: C563. Similar to letter of Jan. 13, 1955, *SL*.

D13 Off-print of poem, THE SWIVELHIPPED AMAZON ([1957]):

D16 Poem, THE GIFT, as Christmas card (1957): THE GIFT | A POEM BY | William Carlos Williams | CHRISTMAS 1957

Broadsheet folded vertically. [4] pp. 7 5/16 × 3 13/16 inches. Fore and bottom edges untrimmed on some cards.

[1:] *Title*. [2–3:] THE GIFT. [4:] Printed at Christmas, 1957 | for the friends of | William Carlos Williams | and New Directions | "The Gift" was first published in | "The Hudson Review" | Copyright © 1957 | by William Carlos Williams

Issued Christmas, 1957; 2500 copies printed by Peter Beilenson at The Walpole Printing Office, Mt. Vernon, N.Y.; 100 copies for Dr. and Mrs. Williams printed with the names "Bill and Floss"; 200 copies for Mr. and Mrs. John C. Thirlwall printed "Fuji and John Thirlwall"; 500 copies for Mr. and Mrs. James Laughlin printed "Ann and J Laughlin"; 1700 copies printed "New Directions."

In *PB;* periodical publication, C526.

D17 Poem, THE GIFT, as Christmas card ([1962]):

Broadsheet folded vertically and horizontally. [4] pp. 8 1/2 × 8 7/16 inches.

[1:] *Color reproduction of Giotto's "Adoration of the Magi"* [2:] THE GIFT [*in very small print at end of poem*:] © William Carlos Williams [*at foot of page*:] Giotto (1267–1337) | Adoration of the Magi | Fresco, Scrovegni Chapel, Padua [3:] GREETINGS | AND BEST WISHES | FOR A | MERRY CHRISTMAS | AND A | HAPPY NEW YEAR [*handwritten signature*:] Bill and Floss [4, *at foot of page*:] Print from the SKIRA Collection | [*device*] | Hallmark | 6015 | © Hallmark Cards, Inc. | Made in U. S. A.

Issued Christmas, 1962, at 60¢.

(THE GIFT is reprinted in *American Christmas,* edited by Webster Schott and Robert J. Myers, Hallmark Cards, Inc., Kansas City, Missouri, 1965, pp. 30–31.)

D18 Poem, TO BE RECITED TO FLOSSIE ON HER BIRTHDAY, (1959): W.C.W.—F.H.W. | April 18, 1959

Broadsheet folded horizontally and vertically. [4] pp. 5 7/16 × 3 1/2 inches. Fore edge untrimmed.

[1:] *Title.* [2:] *Blank.* [3:] TO BE RECITED TO FLOSSIE ON HER BIRTHDAY. [4:] One hundred Copies of this Poem | have been printed for Florence Williams | at the Press of Igal Roodenko | © 1959 by William Carlos Williams

In *PB*; periodical publication, C594.

D19 *Statement in theater program (1960): THE | LIVING | THEATRE [*line drawing*] | REPERTORY | 1960 [New York]

[16] pp. with rough tan paper covers printed in black; stapled at fold.

WCW's statement, an excerpt from a letter he had written to Judith Malina and Julian Beck in praise of The Living Theatre's first production, Gertrude Stein's *Doctor Faustus Lights the Lights,* is on p. [5] in an essay, "A History of the Living Theatre."

Three plays are listed in this program: Jack Gelber's *The Connection,* which opened July 15, 1959; and Jackson MacLow's *The Marrying Maiden* and Sophokles' *Women of Trachis* (in a version by Ezra Pound), which were added to The Living Theatre Repertory June 22, 1960.

D20 *Statement for theater program (1960): THE | '92 THEATER PRESENTS | UNDER THE STARS | AND A DREAM OF LOVE

| A POET IN THE THEATER: TWO PLAYS | ADMISSION FREE—NO RESERVED SEATS | SATURDAY, 14 MAY 1960 8:00 P.M. [*vertically on left side:*] WILLIAM CARLOS | WILLIAMS [*Directed by Clinton J. Atkinson, Jr., Wesleyan University, Middletown, Conn.*]

Broadsheet folded vertically in thirds. [6] pp. 4 × 6 inches (opens to 18 inches). Buff paper.

WCW's statement, pp. [2–3], is about UNDER THE STARS, a "ten or twelve page dialogue" never before produced, and about his wanting "to write for the stage but it has always proved a will-o-the-wisp for me, production has always escaped me by a hair's breadth."

First publication of *UNDER THE STARS, C350; of A DREAM OF LOVE, A27.

D21 *Statement for announcement of art exhibition (1962): FEBRUARY 13 – MARCH 3 PREVIEW FEBRUARY 13, 7–9 | SEYMOUR SHAPIRO | STABLE GALLERY 33 EAST 74TH STREET, NEW YORK 21 [*artist's name in yellow*]

Broadsheet folded vertically. [4] pp. 5 3/4 × 5 inches.

[1:] *Title.* [2:] *Statement of one sentence by WCW.* [3:] *Reproduction of painting, untitled, by Seymour Shapiro.* [4:] *Blank.*

Issued gratis 1962; 1000 copies printed.

Seymour Shapiro was a neighbor and friend of WCW in Rutherford, N.J. The original draft of the announcement, with WCW's corrections and signature, is in Shapiro's possession. WCW's statement: "The artist, divorced from sense, might as well be called a poet unless he has not forgot the prime importance of measure."

D22 *Poem, BIRD SONG, on broadsheet ([1963]): 12 × 8 5/16 inches. Printed on one side only. Proof of advertisement by Steuben Glass that appeared in the New York Philharmonic Hall program, May 13 to 19, 1963; 100 copies of proof printed and distributed after publication of *Poetry in Crystal* (B91).

Photograph of crystal piece on top left of sheet, BIRD SONG on top right, advertising below.

Poem reprinted in *WFLN Philadelphia Guide* (Feb. 1965) p. 9.

D23 *"CONSTRUCTS" by David Lyle, Rock Hill, Wanaque, N.J. From 1938 to the present Lyle has distributed thousands of his constructs or montages to friends of WCW. The constructs, on sheets (11 × 8 1/2 inches) of different colors and weights, are made through various duplicating processes (mimeographing, Xeroxing, etc.) in several colors, typing, handwriting, drawing, pasting, and stapling, so that no two constructs are exactly alike. They contain fragments of poems and quotations from unpublished letters by WCW, freely arranged. For an example, see *Trace,* Hollywood, Calif., No. 49 (Summer 1963) 160, which contains a reproduction, reduced in size, of "Arrangement from Paterson · In honor of William Carlos Williams" by Lyle. For an article about Lyle's relationship to Williams' writing of *Paterson,* see "The poet and the engineer, or, birth of a masterpiece" by Ann Marie Sullivan in the biweekly newspaper *Trends,* Riverdale, N.J. (Thurs., May 5, 1966) 23.

E. MUSICAL SETTINGS

E1 Poem, DANSE RUSSE, set to music ([1935]): SECOND RHAP-
SODY for Tenor and Piano (four hands) by Irwin Heilner.
 Broadsheet folded vertically. [4] pp. 13 13/16 × 10 1/4 inches.
 New Music Edition, regular series, Henry Cowell, Editor. Published
by Golden West Music Press, San Francisco and Los Angeles, at 75¢
for one or $2.00 for four.
 Poem is in *CEP*; first publication, C15.

E2 Poem, CHORAL: THE PINK CHURCH, set to music (1946). See
C374.

E3 Poem, ROGATION SUNDAY, set to music (1950): HYMN FOR
ROGATION SUNDAY, with music for chorus and orchestra by
Thomas S. Canning.
 10 pp. 11 1/16 × 8 9/16 inches.
 Performed August 13, 1950, by the Linwood Music School, Linwood,
Livingston County, New York.
 Poem is in *CEP*; see D3.

E4 Poem, DAWN, set to music (1961): DAWN for soprano and piano
by Vincent Di Fiore.
 5 pp. 12 1/4 × 9 7/16 inches. One copy only in pencil. Music composed by Vincent Di Fiore at Rocky Ridge Music Center, Estes Park,
Colorado, summer, 1961.
 Poem is in *CEP.*

E5 *Poem set to music (1964): REVERIE AND INVOCATION for
choir and organ or piano by Stanley A. Purdy.
 11, [1] pp. 11 × 7 inches.
 Fairleigh Dickinson University Choral Series, No. 302. Editorial
Notes by Thomas N. Monroe, Chairman, Music Department, Fairleigh
Dickinson University, Rutherford, N.J. *At foot of p. 3:* "© 1964 Fair-
leigh Dickinson University Press"
 The poem is not reprinted.

F. RECORDINGS AND RADIO SCRIPTS OR TRANSCRIPTS

Recordings that are for sale or that are deposited in library collections are listed here, as well as radio scripts or transcripts.

Although the libraries that hold the recordings are indicated, some of the recordings are not at present available to the public. The Free Public Library, Rutherford, New Jersey, has duplicate copies on tape of each of the recordings it holds, but does not at present have listening facilities for the public, and the tapes may not be removed from the library.

Not described here are recordings in private collections and television programs dramatizing Williams' life and work. The television programs include a dramatization of three of Williams' short stories on "Camera 3," CBS, November 10, 1963, produced by Sid Maglen; a CBS film about Williams made in 1966 (see F7); and a National Educational Television program about Williams made in 1967.

F1 [Eight poems] On January 9, 1942, Williams recorded for the National Council of Teachers of English, Columbia University Press, Contemporary Poets, Series 55-56 (78 rpm) the following poems: THE RED WHEELBARROW—TRACT—A CORONAL—THE DEFECTIVE RECORD—TO AN OLD WOMAN—TO ELSIE—THE WIND INCREASES—CLASSIC SCENE. In a typed list in a small notebook, YALC, Williams refers to this record as "my first disc."

F2 [Forty-nine poems and one short story] On May 5, 1945, Williams recorded in The Library of Congress Recording Laboratory (acetate discs; not for sale) the following: SONNET: 1909 [*also titled* MARTIN AND KATHERINE *and* THE WARTBURG]—PATERSON: THE FALLS—PEACE ON EARTH—POSTLUDE—PASTORAL (When I was younger)—PASTORAL (The little sparrows)—DAWN —PORTRAIT OF A WOMAN IN BED—SYMPATHETIC PORTRAIT OF A CHILD—SPRING STRAINS—DEDICATION FOR A PLOT OF GROUND—LOVE SONG (I lie here thinking of you) —OVERTURE TO A DANCE OF LOCOMOTIVES—COMPLAINT—THE COLD NIGHT—PRIMROSE—QUEEN-ANN'S-LACE—TO A FRIEND CONCERNING SEVERAL LADIES— YOUTH AND BEAUTY—THE THINKER—THE NIGHTIN-

259

GALES—THE WIDOW'S LAMENT IN SPRINGTIME—LIGHT
HEARTED WILLIAM—SPRING AND ALL—THE FARMER—
THE EYEGLASSES—SHOOT IT JIMMY!—TO ELSIE—THE
RED WHEELBARROW—RIGAMAROLE—IT IS A LIVING
CORAL—THE BULL—THE BOTTICELLIAN TREES—FLOW-
ERS BY THE SEA—THE YACHTS—THE TERM—A SORT OF
A SONG—THE DANCE (In Breughel's great picture)—BURNING
THE CHRISTMAS GREENS—IN SISTERLY FASHION—THE
WORLD NARROWED TO A POINT—THE HOUNDED LOV-
ERS—THE CURE—THE ROSE (The stillness of the rose)—PER-
FECTION—THE LAST TURN—THE AFTERMATH—THE
YELLOW CHIMNEY—THE YELLOW CHIMNEY [*rereading*]—
RALEIGH WAS RIGHT—[*short story*] A NIGHT IN JUNE.

In 1958 these poems and the short story were transferred by The
Library of Congress from the acetate discs to tape LWO 2689 (reel
11). See also F4, 11 and 21.

F3 [Three poems and three selections from *Paterson*] On October 18,
1947, a reading by Williams was scheduled, under the sponsorship of
Robert Lowell, in The Library of Congress Recording Laboratory, but
the recording was actually made at the NBC Studio in Washington
and sent to the Library (acetate discs; not for sale): THE SEM-
BLABLES—THE CATHOLIC BELLS—PERPETUUM MOBILE:
THE CITY—*from* PATERSON, TWO, III: [*first and last lines*]
Look for the nul . . . . Alone, watching the May moon above the trees
—*from* PATERSON, ONE, I: [*first and last lines:*] Paterson lies in
the valley under the Passaic Falls . . . . after a long flight to his cote
—*from* PATERSON, ONE, II: [*first and last lines:*] There is no
direction. Whither? I . . . . it drives in among the rocks fitfully.

In 1958 these poems were transferred by The Library of Congress
from the acetate discs to tape LWO 2689 (reels 10 and 11); this reading was transferred to tape before the reading of 1945 (F2).

F4 [Six poems] In 1949 six poems from the 1945 reading (F2) were made
available for commercial sale by The Library of Congress, Twentieth
Century Poetry in English, Album IV, P-16 (78 rpm; $1.65 plus post-
age): PEACE ON EARTH—LIGHT HEARTED WILLIAM—

D—H: *Miscellanea*

SPRING AND ALL—IT IS A LIVING CORAL—QUEEN-ANN'S-LACE—THE YACHTS. See F11.

F5 [Six poems] On May 20, 1949, Williams recorded poems for Columbia Records, which were released December 5, 1949, in *Pleasure Dome,* "an audible anthology of modern poetry read by its creators and edited by Lloyd Frankenberg," MM877 (4 records, 78 rpm) and ML4259 (33 1/3 rpm): THE YOUNG HOUSEWIFE—THE BULL —POEM (As the cat)—LEAR—THE DANCE (In Breughel's great picture)—EL HOMBRE. The other poets on this record are Eliot, Marianne Moore, Cummings, Ogden Nash, Auden, Dylan Thomas, and Elizabeth Bishop.

F6 [Statements about writing] "Symposium on Writing," under the direction of Richard Wirtz Emerson, broadcast October 7, 1950, Station WOSU, Columbus, Ohio—see C460.

F7 [Interview and five poems] On January 13, 1951, at Williams' home in Rutherford, Jack Gerber recorded an hour's interview on tape (15 ips), from which acetate discs were made. The original tape was destroyed, but from the discs, several recordings (2 tapes, 7 1/2 ips) were made, one of which is in the Rutherford Free Public Library, one at the University of Puerto Rico, and others in private collections. There are also several typescripts of the interview. Part of the interview (28 min.) was broadcast on Jack Gerber's weekly radio program on WNBC, and a longer version was later broadcast on WNYC. The complete interview offers a precise and full discussion by Williams of many aspects of his life as a doctor and poet. He also reads and comments on five poems: DANSE RUSSE—THIS IS JUST TO SAY—OL' BUNK'S BAND—PORTRAIT OF A LADY—EL HOMBRE.

Excerpts from the tape recording were used in a CBS television program (30 min.) about Williams made by Alfred Waller in 1966 and titled "In the American Grain." (The 16 mm. film may be borrowed for educational purposes, with special permission, from the Rutherford Free Public Library.)

F8 [Eight poems and one selection from *Paterson*] On June 21, 1951, Williams recorded nine poems on tape at Kenneth Burke's home in Andover, New Jersey: THE DESERT MUSIC—THE COD HEAD —BURNING THE CHRISTMAS GREENS—A SORT OF A

SONG—*from* PATERSON, ONE, III: [*first and last lines:*] How strange you are, you idiot! . . . his mind drinks of desire]—TRACT —APRÈS LE BAIN—SPRING IS HERE AGAIN, SIR—MAY 1ST TOMORROW. This recording (one tape, 7 1/2 ips; approx. 30 min.), unedited, includes brief comments between the poems and music at the end; on deposit in YALC—the permission of Mrs. Williams is required to hear the tape. Also on tape at the Rutherford Free Public Library, but not presently (1968) available to the public.

F9 [Twenty poems] In 1952 Williams recorded twenty poems on wire at Ivan Earle's home in California: IN SISTERLY FASHION— TRACT—SMELL!—FLOWERS BY THE SEA—THE POOR (It's the anarchy of poverty)—TO ELSIE—THIS IS JUST TO SAY— IMPROMPTU: THE SUCKERS, 1927—ALL THE FANCY THINGS—IT IS A LIVING CORAL—YOUNG SYCAMORE— THE COD HEAD—THE BULL—POEM (As the cat)—PER-PETUUM MOBILE: THE CITY—THE WIDOW'S LAMENT IN SPRINGTIME—ARRIVAL—GREAT MULLEN—QUEEN-ANN'S-LACE—OVERTURE TO A DANCE OF LOCOMOTIVES [*broken off in the middle, apparently because the end of the wire had been reached*]. This recording, unedited, includes brief comments between the poems; transferred to tape (one tape, 7 1/2 ips; approx. 30 min.), it is on deposit in YALC—the permission of Mrs. Williams is required to hear the tape. Also on tape at the Rutherford Free Public Library, but not presently (1968) available to the public.

F10 [Statements about poetry] On March 5, 1952, Eli Siegel gave a talk, "Williams' Poetry Looked At: A Critical Poem," which Williams heard and responded to in spontaneous discussion afterwards. The talk and discussion were recorded and prepared for publication in book form by Martha Baird—see B94 for more complete information. The recording has not been released.

F11 [Six poems] In 1954 the recording of 1949 (F4) was reissued by The Library of Congress, Twentieth Century Poetry in English, PL-4 (33 1/3 rps; $4.95). The other poets on this record are John Gould Fletcher, John Malcolm Brinnin and Robert Penn Warren.

F12 [Interview and three poems] On March 26, 1954, on an NBC radio program called "Anthology," Williams answered questions asked by the announcer, Fleetwood, and read three poems: THE DESCENT— THE HOST—THE ORCHESTRA. The thirty minute program, produced by Draper Lewis, was recorded on an acetate disc (33 1/3 rpm; labeled "Aura Recording, Inc., 136 West 53rd Street, New York 19, N.Y."), from which a tape (7 1/2 ips) was made. At the Rutherford Free Public Library, but not presently (1968) available to the public.

F13 [Talk about poetry] On March 28, 1954, Williams talked about poetry and the American language on NBC for a fifteen minute program probably introduced by Roger Kennedy, who says that Williams previously had read his poems on this program. The talk was recorded on side two of an acetate disc (33 1/3 rpm) labeled " 'Collectors Item' Exc 3/28/54 | William Carlos Williams Portion . . . | Sales 4/24/54 Dubb"; side one contains other material from the program. At the Rutherford Free Public Library, but not presently (1968) available to the public.

F14 [Fourteen poems and commentary] In April, 1954, Williams gave a public reading at the University of Puerto Rico, which was recorded on "CBS magnetic recording tape" (3 3/4 ips; double track; 1 hr., 15 min.; CBS is the brand name of the tape, not the broadcasting station; handwritten identification on the box: "William Carlos Williams . . . Recorded by Audio Visual"). This reading, unedited, includes several long statements about poetry and many brief comments about the individual poems: Introduction about adventurous and revolutionary voyages made by sailors and by poets—TO WAKEN AN OLD LADY—PRIMROSE—SPRING AND ALL—ON GAY WALLPAPER—EVE—THE SUN—translations by Kenneth Rexroth of two poems by García Lorca—A SORT OF A SONG—A PLACE (ANY PLACE) TO TRANSCEND ALL PLACES—THE HORSE SHOW —statement about the American idiom and a new measure, a "flexible foot"—THE DESCENT [taken from *Paterson*]—TO DAPHNE AND VIRGINIA—THE YELLOW FLOWER—THEOCRITUS: IDYL 1—ASPHODEL, THAT GREENY FLOWER, Book 1. At the Rutherford Free Public Library, but not presently (1968) available to the public.

F15 [Interview and one poem] "Voice of America . . . . Interview with Dr. William Carlos Williams." On June 18, 1954, Francis Mason's interview of Williams for the Voice of America, Department of State, International Broadcasting Services, International Information Administration, was recorded on side one of a disc (33 1/3 rpm; approx.

30 min.); side two is blank. Williams reads during the interview one poem: THE DESCENT. Also preserved in typescript, 2 single spaced pages.

[Six poems] On a tape (7 1/2 ips; approx. 10 min.) labeled "Voice of America, United States Information Agency," Williams reads six poems: POEM (As the cat)—THE YOUNG HOUSEWIFE—LIGHTHEARTED WILLIAM—THE DANCE—THE BULL—THE YACHTS. The date is unknown. The Voice of America interview and typescript and the recording of six poems are at the Rutherford Free Public Library, but are not presently (1968) available to the public.

F16 [Twenty poems] In 1955 Williams again (see F9) recorded twenty poems on tape at Ivan Earle's home in California: Reel One: PEACE ON EARTH—THE BOTTICELLIAN TREES—FLOWERS BY THE SEA—PRIMROSE—SPRING AND ALL—ON GAY WALL-PAPER—THE RED LILY—THE SUN—A SORT OF A SONG—MAY 1ST TOMORROW—A UNISON—statement about the variable foot—THE DESCENT—TO DAPHNE AND VIRGINIA. Reel Two: THE ORCHESTRA—THE YELLOW FLOWER—THE HOST—THE MENTAL HOSPITAL GARDEN—WORK IN PROGRESS [Asphodel, That Greeny Flower: *a few lines not in final version followed by the last part of* Book 1, *beginning* "All women are not Helen" *to end of* Book 1]—THE IVY CROWN—SHADOWS—WORK IN PROGRESS [Asphodel, That Greeny Flower: Coda: *cut off at* "and that not the darker/ which John Donne," *apparently because the end of the tape had been reached*]. This recording, unedited, includes brief comments between the poems; on deposit (two tapes, 7 1/2 ips, "Reel One" and "Reel Two"; approx. 1 hr.) in YALC—the permission of Mrs. Williams is required to hear the tapes. Also on tape at the Rutherford Free Public Library, but not presently (1968) available to the public.

F17 [Description of Rutherford, New Jersey] In July, 1955, "William Carlos Williams on Rutherford, New Jersey," number 13 of the "This Is America" series broadcast by the Voice of America, was read by John Pauker. 4 double spaced typed pages. At foot of p. 4: "(Material for this script was drawn, with the permission of the author and the Curtis Publishing Company, from a longer article written by William

Carlos Williams for Holiday Magazine [C502].)" The series offered
descriptions by twenty-eight writers, including Wallace Stevens on
Connecticut, James T. Farrell on Chicago, John Steinbeck on New
York, Kenneth Rexroth on San Francisco, Robert Lowell on Boston,
Marianne Moore on Brooklyn, Elizabeth Gray Vining on Philadelphia,
Louise Bogan on New York. The scripts were translated into many of
the thirty-seven languages used by the Voice of America in its daily
schedule.

F18 [Statement about Ezra Pound] "A Tribute to Ezra Pound," broadcast December 5, 1955, on WYBC, the Yale Broadcasting Company.
Narration by Joel T. Daly. Editing and technical supervision by
Edmund L. Dana, Jr. Written and produced by Frederic D. Grab
and Reid B. Johnson in honor of Pound's seventieth birthday. The 16
double spaced pages of the typescript contain many statements by
Williams. See also T23.

F19 [Eighteen poems] On June 6, 1954, Williams recorded a number of
poems at his home in Rutherford for Caedmon Publishers, New
York. In 1956 eighteen poems were released by Caedmon on record
TC 1047 (33 1/3 rpm; $5.95), *William Carlos Williams Reading His
Poems:* Side A: THE DESCENT—TO DAPHNE AND VIRGINIA
—THE ORCHESTRA—FOR ELEANOR AND BILL MONAHAN
—THE YELLOW FLOWER—THE HOST—WORK IN PROG-
RESS [*the last 21 lines of* Asphodel, That Greeny Flower, Book 1].
Side B: THE BOTTICELLIAN TREES—FLOWERS BY THE SEA
—THE YACHTS—THE CATHOLIC BELLS—SMELL!—FISH—
PRIMROSE—TO ELSIE—BETWEEN WALLS—ON GAY WALL-
PAPER—THE RED LILY. On the sleeve of the record is a photo-
graph of Williams by Paul Bishop and a brief statement by the poet.

F20 [One poem] In 1957 one poem from the June, 1954, reading (F19
above) was released by Caedmon Publishers, TC 2006 (2 records,
33 1/3 rpm; $11.90), *The Caedmon Treasury of Modern Poets Read-
ing:* THE SEAFARER. The other poets on these records are Eliot,
Yeats, Auden, Edith Sitwell, Dylan Thomas, MacNeice, Graves,
Gertrude Stein, MacLeish, Cummings, Marianne Moore, Empson,
Spender, Aiken, Frost, Stevens, Eberhart, Elizabeth Bishop, and
Wilbur.

F21 [One poem] In 1959 one poem from the 1945 reading (F2) was included in *An Album of Modern Poetry,* The Library of Congress,

Twentieth Century Poetry in English, PL 20, 21, and 22 (33 1/3 rpm; $14.05): THE YACHTS. Edited by Oscar Williams, the album contains forty-six poets reading a total of seventy-eight poems. Williams is on PL20.

G. BRIEF STATEMENTS ON BOOK AND PERIODICAL COVERS AND IN ADVERTISEMENTS

For statements by WCW on the dust jackets of his own books, see *In the American Grain*, A9a, c; *First Act*, A21b; *Paterson (Three)*, A30a; *Paterson (Five)*, A44a; he may also have written or contributed to the statement on the jacket of *Al Que Quiere!*, A3.

G1 *Pagany*, Boston, III. 4 (Fall–Winter 1932–1933) i.
   Statement by WCW about *The Water Wheel* by Julian L. Shapiro in an advertisement of The Dragon Press, Ithaca, N.Y.

G2 *Dune Forum*, Oceano, Calif., Subscribers' Number ([1933–1934]) 17. [Issued prior to I. 1 (Jan. 15, 1934).]
   Statement by WCW, from a letter to the editor, Gavin Arthur, says: "Nothing to send just now, so tho't I'd send it. Best luck—or say best wind, to Dunes."

G3 *A Test of Poetry* by Louis Zukofsky (Brooklyn: The Objectivist Press, 1948).
   Hard covers, 165 pp. Statement by WCW on front of dust jacket about the book, which is a comparative study of world poetry in English from Homer to the present.

G4 *Gutbucket and Gossamer, A Short Story* by Fred Miller (Yonkers, New York: The Alicat Bookshop Press, 1950).
   Paper covers, 28 pp. Statement by WCW in "Publisher's Note" on p. [1] about Fred Miller's story.

G5 *Delta Return* by Charles G. Bell (Bloomington: Indiana University Press, 1956).
   Hard covers, 95 pp. Statement by WCW on front flap of dust jacket about Bell's poems. See C529.

G6 *Edge*, Melbourne, Australia, No. 5 (May 1957) and No. 7 (Aug. 1957).
   Statement by WCW, from a letter to the editor, Noel Stock, on inside back covers (second statement excerpted from the first), praises *Edge* for publishing Thaddeus Zielinski's "The Sibyl," three essays on ancient religion and Christianity, in *Edge*, No. 2 (Nov. 1956) 1–47 [entire issue].

G7 *The Maximus Poems* by Charles Olson (New York: Jargon-Corinth Books, 1960).

Paper covers, 160 pp. Statement by WCW on back cover about Olson's poems.

G8 *The Materials* by George Oppen (New Directions, New York [James Laughlin] and *San Francisco Review* [June Oppen Degnan], 1962).

Paper covers, 52 pp. Statement by WCW on back cover about Oppen's poems.

G9 *Love & Death, A Study in Censorship* by Gershon Legman (New York: Hacker Art Books, 1963).

Paper covers, 95 pp. Statement attributed to WCW on inside back cover. The statement is about the first edition published at Breaking Point, New York, 1949, and the source cited for the statement is "(N.Y. Times)," the date "(1948)."

G10 *Stand Up, Friend, with Me* by Edward Field (New York: Grove Press, Inc., 1964).

Paper covers, 77 pp. (first published in hard covers by The Academy of American Poets as The Lamont Poetry Selection for 1962). Statement by WCW on back cover about Field's poems.

G11 *All, The Collected Short Poems 1923–1958* by Louis Zukofsky (New York: W. W. Norton & Company, Inc., 1965).

Paper covers, 157 pp. Statement by WCW on back cover about Zukofsky's poems, taken from essay, "A New Line Is a New Measure," C392.

G12 *saint thomas. poems.* by Tram Combs (Middletown, Conn.: Wesleyan University Press, 1965).

Paper covers, 83 pp. Statement by WCW on back cover about Tram Combs's poems. See also B74.

H. MEDICAL ARTICLE IN MEDICAL JOURNAL

H1 *Archives of Pediatrics,* A Monthly Journal Devoted to Diseases of Infants and Children, New York, XXX (Aug. 1913) 603–607.
*THE NORMAL AND ADVENTITIOUS DANGER PERIODS FOR PULMONARY DISEASE IN CHILDREN.

The author is identified as "William Carlos Williams, M.D., Medical Inspector of Schools, Rutherford, N.J." This is the only published medical article by William Carlos Williams that has been found, although there are many articles by W. C. Williams, M.D., F.A.P.H.A., Commissioner, Tennessee Department of Public Health, Nashville, Tennessee.

MISCELLANEA
ADDENDA

T

A CHECKLIST OF TRANSLATIONS
INTO FOREIGN LANGUAGES OF POEMS AND PROSE
BY WILLIAM CARLOS WILLIAMS

The difficulties of locating foreign editions of Williams' work make a complete bibliography of translations impossible at this time. Even when a contract was signed by a foreign publisher with Mrs. Williams or James Laughlin of New Directions, it has not always been possible to discover if a book were finally published. (In 1963, for example, a publisher in Viet Nam paid the permission fee for publishing 1000 copies of a translation of *In the American Grain,* but the book has apparently not been completed. Other foreign translations are scheduled, one of particular interest being a Romanian edition of selected poems.) The checklist offered here includes every book, anthology, and periodical definitely known to have published translations of Williams' poems and prose, but there are no doubt many others.

An item not seen by me is marked by a dagger. Square brackets enclose English translations of foreign titles. Accents are given as they appear in the foreign printing. When the original English and the translation are on facing pages, the titles are separated by a double vertical rule, *e.g.,* "The Term || Le Terme." If the translation is the first or the only printing of a poem or essay, the reader is directed to a more complete description in earlier sections of the bibliography.

I am especially indebted to the late Sylvia Beach, John Brown, Cristina Campo, James Laughlin, Mary de Rachewiltz, and Florence Williams for allowing me to examine foreign editions in their collections; to Vilmos Benczik, Cristina Campo, Donald Gallup, Ants Mikk, Humphrey Tonkin, Michael Weaver, Walerian Włodarczyk, and Vera Zlotnikova for supplying descriptions; and to the following persons who helped translate titles back into English: Wadad Ajami and Aryeh L. Motzkin (Arabic), Milan Lasek (Czechoslovakian), Catherine and Christoph Schweitzer (German), Richmond Lattimore (Greek), Vilmos Benczik (Hungarian), Hideko Matsuno and Nancy Cheng (Japanese), Florence Williams (Norwegian), Walerian Włodarczyk (Polish), and Vera Zlotnikova (Russian).

ARABIC

Anthologies:

T1 [ANTHOLOGY OF AMERICAN VERSE, collected and translated into Arabic by Yūsef El-Khal, Dar Majallat Sher, Beirut, Lebanon, 1958] 1 blank leaf, 205 pp. 7 15/16 × 5 1/2 inches. Contains translations by El-Khal, pp. 131–134, of three poems: [Portrait of a Lady—Pastoral (When I was younger)—Gulls]. Arabic only.

T2 [FIFTY POEMS FROM CONTEMPORARY AMERICAN POETRY, edited by Tawfiq Sayegh, Dar El-Yaqza, Beirut, Lebanon, 1963.] 1 blank leaf, 318 pp., 1 blank leaf. 9 9/16 × 6 5/8 inches. 5 L.L. (about $1.65). Contains translation by Sayegh, pp. 37–80 [65–80 are not in numerical order], of one poem: [Asphodel, That Greeny Flower]. Arabic only.

BENGALI

Periodical:

T3 *Kavita*, Calcutta, XVI. 1, Series 67, Special Bilingual Issue (Dec. 1950) 4, 42–43. See C451.

CZECHOSLOVAKIAN

Book:

T4 HUDBA POUŠTĚ, Přeložila Jiřina Hauková, Státní Nakladatelstvi Krásné Literatury a Umění, Praha, 1964 [THE DESERT MUSIC, translated by Jiřina Hauková, State Publisher of Aesthetic Literature and Art, Prague]. 1 blank leaf, 144 pp., 3 leaves, 1 blank leaf. 7 3/4 × 4 3/4 inches. Translations by Hauková of thirty-eight poems: Má píseň [A Sort of a Song]—Jaro a tak dál [Spring and All]—Květiny v kořenáči [The Pot of Flowers]—Růže [The Rose (The rose is obsolete)]—Pro Anku [To Elsie]—Červený trakař [The Red Wheelbarrow]—Meziměstská expresní [Rapid Transit]—Růžek fialové [Horned Purple]—Topolová alej [The Avenue of Poplars]—Traktát [Tract]—Déšť [Rain]—Milostná píseň [Love Song (I lie here thinking of you)]—Pastorále [Pastoral (The little sparrows)]—Pro chudou stařenu [To a Poor Old Woman]—Proletářský portrét [Proletarian Portrait]—Mezi zdmi [Between Walls]—Abys to věděla

[This Is Just to Say]—Mladá žena u okna [Young Woman at a Window]—Černoška [A Negro Woman]—Lék [The Cure]—Chudý [The Poor (It's the anarchy of poverty)]—Perpetuum mobile: Město [Perpetuum Mobile: The City]—Jachty [The Yachts]—Vdovin nářek na jaře [The Widow's Lament in Springtime]—Aby stará paní procitla [To Waken an Old Lady]—Bezútěšné pole [The Desolate Field]—Toto [These]—Pálení vánočního chvojí [Burning the Christmas Greens]—Předehra k zimě [Prelude to Winter]—Mlhy nad řekou [Mists over the River]—Probuzení [The Rewaking]—Souznění [A Unison]—Sestup [The Descent]—Orchestr [The Orchestra]—Psovi, kterého prějeli na ulici [To a Dog Injured in the Street]—Hudba pouště [The Desert Music]—Uznání malířům [Tribute to the Painters]—PATERSON, První kniha [PATERSON, Book One]. Czechoslovakian only.

FRENCH

Books:

T5 *SWISS:* PASSAIC, PASSAIC!, traduit de l'américain par Susanne et Jean Vermandoy, Abbaye du livre, Lausanne, Switzerland, 1948 (Book two of the collection "Amica America"). 133, [2] pp. 7 1/16 × 5 5/8 inches. 6.50 fr. Translations by the Vermandoys of ten short stories from *Life Along the Passaic River:* Ainsi va la vie sur les rives du Passaic [Life Along the Passaic River]—La gosse aux boutons sur la figure [The Girl with a Pimply Face]—Une nuit de juin [A Night in June]—A dormir debout [To Fall Asleep]—Un visage de pierre [A Face of Stone]—Corvée de nuit [The Cold World]—Un homme peu commode [A Difficult Man]—Sous l'ombrage de ces bois [Under the Greenwood Tree]—Serait-ce la fin du monde? [World's End]—Danse pseudo-macabre [Danse Pseudomacabre]. French only.

T6 POÈMES, Préfacés et traduits de l'Anglais par William King, Pierre Seghers, Éditeur, Paris–XIV, 1963. Unauthorized edition. 1 blank leaf, 2 leaves, 7–93 pp., 1 leaf. 7 1/2 × 5 1/16 inches. 6.75 fr. Translations by King of twenty-nine poems: The Poem || Le Poème—A Sort of a Song || Espèce de Chanson—The Mind Hesitant || L'Esprit hésitant—January || Janvier—Smell || Odeur—Illegitimate Things || Choses illicites—These ‖ Elles—A Goodnight ‖ Un Bonsoir—(By the road to the contagious hospital) ‖ (Sur la route qui mène à l'hôpital contagieux)—Dawn ‖ Aurore—Peace on Earth ‖ Paix sur la Terre—The Yellow Season ‖ La Saison jaune—Metric Figure ‖ Image métrique—Love Song (Sweep the house clean) ‖ Chanson d'amour—Flowers by the Sea ‖ Des Fleurs près de la mer—Queen Ann's Lace ‖ Queen Ann's Lace—Daisy ‖ Marguerite—Nantucket ‖ Nantucket—The Red Wheelbarrow ‖ La Brouette rouge—On Gay Wallpaper ‖ Sur une gaie tapisserie—The Term ‖ Le Terme—Portrait of a Lady ‖ Portrait d'une Dame—The Widow's Lament in Springtime ‖ Lamentation d'une veuve au printemps—To Waken an Old Lady ‖ Pour réveiller une vieille dame—El Hombre ‖ El Hombre—The Forgotten City ‖ La Cité oubliée—The Poor ‖ Les pauvres—Paterson I (*first 36 lines of One,* I: Paterson lies in the valley . . . . only one man—like a city) ‖ Paterson, I—Tract ‖ Tract. English and French.

Anthologies:

T7 ANTHOLOGIE DE LA NOUVELLE POÉSIE AMÉRICAINE, par Eugène Jolas, Kra, 6 Rue Blanche, Paris, 1928. 1 blank leaf, 3 leaves, 266 pp., 1 leaf. 7 3/8 × 4 11/16 inches. 25 N.F. Contains translation by Jolas, pp. 249–251, of one poem: Portrait de l'auteur [Portrait of the Author]. French only.

T8 PROSATEURS AMÉRICAINS DU XXe SIÈCLE, Récits choisis et présentés par Albert J. Guérard, avec vingt-quatre portraits hors texte, Robert Laffont, Pavillons, Paris, 1947. 1 blank leaf, 2 leaves, [7]–461 pp., 3 leaves, 1 blank leaf. 8 5/8 × 5 7/16 inches. Contains translation by Georges Fradier, pp. 65–76, of one essay from *In the American Grain:* La Destruction de Tenochtitlan. (Charles Sheeler photograph of WCW faces p. 64.) French only.

T9 PANORAMA DE LA LITTÉRATURE CONTEMPORAINE AUX ÉTATS-UNIS, Introduction, illustrations, documents, par John Brown, Librairie Gallimard, Paris, 1954. 1 blank leaf, 3 leaves, 9–653 pp., 1 blank leaf. 7 9/16 × 5 5/8 inches. 1.350 fr. Contains translation by Raymond Queneau, pp. 526–527, of one poem, and translations by M. P., pp. 528–530, of three poems: Spring and All ‖ Le Printemps et le Reste—The Widow's Lament in Springtime ‖ Plainte de la

Veuve au Printemps—Poem (So much depends) || Poème (Que de choses/dépendent)—A Chinese Toy || Jouet Chinois. English and French.

T10 ANTHOLOGIE DE LA POÉSIE AMÉRICAINE DES ORIGINES À NOS JOURS, par Alain Bosquet, Librairie Stock, Delamain et Boutelleau, 6, rue Casimir Delavigne, Paris, 1956. 1 blank leaf, 2 leaves, 7–314 pp., 3 leaves. 7 11/16 × 5 3/8 inches. 1.200 fr. and 1.500 fr. (Ex. de luxe). Contains translations by Bosquet, pp. 144–147, of four poems: A Sort of a Song || Une sorte de Chanson—The Poem || Le Poème—The Mind Hesitant || L'Esprit Hésitant— These || Celles-ci. English and French.

Periodicals:

T11 *Le Navire d'Argent,* Paris, II. 10, American Number (1 er mars 1926) 127–135. Translation by Auguste Morel (translator of Joyce's *Ulysses*) of fragments of *Le Grand Roman américain* [*The Great American Novel*]. French only.

T12 *Le Navire d'Argent,* II. 10 (1 er mars 1926) 136. Translation by Morel of introductory statement to *In the American Grain.* French only.

T13 *Bifur,* Paris, No. 2 (25 juillet 1929) 95–103. See C135.

T14 *Demain,* Lawrenceville, N. J., III. 1 (15 novembre 1932) [2]. See C166.

T15 *Mesures,* Paris, V. 3, American Number (15 juillet 1939) 359–372. Translations by Raymond Queneau of four poems: La Fleur [The Flower]—Le Printemps et le reste [Spring and All]—Destruction Totale [Complete Destruction]—Guillaume au Cœur Léger [Light Hearted William]. French only.

T16 *Mesures,* V. 3 (15 juillet 1939) 372–377. Translation by Queneau of an essay from *In the American Grain:* La Venue des Esclaves [The Advent of the Slaves]. French only.

T17 *Fontaine,* Paris, Nos. 27–28, Écrivains et Poètes des États-Unis d'Amérique, Numéro Spécial (juin–juillet 1943) 89–95. Translation by Dolly Chareau of an essay from *In the American Grain:* Dialogue sur la fondation de Québec [The Founding of Quebec]. Also translation of excerpt from a letter by WCW to the translator about the essay. French only.

T18 *Fontaine*, Nos. 27–28 (juin–juillet 1943) 156–157. Translation by Jean Wahl of two poems: Le poète et ses poèmes [The Poet and His Poems—see C282]—Figure métrique [Metric Figure]. French only.

T19 *Profils*, Paris, I (octobre 1952) 9–18. Translation by Alain Bosquet of one short story: Comédie au Tombeau: 1930 [Comedy Entombed]. French only. See C319.

T20 *Profils*, I (octobre 1952) 19–24. Translations by M.P. of ten poems: The Locust Tree in Flower || Le carboubier en fleurs—Young Woman at a Window || Jeune femme à la fenêtre—Between Walls || Entre les murs—Poem (So much depends) || Poème—A Chinese Toy || Jouet chinois—This Is Just to Say || Simple prétexte—Proletarian Portrait || Portrait prolétarien—Complete Destruction || Destruction totale—The Great Figure || Le grand chiffre—Poem (As the cat climbed) || Poème. English and French. See C474, 474a.

T21 *Profils*, I (octobre 1952) 84–93. Translations by M.P. of four poems: To Waken an Old Lady || Pour réveiller une vieille dame—These || Celles-Ci—The Widow's Lament in Springtime || Plainte de la veuve au printemps—The Yachts || The Yachts. English and French. See C473.

T22 *Europe*, Paris, XXXVII. 358–359, Littérature États-Unis (février–mars 1959) 117–125. Translations by Renaud de Jouvenel of six poems: Mouettes [Gulls]—Au Port [In Harbor]—Riposte [Riposte]—Perpetuum Mobile: La Ville [Perpetuum Mobile: The City]—Les Amants Pourchassés [The Hounded Lovers]—La Naissance de Vénus [The Birth of Venus]. French only.

T23 *Les Cahiers de L'Herne*, Paris, No. 6, "Ezra Pound Vol. I" (1965) 111–112. Translation by Pierre Alien titled "Souvenirs de William Carlos Williams": Extrait de 'A Tribute to Ezra Pound', émission radiophonique de la Station WYBC (Yale University), 1955. French only. See F18.

T24 *Les Cahiers de L'Herne*, No. 7, "Ezra Pound Vol. II" (1965) 369–374. Translation by Pierre Alien of an essay in *Selected Essays:* Extraits d'une description critique: XXX Cantos par Ezra Pound [Excerpts from a Critical Sketch: A Draft of XXX Cantos by Ezra Pound]. French only.

GERMAN

Books:

T25 GEDICHTE AMERIKANISCH UND DEUTSCH, Übertragung und Nachwort von Hans Magnus Enzensberger, Suhrkamp Verlag, Frankfurt am Main, 1962. 198 pp., 5 leaves. 7 1/4 × 4 7/16 inches. Translations by Enzensberger of fifty-nine poems: Aus *The Collected Earlier Poems:* To Mark Anthony in Heaven || An Marcus Antonius im Himmel—A Coronal || Ein Kranz—Portrait of a Lady || Bildnis einer Dame—Winter || Winter—A Portrait of the Times || Ein Zeitbild—To A Poor Old Woman || Eine arme alte Frau—Proletarian Portrait || Proletarisches Porträt—The Yachts || Die Jachten—Pastoral (When I was younger) || Pastorale—Pastoral (The little sparrows) || Pastorale—Tract || Traktat—The Young Housewife || Die junge Hausfrau—Danse Russe || Danse Russe—Portrait of a Woman in Bed || Bildnis einer Frau im Bett—Dedication for a Plot of Ground || Widmung für ein Stück Land—Fish || Fische—To Waken an Old Lady || Um eine alte Dame zu wecken—Thursday || Donnerstag— Time the Hangman || Henkerin Zeit—Spring || Frühling—Complete Destruction || Völlige Zerstörung—Primrose || Schlüsselblume—The Widow's Lament in Springtime || Witwenklage im Frühjahr—The Red Wheelbarrow || Der rote Handkarren—Rapid Transit || Transit-Schnellverkehr—The Jungle || Der Dschungel—Between Walls || Zwischen Mauern—This Is Just to Say || Nur damit du Bescheid weißt—Young Woman at a Window || Junge Frau am Fenster— Morning || Der Morgen—The Term || Eine Frage der Zeit—To a Dead Journalist || Auf einen toten Journalisten—The Defective Record || Die Platte hat einen Sprung—A Fond Farewell || Ein freundlicher Abschied—The Unknown || Das Unbekannte—Breakfast || Frühstück —The Last Words of My English Grandmother || Die letzen Worte meiner englischen Großmutter—Sparrow Among Dry Leaves (The sparrows/by the iron) || Sperling unter dürrem Laub. Aus *The Collected Later Poems:* A Sort of a Song || Eine Art Lied—Perfection || Volkommenheit—These Purists || Immer diese Puristen—The

278

Storm || Das Gewitter—The Yellow Chimney || Der gelbe Kamin—The Bare Tree || Der kahle Baum—Prelude to Winter || Vorspiel zum Winter—The Gentle Rejoinder || Sanfte Entgegnung—To a Lovely Old Bitch || Auf ein anmutiges altes Luder—The Motor-Barge || Der Motorkahn—The Act || Die Tathandlung—Suzanne || Suzanne—Picture of a Nude in a Machine Shop || Weiblicher Akt in einer Maschinenhalle—The Red-Wing Blackbird || Die rotgeflügelte Amsel—The Girl || Das Mädchen—The Words, the Words, the Words || Die Worte, die Worte, die Worte—Approach to a City || Stadteinfahrt—Song (Pluck the florets) || Lied—Song (Russia! Russia!) || Lied—The Rose (The stillness of the rose) || Die Rose. English and German.

T26 NEW PLACES · NEUE ORTE, Deutsch von Gertrude C. Schwebell, J. G. Bläschke Verlag, Darmstadt, 1966. 28 leaves. 8 3/16 × 5 13/16 inches. Translations by Schwebell of fourteen poems: PICTURES FROM BRUEGHEL || BILDER VON BRUEGHEL: II. Landscape with the Fall of Ikarus [*sic*] || II. Landschaft mit dem Sturz des Ikarus—V. Peasant Wedding || V. Bauernhochzeit—VI. Haymaking || VI. Heumachen—IX. The Parable of the Blind || IX. Die Parabel von den Blinden—X. Children's Games (I, III) || X. Kinderspiele (I, III)—The Polar Bear || Der Polarbär—SOME SIMPLE MEASURES IN THE AMERICAN IDIOM AND THE VARIABLE FOOT: IV. The Blue Jay || IV. Der Blauhäher—VIII. The Cocktail Party || VIII. Cocktail Party—IX. The Stolen Peonies || IX. Die Gestohlenen Päonien. Calypsos (I–III) || Kalypso Sängerinnen (I–III)—An Exercise || Exerzitium—The Descent || Der Abstieg—A Negro Woman || Eine Negerin—Classic Picture || Klassisches Bild. English and German.

Anthologies:

T27 GEDICHTE AUS DER NEUEN WELT, AMERIKANISCHE LYRIK SEIT 1910, Eingeleitet und übertragen von Kurt Heinrich Hansen, R. Piper & Company, Verlag, München, 1956. 76 pp., 2 leaves. 7 1/2 × 4 13/16 inches. Contains translation by Hansen, pp. 13–15, of one poem: Die Kronung [The Ivy Crown]. German only.

T28 MUSEUM DER MODERNEN POESIE, Eingerichtet von Hans Magnus Enzensberger im Suhrkamp Verlag, Frankfurt am Main,

1960. 421 pp., 1 leaf. 9 5/16 × 6 5/8 inches. Contains translations by Enzensberger (first, third and fifth) and by Erich Fried (second and fourth), pp. 32, 56, 73, 75, 255, of five poems: Die Tathandlung || The Act—Völlige Zerstörung || Complete Destruction—Die letzten Worte meiner englischen Großmutter || The Last Words of My English Grandmother—Junge Frau am Fenster || Young Woman at the [sic] Window—Eine Art Lied || A Sort of a Song. German and English.

Periodicals:

T29 *Fragmente,* Freiburg im Breisgau, I (1951) 17. Translation by Rainer M. Gerhardt of one poem: The R R Bums. German only.

T30 *Fragmente,* Karlsruhe in Baden, II (1952) 6–64. Translation of one poem: Die rote Kirche [The Pink Church]. German only.

T31 *Perspektiven,* Frankfurt am Main, I (Oktober 1952) 11–21. Translation of an essay from *In the American Grain:* Die Zerstörung der Stadt Tenochtitlan [The Destruction of Tenochtitlan]. German only. See C77.

T32 *Perspektiven,* I (Oktober 1952) 22–27. Translations by Christine Koller of ten poems: Akazienbaum in Blüte || The Locust Tree in Flower —Gedicht || Poem (As the cat)—Junge Frau am Fenster || Young Woman at a Window—Zwischen Mauern || Between Walls—Porträt einer Arbeiterin || Proletarian Portrait—Vollständige Vernichtung || Complete Destruction—Die grosse Zahl || The Great Figure— Gedicht || Poem (So much depends)—Ein Chinesisches Spielzeug || A Chinese Toy—Was ich noch Sagen wollte || This Is Just to Say. German and English. See C474, 474a.

T33 *Perspektiven,* I (Oktober 1952) 28–37. Translation of one short story: Grabstein eines Lustspiels [Comedy Entombed]. German only. See C319.

T34 *Perspektiven,* I (Oktober 1952) 38–47. Translations by Kurt Erich Meurer (first and third) and by Alexander Koval (second and fourth) of four poems: Eine alte Dame Aufzumuntern || To Waken an Old Lady—Dies || These—Der Witwe Klage im Frühling || The Widow's Lament in Springtime—Die Yachten || The Yachts. German and English. See C473.

T: Translations

GREEK

Periodical:

T35 [*New Epoch,* World Review of Fine Arts Quarterly, Athens, Winter] 1957, 196–208. Translations by [Zöe Karelli] of twelve poems: [Tract—The Yachts—The Monstrous Marriage—In Sisterly Fashion—A Flowing River—Burning the Christmas Greens—The Clouds, I–IV—Complete Destruction—Between Walls—Young Woman at a Window—The Great Figure—The Orchestra]. Greek only. *On p. 208:* "[The translator gives her personal thanks to Mr. Kimon Friar for his assistance in the selection and the translation.]"

HUNGARIAN

Periodical:

T36 †*Nagyvilág,* Budapest (June 1965) 820. Translations by István Vas of two poems: Tavasz és minden [Spring and All]—Egy öreg hölgy ébresztésére [To Waken an Old Lady]. Hungarian only.

ITALIAN

Books:

T37 POESIE, Versioni di Vittorio Sereni, Immagini di Sergio Dangelo, Milano, Edizioni del Triangolo, 1957. 1 blank leaf, 2 leaves, 7–[29] pp., 1 leaf. 8 13/16 × 7 9/16 inches. L. 700. Translations by Sereni of five poems: Viene l'Inverno (frammento)—La Strada Solitaria—Lamento della Vedova in Primavera—Unisono—Le Nuvole, IV. The Descent of Winter (a fragment)—The Lonely Street—The Widow's Lament in Springtime—A Unison—The Clouds, IV. Italian in first half of book, English in last half.

T38 IL FIORE È IL NOSTRO SEGNO, POESIE DI WILLIAM CARLOS WILLIAMS, Tradotte da Cristina Campo, All'Insegna del Pesce d'Oro, Milano, Vanni Scheiwiller, 1958. 68 pp., 2 leaves. 4 3/4 × 3 9/16 inches. L. 600. Translations by Cristina Campo of sixteen poems: Man in a Room ‖ Uomo in una stanza—Spring Song ‖ Canzone di primavera—Love Song (I lie here thinking of you) || Canzone d'amore—April || Aprile—The Widow's Lament in Springtime || Lamento della vedova a primavera—Spring and All || Primavera eccetera—From "Birds and Flowers" [I, III] || Da "Uccelli e fiori"—Rain || Pioggia—A Marriage Ritual || Rito coniugale—A Sort of a Song || Una specie di canto—The Hard Listener || L'ascoltatore intento—Franklin Square || Franklin Square—Every Day || Ogni giorno —The Quality of Heaven || La qualità del cielo—[From *Paterson, Two*, III:] On this most voluptuous night of the year . . . . and nothing disturb the full octave of its run || In questa notte . . . .—[From *Paterson, Three*, II:] like a mouse, like a . . . . the night was made day by the flames, flames || come un sorcio . . . . English and Italian.

T39 POESIE, Tradotte e presentate da Cristina Campo e Vittorio Sereni, Giulio Einaudi Editore, Torino, 1961. 1 blank leaf, 2 leaves, 7–318 pp., 1 leaf, 2 blank leaves. 8 9/16 × 6 1/4 inches. L. 2000. Reissued in 1967 at L. 2500, with Charles Sheeler photograph of Williams on front. Translations by Campo and Sereni of fifty-five poems; translator's initial given after Italian title: Da *The Collected Earlier Poems*: Man in a Room || Uomo in una stanza [C.]—The Locust Tree in Flower (Among/of/green) || L'Acacia in fiore [S.]—Spring Song || Canzone di primavera [C.]—Rain || Pioggia [C.]—To a Solitary Disciple || A un solitario discepolo [C.]—Love Song (I lie here thinking of you) || Canzone d'amore [C.]—April || Aprile [C.]—The Flowers Alone || I fiori soli [C.]—The Widow's Lament in Springtime || Lamento della vedova a primavera [C.]—Dedication for a Plot of Ground || Dedica per un pezzo di terra [S.]—The Bird's Companion || Il compagno degli uccelli [S.]—Proletarian Portrait || Ritratto proletario [S.]—Complaint || Lamento [S.]—The Young Housewife || La giovane casalinga [S.]—To Waken an Old Lady || A una vecchia signora, per svegliarla [S.]—Complete Destruction || Distruzione totale [S.]—The Lonely Street || La strada solitaria [S.]—The Great Figure || La grande cifra [S.]—The Red Wheelbarrow || La carriola rossa [S.]—The Descent of Winter 9/30 || Viene l'inverno 9/30 [S.]—Between Walls || Tra muri [S.]—Young Woman at a Window || Giovane donna alla finestra [S.]—Poem (As the cat) || Poesia [S.]—Adam || Adamo [S.]—Eve || Eva [S.]—Spring and All || Primavera eccetera [C.]—Portrait of the Author || Autoritratto [C.]—Birds and Flowers

[I, III] || Uccelli e fiori [C.]—To an Elder Poet || A un poeta piú anziano [C.]—Perpetuum Mobile: The City || Perpetuum mobile: la città [C.]—The Crimson Cyclamen || Il ciclamino cremis [C.]— A Marriage Ritual || Rito coniugale [C.]—These || Queste sono [S.] —The Men || Gli uomini [S.]. Da *The Collected Later Poems*: A Sort of a Song || Una specie di canto [C.]—The Hard Listener || L'ascoltatore intento [C.]—Paterson: The Falls || Paterson: le cascate [S.]—Burning the Christmas Greens || Bruciando il verde natalizio [S.]—A Flowing River || Corrente [S.]—The Clouds, IV || Le nuvole, IV [S.]—Seafarer || Navigatore [S.]—Franklin Square || Franklin Square [C.]—The Quality of Heaven || La qualità del cielo [C.]— The Woodpecker || Il picchio [C.]—A Unison || Unisono [S.]—New Mexico || Nuovo messico [S.]—The Horse Show || La fiera dei cavalli [S.]—Approach to a City || In vista d'una città [S.]—The Hard Core of Beauty || Il duro nocciolo della bellezza [S.]. Da *Paterson*: [*Two*, III:] On this most voluptuous night of the year . . . . and nothing disturb the full octave of its run || In questa notte . . . . [C.]— [*Three*, II:] —the whole city doomed and . . . . the night was made day by the flames, the flames || —condannata l'intera città . . . . [C.]—[*Two*, II:] If there is subtlety . . . . despair || Se vi è finezza al mondo . . . . [C.]—[*Three*, I:] So much talk of the language . . . . and clouds || A che parlare di linguaggio . . . . [C.]. Da *The Desert Music and Other Poems*: The Desert Music || La musica del deserto [S.]. *Un inedito*: The World Contracted to a Recognizable Image || L'universo contratto a un'immagine riconoscibile [C.]. English and Italian. This is the first book publication of "The World Contracted to a Recognizable Image" (see B89) and the only publication of a comment by WCW about the poem in an unpublished letter (2 ottobre 1959) to Cristina Campo, Notes, p. 311, Italian only. Also in the Notes, pp. 307-311, are Italian translations of brief excerpts from published letters and books by Williams.

T40 I RACCONTI DEL DOTTOR WILLIAMS, Introduzione di Van Wyck Brooks, Giuilo Einaudi, Torino, 1963. 398 pp., 1 leaf. 8 13/16 × 5 7/16 inches. L. 3000. Translations by Lorenzo Bassi of all the stories in *The Farmers' Daughters*, A46. Italian only.

T41 PATERSON, Traduzione, prefazione, note bio-bibliografiche di Alfredo Rizzardi, Lerici Editori, Milano, 1966. 532 pp. 8 9/16 × 5 1/4 inches. L. 4800. Translation by Rizzardi of all of *Paterson*, including Williams' notes for a projected Book 6. English and Italian.

Anthologies:

T42 L'IMAGISMO, CON UNA PICCOLA ANTOLOGIA (Guide di cultura contemporanea, 11), a cura di G. Flores D'Arcais, R. Mazzetti, G. Vigorelli, Luigi Berti, Cedam, Padova, 1944. 1 blank leaf, 2 leaves, [7]-120 pp., 1 leaf, 1 blank leaf. 7 1/16 × 5 inches. L. 120. Contains translation by Luigi Berti, pp. 109-110, of one poem: Alberi Botticelliani [The Botticellian Trees]. Italian only.

T43 ORFEO, IL TESORO DELLA LIRICA UNIVERSALE INTER-PRETATO IN VERSI ITALIANI, a cura di Vincenzo Errante e Emilio Mariano, Sansoni, Firenze, 1949. Reissued in 1961. Second printing: 2 vols., slipcase; Vol. I: 1 blank leaf, xxvii, 955 pp., 1 leaf; Vol. II: 1 blank leaf, 4 leaves, 961-1986 pp., 1 leaf, 1 blank leaf. 8 1/4 × 5 1/4 inches. L. 8000. Contains translations by Alfredo Rizzardi, Roberto Sanesi, Carlo Izzo, Vittorio Sereni, Cristina Campo, Glauco Cambon, and Sanesi, pp. 1672-1679, of seven poems (translators' names given in the order of the poems): È uno strano coraggio [El Hombre]—A Marco Antonio in cielo [To Mark Anthony in Heaven]—La giungla [The Jungle]—Dedica per un pezzo di terra [Dedication for a Plot of Ground]—Lamento della vedova a primavera [The Widow's Lament in Springtime]—Una eternità [An Eternity]—Canto d'amore [Asphodel, That Greeny Flower, Book 1 (When I speak/of flowers/it is to recall . . . . and every man/who wants to die at peace in his bed/besides). Italian only.

T44 †POETI AMERICANI (1662-1945), a cura di Gabriele Baldini, Francesco De Silva, Torino, 1949. 1 blank leaf, 3 leaves, ix-xxxiii, 434 pp., 1 leaf, 1 blank leaf. L. 1600. Contains translations of several poems.

T45 POESIA AMERICANA CONTEMPORANEA E POESIA NEGRA, Introduzione, versione e note di Carlo Izzo, Guanda, Parma, 1949. xxxii, 596 pp., 9 3/16 × 5 15/16 inches. L. 2500. Reissued in 1955. Contains translations by Carlo Izzo, pp. 202-209, of three poems: Tract || Sermone—The Poor (It's the anarchy of poverty) || I poveri —The Jungle || La giungla. English and Italian.

T46 LIRICA DEL NOVECENTO, ANTOLOGIA DI POESIA ITALI-
ANA, a cura di Luciano Anceschi e Sergio Antonielli, Vallecchi
Editore, Firenze, 1953. Reissued, 1961. Second printing: cvi pp., 2
leaves, 3–897 pp., 1 blank leaf. 7 5/8 × 5 inches. L. 3800. Contains
translation by Vittorio Sereni, pp. 686–688, of one poem: Adamo.
Italian only.

T47 LIRICI AMERICANO, Traduzione di Alfredo Rizzardi, Edizioni
Salvatore Sciascia, Caltanissetta, Roma, 1955. 1 blank leaf, 196 pp.,
1 leaf. 7 7/8 × 5 1/4 inches. L. 1200 (Brossura) and L. 1500 (Rile-
gato). Contains translations by Rizzardi, pp. 72–83, of three poems
and two selections from *Paterson*: The Red Wheelbarrow || La
carriola rossa—El Hombre || El hombre—Paterson || Paterson—
[*Paterson, One,* III:] How strange you are, you idiot || Come sei
stranno, idiota!—[*Paterson, Four,* III:] Trip a trap o'troontjes || Trip
a trap o'troontjes. English and Italian.

T48 POETI STRANIERI DEL '900 TRADOTTI DA POETI ITALI-
ANI, a cura di Vanni Scheiwiller, All'insegna del pesce d'oro, Mi-
lano, 1956. 140, [1] pp., 2 leaves. 5 3/8 × 4 1/16 inches. L. 800.
Contains translation by Vittorio Sereni, pp. 110–111, of one poem:
Dedica per un pezzo di terra [Dedication for a Plot of Ground].
Italian only.

T49 POESIA STRANIERA DEL NOVECENTO, a cura di Attilio Berto-
lucci, Garzanti, Milano, 1958. 1 blank leaf, 3 leaves, ix–xii, 875 pp.,
1 leaf. 8 5/8 × 5 5/8 inches. L. 6000. Reissued in 1960. Contains
translations by Vittorio Sereni, pp. 432–447, of four poems: Paterson:
The Falls || Paterson: Le cascate—Adam || Adamo—These || Questo
sono—Dedication for a Plot of Ground || Dedica per un pezzo di
terra. English and Italian.

T50 POETI AMERICANI DA E. A. ROBINSON A W. S. MERWIN
(1900–1956). Traduzione di Roberto Sanesi, Feltrinelli Editore, Milano, 1958. 1 blank leaf, 1028 pp., 1 leaf. 8 1/8 × 5 1/16 inches.
L. 6000. Contains translations by Sanesi, pp. 255–333, of nine poems,
four selections from *Paterson*, and "Work in Progress": To Mark
Anthony in Heaven || A Marco Antonio in cielo—Sicilian Emigrant's
Song || Canto dell'emigrante siciliano—The Yachts || I panfili—The

Widow's Lament in Springtime || Il lamento della vedova a prima-vera—The Farmer || Il fattore—The Red Wheelbarrow || La carriola rossa—The Avenue of Poplars || Il viale dei pioppi—These || Queste —A Sort of a Song || Una Specie di canzone—From *Paterson*: The Delineaments of the Giants || From *Paterson*: Il delinearsi dei giganti —From *Paterson*: Sunday in the Park || Da *Paterson*: Domenica nel parco—From *Paterson*: The Library || Da *Paterson*: La biblioteca— From *Paterson*: The Run to the Sea || Da *Paterson*: La corsa al mare —Work in Progress [Asphodel, That Greeny Flower, Book 1] || Work in Progress. English and Italian.

T51 LE PIÙ BELLE PAGINE DELLA LETTERATURE NORD-AMERICANA, a cura di Carlo Izzo (PAGINE DELLE LET-TERATURE DI TUTTO IL MONDO, Direttore, Eugenio Montale), Nuova Accademia Editrice, Milano, 1959. 1 blank leaf, 7 leaves, 7–841 pp., 6 leaves, 1 blank leaf. 8 1/2 × 5 1/2 inches. L. 6000 (in tela) and L. 7000 (in pelle). Contains translations by Alfredo Rizzardi, pp. 668–673, of three poems: To Waken an Old Lady || Per destare una vecchia signora—Franklin Square || Piazza Franklin —These || Queste. English and Italian.

T52 IL NATALE, ANTOLOGIA DI POETI DEL '900, a cura di Mary de Rachewiltz e Vanni Scheiwiller, All'insegna del pesce d'oro, Milano, 1961. 1 blank leaf, 2 leaves, 7–135 pp., 1 leaf, 1 blank leaf. 5 5/16 × 4 1/16 inches. L. 1000. Contains translation by Vittorio Sereni, pp. 114–117, of one poem: From 'Burning the Christmas Greens' || Da 'Bruciando Il Verde Natalizio.' English and Italian.

T53 †POESIA AMERICANA DEL '900, a cura di Carlo Izzo, Ugo Guanda, Parma, 1963. lx, 1000 pp. Contains translations of several poems.

Periodicals:

T54 *La fiera letteraria,* Rome, X. 26 (domenica, 26 giugno 1950) 1–2. See C508.

T55 *Prospettive USA,* Firenze, I (autunno 1952) 30–41. Translation by Roberto Bazlen of an essay from *In the American Grain*: La distruzione di Tenochtitlan [The Destruction of Tenochtitlan]. Italian only. See C77.

T56 *Prospettive USA*, I (autunno 1952) 42–51. Translation by Marcella Bonsanti of four poems: The Yachts || I Panfili—These || Queste—To Waken an Old Lady || Per Destare una Vecchia Signora—The Widow's Lament in Springtime || Lamento della Vedova a Primavera. English and Italian. See C473.

T57 *Prospettive USA*, I (autunno 1952) 52–61. Translation by Roberto Bazlen of a short story: Commedia morta e sepolta: 1930 [Comedy Entombed]. Italian only. See C319.

T58 †*Inventario*, Nos. 5–6 (ottobre–dicembre 1953). Translations by Vittorio Sereni of several poems.

T59 *La fiera letteraria*, X. 1 (domenica, 2 gennaio 1955) 3. Translations by Glauco Cambon of seven poems and three selections from *Paterson*: La pausa [The Pause]—Avvicinamento a una città [Approach to a City]—Navigatori [Seafarer]—Parole in ozio [The Words Lying Idle]—Nebbie sul fiume [Mists over the River]—Venere sul deserto [Venus over the Desert]—Una eternità [An Eternity]—Sezione del fuoco [*Paterson, Three*, II, pp. 141–143: Beautiful thing . . . . heat] —Il moto dello spirito [*Paterson, Two*, III, pp. 96–97: The descent beckons . . . . endless and indestructible]—Redenzione del tempo [*Paterson, Three*, III, pp. 172–173: The past above, the future below . . . . is real]. Italian only.

T60 †*Stagione*, Rome, IV. 14 (1957[?]) 3. Translation by Cristina Campo of one poem: Una specie di canto [A Sort of a Song].

T61 †*Il Verri*, Milan, No. 6 (1957). Translations by Alfredo Rizzardi of several poems.

T62 *La posta letteraria*, Lodi, V. 22 (14 dicembre 1957) 3. Translation by Cristina Campo of one poem: Nebbia sul fiume [Mists Over the River]. Italian only.

T63 †*Corriere d'informazione*, Milan (febbraio 1959). Translation by Cristina Campo of a selection from *Paterson*: In questa notte [*Paterson, Two*, III: On this most voluptuous night of the year . . . . and nothing disturb the full octave of its run].

T64 *Marsia*, Nos. 6–7 (maggio–dicembre 1959) 113–115. Translation by

Ariodante Marianni of one poem: La nascita di venere [The Birth of Venus]. Italian only.

T65 *La posta letteraria* (27 giugno 1959) 3. Translations by Cristina Campo of two poems: Canzone di primavera [Spring Song]—Una specie di canto [A Sort of a Song]. Italian only.

T66 *Chelsea Twelve*, New York (Sept. 1962) 122–127. Translations by Vittorio Sereni and Cristina Campo of three poems (the second translation is by Campo): To Waken an Old Lady || A una vecchia signora, per svegliarla—Spring and All || Primavera eccetera—Approach to a City || In vista d'una citta. English and Italian. C51, 82, 375.

JAPANESE

Periodical:

T67 [*Mugen*, Tokyo], Quarterly Magazine of Poetry, IX ([Dec. 1] 1961) 46–54. This issue is dedicated to William Carlos Williams and prints, in addition to the translations of poems and prose, in English a letter from Williams expressing his appreciation (C610) and in Japanese several critical essays and a symposium about Williams, as well as two photographs of Williams. Translations by [Hanshiro Murano] and [Rikutaro Fukuda] of seventeen poems (the first six by Murano, the last eleven by Fukuda) and by [Ichiro Ando] of one selection from *Paterson*: Complete Destruction—The Desolate Field—Hero—To Waken an Old Lady—Proletarian Portrait—Metric Figure—The Yachts—Illegitimate Things—The Term—The Red Wheelbarrow—This Is Just to Say—The Young Housewife—Young Woman at a Window—Nantucket—Riposte—The Forgotten City—January—Patterson [*sic*] V. The last poem is from *Paterson, Five*, III, 268–273: Paterson has grown older . . . . among the oak trees. The titles are in English, but the texts of the poems are in Japanese only.

T68 [*Mugen*], IX ([Dec. 1] 1961) 55. Translation by [Hanshiro Murano] of one poem: [The Children]. Japanese only except acknowledgment at foot of page: "Harper's Magazine, June 1961."

T69 [*Mugen*], IX ([Dec. 1] 1961) 57–65. Translations titled [Casual Thoughts] by [Terasuko Tanaka] of four prose selections: excerpts from [A Look Back], Chapter 42 of [*The Autobiography*]—excerpts from [Preface to *Selected Essays*]—[The Poem Paterson], Chapter 58 of [*The Autobiography*]—excerpts from [Foreword to *The Autobiography*]. Japanese only.

T70 [*Mugen*], IX ([Dec. 1] 1961) 86–93. In an essay about Williams by [Yuzuru Katagiri] are translations of four complete poems (as well as lines from other poems): The Widow's Lament in Springtime—Poem (So much depends)—The Lily—The Yachts. The four poems are printed in both English and Japanese.

NORWEGIAN

Anthologies:

T71 AMERIKANSK LYRIKK, Et Utvalg i Norsk Gjendiktning ved Paal Brekke, Forlagt av H. Aschehoug & Co. (W. Nygaard), Oslo, 1957. 150 pp., 1 leaf, 1 blank leaf. 8 5/8 × 5 5/8 inches. Contains translations by Brekke, pp. 63–65, of four poems: For å Vekke en Gammel Dame [To Waken an Old Lady]—Blomster og Sjø [Flowers by the Sea]—Lukt [Smell]—Pastorale [Pastoral (When I was younger)]. Norwegian only.

T72 UNDER NYE STJERNER [UNDER NEW STARS], AMERIKANSK LYRIKK GJENNOM 300 ÅR [AMERICAN LYRICS OF 300 YEARS], Utvald Omsett av Sigmund Skard, Gyldendal Norsk Forlag, Olso, 1960. 225 pp., 1 leaf. 9 1/8 × 6 1/8 inches. Contains translations by Skard, pp. 174–178, of six poems: Oksen [The Bull] —Klassisk Scene [Classic Scene]—Feil i Plata [The Defective Record] —Den Raude Trillebåra [The Red Wheelbarrow]—Nantucket Øy [Nantucket]—Dette er Berre for å Seia at [This Is Just to Say]. Norwegian only.

Periodical:

T73 *Morgen Posten*, Oslo (Mandag, 30 Desember 1957) 5. Translations by Paal Brekke of two poems: Blomster og Sjø [Flowers by the Sea]— Lukt [Smell]. Norwegian only.

POLISH

Anthology:

T74 CZAS NIEPOKOJU, ANTOLOGIA WSPÓŁCZESNEJ POEZJI BRYTYJSKIEJ I AMERYKAŃSKIEJ, Wybrał i opracował Paweł Mayewski, Wstęp napisał Karl Shapiro. Wydano staraniem The East Europe Institute przez Criterion Books, Nowy Jork, 1958. xviii, 382 pp. 7 5/8 × 5 1/16 inches. Contains translations by Józef Wittlin (first three) and Zbigniew Chałko (fourth), pp. 82–95, of four poems: Poem (By the road to the contagious hospital) [Spring and All] || Wiersz (Na drodze do szpitala chorób zaraźliwych—January || Styczeń— The Poor || Biedni ludzie—To Daphne and Virginia || Dafnie i Wirginia. English and Polish.

Periodical:

T75 †*Życie Literackie*, Kraków, XXXVIII. 296 ([Sept.] 1957) 7. Translation by Stanisław Czycz of one poem: (Drogę do szpitala chorób zakaźnych) [Spring and All: By the road to the contagious hospital]. Polish only.

PORTUGUESE

Periodical:

T76 *Pensamento da America,* Supplemento panamericano de A Manhã, V. 4 (Domingo, 5 de Maio de 1946) 56. Translation by Joaquim Cardozo of one poem: Figura Metrica [Metric Figure]. Edited by Charles Edward Eaton, who was preparing (according to an announcement on p. 49, the first page of this section of the newspaper) an anthology of North American poets translated into Portuguese. Photograph of WCW on p. 49.

RUSSIAN

Anthologies:

T77 [AMERICAN POETS, XX CENTURY, State Literary Publishing House, Moscow], 1939. 288 pp. Contains translations by [Michail Zenkevich] (three selections from "The Wanderer") and [Ivan Kash-

kin] (last three poems), pp. 170–174, of four poems: The Wanderer:
(Advent—Broadway—Paterson, The Strike)—Peace on Earth! [*sic*]
—Metric Figure—Dawn. The titles are in English and Russian, but
the texts of the poems are in Russian only. An exclamation point
follows both the Russian and English title "Peace on Earth!"

T78 †[I LISTEN, AMERICA SINGS: POETS OF THE U.S.A., Compiled and translated by [Ivan Kashkin], Foreign Literature Publishing House, Moscow], 1960. 174 pp. Contains translations by Kashkin,
pp. 144–145, of three poems: [Peace on Earth!—Metric Figure—
Dawn]. Russian only.

Periodicals:

T79 †[*International Literature,* Moscow], No. 2 (1937) 130–131. Translations by [Ivan Kashkin] of two poems: [Metric Figure—Dawn]. Russian only.

T80 †[*Foreign Literature,* Moscow], No. 8 (1961) 173–174. Translation
by [Andrej Sergejev] of one poem: [To a Dog Injured in the Street].
Russian only.

SPANISH

Books:

T81 ASÍ COMIENZA LA VIDA [Thus Life Begins], Traducción del
inglés por Federico López Cruz, Santiago Rueda, Editor, Buenos Aires,
1946. [Half title:] Título del original en inglés: "WHITE MULE".
2 leaves, 7–345 pp., 1 leaf. 8 3/4 × 5 13/16 inches. $8. –m/n. Spanish
only.

T82 EL CUERNO DE LA ABUNDANCIA [The Horn of Plenty], Tra-
ducción del inglés por Federico López Cruz, Santiago Rueda, Editor,
Buenos Aires, 1947. [Half title:] Título del original en inglés: "IN
THE MONEY". 2 leaves, 7–414 pp., 1 leaf. 8 3/4 × 5 13/16 inches.
$7. –m/n. Spanish only.

Periodical:

T83 *Orígenes,* Revista de Arte y Literatura, Habana, Cuba, I. 3 (otoño
1944) 22–23. See C351.

TRANSLATIONS
ADDENDA

INDEX

Titles of books and pamphlets by or translated by Williams or with contributions by him are set in all capitals, followed by the date of publication; the reference number for the major descriptive entry is set in boldface. Other titles are italicized or are within quotation marks and are followed by the author's name. Titles of periodicals are italicized, followed by the place(s) of publication. Titles of poems, essays, short stories, chapters for novels, improvisations, and plays by Williams are within quotation marks; first lines of untitled poems, improvisations, and translations are within parentheses. After the titles of Williams' work, the following abbreviations, set within square brackets, are used to indicate the genre: [D] drama; [E] essay, including review, editorial, and short prose statement; [Imp] improvisation; [P] poem; [S] story; [T] translation.

293

La fiera letteraria, Rome, C508; T54, 59
"Fierce Singleness" [E], A12
"15 Years Later" [P], A48; C574
FIFTY POEMS FROM CONTEMPO-RARY AMERICAN POETRY (in Arabic by Sayegh), T2
55 Poems (Zukofsky), C324
FIFTY POETS, AN AMERICAN AUTO-ANTHOLOGY, 1933, B20
"The Fight" (for Horace Gregory) [P], C528
"Figueras Castle" [P], A23, 31; C284
Figueredo, Alvaro, C564
"The Final Embarrassment" [S], A32, 46; T40
"A Final Offer [IN THE MONEY]," A21
Fine Arts Production Committee, University of California, B65, 67
"Fine Work with Pitch and Copper" [P], A17, 20, 28, 36; B34; C230
Finnegans Wake (Joyce), B8, 11, 36
IL FIORE È IL NOSTRO SEGNO, POESIE DI WILLIAM CARLOS WILLIAMS (Campo), T38
"Fire Spirit" [P], A20, 36; C15
Firmin-Didot et Cie Mesnil-sur-l'Estrée (Eure), B92
FIRST ACT, 1945, A18b, **A21b,** 32n
"The First Book [AUTOBIOGRA-PHY]," A35
"First Days [A VOYAGE TO PA-GANY]," A10
"First Memories [AUTOBIOGRA-PHY]," A35
"First Praise" [P], A2, 20, 36
"The First President: Libretto for an Opera (and Ballet)" [D], A47; B26; C350
(The first snow) [Imp], "The Descent of Winter 12/2," C122; *and in* "Notes in Diary Form," A40
"First Version: 1915" [P], A36; *first titled* "Love Song (What have I to

say to you)," C14, *and* "A Love Song, First Version: 1915," A22
"First Week [A VOYAGE TO PA-GANY]," A10
"First Years of Practice [AUTOBIOG-RAPHY]," A35
"Fish" [P], A36; C71; F19; T25; [section in *CEP*], A36
"The Fistula of the Law" [E], C425
Fitts, Dudley, B31
"The Five Dollar Guy" [S], C105
"Five to the Fifth Power" [E], C529
(a flash of juncos) [Imp], "The Descent of Winter 10/28," C122; *and in* "Notes in Diary Form," A40
"Flattery (For F. W.)" [P], C528
Fleetwood, F12
Fletcher, John Gould, B14, 45, 76; F11
"Flight [WHITE MULE]," A18; C214
(A flight of birds), PATERSON, C558; *included in* (Paterson has grown older), C558; T67
"Flight to the City" [P], A7, 8, 15, 20, 36; *first titled* "Cornucopia," C80
Flint, F. S., B14
"The Flirtation [WHITE MULE]," A18; C201
"La Flor (For E. P.)" [P], C5, 528
"Florence [Italy, A VOYAGE TO PAGANY]," A10
Flores, Angel, A13
Floss, Flossie. *See* Williams, Florence
"The Flower (A petal, colorless)" [P], A15, 20, 36; B14; C143; T15; [Section in *CEP*], A36
"The Flower (This too I love)" [P], A26, 31
(The flower), "Two Sentimental Little Poems," C540; *later titled* "The Loving Dexterity"
"A Flower from the Park [WHITE MULE]," A18; C156
"The Flowers Alone" [P], A36; B21; C191; T39
"Flowers by the Sea" [P], A16, 20,

Hueffer, Ford Madox. *See* Ford, Ford Madox
Hughes, Glenn, B14
Hughes, Langston, B43
"Hula-Hula" [P], C72
The Human Body (Logan Clendening), A12
Humphries, Bruce, B18, 29
Humphries, Rolfe, B28, 64
Hunt, Sidney, B16
"The Hunter" [P], A5, 20, 28, 36; C47
Hunter, Naomi, letter to, C539
"The Hunters in the Snow" [P], A48; C580
"The Hurricane" [P], A26, 31; *first titled* "Address," C352
"Hymn for Rogation Sunday" [poem "Rogation Sunday" set to music by Thomas Canning], E3
"Hymn to Love Ended" [P], A16, 20, 36; C216
"Hymn to Perfection" [P], A1
"Hymn to the Spirit of Fraternal Love" [P], A1
HYPNOS WAKING (René Char), 1956, B69; C522
Hyslop, Jim. See "The Old Worshipper," C528

(I bought a new), "From the Poem 'Patterson' [*sic*]," A17; "Unnamed: From 'Paterson,'" A20, 36
(I had a misfortune in September), "Detail" [P], A36
I LISTEN, AMERICA SINGS: POETS OF THE U.S.A. (in Russian by Kashkin), T78
(I make really very little money) [P], "The Descent of Winter 11/28," A20, 36; C122; (I make very little money), A15; B18
"I Saw the Figure 5 in Gold" (Charles Demuth), A5n
I WANTED TO WRITE A POEM, 1958, A1n, 2n, 3n, 4n, 5n, 7n, 9n, 10n, 11n, 12n, 13n, 14n, 15n, 16n, 17n, 18n, 19n, 20n, 21n, 23n, 24n, 26n, 29n, 32n, 33n, 35n, 37n, 38n, 39n, 40n, 41n, **A43**, 46; B75; C556
(I will make a big, serious portrait) [Imp], "The Descent of Winter 10/23," C122; *and in* "Notes in Diary Form," A40
"'I would Not Change for Thine'" [P], A29, 31
"The Ideal Quarrel" [Imp], C30
(If genius is profuse) [Imp], "The Descent of Winter 11/24," C122; *and in* "Notes in Diary Form," A40
(If I could clap this in a cage and let that out), KORA, A4; C38
(if there is subtlety), PATERSON, T39
Ignatow, David, C419
"L'Illégaltié aux États-Unis" [E], C135
Illegitimate Sonnets (Merrill Moore), D6
"Illegitimate Things" [P], A22, 36; C282, 451; T6, 67
"Image and Purpose" [E], C262
Imagi, Baltimore, Md., C409, 425; Allentown, Pa., C442, 480
(Imagine a family of four grown men) [Imp], "The Descent of Winter 12/9," C122; *and in* "Notes in Diary Form," A40
Imagism, A15n, 42
L'IMAGISMO, CON UNA PICCOLA ANTOLOGIA (D'Arcais), T42
IMAGIST ANTHOLOGY, 1930, B14
"Imitation of a Translation" [P], C432; *also titled* "Translation," C421; A31e
"Imitations" [P], A1
Imitations (Robert Lowell), C613
"The Immemorial Wind" [P], A16; *also titled* "The Black Winds," A7, 20, 36
"Immortal" [P], A2, 20, 36; *first titled* "Proof of Immortality," C2
"Impasse and Imagery" [E], C125

Terre Reviews the Fathers," B76; *and see* "Landless John . . ."

Jeffers, Robinson, B43

Jefferson and/or Mussolini (Ezra Pound), C234; "Jefferson and/or Mussolini" [E], C234

"Jersey Lyric" [P], A48; C609

"Jew" [S], C291

"Jingle" [P], A31

JOHN MARIN MEMORIAL EXHIBITION, 1955, B67

Johns, Jasper, A5n

Johns, Richard, A18, 21; B16

Johnson, Ray, A9d; B85

Johnson, Reid B., F18

Jolas, Eugene, A12; B11, 16, 56; T7; letter to, C115

Jones, Frank, B41

Jones, Glyn, B41

Jones, Howard Mumford, A43

Jones, J., B16

Jones, John Paul, A9

Jones, LeRoi, B80

Joseph Conrad (Albert Guerard, Jr.), A27

Josephson, Matthew, A11

Josephy, Robert S., A10

The Journal of Albion Moonlight (Kenneth Patchen), C310

Jouvenel, Renaud de, T22

JOURNEY TO LOVE, 1955, **A41**, 48; C476, 486, 488, 492, 497, 498, 499, 504, 506, 507, 508, 509

Joyce, James, A10n, 12; B8, 14, 17, 19; C44, 113, 546; T11; *and see* "A Note on the Recent Work of James Joyce," A12, 40; C113; *and* "A Point for American Criticism," A40, 50; B11; C129

"Juan Gris" [E], A12

"July" [P], A1

"June" [P], A1

"June 9" [P], C456; 459

"The Jungle" [P], A15, 20, 36; B18; C70; T25, 43, 45

(The justice of poverty) [P], "The Descent of Winter 10/29," A15, 20, 36, 50; C122

"K. McB." [P], A3, 20, 36; *first titled* "K. McD.," C15

Kaplan, Maurice Serle, A31a, e, 32, 36a, 46a, 47a, 48a, 49g

Karelli, Zöe, T35

Kashkin, Ivan, T77, 78, 79

Katagiri, Yuzuru, T70

Kavita, Calcutta, India, A31; C282, 451; T3

Kazin, Alfred, A32

Keats, John, C616

Keep, O. Davis, letter to, C63

Kees, Weldon, B43, 51

"Keller Gegen Dom" [P], A3, 20, 36; B5; C15

Kennedy, Roger, F13

Kenner, Hugh, A49g

"Kenneth Burke" [E], A12, 40; C127

"Kenneth Lawrence Beaudoin" [E], C471

Kent, George, B16

Kent, Rockwell, B13

The Kenyon Review, Gambier, Ohio, C270, 380, 381, 408, 484, 486, 509

Kimball, Dudley, A27

"The King" [P], A41, 48

King, Basil, B80

King, William, T6

Kinnell, Galway, B76

Kipling, Rudyard, A6n

Kirgo's, New Haven, C461

Kirstein, Lincoln, letter to, C157

Klee, Paul, B62

THE KNIFE OF THE TIMES AND OTHER STORIES, 1932, **A13**, 19n, 32, 46; T40; "The Knife of the Times" [S], A13, 32, 46; T40

"The Knight" [TP], C631

Knoll, Robert E., A6; B81; C559

Knopf, Alfred A., B3, 5, 63

Koch, Vivienne, B57, 58

INDEX

A BIBLIOGRAPHY OF
William Carlos Williams